Boomer Bust?

Boomer Bust?

Economic and Political Issues of the Graying Society

Edited by
Robert B. Hudson

Praeger Perspectives

Westport, Connecticut
London

Library of Congress Cataloging-in-Publication Data

Boomer bust? : economic and political issues of the graying society / edited
by Robert B. Hudson.
    p. cm.
  Includes bibliographical references and index.
  ISBN 978-0-275-99549-2 (set : alk. paper) — ISBN 978-0-275-99551-5
(vol. 1 : alk. paper) — ISBN 978-0-275-99553-9 (vol. 2 : alk. paper)
  1. Population aging—United States. 2. Baby boom generation—
Retirement—United States. 3. United States—Population—Economic aspects.
I. Hudson, Robert B., 1944–
HQ1064.U5B66 2009
306.3'808440973—dc22   2008024968

British Library Cataloguing in Publication Data is available.

Library of Congress Catalog Card Number: 2008024968
ISBN: 978-0-275-99549-2 (set)
     978-0-275-99551-5 (vol. 1)
     978-0-275-99553-9 (vol. 2)

First published in 2009

Praeger Publishers, 88 Post Road West, Westport, CT 06881
An imprint of Greenwood Publishing Group, Inc.
www.praeger.com

Printed in the United States of America

The paper used in this book complies with the
Permanent Paper Standard issued by the National
Information Standards Organization (Z39.48–1984).

10 9 8 7 6 5 4 3 2 1

Contents

Preface

Having grown from infancy through adolescence to adulthood, 76 million baby boomers are now about to enter old age. In the course of their lifetimes, the boomers have forced double shifts in elementary schools, generated an enormous growth in higher education, created new consumer markets, and enjoyed historically unprecedented levels of prosperity. Having massively impacted every social institution they have encountered thus far, the boomers are widely expected to revolutionize old age as well.

The two volumes that comprise *Boomer Bust? Economic and Political Issues of the Graying Society* examine in great detail what the boomers will look like in old age, how they are likely to behave, and the impact they may have on the larger society. There is no question that the boomers will comprise the largest cohort of older Americans ever, but beyond numbers alone there are many unknowns about the actual effect they may have (or be associated with or blamed for). Because of their very size, the boomers may displace or replace other age groups in various roles (workers, consumers, caregivers, voters, Social Security recipients), but questions remain about how singularly they will behave and how salient their generational impact will be. Despite their iconic demographic standing, the boomers by no means all look the same, and equally important, they also very much resemble people from other generations in obvious ways. Boomers and nonboomers alike are male or female, black or white, rich or poor, urban or rural, healthy or ill. In short, the world of the boomers is marked both by intracohort differences and intercohort similarities.

These interrelated attributes—cohort size, cohesion, and distinctiveness—are central to any discussion about the impact the boomers are likely to have on American life. A number of critical questions flowing logically from this formulation are addressed in the chapters that follow:

- How singularly will the boomers behave in old age?
- How different will they be from older and younger people?
- How important will their age (the effect of how old they are) and their generation (the effect of when they were born) be in affecting their late-life behavior?
- Will there be just one boomer cohort or a "first wave" and a "second wave"?
- Will younger generations resent the size and standing of older boomers?
- Will boomers be a healthier older cohort even though they are living longer?
- Does the rise of "productive aging" mean that elders will become net contributors to the social and economic resource base or will they continue to be draws on it?
- How many older boomers will be care recipients, care providers, or both?
- Will older boomers work longer, or will they enjoy longer retirement, or both?
- Can boomers save and invest enough for a decent retirement?
- Will the boomers contribute to or hinder future economic growth?
- Will older boomers be "the most powerful lobby in Washington"?

How the larger society and the boomers themselves understand their needs, contributions, and standing will very much affect how the nation responds to the boomers' imposing presence. The boomers in old age will represent complete realization of the institutional standing older people have come to assume in American life over the past half-century. No longer a marginal presence, seniors today (and certainly tomorrow) are demanding and receiving recognition of their new prominence. A range of societal institutions are being forced to accommodate older people's new preferences and concerns. Employers are wrestling with a rising need to retain older workers after years of easing them out the door; families are struggling with growing "work/family" pressures as older relatives require care and attention in unprecedented numbers; communities are realizing that long-established housing and transportation patterns (many generated by the boomers earlier in life) are not congruent with the needs and preferences of older residents; and government is confronted with the costs associated with pension and health care policies that are expected to grow at what many consider to be an alarming rate.

How society will respond to the boomers in old age raises a host of additional questions:

- Will there be a labor shortage when boomers retire, and how will society respond?
- How willing are employers to retain and recruit older workers?
- Under what circumstances will the boomers be willing to work in late life?
- How will erosion of retired employee health care insurance affect late-life work?
- Can Social Security survive the boomers in retirement?
- Can increases in health care expenditures be contained as the boomers age?
- Will older boomers be the victims of age discrimination, or will they be the beneficiaries of age affirmation?

- Can communities modify transportation and housing policies to accommodate the needs and desires of aging boomers?
- Will there be a geriatric labor force in place able to meet the needs of very old boomers?
- How will families adjust to the combination of more older relatives, fewer children, and more adult members in the labor force?

The separate volumes of *Boomer Bust?* examine these questions from two overarching perspectives. Volume 1 takes a "macro view," assessing the presence of the boomers from a societal perspective. How may the boomers impact society, and how is society likely to respond? What are the critical demographic, economic, political, and policy considerations to be kept in mind? Volume 2 is directed more to the boomers themselves. How should they think about extended work lives, retirement, and retirement planning? What other roles are there for them, and how can they contribute through civic engagement, volunteering, late-life learning, and working intergenerationally? How will older boomers get around, adapt to new or existing communities, and be cared for when health care needs arise?

The chapters in volume 1, part 1, examine the boomer population as the imposing demographic phenomenon it will be. Chapter 1 previews the older boomers in broad brush, addressing a series of "frequently asked questions" about how big an impact the boomers will have. Chapter 2 sets forth the vast diversity to be found among the boomer population, making it hard to reach unconditional conclusions about their overall well-being and noting that many older boomers will continue to be in dire circumstances. Chapter 3 highlights the improvements that have been made in elders' well-being in recent decades and introduces the truly modern concept of "productive aging."

Part 2 assesses the likely economic effects of the boomers in old age. Chapter 4 emphasizes the relative prosperity of the boomers in their early years, the emergence of "leading-edge" and "trailing-edge" boomer subcohorts with different economic histories, and what will be required for boomers to assure themselves adequate income in retirement. Chapter 5 explores how different the labor market participation of boomers will be from current older adults, concluding that the changes are not likely to be as dramatic as many foretell and that men's and women's work trajectories may follow somewhat different paths. Chapter 6 reviews the impact aging boomers will have on the health care system and, in turn, how boomers must expect to deal with ever-rising health care costs. Importantly, the aging of the population—soon to be associated with the boomers—is not the principal factor of health cost increases, technology and reimbursement being bigger drivers.

Part 3 of volume 1 examines the boomers in the context of politics, government, and public policy. Chapter 7 reviews the dramatic increase in public-sector policies and expenditures on behalf of the aged, examines factors accounting for these increases, and suggests that the size of the boomer cohort in the face of spending pressures on the big entitlement programs have the makings of a political "perfect storm." Chapter 8 investigates the political attitudes and behaviors of older voters, projects these patterns onto how the boomers may behave in coming decades, and concludes that the boomers, numerically important as they may be as voters and constituents, will not constitute a solid voting block concerned with only a narrow political agenda. Chapter 9 assesses the "intergenerational equity" debate in which older and younger generations are said to be pitted one against the other, concluding that the evidence of that friction is weak, although the desire for some actors to continuing framing the debate in those terms is strong.

Part 4 contains a series of chapters addressing public policies directed to older Americans. Beyond providing important information about these programs' aims, successes, and shortcomings, each of the chapters renders judgment on how the boomers will affect these programs' workings and how well suited they may prove to be in meeting the diverse needs of the boomers. Chapter 10 provides an exhaustive review of so-called entitlement spending directed toward seniors, addressing the question of whether the nation can continue to afford these programs given how expensive they are becoming. The chapter juxtaposes aging-related spending against other large expenditure categories, uses the size and growth of the gross domestic product as a benchmark against which to assess old-age spending, and concludes that a series of tax, savings, and expenditure reforms can make these programs sustainable in the long run (Medicare and overall health care spending being the most challenging). Chapter 11 provides an overview of private pensions and uses different economic models to forecast how well they will help meet retirement needs of the boomers. Divergent patterns of coverage and contributions yield mixed conclusions, but the authors express guarded optimism that reforms enacted in 2006 will lead to more widespread participation and higher benefits.

Chapter 12 calls for a fundamental rethinking of Medicare's current approach to old-age health concerns. Historically directed at acute care illness and associated overwhelmingly with hospitals and physicians, Medicare must be reworked to better recognize the shifting health profile of contemporary elders, specifically, to better cover long-term care, mental health care, and disease management. Chapter 13 turns attention directly to long-term care, a policy arena where public policy has not been nearly as extensive as those addressing income security and acute health care. Beyond elevating the place of long-term care in public policy, the author urges that the existing paradigm be modified to better recognize consumer preferences, lifelong rather than late-life-only disabilities, and the role of both high- and low-tech innovations.

Chapter 14 explores the intriguing question of how well and how appropriately age discrimination legislation protects older people. Should the aged be legally protected against discrimination in a manner analogous to people of color and women? Does such legislation give older people needed protections or special privileges? Advanced age has historically been used as a proxy for demonstrable need, and this chapter raises the question of whether that—unmodified—should continue to be the case or some reassessment is called for. The volume's final chapter examines family leave policy and what programmatic changes may be in order to better meet the needs of individuals wearing both worker and caregiver hats. It also reviews employer policies and the contributions and limitations of what the private sector is doing to promote work/family balance.

The contributors to both volumes come from a rich array of academic, research, foundation, and frontline organizations involved with investigating and improving the lives of seniors. I am indebted to each of these contributors for their care and diligence in preparing these chapters and, in particular, for directing their attention to the older boomer question. Because most boomers *are not yet old*, this task is not as straightforward as it might first appear. Through modeling, extrapolation, and historical and longitudinal investigation, these authors have succeeded in giving informed and nuanced appraisals of how the boomers may fare in tomorrow's economic and political worlds and how those worlds may experience them, the largest old-age population in history.

Among many others, I would like to thank my colleague Judith Gonyea for the clarity of her conceptual thinking around the project's overall organization and Jeff Olson from Praeger Publishers, who shepherded these materials through the labyrinthian approval and production process. As always, thanks to my wife Perry (who believes rounding up academics is like herding cats) and my stepson Tim (who thinks none of us works hard enough).

I
DEMOGRAPHIC AND SOCIAL PROFILE

The Baby Boom Age Wave: Population Success or Tsunami?

GREG O'NEILL

THE SILVER TSUNAMI

In 2008, the first wave of the baby-boom generation—the 77 million Americans born between 1946 and 1964—will turn 62 and become eligible for Social Security benefits. Just three years later, they'll be eligible for Medicare benefits. By 2030, the entire cohort will have reached age 65 and one in five Americans will be 65 or over, compared to about one in eight today.

The aging of the baby-boom generation is often seen as a "crisis," with headlines warning that boomers will "bankrupt" Social Security and Medicare, shrink the size of the labor force, and trigger a stock market "meltdown" (Kosterlitz and Serafini 2005). Books with apocalyptic titles like *Gray Dawn* and *The Coming Generational Storm* have used the specter of population aging as a justification for major structural changes to the nation's old-age entitlement programs (Schulz and Binstock 2006). In 2007, David Walker, head of the Government Accountability Office (GAO)—Congress's nonpartisan watchdog agency—testified that the "demographic tidal wave ... represented by the retirement of the baby-boom generation" had the potential to create a "tsunami of spending that could swamp our ship of state" (Greenblatt 2007).

This chapter will review some of the most popular "doom and gloom" arguments typically expressed in the media and public policy debates. It also will present counterarguments—drawing from the academic and public policy literature—that offer a more nuanced and optimistic view of both the challenges and opportunities of an aging society.

BOOMERS AND THE GRAYING OF THE POPULATION

The United States has an aging population. Between 1960—when the baby boom was still under way—and 2030, the share of the population age 65 or older will more than double (from 9 percent to 20 percent). This has led commentators to describe the future United States as "a nation of Floridas"— since about one in five Floridians today is over 65.

Although current anxiety over the "graying of the population" is often discussed as though it were associated solely with the impending retirement of the baby-boom generation, the American population was aging long before the boomers came along and will continue to age even after the youngest boomer has passed away. The population is growing older as a result of two long-term demographic trends: women are having fewer children and people are living longer.

In the United States, the total fertility rate—defined as the average number of children born to each woman—had been declining steadily for nearly two hundred years when suddenly, in the mid-twentieth century, it went up and stayed up for almost two decades. But the postwar "baby boom" was a temporary phenomenon. By the mid-1960s, birthrates reverted back to historical trends, dropping sharply from 3.7 children per woman at the height of the boom in 1957 to a historic low of 1.7 children by the mid-1970s. The rate has since recovered to 2.1 children per woman—or what is commonly called the replacement rate—but the drop in the fertility rate relative to the baby-boom period is pushing up the average age of the population (Munnell 2004).

The other factor behind the demographic transformation is increasing life expectancy. Better medical care and healthier lifestyles mean that people live much longer than they did fifty years ago. And, as people live longer, the proportion of the population at older ages becomes larger. In the United States, life expectancy at birth was 69.7 years in 1960. By 2004, it had moved up more than eight years to 77.9 years. Moreover, life expectancy in 1960 for those age 65 was about thirteen years for men and fourteen years for women. By 2004, it had risen to almost seventeen years for men and nineteen years for women.

The aging of the baby-boom generation, increased life expectancy, and fertility rates at about the replacement level are expected to significantly increase the elderly dependency ratio—the estimated number of people age 65 and over compared to the working-age population, ages 15 to 64. There were more than seven workers for every retiree in 1950, but now there are only about five workers per retiree—and that is projected to decline to three by 2030 (GAO 2005).

There is no evidence that these trends will reverse in the near future. Experts are not expecting any significant increase in the birthrate or a change in the trend toward longer life (Munnell 2004). The U.S. Census

Bureau projects that life expectancy will increase over the next several decades, that about one in every nine baby boomers (or nine million boomers) will survive into his or her late 90s, and that three million boomers will reach 100 (Sonnega 2006).

Furthermore, there is widespread agreement among researchers that current and projected levels of immigration—around a million net immigrants per year—are not nearly large enough to offset the aging of the U.S. population. Although immigration makes the population larger, differences between the average age and fertility rates of immigrants and natives do not significantly affect the overall *age composition* of the population, because immigrants make up a relatively small percentage of the total population (Camarota 2007; United Nations 2001). Thus, studies show that it would require almost four million additional immigrants every year through 2025 to maintain the elderly dependency ratio at the year-2000 level. But experts agree that such a large increase in the gross immigration quota seems unrealistic from a social and political standpoint (Lee and Haaga 2002).

"ONE EVERY EIGHT SECONDS ..."

As the baby-boom generation begins to reach traditional retirement ages, at the rate of "one every eight seconds" (Greenblatt 2007), the pace of population aging will rapidly accelerate. Although this commonly cited statistic succinctly conveys the speed with which the population will age, it conceals an important detail about the size and distribution of the nineteen-year baby-boom cohort—namely, that there are more boomers in the cohort's younger, second half (see table 1-1). Thus, although boomers born in 1946 will soon reach retirement age at the rate of one every 11.5 seconds,

TABLE 1-1.   U.S. Population by Age Group, 1960–2030 (millions)

Age Group	1960	1970	1980	1990	2000	2010*	2020*	2030*
0 to 4	20.3 B	17.2	16.5	18.4	19.2	21.4	22.9	24.3
5 to 14	35.7 B	40.8 A	34.8	35.2	41.1	40.5	44.5	47.3
15 to 24	24.2	35.8 A	42.5 B	36.8	39.4	43.0	42.2	46.6
25 to 34	22.7	25.1	37.4 B	43.2 Y	39.8	41.6	45.1	44.9
35 to 44	24.1	23.0	25.8	37.6 Y	45.1 B	41.1	42.8	46.7
45 to 54	20.6	23.3	22.7	25.2	38.0 B	44.8 O	40.9	42.9
55 to 64	15.6	18.7	21.8	21.1	24.4	36.2 O	42.7 O	39.4
65 to 74	11.0	12.5	15.7	18.1	18.4	21.3	31.8 O	37.9 M
75 and over	5.6	7.6	10.1	13.1	16.7	19.0	22.9	33.5 M
TOTAL	180	204	227	249	282	309	336	364

*Estimated Population

Source: U.S. Census Bureau, CPS Reports P-25, Numbers 917, 1095.

TABLE 1-2.   U.S. Population Growth by Age, 1960–2030 (percent)

Age Group	1960– 1970	1970– 1980	1980– 1990	1990– 2000	2000– 2010*	2010– 2020*	2020– 2030*
0 to 4	−15.0	−4.1	11.5	4.3	11.5	7.0	6.1
5 to 14	14.3 B	−14.7	1.1	16.8	−1.5	9.9	6.3
15 to 24	48.0 B	18.7 A	−13.4	7.1	9.1	−1.9	10.4
25 to 34	10.6	49.0 A	15.5 B	−7.9	4.5	8.4	−0.4
35 to 44	−4.6	12.2	45.7 B	19.9 Y	−8.9	4.1	9.1
45 to 54	13.1	−2.6	11.0	50.8 Y	17.9 B	−8.7	4.9
55 to 64	19.9	16.6	−3.2	15.6	48.4 B	18.0 O	−7.7
65 to 74	13.6	25.6	15.3	1.7	15.8	49.3 O	19.2 O
75 and over	35.7	32.9	29.7	27.5	13.8	20.5	46.3 O
TOTAL	13.3	11.4	9.5	13.3	9.6	8.7	8.3

*Projected growth

Source: U.S. Census Bureau, CPS Reports P-25, Numbers 917, 1095.

boomers born in 1960 (the peak birth year of the baby boom) will retire at the rate of one every 7.5 seconds.

From a public policy perspective, the first wave of boomer retirees will be a harbinger of trends that will intensify when the larger, second half of boomers retire a decade later. In the meantime, however, one should not forget that the oldest boomers have just entered their 60s, whereas the youngest are still in their early 40s. Today, the fastest-growing age group is the one that contains the first half of the baby boom—55- to 64-year-olds (see table 1.2). Indeed, the over-65 population, the much smaller generations born in the Great Depression and the baby-bust years of World War II, is growing slowly today (Frey 2007). Attention to these demographic facts is important because, if policy makers and politicians believe the graying of the population is already in full flight, they may not be prepared for when it actually arrives.

BABY BOOMERS AND SOCIAL SECURITY: TROUBLE ON THE "INFINITE HORIZON"?

As the first wave of baby boomers approaches retirement, there is considerable debate about the magnitude of Social Security's financial problems. At the center of the debate is the annual *Social Security's Trustees Report.* One side—including most media coverage—claims that the Trustees Report clearly indicates that the retirement of the baby-boom generation will "bankrupt" Social Security and that drastic structural changes (such as privatization) are required to restore the program's long-term solvency. Meanwhile, the other side argues that the report only confirms that Social

Security faces a challenging but manageable long-term funding shortfall that can be closed through a mix of moderate benefit changes and new revenues.

The 2007 Trustees Report forecasts that benefit payments will begin to exceed Social Security's *tax* revenues in 2017. After that date, the program would have to begin drawing upon assets in the Social Security trust funds to continue full payment of scheduled benefits—although initially it would only have to draw on interest from the trust fund's bonds (i.e., U.S. Treasury notes). By 2041, the report projects that there will be no more bonds left to sell and the trust funds will be depleted. This date is often described as the point at which Social Security is "bankrupt," giving the impression that there will be no money in the program. In reality, upon exhaustion of the trust funds, Social Security will continue to receive annual revenues from payroll taxes and from the partial taxation of the Social Security benefits that higher-income beneficiaries receive. This revenue will be sufficient to pay 75 percent of promised benefits in 2041 and will gradually fall to 70 percent of benefits in 2081—assuming the Social Security Act is not changed.

The Trustees Report also presents Social Security's financial shortfall in dollar terms, and these very large numbers often appear in the press. In the 2007 report, the present discounted value of the seventy-five-year shortfall between projected revenues and expenditures was placed at $4.7 trillion. (The seventy-five-year period is chosen because it includes the entire lifetimes of nearly all current participants.) The report also estimated Social Security's "infinite horizon" shortfall to be $13.6 trillion—the present discounted value of the difference between projected revenues and benefits from now through *eternity*.

Although it is widely agreed that Social Security faces a significant long-term funding shortfall if no changes are made to the program, many analysts question the reliability or usefulness of calculating Social Security's unfunded obligation over seventy-five years, given the uncertainty of economic and demographic trends over such a long period. Likewise, the infinite horizon measure, which was first included in the 2003 Trustees Report, has been strongly criticized by actuaries and other Social Security analysts as a highly speculative and misleading measure (see Stone and Greenstein 2007).

Indeed, observers note that the outlook for Social Security presented in the Trustees Report has changed significantly in just the past decade (see table 1-3). From 1997 to 2007, the date by which the trust fund was projected to be exhausted rose by twelve years—from 2029 to 2041. In other words, although the outlook for Social Security tends to change little year to year, the recent trend has been one of an *improving* outlook for Social Security, rather than a worsening one. Furthermore, the nonpartisan Congressional Budget Office (CBO) does not project a shortfall for Social Security until 2052, a decade longer than the prediction of the Social Security trustees (Congressional Budget Office 2005).

TABLE 1-3. History of Social Security Trustees' Estimates

Report Year	75-year Deficit as a Percent of Taxable Payroll	Infinite Horizon Deficit as a Percent of Taxable Payroll	Year When Costs First Exceed Total Revenues	Year When Trust Fund is Exhausted
1997	2.23%	NA	2019	2029
1998	2.19	NA	2021	2032
1999	2.07	NA	2022	2034
2000	1.89	NA	2025	2037
2001	1.86	NA	2025	2038
2002	1.87	NA	2027	2041
2003	1.92	3.8%	2028	2042
2004	1.89	3.5	2028	2042
2005	1.92	3.5	2027	2041
2006	2.02	3.7	2026	2040
2007	1.95	3.5	2027	2041

Source: Trustees Reports, various years, as cited in Chad Stone and Robert Greenstein, "What the 2007 Trustees' Report Shows about Social Security," Center on Budget and Policy Priorities, April 24, 2007, available at http://www.cbpp.org/4-24-07socsec.pdf.

In addition, many economists and policy analysts question the Trustees Reports' specific assumptions about future economic growth and demographic change. In particular, they argue that the trustees' assumptions about the performance of the economy are overly pessimistic and thus overstate the program's financial problems. Historically, gross domestic product (GDP) growth has averaged 3.4 percent annually after accounting for inflation, according to the Bureau of Economic Analysis (GAO 2006). But in their assumption of long-run real economic growth, the Social Security trustees use a range between 1.1 percent and 2.7 percent, with 2.0 percent assumed for the intermediate (best estimate) assumptions. If the trustees' intermediate assumption is right, growth will be 41 percent *slower* in the future than it has been in the past. This has important implications for the Social Security debate. As Friedland and Summer (2005) argue, small differences in sustained economic growth can have a dramatic impact on the fiscal future of society. According to their analysis, if real economic growth averages about 2.6 percent per year between now and 2050, then projected government expenditures could be about the same proportion of GDP as today. Indeed, it is worth noting that under what the trustees label their "optimistic" assumptions, the trust fund would remain solvent over the entire seventy-five-year projection period (and, in fact, their "optimistic" projections have proven to be correct in the past decade).

Although it would be foolish to assume that the United States will simply grow its way out of the fiscal challenges presented by the retirement of the baby-boom generation, Friedland and Summer argue that it would be equally foolish to assume that the future will be completely dismal without radical restructuring of government programs such as Social Security. "Population growth and change will affect society," they write, "but so too will policy choices" (2005, 4). Indeed, prominent economists such as Peter Diamond and Peter Orszag, Henry Aaron and Robert Reischauer, and former Social Security commissioner Robert Ball have put forth a range of proposals to restore Social Security solvency that offer various combinations of modest benefit reductions and revenue increases (for an excellent summary, see Sass, Munnell, and Eschtruth 2007).

These proposals include, among other ideas, raising the cap on earnings subject to the Social Security payroll tax. Currently, Social Security benefits are financed by a 12.4 percent tax on earnings (split evenly between workers and employers) with a cap on wages subject to the tax of $97,500 in 2007. When the current cap was put in place, Social Security taxed about 90 percent of all U.S. earnings. But growing income inequality has shrunk the Social Security tax base. Today, with the increased concentration of income among the highest-paid, Social Security covers only 84 percent of all wage and salary income earned in the United States. To once again cover 90 percent of wages, the cap would have to rise to $177,600. Although this change would affect only 6 percent of workers—whose benefits would be increased as well—it would eliminate 45 percent of the seventy-five-year projected shortfall (Sass, Munnell, and Eschtruth 2007). Eliminating the earnings cap altogether, without increasing benefits for the highest-paid, would produce a *surplus* in the system over the next seventy-five years (Spriggs 2005).

Opponents argue that raising the cap could undermine political support for the program in Congress and among those with the highest earnings. But this is hardly a radical idea—in 1993, the Medicare tax cap was completely eliminated without increasing benefits at all, and it was accomplished with almost no political debate (Schulz and Binstock 2006). Moreover, those who would be affected by this change tend to earn a large percentage of their income from capital gains, interest income, and dividends—and Social Security taxes are not assessed on this income. In addition, income from these sources is taxed at a much lower rate than wage/salary income—a maximum of 15 percent under the Bush administration's 2003 tax cuts.

Although the different proposals can be debated, it is clear that the issue is not a lack of options but rather a lack of political will. In any case, by 2041 time will have taken its toll on the baby boomers. The oldest members of this generation will be in their 90s, and the youngest will be 77. Even if no changes have been made to the system by that time, Social Security benefits will still be available to support them in their retirement.

THE RISING TIDE OF HEALTH CARE COSTS: ARE AGING BOOMERS TO BLAME?

For years, pundits and politicians have predicted that the retirement of the baby boomers will accelerate growth in health care spending and that such growth will "bankrupt" the government's health care programs (Pan, Chai, and Farber 2007). This scenario has powerful face validity. On average, acute and chronic illnesses increase with age, and per-capita health expenditures rise very rapidly after 65. Indeed, as a share of the U.S. economy, federal spending for Medicare and Medicaid together already exceeds outlays for Social Security—4.5 percent versus 4.3 percent of GDP in 2006. And the CBO projects that if health care costs continue growing faster than the economy, federal spending on Medicare and Medicaid alone would rise to about 20 percent of GDP by 2050—roughly the same share of the economy that the *entire* federal budget accounts for today! (Orszag 2007).

Yet a closer analysis of the CBO projections shows that population aging is not the primary factor driving the rise in America's health care costs. By itself, growth in the share of the older population accounts for less than 20 percent of the projected growth in federal Medicare and Medicaid spending over the next fifty years, whereas *growth in medical spending* per person above and beyond the increase attributable to population aging and economic growth accounts for about 80 percent.

Indeed, research has consistently found that the aging of the population alone is not likely to be a major driver of the annual growth in the demand for health care and in national health spending (Reinhardt 2003). Other factors, such as new diagnostic and curative technologies and more sophisticated prescription drugs, play a much bigger role. Other reasons relate to characteristics of the health care system—including fee-for-service payment, medical price inflation, health care workforce shortages, and weak controls on the supply and use of services (Strunk and Ginsburg 2002). Together, these characteristics encourage the provision of more health care services, rather than the more efficient use of health care resources.

Reforms that eliminate the health care system's inefficiencies may help reduce Medicare and Medicaid's growth rate, but are unlikely to hold health care expenditures in the public sector at their current share of the economy. This is because new medical technologies and therapies have enabled baby boomers to live longer and healthier lives—and it is hard to believe that Americans will not want to avail themselves of such medical advances in the decades ahead, even if they entail significant costs. The challenge for political leaders and policy makers therefore "is to pursue major reforms that eliminate inefficiencies in the health care system and restrain costs in the system to the greatest extent possible without unduly constraining medical progress" (Kogan et al. 2007, 4).

New evidence suggests that there are opportunities to reduce health care costs without incurring adverse health consequences. Although the United States outspends all other nations in health care (including those whose populations already have the age structure that the U.S. population will reach only in 2020–2025), its higher costs are not accompanied by measurable advances in overall health outcomes (McKinsey Global Institute 2007).

Indeed, within the United States there is significant evidence that "more expensive care doesn't always mean higher quality care" (Orszag and Ellis 2007, 1794). Perhaps the most compelling evidence comes from the substantial differences in per-enrollee Medicare spending in various regions of the country—and the fact that higher-spending regions do not generate better health outcomes than lower-spending regions, controlling for differences in the health of the population and medical prices (Fisher et al. 2003).

WILL RETIRING BOOMERS SINK THE STOCK MARKET?

In addition to concerns about how the boomers' retirement will strain the nation's retirement and health systems, worries about a future market "meltdown" as a result of demographic changes have frequently appeared in the media over the past decade. In 2006, *Fortune* featured an article with this provocative headline: "The Boomer Bust: Will Aging Boomers Pull Their Money Out of the Market and Cause an Asset Meltdown on Their Way to Retirement?" The article speculated that just as the boomers helped fuel a spectacular bull market in the 1980s and 1990s by buying stocks, they will trigger a lengthy bear market when they retire and begin selling stocks.

The reason that these "demography is destiny" stories attract a lot of attention in the financial press is that "there is an underlying link between the age structure of the population, the demand for assets, and the prices of assets" (Poterba 2004, 45). However, as Poterba notes, the critical issue is to quantitatively determine how important demographic factors are in relation to other factors that influence asset prices.

Several empirical studies argue that the rise in stock market prices in the 1990s can be attributed to the entry of the baby-boom cohort into its "peak saving years," and some have forecast a sharp and sudden decline in asset prices in coming decades as boomers sell their assets to the smaller baby-bust cohort that follows them (see, for example, Schieber and Shoven 1997; Brooks 2002; Geanakoplos, Magill, and Quinzii 2004; Siegel 2005). In a survey of the literature, Poterba (2004, 47) concludes that a "reasonable consensus analysis" would suggest that the large number of baby-boom retirees may reduce the market's annualized return by about one-half of 1 percent (or fifty basis points) over the next couple of decades.

Although a half-point decline seems somewhat small in comparison to real annual U.S. stock returns (which have averaged about 8 percent from 1946 to 2004), the effect is more substantial when considered in terms of its accumulation over a long period. Compounded annually over thirty years, this would mean that for two investors—one who earns 8 percent and the other 7.5 percent—the former investor's assets would be worth about 13 percent more. (The proportional effect of a 0.5 percent decline in annual return would be smaller if the baseline level of the return was higher, but the absolute effect in terms of dollars would be larger.) Even so, Poterba concludes that the evidence suggests only modest effects, if any, of demographics on returns and does not support the alarmist asset market "meltdown" view.

A subsequent report from the GAO (2006) on the market impact of the baby boom's retirement came to a similar conclusion. Based on a survey of academic studies as well as its own empirical research, the GAO determined that, although there is some evidence to suggest that the baby-boom retirement will have a negative effect on financial asset returns, it does not support the claim that it will cause a "dramatic decline" in stock prices or returns. The GAO found that demographic variables explained on average about 6 percent of the variation in annual stock returns from 1948 to 2004, but other macroeconomic and financial variables in their statistical model explained nearly half of the variation in historical stock returns. This suggests that such factors outweigh any demographic effect on stock returns.

Furthermore, the GAO report argues that the potential for the baby-boom generation to precipitate a market meltdown in retirement may be substantially reduced because a small minority of this population holds the majority of the generation's financial assets. According to the GAO's analysis of the 2004 Survey of Consumer Finances, the wealthiest 10 percent of boomers owned more than two-thirds of the generation's financial assets, including stocks, bonds, mutual funds, individual retirement accounts (IRAs), and other account-type retirement savings plans (see figure 1-1). In fact, about a third of boomers do not own *any* financial assets. This concentration of wealth means that boomers may be less pressured to spend down their financial assets in retirement. Research on current retirees indicates that the wealthiest are able to support themselves on the income these investments generate without spending them down significantly (Carroll 2000). The

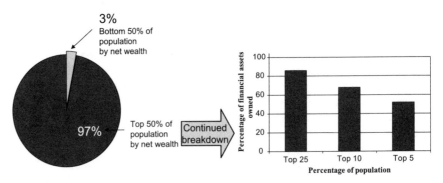

FIGURE 1-1.   Distribution of Baby Boomer Financial Assets, by Wealth Percentiles

Note: Financial assets include stocks, bonds, mutual funds, IRAs, Keogh plans, and other account-type retirement savings plans. The distribution of baby boomers is based on total wealth, defined as the net of all assets that each household owns and all outstanding debts.

Source: GAO analysis of 2004 Survey of Consumer Finances.

GAO also noted that boomers will retire not all at once, but over a nineteen-year span, which mitigates the risk of a shock to financial markets.

Other scholars, mostly economists, have noted several other scenarios that might ease the impact of the aging of the baby boom on the performance of U.S. financial markets. For example, increases in life expectancy and the expectation of many boomers to work past traditional retirement ages will likely spread asset sales over a longer period of time than was typical for earlier generations. In addition, rather than face the prospect of a sharp sell-off in stocks, companies will most likely find ways to make stocks more attractive to the shrinking number of buyers by increasing their dividends—allowing retirees who need income to continue holding their assets. Another counter to the asset "meltdown" theory is that boomers may use their homes to finance retirement through instruments like reverse mortgages, since houses are generally older Americans' largest assets—not stocks, bonds, or mutual funds. Also, some have noted that the emergence of global capital markets means aging boomers in the United States need not sell exclusively to young Americans. Indeed, some noted economists (Siegel 2005; Fehr, Jokisch, and Kotlikoff 2005) predict young investors in emerging economies such as India and China will be net buyers of capital when aging American boomers begin to sell.

WILL THE BOOMERS DRAIN THE LABOR POOL?

For several years now, the business press and media have been warning that the U.S. economy will soon experience widespread job vacancies because of a shortage of workers. Behind the predictions of a coming labor crisis are demographic forecasts that the U.S. labor force will grow more slowly than in the past as the baby-boom generation retires and is replaced by the smaller baby-bust generation. Labor force projections from the Bureau of Labor Statistics (BLS) point to a lower labor force growth rate of 0.8 percent per year for the 2006–2016 period, compared to an annual growth rate of 1.2 percent during the 1996–2006 decade. In addition, as the population ages, the labor force's age composition will change dramatically. According to BLS projections, the overall labor force (16 years and older) will increase by just 9 percent between 2006 and 2016, but the age-55-and-older workforce will increase by 47 percent. The BLS also forecasts that the median age of the labor force will increase to 42.1 years in 2016, from 35.4 years in 1986 (Toossi 2007). The concern among business and government leaders is that low labor force growth associated with population aging will lead to slower economic growth and, in turn, declines in overall living standards (Cappelli 2004).

Although the baby-bust cohort—those born after 1964 and through the 1970s—is smaller than the baby boom, Cappelli (2004) argues that it is wrong to assume that a smaller cohort of workers will necessarily lead to a labor shortage. He points out that, even though entry-level cohorts may be smaller in the future, the overall number of college graduates will actually rise—and it is college graduates who employers most demand. When baby boomers were in high school in the 1960s and 1970s, fewer than 50 percent of graduates went on to college. Now, according to the National Association for College Admission Counseling, about two-thirds move directly into post-secondary education. Moreover, Cappelli notes that behind the baby-bust cohort is another large generation—the "echo" children of the baby boom (now in their teens and 20s)—that is just beginning to enter the workforce. According to Census Bureau data, births in 1990 were the highest recorded since the baby-boom days of the early 1960s. Now, eighteen years later, the children of baby boomers are making news headlines as the largest high school class in the history of the United States sets its sights on college (Hofius Hall 2008).

As for the fear that baby boomers' retirement will contribute to a serious labor shortage, Cappelli argues that it is unrealistic to assume boomers will retire at age 65, given the lengthening average life span. As baby boomers approach traditional retirement age, there is evidence that they are choosing to stay in the workforce longer, alleviating the threat of a sudden and severe labor shortage. According to the BLS, the number of older people in the work-force has doubled in the past twenty years. Almost 20 million men and women aged 55 to 64 were employed in 2006, representing 13 percent of the total labor force—up from 12 million (10 percent) in 1986. At the same time, the overall labor force participation rate for this group increased from 54 per-cent to 64 percent. This is an important trend, since most of this age group are members of the (smaller) front end of the baby-boom cohort, and their labor market attachment suggests increased numbers of older workers in the near future as the later and larger part of the baby-boom generation ages.

Retirement experts say the increase in older workers primarily reflects inad-equate retirement savings, the erosion of traditional defined-benefit pensions, and rising health care costs. In addition, there is evidence that labor force par-ticipation among older workers has risen in response to the increase in the eli-gibility age for full Social Security benefits and the elimination of the earnings test for workers at full retirement age and beyond (GAO 2007). Beyond finan-cial incentives, surveys by AARP (2004) and Civic Ventures/MetLife Founda-tion (2005) also have found that the majority of baby boomers—upwards of 70 percent—plan to work past traditional retirement age for reasons associated with feelings of social and mental well-being. Furthermore, higher education levels, improved health status among today's older workers, and a decline in physically demanding jobs imply a continued upward trend in labor market participation (Turner 2007). Whatever the reasons, even a modest increase in the labor force participation rate of baby boomers will increase the labor sup-ply significantly because of the cohort's large size.

However, significantly higher boomer labor force participation rates are not inevitable. Munnell (2006) cites a number of factors that could adversely affect the demand for and supply of older workers. On the demand side, cost is the paramount issue. At the same productivity level, older workers' higher wages and benefits—health insurance and pensions—make them more expensive than younger workers. On the supply side, health conditions and few flexible work/retirement options are major hurdles to continued employment. In addition, employment-based age discrimination, although illegal, remains pervasive (McCann 2004). A study of age bias conducted by the Center for Retirement Research at Boston College found a younger worker is 40 percent more likely to be called in for an interview than a worker age 50 or over (Lahey 2005).

Furthermore, although most baby boomers plan to work longer than their predecessors, it is too early to assume that this is what they will actually do. The annual Retirement Confidence Survey has consistently found that approximately four in ten retirees leave the workforce earlier than planned (37 percent in 2007). Many retirees who retire early cite health problems, disability, or changes at their company (such as downsizing or closure). Others indicate work-related reasons, such as obsolete skills (Employee Benefit Research Institute 2007).

Yet, even if baby boomers' retirements lead to a slowdown in labor force growth, it does not necessarily mean that overall living standards will decline, as many observers fear. Certainly, the concern is understandable, since workforce growth has been a key to U.S. economic growth for most of the past half-century. However, the economy's growth rate is determined by the rate of increase in the labor force *plus* the rate of increase in productivity. Indeed, the steady rise in U.S. living standards is due to productivity (output per worker) that has outpaced the labor force growth rate: The U.S. economy today is about eight times bigger than it was at the end of World War II, but the workforce is only twice as big (Friedland and Summer 2005). Although future economic growth will likely have to rely less on labor force growth and more on higher productivity, many economists expect productivity to continue to grow enough over the next half-century to ensure rising standards of living for everyone (Wray 2006).

In fact, some argue that an aging society could help achieve higher productivity growth. Alan Greenspan, former chairman of the Federal Reserve, has speculated that a slowed rate of growth or a decline in the working-age population associated with aging should increase the incentives for developing labor-saving technologies and may actually spur technological innovation—a critical determinant of labor productivity (Greenspan 2003). Mérette (2002) predicts that a rising ratio of retirees to workers will result in tight labor markets that will create upward pressure on wages in general. These labor conditions, he argues, will propel investments in human capital (education and training), "whose importance as an engine of growth is increasingly being recognized as industrialized countries shift away from resource-based and toward knowledge-based economies" (2002, 3). Mérette points out that rising wages should also induce many older workers to keep working, further limiting labor shortages.

Thus, one cannot conclude that the retirement of the baby boomers will lead to widespread labor shortages. Although there may be a possibility of "spot" shortages in specific geographic areas and occupations (Kuhn 2003), even this scenario will depend on the ability of the labor market to make adjustments as needs emerge. Just as the labor market adapted to the baby boomers' entrance into the workforce, many economists predict that employers and governments will proactively adjust their policies and practices to accommodate older workers and prevent labor shortages (Wray 2006; Greenspan 2003).

HARNESSING THE POWER OF THE AGE WAVE

Currently, much of the discussion about an aging society focuses on its cost and perpetuates the stereotype that older adults place a burden on society. In reality, older Americans' social and economic contributions are considerable. According to data from the 2006 Current Population Survey (CPS), about 17.3 million adults age 55 and over are engaged in formal volunteer activities (defined as volunteering for a religious, educational, health-related, or other charitable organization). Americans age 65 and over devoted the most time to community activities—double the national median annual hours for all ages. Using a moderate cost assumption, Johnson and Schaner (2006) estimate that adults age 55 and over contributed $44.3 billion through formal volunteer activities in 2002.

Volunteers' contributions are increasingly important given the government's growing reliance on nonprofits to deliver public services. Baby boomers could boost the volunteer sector, not just because of the generation's size but also because of its members' relatively high levels of education, wealth, and skills. Although some research argues that baby boomers have been less civically engaged than preceding generations (Putnam 2002), more recent studies find that baby boomers are volunteering at higher rates than previous generations. According to Census Bureau surveys of volunteer activity, an estimated 31 percent of baby boomers volunteered when they were age 46 to 57, compared with an estimated 25 percent of the "greatest generation" (born between 1910 and 1930) at the same ages (Foster-Bey, Grimm, and Dietz 2007).

In addition, new research finds a high commitment to formal volunteer work among the newly retired. Using data from the Health and Retirement Study, Zedlewski (2007) examined transitions from work to volunteering for adults age 55 to 64 who retired between 1996 and 2000. Among those who retired, 45 percent engaged in formal volunteer activities within a four-year postretirement period—even though only 34 percent had volunteered while working. Noting that the population age 55 to 64 will be about 75 percent larger by 2020 than in 2000, Zedlewski remarks that "nonprofit organizations seem destined to benefit from a significant growth in the services of retirees" (2007, 6).

However, surveys find that most nonprofit and voluntary organizations are not prepared for the challenge of engaging large numbers of baby boomers in meaningful service (Casner-Lotto 2007). For the last two decades, the voluntary sector has benefited from the substantial contributions of older volunteers whose strong community values were shaped in the World War II era. Despite being placed mostly in routine administrative or fundraising roles, this small cohort of older volunteers has been giving a disproportionate share of volunteer hours (Reed and Selbee 2001). Now the "greatest generation" members are rapidly aging out of the volunteer ranks, leaving behind gaps that must be filled. But a growing body of evidence suggests that baby boomers are not willing to perform the traditional "envelope-stuffing" tasks that their predecessors have been doing. Consistent with their higher levels of education and professionalism, boomers demand "interesting, growth-producing, mission-critical, productive, high-level, high-impact work that allows them the freedom to apply their high skills and influence" (Graff 2007). In fact, studies show that baby boomers who engage in professional or management activities such as strategic planning, marketing, or volunteer coordination are the most likely to continue volunteering from one year to the next, while those involved in general labor and routine tasks such as driving, fundraising, and meal preparation are the least likely (Foster-Bey, Grimm, and Dietz 2007).

Experts on civic engagement and aging agree that attracting baby-boomer volunteers to the nonprofit world will be critical to solving a wide range of social problems in the years ahead. According to Marc Freedman, founder of Civic Ventures, the aging of the baby boom and its improved circumstances could provide a windfall for civic life in the twenty-first century by greatly increasing the number of people available to address the needs of American communities (Freedman 1999). In addition, there is substantial evidence that older adults who volunteer live longer and enjoy better physical and mental health than their counterparts who do not volunteer (Grimm, Spring, and Dietz 2007). Recipients of volunteer services, children in particular, also benefit from older adults' engagement—especially in educational activities. And increased volunteerism potentially reduces costs, as healthier older adults require fewer health care dollars (Zedlewski and Butrica 2007).

CONCLUSION: DEMOGRAPHY IS NOT DESTINY

Although the aging of the baby-boom generation is commonly depicted in the popular press as cause for alarm, the empirical evidence reviewed here suggests there is no reason to fear the coming demographic shift. In fact, the benefits of an aging population may outweigh the costs as millions of boomers—buoyed by gains in longevity, education, and health—are expected to reinvent retirement as a more active stage of life that mixes work, leisure, and national service (Harvard School of Public Health/MetLife Foundation

2004). But this will require that we create new public policies and institutions that enable older adults to make continuing contributions to society. Fortunately, recent years have seen the growth of a wide range of organizations—in the private, public, and nonprofit sectors—that help advance the goal of "civic engagement" in later life (e.g., see "The Civic Enterprise" at http://www.civicengagement.org). We have also reviewed good evidence to suggest that an aging population and slower labor force growth does not necessarily imply lower productivity growth. Indeed, as Fogel and Prusiner (2007) and Moody (2005) have argued, an aging society can be expected to spur "silver industries" (especially in the area of health care services) that will be the new drivers of the American economy.

REFERENCES

AARP. 2004. Baby boomers envision retirement II: Survey of boomers' expectations for retirement. Washington, DC: AARP.

Brooks, R. 2002. Asset-market effects of the baby boom and social security reform. *American Economic Review* 92 (2): 402–6.

Camarota, S. A. 2007. Immigration's impact on American workers. Testimony prepared for the House Judiciary Committee, May 9, 2007. Available at http://www.cis.org/articles/2007/sactestimony050907.pdf.

Cappelli, P. 2004. Will there really be a labor shortage? *Public Policy & Aging Report* 14 (3): 1–6.

Carroll, C. D. 2000. Portfolios of the rich. National Bureau of Economic Research (NBER) Working Paper No. 7826. Cambridge, MA: NBER.

Casner-Lotto, J. 2007. Boomers are ready for nonprofits, but are nonprofits ready for them? Conference Board Report E-0012-07-WG. Available at http://www.conference-board.org/publications/describe.cfm?id=1319.

Civic Ventures/MetLife Foundation. 2005. *New face of work survey.* San Francisco: Civic Ventures.

Congressional Budget Office. 2005. *The long-term budget outlook.* Washington, DC: CBO. Available at http://www.cbo.gov/ftpdocs/69xx/doc6982/12-15-LongTerm Outlook.pdf.

Employee Benefit Research Institute. 2007. The retirement system in transition: The 2007 Retirement Confidence Survey. EBRI Issue Brief No. 304. Available at http://www.ebri.org/pdf/briefspdf/EBRI_IB_04a-20075.pdf.

Fehr, H., S. Jokisch, and L. J. Kotlikoff. 2005. Will China eat our lunch or take us to dinner? Simulating the transition paths of the U.S., the EU, Japan, and China. NBER Working Paper No. 11,668. Washington, DC: NBER.

Fisher, E. S., D. E. Wennberg, T. A. Stukel, D. J. Gottlieb, F. L. Lucas, and E. L. Pinder. 2003. The implications of regional variations in Medicare spending: Health outcomes and satisfaction with care. *Annals of Internal Medicine* 138:288–98.

Fogel, R., and S. Prusiner. 2007. Health, Science, and Wealth. New York: International Longevity Center. Available at http://www.ilcusa.org/media/pdfs/Health_Science_Wealth.pdf.

Foster-Bey, J., R. Grimm Jr., and N. Dietz. 2007. Keeping baby boomers volunteering: A research brief on volunteer retention and turnover. Washington, DC: Corporation for National and Community Service. Available at http://www.nationalservice.gov/pdf/07_0307_boomer_report.pdf.

Freedman, M. 1999. *Prime time: How baby boomers will revolutionize retirement and transform America.* New York: Public Affairs.

Frey, W. H. 2007. *America's regional demographics in the '00s decade: The role of seniors, boomers and new minorities.* Washington, DC: Research Institute for Housing America and the Brookings Institution.

Friedland, R., and L. Summer. 2005. *Demography is not destiny, revisited.* Washington, DC: Center on an Aging Society.

GAO (Government Accountability Office). 2005. *Redefining retirement: Options for older Americans.* GAO-05-620T. Washington, DC: GAO.

————. 2006. Baby boom generation: Retirement of baby boomers is unlikely to precipitate dramatic decline in market returns, but broader risks threaten retirement security. GAO-06-718. Washington, DC: GAO.

————. 2007. Retirement decisions: Federal policies offer mixed signals about when to retire. GAO-07-753. Washington, DC: GAO.

Geanakoplos, J., M. Magill, and M. Quinzii. 2004. Demography and the long-run predictability of the stock market. Cowles Foundation Paper No. 1099. New Haven, CT: Cowles Foundation for Research in Economics, Yale University.

Graff, L. 2007. Boom or bust? Will baby boomers save us? Http://www.lindagraff.ca/musings.html#boom.

Greenblatt, A. 2007. Aging baby boomers: Will the "youth generation" redefine old age? *CQ Researcher* 17 (37): 865–88.

Greenspan, A. 2003. Statement of Alan Greenspan, Chairman, Board of Governors of the Federal Reserve System, before the Special Committee on Aging, United States Senate, February 27, 2003. Available at http://www.federalreserve.gov/boarddocs/testimony/2003/20030227/default.htm.

Grimm, R., Jr., K. Spring, and N. Dietz. 2007. The health benefits of volunteering: A review of recent research. Washington, DC: Corporation for National and Community Service. Available at http://www.nationalservice.gov/pdf/07_0506_hbr.pdf.

Harvard School of Public Health/MetLife Foundation. 2004. *Reinventing Aging: Baby Boomers and Civic Engagement.* Boston, MA: Harvard School of Public Health. Available at http://www.reinventingaging.org/.

Hofius Hall, S. 2008. Largest high school crop in history competes for admission. *Times-Tribune* (Scranton, PA). January 14. Available at http://www.thetimes-tribune.com/site/news.cfm?newsid=19195091&BRD=2185&PAG=461&dept_id=415898&rfi=6.

Johnson, R. W., and S. G. Schaner. 2006. Value of unpaid activities by older Americans tops $160 billion per year. Perspectives on Productive Aging, No. 4. Available at http://www.urban.org/uploadedpdf/311227_older_americans.pdf.

Kogan, R., M. Fiedler, A. Aron-Dine, and J. Horney. 2007. The long-term fiscal outlook is bleak: Restoring fiscal sustainability will require major changes to programs, revenues, and the nation's health care system. Center on Budget and Policy Priorities, http://www.cbpp.org/1-29-07bud.htm.

Kosterlitz, J., and M. W. Serafini. 2005. Must it be gloom and doom for the baby boom? *National Journal* (December 3): 3698–3705.

Kuhn, P. 2003. Effects of population aging on labour market flows in Canada: Analytical issues and research priorities. Department of Economics, University of California, Santa Barbara. Available at http://www.econ.ucsb.edu/~pjkuhn/Research%20Papers/Aging.pdf.

Lahey, J. N. 2005. Do older workers face discrimination? Center for Retirement Research at Boston College. Available at http://crr.bc.edu/images/stories/Briefs/ib_33.pdf.

Lee, R., and J. Haaga. 2002. *Government spending in an older America*. Reports on America, vol. 3, no. 1. Washington, DC: Population Reference Bureau.

McCann, L. A. 2004. Age discrimination in employment: Why its predicted demise is off the mark. *Public Policy & Aging Report* 14 (3): 7–10.

McKinsey Global Institute. 2007. *Accounting for the cost of health care in the United States*. San Francisco: McKinsey.

Mérette, M. 2002. The bright side: A positive view on the economics of aging. *Choices* 8(1). Available at http://www.irpp.org/choices/archive/vol8no1.pdf.

Moody, H. R. 2005. Silver Industries and the New Aging Enterprise. *Generations* 28(4). Available at http://www.generationsjournal.org/GENERATIONS/GEN28-4/ARTICLE.CFM.

Munnell, A. H. 2004. Population aging: It's not just the baby boom. Center for Retirement Research at Boston College Issue Brief No. 16. Available at http://crr.bc.edu/briefs/population_aging_its_not_just_the_baby_boom.html.

———. 2006. Policies to promote labor force participation of older people. Center for Retirement Research at Boston College Working Paper No. 2006-2. Available at http://crr.bc.edu/working_papers/policies_to_promote_labor_force_participation_of_older_people.html.

Orszag, P. R. 2007. *Health care and the budget: Issues and challenges for reform*. Statement before the Committee on the Budget, U.S. Senate, June 21, 2007. Available at http://www.cbo.gov/ftpdoc.cfm?index=8255.

Orszag, P. R., and P. Ellis. 2007. The challenge of rising health care costs: A view from the Congressional Budget Office. *New England Journal of Medicine* 357:1793–95.

Pan, C. X., E. Chai, and J. Farber. 2007. Myths of the high medical cost of old age and dying. New York: International Longevity Center. Available at http://www.ilcusa.org/media/pdfs/Myths%20of%20High%20Medical%20Cost.pdf.

Poterba, J. M. 2004. Impact of population aging on financial markets in developed countries. In *Economic Review, Fourth Quarter*. Kansas City: Federal Reserve Bank of Kansas City.

Poterba, J. M. 2004. The impact of population aging on financial markets. NBER Working Paper No. 10851. Cambridge, MA: NBER.

Putnam, R. 2002. Bowling together. *American Prospect* 13 (3): 20–22.

Reed, P. B., and L. K. Selbee. 2001. The civic core in Canada: Disproportionality in charitable giving, volunteering, and civic participation. Ottawa: Statistics Canada and Carleton University.

Reinhardt, U. E. 2003. Does the aging of the population really drive the demand for health care? *Health Affairs* 22 (6): 27–39.

Sass, S., A. H. Munnell, and A. Eschtruth. 2007. *The social security fix-it book*. Boston: Trustees of Boston College. Available at http://crr.bc.edu/special_projects/the_social_security_fix-it_book.html.

Schieber, S., and J. Shoven. 1997. The consequences of population aging on private pension fund saving and asset markets. In *Public policy toward pensions*, ed. S. Schieber and J. Shoven, 219–45. Cambridge, MA: MIT Press.

Schulz, J. H., and R. H. Binstock. 2006. *Aging nation: The economics and politics of growing older in America*. Westport, CT: Praeger.

Siegel, J. 2005. *The future for investors*. New York: Crown Business.

Sonnega, A. 2006. The future of human life expectancy: Have we reached the ceiling or is the sky the limit? *Research Highlights in the Demography and Economics of Aging*, no. 8. Available at http://www.prb.org/pdf06/NIA_FutureofLifeExpectancy.pdf.

Spriggs, W. E. 2005. Pulling a fast one? The facts about Social Security. *Crisis* (March/April): 17–21. Available at http://www.epi.org/issueguides/socialsecurity/spriggs.naacp.crisis.20050304.pdf.

Stone, C., and R. Greenstein. 2007. *What the 2007 Trustees' Report shows about Social Security*. Center on Budget and Policy Priorities, http://www.cbpp.org/4-24-07socsec.pdf.

Strunk, B. C., and P. B. Ginsburg. 2002. Aging plays limited role in health care cost trends. Center for Studying Health System Change Data Bulletin No. 23. Available at http://www.hschange.org/CONTENT/473/.

Toossi, M. 2007. Labor force projections to 2016: More workers in their golden years. *Monthly Labor Review* 130 (11): 33–52. Available at http://www.bls.gov/opub/mlr/2007/11/art3full.pdf.

Turner, J. A. 2007. Promoting work: Implications of raising social security's early retirement age. Center for Retirement Research at Boston College. Available at http://crr.bc.edu/briefs/
promoting_work_implications_of_raising_social_securitys_early_retiremen.html.

United Nations. 2001. *Replacement migration: Is it a solution to declining and ageing populations?* New York: United Nations, Department of Economic and Social Affairs, Population Division. Available at http://www.un.org/esa/population/publications/ReplMigED/migration.htm.

Wray, L. R. 2006. The burden of aging: Much ado about nothing, or little to do about something? Levy Economics Institute of Bard College Policy Note 2006/5. Available at http://www.levy.org/pubs/pn_5_06.pdf.

Zedlewski, S. R. 2007. Will retiring boomers form a new army of volunteers? Perspectives on Productive Aging, No. 7. Available at http://www.urban.org/UploadedPDF/411579_retiring_boomers.pdf.

Zedlewski, S. R., and B. A. Butrica. 2007. Are we taking full advantage of older adults' potential? Perspectives on Productive Aging, No. 9. Available at http://www.urban.org/UploadedPDF/411581_adult_potential.pdf.

Boomer Diversity and Well-Being: Race, Ethnicity, and Gender

JAN E. MUTCHLER AND JEFFREY BURR

Between 1946 and 1964, 76 million children were born in the United States as part of an upswing in births that began at the end of World War II and continued for almost twenty years (National Center for Health Statistics 2002). The "baby boom" cohort is now firmly embedded in midlife, with members of this generation being between 42 and 60 years of age in 2006. Although decades of mortality have taken a toll, the baby boomer population paradoxically now numbers 78 million individuals (U.S. Census Bureau 2006). This apparent "growth" of the boomer population occurred because birth cohort losses through mortality were more than offset by the immigration of boomer-aged, foreign-born individuals who arrived in the United States at some point during their lifetimes, a process facilitated by a massive transformation of immigration policy occurring just as the baby boom was ending (Haaga 2007). Almost one in six of today's aging boomers is an immigrant, the vast majority of whom were born in Latin America or Asia. Boomers represent not only the largest cohort in American history to find themselves on the doorstep of later life, but, due in part to these immigration trends, the boomer generation also contains patterns of race and ethnic diversity not seen in previous cohorts.

Our goal in this chapter is to examine the implications of this diversity for the well-being of boomers as they approach later life. To begin, we briefly comment on the historical and demographic context shaping the experience of boomers, especially factors that have redefined the significance of race, ethnic, and gender group membership for this cohort.[1] Next, we build on this discussion by presenting current evidence on two dimensions of well-being that become increasingly important as individuals enter the later stages of life: economic well-being and health status. These dimensions are important at all ages, but especially so in later life when lifelong processes of inequality in economic and health-related experiences become personal challenges for many individuals and their families, as well as public concerns for governmental and nongovernmental programs and organizations serving seniors.

THE HISTORICAL AND DEMOGRAPHIC CONTEXT OF THE BABY BOOM AND DIVERSITY

Prior to 1946, birthrates had been declining for several decades, leading many scholars at the time to proclaim an imminent end to population growth in the United States. In a sharp turnaround, more than three million babies were born in 1946, half a million more than had been born in the previous year (National Center for Health Statistics 2002). Rather than reflecting a short-term pattern of making up for lost time associated with the separation of couples and families during World War II or compensating for longer-term deferred childbearing during the Depression, this surge in births reflected the start of a long-term trend in fertility that would continue for nearly twenty years. During the baby boom era, the number of births rose progressively higher each year until 1957, when 4.3 million children were born. As the boomers moved through childhood and early adulthood, they would leave an impression on virtually every major social and economic institution in America, including schools, workplaces, and health care settings. Boomers represent 26 percent of the total U.S. population and are more numerous than any previous twenty-year birth cohort in American history. As the leading edge of the baby boom approaches later life, with those born in 1946 reaching age 65 in 2011, their decisions about work, retirement, and leisure, as well as their resources in terms of health, income, and wealth, take on unprecedented national significance (Eggebeen and Sturgeon 2006).

The baby boom era opened on a society that drew sharp lines separating men from women, and race and ethnic groups from one another, in terms of social and economic opportunity. Although during the war women had become actively involved in paid work and other activities that had previously been closed to them, the return of GIs to the workplace signaled a resumption of domesticity for many of America's wives, mothers, and daughters. Schweitzer (1980) reports that just before World War II, 27 percent of women age 14 and over were in the labor force (many of whom were unemployed), and by 1943 the female labor force had increased to 37 percent. As of 1947, the female labor force participation rate returned to prewar levels, and it would take a number of years and many social and legal changes for women to return to the labor force with equal and even greater commitment.

Race relations in the mid-1940s were focused heavily on the African American population vis-à-vis the white population. Other than the whites, the most sizable racial group was U.S.-born African Americans, many of whom were only a generation or two removed from slavery. Jim Crow laws were in effect throughout the Southern states, and race segregation was a fact of life in schools and communities nationwide. Although demographic data on the Hispanic population was not systematically collected during this time, estimates suggest that this group was considerably smaller than the African American population and heavily concentrated in a relatively small number of southwestern and western states (Gibson and Jung 2002). The share of the population that was of Asian or Native American origin was also quite small and regionally concentrated.

Boomers born during this era witnessed and participated in momentous sociopolitical movements challenging inequalities then in place, many of which were a response to long-present divisions associated with race, ethnicity, and gender. The civil rights movement of the 1960s and 1970s, the transformation of immigration policy in 1965, and the struggle for the Equal Rights Amendment for women in the 1970s were markers of a cultural reshaping of group and self-identity, opportunities, and expectations among women and members of nonwhite racial and ethnic groups. For boomers, the sheer density and timing of these movements—most of these occurring as the leading edge of the boomers approached adulthood—and the associated challenges to the status quo had special significance. As a result, this diverse cohort is poised to reshape the character of later life in part because they bring with them unique views of the meaning and significance of race, gender, and ethnicity.

These social and cultural revolutions were accompanied by another demographic revolution that continues today, as the United States continues on a path of ever-growing racial and ethnic diversity. Baby boomers represent not only the largest cohort to reach later life in the history of the United States but also the most racially diverse. In 2006, 27 percent of the boomer cohort was either nonwhite or Hispanic, a far larger share than similarly aged individuals just a generation ago. For example, in 1980 just 16 percent of adults ages 42–60 were either nonwhite or Hispanic (calculated from the 1980 Census [Ruggles et al. 2004]). African Americans currently make up 11 percent of the boomer population, with the Hispanic proportion nearly as large (10 percent in 2006). The Asian-origin population contributes 4 percent, while 2 percent of boomers are of some other race (see figure 2-1).[2]

A significant factor driving the racial and ethnic diversity of the boomer cohort is the pattern of immigration to the United States over the past several decades. Following the large flows of mostly European immigrants to the United States at the turn of the twentieth century, the number of new immigrants declined precipitously until 1970, when increasing immigration levels resumed. The largest share of these post-1970 immigrants are from Asia and Latin America (Bean and Stevens 2003). Many new arrivals in the

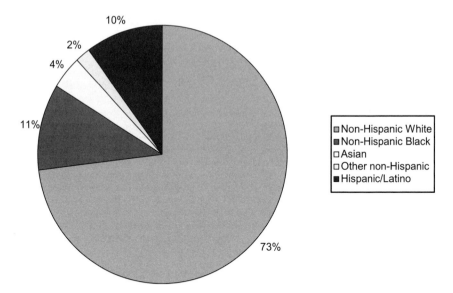

FIGURE 2-1.   Baby Boom Population by Race and Ethnicity, 2006
Note: Calculations based on people aged 42–60 only.
Source: Calculated by the authors from 2006 American Community Survey microdata.

1970s and 1980s came as young adults, further swelling the size of the boomer cohort. Indeed, two-thirds of the Hispanic boomers, and nearly nine out of ten Asian boomers, were born outside of the United States (see table 2-1). Because immigration persists at high levels and new entrants continue to be drawn largely from Asian and Latin American countries, the increasing diversity of the United States population is fueled in large part by immigration flows. As a result, birth cohorts younger than the boomers (cohorts including the children and grandchildren of the boomer generation) are even more diverse than the boomers themselves (Myers 2007).

Visualizing the implications of these joint processes of aging and ethnic diversity is aided by reference to figure 2-2. This graph represents a modified population pyramid, with age pyramids displayed for 2006 (on the left) and for the projected 2030 population (on the right). Pyramids for the combined Hispanic and nonwhite populations are superimposed on equivalent pyramids for the non-Hispanic white population at each time point in order to show the relative size of each segment of the population as it differs by age group and as it is expected to change over time. As seen in the pyramid, the baby-boom cohort constitutes a "bulge" in the age structure at each time point, but is noticeable only for the non-Hispanic white population. Thus the baby boom has had a far more substantial impact on the age structure of the non-Hispanic white population than it has for the rest of the population. The ongoing immigration patterns, and the fact that the immigrant

TABLE 2-1.   Baby Boomers by Race and Ethnic Status and Immigrant Status, 2006

	Number of Boomers	Percent born in the U.S.*	Percent born outside the U.S.
Non-Hispanic:			
White	56,561,617	95%	5%
African American	8,762,138	89	11
Asian	3,425,842	12	88
Other Race	1,357,080	86	14
Hispanic/Latino	8,013,427	35	65
Total	78,120,104	84	16

*Reflects the share born in one of the fifty states. Alternative definitions of U.S.-born (including people born abroad to U.S. parents and/or people born in a U.S. territory) yield similar findings for all groups except for Hispanics. Classifying people born in a U.S. territory or elsewhere to U.S. parents as born in the United States results in the percentage of Hispanics who are classified as U.S. born increasing from 35 percent to 42 percent.

Note: Calculations based on people aged 42–60 only.
Source: Calculated by the authors from 2006 American Community Survey.

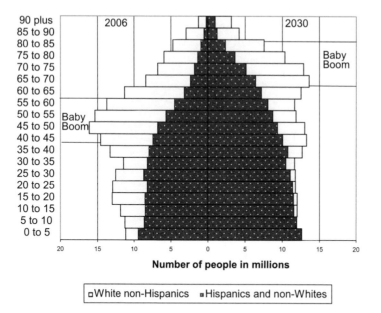

Number of people in millions

□White non-Hispanics   ■Hispanics and non-Whites

FIGURE 2-2.   Age Distribution of the U.S. Population for 2006 (estimated) and 2030 (projected), by Race and Ethnicity
Note: Baby boomers are aged 42–60 in 2006 and 66–84 in 2030.
Source: Data for 2006 are from the population estimates series, U.S. Census Bureau (2006). Data for 2030 are from the population projection series, U.S. Census Bureau (2004).

population is far younger than the U.S.-born population, will continue to be reflected in the size and age composition of the segment of the population that is either nonwhite or Hispanic.

Considering the left-hand side of the pyramid in figure 2-2, which represents the age structure of the U.S. population in 2006, it is noteworthy that in the youngest age groups, the non-Hispanic white and the other racial and ethnic groups are more balanced in size. Indeed, in 2006, Hispanics and nonwhites together constituted 42 percent of the U.S. population under age 30, but only 19 percent of the population aged 65 and over. Among boomers, who were aged 42 to 60 in 2006, about one-third were persons of color. Looking ahead to 2030 with the aid of projections generated by the U.S. Census Bureau (2004; right-hand side of the pyramid), it is anticipated that people who are either nonwhite or Hispanic will be a significantly larger segment of the population as a whole, but especially among younger age groups. This time frame is important because by 2030 the entire boomer cohort will have entered later life, with the youngest members being age 66. The movement of boomers into later life means that the population age 65 and over will include larger segments of Hispanics and nonwhites (28 percent, as compared to 19 percent in 2007). However, the presence of nonwhites and Hispanics will be still more significant among those younger than the boomers. Indeed, persons of color are expected to make up 43 percent of those aged 30 to 64 in 2030 and fully *half* of those under age 30.

The boomer generation will move through later life embedded in a population that is increasingly composed of nonwhite and Hispanic youth and younger adults, many of whom will be immigrants or children of immigrants. The increasing diversity among younger cohorts is important because these persons will make up larger shares of the labor force and thus contribute to the payroll and other taxes that support programs aimed at assisting elderly boomers. As well, if boomers are to be able to downsize housing, make retirement-based amenity moves, or sell their homes for any other reason, the diverse population of younger adults will need adequate resources to purchase the homes boomers leave behind. Furthermore, a large share of the health care service industry, expected to expand dramatically as boomers' needs for care increase, will be composed of persons of color (see Myers 2007).

THE IMPLICATIONS OF RACE, ETHNIC, AND GENDER INEQUALITY FOR LATER LIFE

A high level of inequality characterizes American society, with the result that some individuals reach old age with far fewer economic and health resources than others (Crystal and Shea 1990). To some extent, the pathway to economic security in later life has its roots in childhood and young adulthood. Although far from a deterministic process, on average children born to parents who have few resources accumulate less education, less income, and less wealth as they move through the life course, as compared to children born to more affluent parents. Lower likelihoods of completing high school or college correspond strongly with higher risk of unstable employment, poorly compensated jobs, and a reduced accumulation of wealth, ultimately extending to fewer Social Security credits and lower or nonexistent private pension benefits. Research shows that accumulated advantages and disadvantages are carried into old age, resulting in a high level of inequality among those 65 years old and over (Crystal, Shea, and Shreeram 1992; O'Rand 1996).

Healthy aging similarly has its origins early in life (George 2003; Hayward and Gorman 2004). Indeed, survivorship itself is distributed unequally in the population, such that those with fewer resources and poorer backgrounds are less likely to survive to old age (Mechanic 2007; Wilson, Shuey, and Elder 2007). Poor health and inadequate access to proper health care cumulates throughout the life course, making it more likely that a person who has been disadvantaged with respect to health care in early life will be disabled in later life. Moreover, because health and disability status have implications for employment and lifetime earnings capacity, poor health and early-onset disability have direct and indirect implications for economic standing in later life.

On average, members of some racial and ethnic groups (most notably, African Americans, Native Americans, and Hispanics) are more likely to be born into families with fewer advantages than are their white counterparts, and they continue to accumulate fewer resources as they age. Gaps in the accumulation of wealth and in homeownership levels are evident across racial and ethnic groups (Sykes 2003). Group differences in morbidity and mortality profiles are also well documented. Members of some groups, most notably African Americans and Native Americans, are less likely to survive to old age and more likely to enter old age in a disabled state than whites and Asian Americans (e.g., Goins et al. 2007; Hayward and Heron 1999). Although women typically have educational achievements that are on par with those of men, they are often less likely to convert this resource directly into income or wealth, in part due to family responsibilities and gender roles (Moen and Chermack 2005). Health disparities by gender take the form of more chronic illnesses and higher levels of disability, although women live longer than men on average (Crimmins 2004).

Though boomers moved through childhood and young adulthood in an era characterized by expanding opportunities for both women and members of racial and ethnic minority groups, pervasive inequalities continue. The remainder of this chapter takes stock of key elements of inequality currently reflected among boomers at midlife, and we will discuss the differential prospects for a secure old age among members of this generation. Our examination will focus on socioeconomic status and indicators of health and physical well-being. These attributes are reflective of well-being throughout the life course and are highly predictive of well-being in later life, yet at the same time, well-being is sharply differentiated by gender, race, and ethnicity.

We draw on data from several sources for this analysis. Information on socioeconomic resources is developed from the 2006 American Community Survey (ACS), a large national sample survey collected by the U.S. Census Bureau. Information on health and health behaviors is drawn from the 2006 National Health Interview Survey (NHIS), a large, nationally representative survey conducted annually by the Centers for Disease Control and Prevention's (CDC) National Center for Health Statistics (CDC 2007). We focus on respondents who were aged 42 to 60 in 2006 (i.e., persons born between 1946 and 1964) and direct our attention to four mutually exclusive racial and ethnic groups: non-Hispanic whites, non-Hispanic African Americans, non-Hispanic Asians, and Hispanics/Latinos. These classifications are based on two survey questions, one focused on self-identified race and another on self-identified Hispanic ethnicity. We acknowledge the heterogeneity of the Asian and Hispanic populations, which include individuals from many different points of geographic origin, immigration histories, and cultural traditions. Sample sizes are inadequate to support separate analyses of the many subgroups within these populations. Sample sizes also preclude analysis of the roughly 2 percent of the boomer population that does not fall into one of these four groups, including persons who self-identify as American Indian, Alaskan Native, Pacific Islander, or Native Hawaiian or who list two or more racial identities.

DIVERSITY IN SOCIOECONOMIC RESOURCES AMONG MIDLIFE BOOMERS: RACE, ETHNICITY, AND GENDER

The opportunities encountered in early and mid-adulthood, and the ensuing human capital and financial investments made during these life stages, have critical implications for well-being in later life. Key among these investments is the accumulation of educational resources and the purchase of a home. Individuals who complete high school experience far greater job security and lifetime earnings than those who do not, and benefits are higher still for those who attain a college degree. Overall, higher levels of education are associated with greater financial stability, increased wealth, and greater likelihood of retiring with a pension. Similarly, the value of an owned home represents the single most significant source of wealth for most older individuals (Di, Belsky, and Liu 2007).

Education

As a cohort, the boomers far outstripped the educational achievements of their parents (see table 2-2). Nearly nine out of ten boomers (age 42–60 in 2006) completed high school, and 29 percent had at least a college degree. In contrast, individuals who were aged 42–60 in 1980, roughly the cohort representing boomer parents, were less educated on average, with only 65 percent having completed high school and 14 percent having college

TABLE 2-2. Socioeconomic Investments by Race, Ethnicity, Gender, and Cohort: Boomers in 2006 Compared to Same-Aged Persons in 1980

Group	Percentage with at least a high school diploma		Percentage with at least a college degree		Percentage owning a home	
	Aged 42–60 in 2006	Aged 42–60 in 1980	Aged 42–60 in 2006	Aged 42–60 in 1980	Aged 42–60 in 2006	Aged 42–60 in 1980
Non-Hispanic:						
White	93%	69%	32%	15%	77%	81%
African American	84%	43%	19%	7%	49%	57%
Asian	85%	73%	46%	27%	64%	65%
Hispanic/Latino	61%	36%	14%	7%	52%	57%
All men	87%	65%	30%	19%	70%	78%
All women	89%	66%	28%	10%	71%	77%
Total	88%	65%	29%	14%	71%	77%

Note: Race and ethnic categorizations used in this table were made consistent between 1980 and 2006 by using the bridged race classification provided in the IPUMS.

Source: Calculated by the authors from 2006 American Community Survey and the 1980 U.S. Census of Population.

degrees. These intergenerational advances in education did not eliminate disparities across race and ethnic groups, however. Substantial differences in educational attainments persist among boomers, as they did for similarly aged individuals in 1980. More than 90 percent of white boomers completed high school, compared to about 85 percent of African Americans and Asians, but just 61 percent of Hispanic boomers.

The educational gap is even starker when comparing the percentage of persons from each group having earned a college degree. About a third of white boomers earned at least one college degree, compared to less than one in five African American or Hispanic boomers. Although African American boomers are far more likely to have a college degree than their parents, they continue to lag behind their white counterparts, due to a range of factors, including fewer opportunities for higher education, lower levels of support for their educational aspirations from communities and schools, and other social and economic barriers. Hispanic boomers faced similar challenges in attaining college degrees, coupled for many with the additional challenge posed by their immigrant status.

Asian boomers are distinctive among the larger population of boomers in terms of their relatively high numbers of college graduates. Among Asian boomers, nearly half (46 percent) have a college degree, perhaps reflecting the higher value placed on education within many segments of the Asian population, as well as the educational opportunities that have drawn many Asian immigrants to the United States. Because so many of the Hispanic and Asian boomers are immigrants, the achievements of their parents may not be reflected in the statistics from 1980. However, it is clear that for all groups, the boomers have attained higher levels of education than midlife members of the same race and ethnic groups from earlier generations (2006 compared to 1980).

In contrast to the human capital differences noted among these race and ethnic groups, comparatively few educational differences are observed between male and female boomers. A slightly larger share of women than men completed high school (89 percent versus 87 percent). Although a somewhat larger share of boomer men completed college (30 percent versus 28 percent), this represents a substantial narrowing of the gender gap in college completion in 1980 (which was then 19 percent for men aged 42–60 and 10 percent for similarly aged women). For female boomers, the significance of educational differences lies less with the years of schooling completed and more with the gendered ways in which educational credentials are translated into earnings, careers, wealth, and pensions.

Homeownership

Homeownership is an additional investment-based indicator of well-being in adulthood. As a reflection of the "American Dream," owning a home is an aspiration shared by many; moreover, the value of an owned home typically reflects the single most significant asset held by people at all ages, including those in later life. Statistics from the 2006 ACS show that similar patterns of homeownership characterize male and female boomers, with about 70 percent of each gender group owning a home.[3] In contrast, racial and ethnic group differences in homeownership are pronounced. More than three-quarters of white boomers own a home (77 percent), followed by 64 percent of Asian boomers, whereas only about half of Hispanic (52 percent) and African American (49 percent) boomers own a home.

These rates of homeownership reflect declines from rates for people of the same age in 1980. For example, 57 percent of African American individuals aged 42–60 in 1980 owned a home, compared to just 49 percent of African American boomers in the same age bracket today. The ability of boomers to translate gains in educational investments into other forms of wealth (here, defined by homeownership) appears to have faltered. The escalating costs of homeownership may have outstripped the rising economic resources associated with improved educational levels. The fact that earnings among American workers have not increased substantially, in constant dollars, may also play a role. These generational differences may be especially prevalent among groups who have experienced persistent racial and ethnic employment discrimination and residential segregation (i.e., Hispanics and African Americans). As well, many boomers' experiences with divorce, including a historically unprecedented rise in divorce rates among Hispanics (Landale, Oropesa, and Bradatan 2006), and other forms of family disruption may have resulted in fewer household resources that otherwise promote homeownership. Whatever the sources of this decline, it is apparent that a smaller share of boomers is approaching later life owning a home than was the case a generation earlier, when their parents were middle-aged.

Earnings and Household Income

Racial, ethnic, and gender differences are also evident in the financial resources reported by boomers at midlife. Among most midlife individuals, earnings from employment are their most important financial resource, and the largest share of individual and household income results from labor force activity. In addition, earnings shape economic well-being in later life through the accumulation of public and private pension credits and private wealth through savings and financial investments (e.g., ownership of real estate, stocks, and bonds). Statistics based on data from the 2006 ACS suggest that 75–80 percent of boomers are working in midlife, with higher rates of labor force participation among whites and among men irrespective of race or ethnic group affiliation (data not presented here). Although part-time and part-year work is not uncommon, more than half of the boomers in all racial and ethnic groups report working full-time, year-round.[4] Men

TABLE 2-3. Median Earnings for Full-Time Full-Year Workers and Median Household Income, by Race, Ethnicity, and Gender among Boomers in the 2006 American Community Survey

Group	Median annual earnings, full-time full-year workers	Median household income
Non-Hispanic:		
White	$46,687	$73,050
African American	$35,217	$46,285
Asian	$44,272	$79,187
Hispanic/Latino	$30,186	$51,316
All men	$50,310	$70,433
All women	$35,217	$64,899
Total	$43,266	$67,415

Note: Calculations based on people aged 42–60 only.
Source: Calculated by the authors using 2006 American Community Survey.

are more likely to work full-time year-round (66 percent) than are women (45 percent).

A substantial share of earnings differentials evident in any population is a function of the amount of time that individuals devote to paid work activities. An exhaustive examination of these issues is beyond the scope of the current chapter; instead, we focus our attention on an examination of the median personal earnings among full-time year-round workers, who typically share similar profiles with respect to time committed to work. This assessment reveals striking group differences in the compensation received for work even among those segments of the boomer workforce with the most extensive participation (see table 2-3). Among boomers, whites earn the most (median annual earnings = $46,687), while Hispanics earn the least ($30,186). Asians working full-time year-round earn somewhat less than whites ($44,272), while African Americans earn substantially less ($35,217). The lower earnings levels of Hispanics and African Americans reflect the educational differences discussed earlier, as well as restricted employment and promotion opportunities, geographic differences in pay rates, and other factors.

Although male and female boomers report similar educational attainments, gender-specific median earnings levels suggest substantial differences in compensation. A typical woman who works full-time year-round earns $35,217, compared to $50,310 for her male counterpart, a difference of 30 percent. These differences may be a reflection of occupational choices, experience levels associated with time spent out of the labor force for child care or other family-related responsibilities, and other factors related to the gendered interpretation of family and work–life experiences, including gender discrimination in the workplace. Regardless of the source of these differences by race, ethnicity, and gender, earnings differentials experienced at midlife will be reflected in resource differentials among boomers and their families in later life.

An alternative indicator of financial well-being is captured by household income, which reflects the economic resources held by all persons living in the same housing unit. Household income is an indicator of the standard of living generated by the pooled resources of household members and therefore is reflective not only of the income level of work-eligible members but also the composition of the household. High household incomes occur among units that include high-income wage earners but also in households that include more working adults. Low household income occurs when members earn low wages, as well as when few or no members are employed. Some research demonstrates that although the average standard of living experienced by boomers, as a whole, is higher than that experienced by their parents, a higher level of inequality characterizes the household incomes of boomers (Hughes and O'Rand 2004).

Table 2-3 provides data that suggest the combination of these forces results in median household incomes that are far lower for African American and Hispanic boomers as compared to white and Asian boomers. African American and Hispanic median household incomes are about one-third less than that of their white counterparts. In contrast, Asian boomers report median household incomes that are about 8 percent greater than the median incomes reported by whites. Further, male boomers live in households with a median income of more than $70,000, while female boomers live in households with a median income of just under $65,000, reflecting the different earnings profiles of men and women, coupled with differences in family structure, number of earners, and level of work participation among those members who do work. For example, women are more likely to live in single-parent, single-earner households, and as reflected in table 2-3, their earnings tend to be lower than that of men even when they work full-time.

Wealth and Pensions

We cannot know with certainty what late life has in store for the economic security of boomers. However, research suggests that many boomers are not adequately prepared for a secure retirement, and that African Americans, Hispanics, and women are especially vulnerable. For example, based on data from the Health and Retirement Study (HRS), a nationally representative survey of older adults in the United States and a leading resource describing the economic, labor force, and health characteristics of older persons, Lusardi and Mitchell (2006) indicate that a high level of wealth inequality characterizes the leading edge of the boomer cohort, the "early boomers," defined in their study as those persons born between 1948 and 1953. Many early boomers have very little wealth; for example, median net worth among African American early boomers is only $27,000 and is just $56,000 for Hispanic early boomers, compared to almost $200,000 for early boomer whites. These differences reflect lower levels of homeownership, lower values of owned homes, and lower levels of other resources, such as savings and financial investments, among members of these groups. As well, male early boomers report much higher net worth than their female counterparts. For most boomers, but especially for racial and ethnic minority group members, their primary asset is their residence, making them especially vulnerable to fluctuations in the housing market.

Low levels of wealth are coupled with limited pension prospects for many boomers. Moore (2006) projects that about half of boomers will be eligible for an employer-sponsored pension at age 62, but eligibility rates are expected to be substantially lower for women than for men, and lower for African Americans and Hispanics than for whites. Projected income received from pensions is also expected to be lower for these groups. Perhaps in response to their perceived constraints in wealth and pension resources, boomers report that they expect to work longer than members of older generations. HRS data reveal that members of the leading edge of the boomer cohort are more likely than previous cohorts to expect to work past age 65 (Mermin, Johnson, and Murphy 2007). U.S. Bureau of Labor Statistics projections also anticipate that a higher labor force participation rate will characterize this generation (Toossi 2005). Among the early boomers who participated in the HRS, males were more likely than females to expect to work past age 65, and African Americans were less likely than others to expect to work that long (Mermin, Johnson, and Murphy 2007). In other words, the groups with lower wealth levels and fewer pension prospects are least likely to expect to work in later life. If these expectations are translated into behavior, patterns of work beyond age 65 may serve to further increase gender, racial, and ethnic economic inequality in retirement among boomers.

LIFE EXPECTANCY, CHRONIC DISEASE, AND HEALTH BEHAVIORS AMONG MIDLIFE BOOMERS: DIFFERENCES BY RACE, ETHNICITY, AND GENDER

Life Expectancy

Racial, ethnic, and gender differences in health profiles and survivorship, or life expectancy, are stubborn reminders of the inequalities that continue to permeate American society. A white infant born at the peak of the baby boom had an expectation of life of seventy-four years if she was a girl, or sixty-seven years if he was a boy. If the infant was African American, she was expected to live only sixty-six years if a girl, sixty-one years if a boy. Improvements in medical interventions and preventive health care have increased expectation of life across all groups, yet gender and race differences persist.[5] Although the total number of years lived, on average, has shifted upward for all groups, a significant gap between whites and African Americans persists. What this means is that, among the baby boomers, men of all races and African Americans of both sexes disproportionately die before reaching midlife. Moreover, mortality differences continue to affect survivorship throughout adulthood. Consider that white female boomers born in 1957 and fortunate enough to survive to the age of 46 in 2003 are expected to live another thirty-six years, whereas African American female boomers can expect to live an additional thirty-three years. White male boomers had a life expectancy of thirty-two years at age 46, while African American male boomers could expect, on average, only twenty-eight years of additional life (Arias 2007).

Chronic Conditions

To elaborate further on the well-being of the boomer generation as captured by health status, we address two questions: What do the boomers' prospects look like for a healthy, disability-free old age? And, in the next section, to what extent are potential late-life health disparities foreshadowed in the health conditions and health behaviors of today's midlife boomers?

Chronic disease not only contributes to premature death but also presents substantial economic costs and burdens in terms of disability, loss of function, and loss of independence. High blood pressure, arthritis, and diabetes are among the most common chronic conditions in later life; further, these conditions have been identified as contributing to disability. Some evidence suggests that these chronic conditions may also be related to cognitive decline (CDC and Merck Company Foundation 2007).

Data from the 2006 National Health Interview Survey demonstrate that chronic conditions are differentially distributed across racial, ethnic, and gender groups among midlife boomers (see table 2-4). Three common conditions considered here—hypertension, arthritis, and diabetes—have implications for long-term risk of disability and premature death. Although these conditions are common within the boomer cohort, they are especially prevalent among African American boomers, 39 percent of whom are hypertensive, one-quarter of whom have been told they have arthritis, and 12 percent of whom are diabetic. Hispanics have the highest rate of diabetes (14 percent), and Asians have the lowest rate of hypertension (22 percent) and arthritis (11 percent). White boomers have a high percentage of their members with arthritis (26 percent) and hypertension (27 percent) but a relatively low percentage with diabetes (7 percent).

Comparing male to female boomers without respect to race or ethnic group, the only sizable gap that emerges is the higher rate of arthritis among women (28 percent) than among men (21 percent). This pattern is consistent with respect to the higher risk of disability that has been observed among older women as compared to older men.

TABLE 2-4. Chronic Health Conditions by Race, Ethnicity, and Gender among Boomers in the 2006 National Health Interview Survey

Group	Diagnosed by a physician or other health care professional as having:		
	Hypertension[a]	Arthritis	Diabetes
Non-Hispanic:			
White	27%	26%	7%
African American	39%	26%	12%
Asian	22%	11%	10%
Hispanic/Latino	23%	18%	14%
Male	29%	21%	9%
Female	27%	28%	8%
Total	28%	24%	9%

[a]Respondent was told by a physician or other health care professional two or more times that he or she has high blood pressure.

Note: Calculations based on people aged 42–60 only.

Source: Calculated by the authors from the 2006 from the National Health Interview Survey.

These indicators suggest that substantial gaps in the prevalence of chronic health conditions exist among boomers. The measures of health conditions provided here are self-reported; respondents are asked if a doctor or other health professional has ever told them they had diabetes, arthritis, or high blood pressure (CDC 2007). Individuals who have not received adequate screening for conditions like diabetes or hypertension or who have not discussed symptoms that might lead to a diagnosis of arthritis with a health provider would not necessarily know that they had these conditions. Actual prevalence rates for these conditions may be higher than reflected here, especially among populations having low or uneven contact with health care professionals.

Health Behaviors

Smoking, obesity, excessive alcohol consumption, and lack of physical activity reflect aspects of an unhealthy lifestyle that can have significant implications for long-term health, disability, and mortality (Wister 2005). The Centers for Disease Control and Prevention estimates that just three behaviors—smoking, consuming a poor diet, and being physically inactive—are the causes of nearly a third of all deaths in the United States. CDC researchers conclude that "adopting healthier behaviors, such as engaging in regular physical activity, eating a healthy diet, leading a tobacco-free lifestyle, and getting regular health screenings ... can dramatically reduce a person's risk for most chronic diseases, including the leading causes of death" (CDC and Merck Company Foundation 2007, 4).

TABLE 2-5. Unhealthy Behaviors by Race, Ethnicity, and Gender among Boomers in the 2006 National Health Interview Survey

Group	Five or more drinks in one day at least once in the past year	Current cigarette smoker	Physically inactive[a]	Obese[b]	Reports two or more unhealthy behaviors
Non-Hispanic:					
White	20%	23%	33%	30%	29%
African American	12%	30%	46%	39%	36%
Asian	7%	11%	42%	11%	12%
Hispanic/Latino	15%	17%	50%	32%	32%
Male	26%	25%	37%	31%	34%
Female	11%	21%	37%	30%	26%
Total	18%	23%	37%	30%	30%

[a] Defined as never engaging in any leisure-time light, moderate, or vigorous physical activity
[b] Defined as having a body-mass index (BMI) greater than or equal to 30, based on self-reported height and weight

Note: Calculations based on people aged 42–60 only.
Source: Calculated by the authors from the 2006 National Health Interview Survey.

Table 2-5 presents information on a set of unhealthy behaviors by population subgroup, based on data from the 2006 NHIS. As a group, nearly one in five boomers engages in risky drinking behavior (i.e., has consumed five or more drinks in a single day at least once in the previous year), and almost one in four was a current smoker. Larger shares (one-third or more) were physically inactive or obese.[6] These unhealthy behaviors clearly place many boomers at increased risk of disease, disability, and premature mortality. This risk may be especially high for the 30 percent of boomers who report two or more of these unhealthy behaviors (see the last column in table 2-5).

Differences among racial and ethnic groups in these behaviors are evident, but do not point to a consistent pattern of unhealthy behavior among any one group (see Adams and Schoenborn 2006, for a similar conclusion). For example, relatively more white boomers engage in high-risk alcohol consumption (20 percent) compared to any other group, but they are most likely to be physically active. Asians are least likely to engage in high-risk alcohol consumption, to smoke, or to be obese, but 42 percent of them are physically inactive. As a group, African Americans are the most likely to be obese (39 percent) or to currently smoke (30 percent), and many are physically inactive (46 percent), but only 12 percent have engaged in high-risk alcohol consumption. Hispanics are at or below the population average of all unhealthy behaviors except for physical inactivity—fully half of Hispanics report never engaging in light, moderate, or vigorous leisure-time physical activity. However, the fact that 32 percent of Hispanics, and 36 percent of African

Americans, report engaging in two or more unhealthy behaviors, may place them at potentially higher risk of health consequences associated with lifestyle.

Patterns by gender suggest that unhealthy behavior is more common among boomer men than women. Although similar levels of physical inactivity and obesity are evident by gender (approximately one in three for each group), men are somewhat more likely than women to be current smokers, and considerably more likely to engage in high-risk drinking behavior. Furthermore, over one-third of the male boomers, but only about one-quarter of women, report engaging in two or more unhealthy behaviors.

Because of these different patterns of unhealthy behaviors, the health consequences realized may take different forms across the subgroups. For example, groups with high obesity levels are at especially high risk for diabetes and heart disease, whereas groups with high rates of smoking are at higher risk for certain types of cancer.

Implications for Health Disparities in Later Life

A considerable amount of past research indicates that disability levels in later life have declined in recent decades (Crimmins 2004; Manton, Gu, and Lamb 2006). These declines have been traced to changes in health-related behaviors and cohort succession, whereby younger, healthier cohorts are moving into later life replacing less healthy and less affluent persons from earlier cohorts. Looking ahead, we anticipate that disparities in health outcomes among boomers are likely to persist despite potential declines in disability across this cohort as a whole. Differences in rates of hypertension, diabetes, arthritis, and other early-onset health conditions may be amplified among boomers by high levels of participation in unhealthy behaviors (e.g., obesity and low physical-activity levels). Moreover, economic resource differences among some racial, ethnic, and gender groups, as documented earlier, influence health trajectories, with the result that disadvantages cumulate into later life. The implications of having diabetes for higher rates of disability and mortality, for example, may be more unfavorable among individuals with fewer financial resources, limited education, or poorer access to health care services. The quality of life experienced by boomers in later life, and the differences among racial, ethnic, and gender groups in those experiences, will be shaped by the intersection of trajectories in health and in socioeconomic resource accumulation, which together reflect accrued advantages and disadvantages for each group over the life course.

DISCUSSION

There is a tendency among policy makers and academicians to fail to embrace the heterogeneity of the boomers when considering the aging of this generation. It is a mistake to do so (see the discussion in Wilmoth and Longino 2006). In this chapter, we sought to highlight the diverse economic and health characteristics of this group by considering differences and similarities by race, ethnicity, gender, and age. While this large population of middle-aged persons lived through and participated in some of the most significant social, political, and cultural changes this country has ever witnessed, the impact of these changes on members of these subgroups is variable.

A common theme in the scholarly literature and the popular media emphasizes that boomers are likely to be different from earlier generations in terms of how they live out their retirement years. As one elderly cohort replaces another through the process of cohort succession, past patterns of aging are often not accurate predictors of attitudes and behaviors among members of incoming replacement generations (Myers 2007; Wister 2005). Noting that boomers, on average, are healthier and better prepared financially for later life, many observers suggest that they will continue to lead productive and fulfilling lives well into old age (Freedman 2006/2007; Greenblatt 2007). It is difficult to disagree with this assessment. Boomers have the opportunity to redefine what "senior citizenship" means because they are generally well equipped educationally and otherwise to advocate on behalf of their own redefinitions.

However, evidence presented in this chapter suggests that resource differences among segments of this cohort—many of the differences being quite substantial—may challenge the ability of some boomers to realize this optimistic vision. African Americans, Hispanics, and some women may not have as many financial resources as white men during these later years. Moreover, the disability outlook appears to be much more unfavorable for some groups than for others. For some boomers, the later stages of life may greatly resemble the model experienced by their parents. For them, old age may fall well short of the promise embedded in the social movements of their youth that were directed toward the elimination of unequal access to opportunities, resources, and outcomes. As a society, we need to be conscious of the "boomer stereotype" that highlights the advances made in education and medical care, and not lose sight of the fact that a substantial fraction of the boomer generation will still be vulnerable in old age.

One aspect of boomer heterogeneity that has been generally overlooked relates to the sizable immigrant population embedded in this cohort. Although space and data constraints do not permit an exhaustive consideration of the immigrant boomer population here, it is well worth remembering that a substantial share of the diversity within the boomer cohort is attributed to immigrants, most of whom were born in Latin America or Asia. Considering the implications of this diversity, then, our attention is drawn not only to factors related to race and ethnicity but also to issues relating to immigration. With the already high levels of first-generation immigrants residing in the United States and the increasing inflows expected in the future, understanding the economic and health issues of boomer immigrants takes on added significance, especially given changes to federal and state policy related to public support for older immigrants (Angel 2003).

One set of factors that conditions the implications of the financial and health-related profiles discussed here is the myriad of family types in which boomers are embedded. Family relationships—encapsulated in spouses and partners, children, and grandchildren as well as siblings and other extended family members—can be a powerful force in buffering the effects of economic and health-related disadvantage. For example, the standard of living for economically disadvantaged older adults may be improved by combining households with relatives (Goldscheider and Goldscheider 1989). As well, the implications of disability and poor health for participation in activities may be minimized when informal, family-based support and assistance are available. Like finances and health, social capital, defined as the potential to draw upon informal support when in need, is distributed unevenly within the boomer population. Divorce and other forms of marital disruption are more common among boomers than among previous generations; however, most boomers have a marital partner, especially among whites and Hispanics, and relatively few live alone (Eggebeen and Sturgeon 2006). Yet changes in family structure, including historically low fertility rates and late marriage, among African American and Hispanic boomers may jeopardize their ability to draw on informal resources for assistance in later life (Wilmoth and Longino 2006).

As the boomers approach later life, primary policy questions have focused on economic support, provision of health care, and the nature of entitlements (Greenblatt 2007). Can the United States continue to provide adequate Social Security and Medicare benefits as the number of seniors explodes over the next twenty years? What are the implications of pulling back from entitlements or redefining the conditions under which benefits are available? Policies such as those promoting a longer worklife are a potential solution for many boomers who are already predisposed to keep working in some capacity and who have the energy and adequate health to continue. For others, however, especially those already on a trajectory leading toward a heavy burden of chronic disease and disability, an extended worklife is unlikely to be a realistic solution to economic shortfalls.

Given that certain groups (for example, African Americans, Hispanics, and women) have poorer economic profiles, future adjustments to Social Security and Medicare will need to take into consideration the differential impact of any potential changes. Indeed, anticipated demographic shifts make it likely that the absolute size of the groups who could most benefit from needs-based transfer programs such as SSI and Medicaid will increase just at a time when policy makers and some members of the general public will be inclined to reduce these programs or shift the burden to families or the private sector (Wilmoth and Longino 2006).

NOTES

1. We use the terms *cohort* and *generation* somewhat interchangeably, albeit advisedly, in this chapter. In demographic terms, baby boomers represent a cohort in that they share the timing of their birth (typically dated as 1946–1964). Insofar as boomers also constitute a "generation," they are thought to share aspects of identity related to a shared cultural history (Alwin, McCammon, and Hofer 2006). The extent to which the history that defines a generation in these terms is, in fact, shared by members of the baby-boom birth cohort is variable by race, ethnicity, and immigrant status.

2. Figures for 2006 were calculated by the authors using data from the 2006 American Community Survey (ACS). Respondents to the ACS may self-identify with more than one race category. Approximately 2 percent of the boomer cohort lists more than one race. Following precedent in the scientific literature, we include only those persons listing a single race in each of the three race categories examined here (white, African American, and Asian). Hispanics may be of any race and may have selected multiple races (e.g., many Hispanics mark both "White" and "Other" in response to the race question).

3. In the ACS, homeowners are identified as people who are either the head of a household or the spouse of a householder, and who live in an owned home.

4. Following convention, full-time year-round work is defined as having worked at least fifty weeks in the previous year and typically working at least thirty-five hours per week.

5. White female children born in 2003 have a life expectancy of eighty years, but that for African American female children is only seventy-six years. For male children, the life expectancy figure is seventy-five years for whites and sixty-nine years for African Americans (Arias 2007).

6. All health behavior assessments were based on self-reports, including obesity, which was based on self-reported weight and height.

REFERENCES

Adams, P. F., and C. A. Schoenborn. 2006. *Health behaviors of adults: United States, 2002–04*. National Center for Health Statistics, Vital and Health Statistics Series 10, No. 230. Washington, DC: GPO.

Alwin, D. F., R. J. McCammon, and S. M. Hofer. 2006. Studying baby boom cohorts within a demographic and developmental context: Conceptual and methodological issues. In *The baby boomers grow up: Contemporary perspectives on midlife*, ed. S. K. Whitbourne and S. L. Willis, 45–71. Mahwah, NJ: Erlbaum.

Angel, J. 2003. Devolution and the social welfare of older immigrants: Who will bear the burden? *Public Administration Review* 63:79–89.

Arias, E. 2007. United States life tables, 2003 [electronic version]. Centers for Disease Control and Prevention. *National Vital Statistics Reports* 54 (14).

Bean, F. D., and G. Stevens. 2003. *America's newcomers and the dynamics of diversity*. New York: Russell Sage.

CDC (Centers for Disease Control and Prevention). 2007. *2006 National Health Interview Survey (NHIS) public use data release, NHIS survey description*. Hyattsville, MD: National Center for Health Statistics.

CDC and the Merck Company Foundation. 2007. *The state of aging and health in America, 2007*. Whitehouse Station, NJ: Merck Company Foundation. Available at http://www.cdc.gov/aging/saha.htm.

Crimmins, E. M. 2004. Trends in the health of the elderly. *Annual Review of Public Health* 25:79–98.

Crystal, S., and D. Shea. 1990. Cumulative advantage, cumulative disadvantage and inequality among elderly people. *Gerontologist* 30:437–43.

Crystal, S., D. Shea, and K. Shreeram. 1992. Educational attainment, occupational history, and stratification: Determinants of later-life economic outcomes. *Journals of Gerontology* 47:S213–S221.

Di, Z. X., E. Belsky, and X. Liu. 2007. Do homeowners achieve more household wealth in the long run? *Journal of Housing Economics* 16:274–90.

Eggebeen, D. J., and S. Sturgeon. 2006. Demography of the baby boomers. In *The baby boomers grow up: Contemporary perspectives on midlife*, ed. S. K. Whitbourne and S. L. Willis, 3–21. Mahwah, NJ: Erlbaum.

Freedman, M. 2006/2007. The social-purpose encore career: Baby boomers, civic engagement, and the next stage of work. *Generations* 30 (Winter): 43–46.

George, L. K. 2003. What life-course perspectives offer the study of aging and health. In *Invitation to the life course: Toward new understandings of late life*, ed. R. A. Settersten, 161–88. Amityville, NY: Baywood.

Gibson, C., and K. Jung. 2002. *Historical census statistics on population totals by race, 1970 to 1990, and by Hispanic origin, 1970 to 1990, for the United States, regions, divisions, and states*. Population Division Working Paper No. 56. Washington, DC: U.S. Census Bureau.

Goins, R. T., M. Moss, D. Buchwald, and J. M. Guralnik. 2007. Disability among older American Indians and Alaska Natives: An analysis of the 2000 Census Public Use Microdata Sample. *Gerontologist* 47:690–96.

Goldscheider, F. K., and C. Goldscheider. 1989. *Ethnicity and the new family economy: Living arrangements and intergenerational financial flows*. Boulder, CO: Westview Press.

Greenblatt, A. 2007. Aging baby boomers. *CQ Researcher* 17 (37): 865–88.

Haaga, J. 2007. Just how many baby boomers are there? Population Reference Bureau, http://www.prb.org/Articles/2002/JustHowManyBabyBoomersAreThere.aspx.

Hayward, M. D., and B. K. Gorman. 2004. Long arm of childhood: The influence of early-life social conditions on men's mortality. *Demography* 41:97–107.

Hayward, M. D., and M. Heron. 1999. Racial inequality in active life among adult Americans. *Demography* 36:77–91.

Hughes, M. E., and A. M. O'Rand. 2004. *The lives and times of the baby boomers*. New York: Russell Sage and the Population Reference Bureau.

Landale, N., S. Oropesa, and C. Bradatan. 2006. Hispanic families in the United States: Family structure and process in an era of change. In *Hispanics and the future of America*, ed. M. Tienda and F. Mitchell, 138–75. Washington, DC: National Academies Press.

Lusardi, A., and O. S. Mitchell. 2006. Baby boomer retirement security: The roles of planning, financial literacy, and housing wealth [electronic version]. University of Michigan, Retirement Research Center, Working Paper No. 2006-114.

Manton, K. G., X. Gu, and V. L. Lamb. 2006. Change in chronic disability from 1982 to 2004/2005 as measured by long-term changes in function and health in the

U.S. elderly population. *Proceedings of the National Academy of Sciences of the United States of America* 103 (48): 18374–79.

Mechanic, D. 2007. Population health: Challenges for science and society. *Milbank Quarterly* 85 (3): 533–59.

Mermin, G. B. T., R. W. Johnson, and D. P. Murphy. 2007. Why do boomers plan to work longer? *Journal of Gerontology: Social Sciences* 62B: S286–S294.

Moen, P., and K. Chermack. 2005. Gender disparities in health: Strategic selection, careers, and cycles of control. *Journal of Gerontology: Social Sciences* 60B (Special Issue II): 99–108.

Moore, J. H., Jr. 2006. Projected pension income: Equality or disparity for the baby-boom cohort? *Monthly Labor Review* 129 (3): 58–67.

Myers, D. 2007. *Immigrants and boomers: Forging a new social contract for the future of America.* New York: Russell Sage.

National Center for Health Statistics. 2002. Live births, birth rates, and fertility rates, by race: United States, 1909–2002. Http://www.cdc.gov/nchs/data/statab/natfinal2002.annvol1_01.pdf.

O'Rand, A. 1996. The precious and the precocious: Understanding cumulative disadvantage and cumulative advantage over the life course. *Gerontologist* 36:230–38.

Ruggles, S., M. Sobek., M. Alexander, C. A. Fitch, R. Goeken, P. K. Hall, M. King, and C. Ronnander. 2004. *Integrated public use microdata series: Version 3.0* [machine-readable database]. Minneapolis: Minnesota Population Center [producer and distributor]. See http://usa.ipums.org/usa/.

Schweitzer, M. W. 1980. World War II and female labor force participation rates. *Journal of Economic History* 40:89–95.

Sykes, L. L. 2003. Income rich and asset poor: A multilevel analysis of racial and ethnic differences in housing values among baby boomers. *Population Research and Policy Review* 22:1–20.

Toossi, M. 2005. Labor force projections to 2014: Retiring boomers. *Monthly Labor Review* 128 (11): 25–44.

U.S. Census Bureau. 2004. *Population projections for 2000–2050 by single years of age, by sex, and race and Hispanic origin.* Population Projections Branch, Population Division, U.S. Census Bureau. Retrieved November 1, 2007, from http://www.census.gov/ipc/www/usinterimproj/.

———. 2006. *Monthly population estimates by age, sex, race and Hispanic origin for the United States: April 1, 2000, to July 1, 2006 (with short-term projections to dates in 2007).* Population Estimates Program, Population Division, U.S. Census Bureau. Retrieved November 1, 2007, from http://www.census.gov/popest/datasets.html.

Wilmoth, J. M., and C. F. Longino. 2006. Demographic trends that will shape U.S. policy in the twenty-first century. *Research on Aging* 28:269–88.

Wilson, A. E., K. M. Shuey, and G. H. Elder Jr. 2007. Cumulative advantage processes as mechanisms of inequality in life course health. *American Journal of Sociology* 112:1886–1924.

Wister, A. V. 2005. *Baby boomer health dynamics: How are we aging?* Toronto: University of Toronto Press.

A History of Productive Aging and the Boomers

W. ANDREW ACHENBAUM

*A*ging, according to the *Oxford English Dictionary* (1971), first entered the English lexicon in 1879. *Aged*, in contrast, appeared more than four centuries earlier. *Old* is the most ancient term associated with the language of age. The word has several meanings in Greek and Latin; it has cognates in Etruscan, Sanskrit, and Armenian.

Productive aging is a modern term. The earliest U.S. reference I could uncover is found in the *Report of the Committee on Economic Security of 1935.* "We deem provision of work the best measure of security for able-bodied workers," the committee declared. "In placing primary emphasis on employment, rather than unemployment compensation, we differ fundamentally from those who see social insurance as an all-sufficient program for economic security" (Committee on Economic Security 1985, 30, 70).

It is not clear that the Committee on Economic Security architects of the 1935 Social Security Act actually had elderly workers in mind when they referred to the importance of employment for "able-bodied" workers. Title I (Old-Age Assistance) of that landmark legislation granted up to $30 a month for needy men and women aged 65 and over who met federal and state criteria. Title II (Old-Age Insurance) provided pensions for employees who had contributed to the system; benefits began at age 65. It is likely, then, that employment compensation under Social Security was earmarked primarily for men in their prime—full-time employees aging in the labor force.

The committee's presumption that it was aging, not aged, workers who contributed to the nation's productivity is consistent with assumptions in other key documents published in the 1930s. Consider how the idea of human resources is framed in *Recent Social Trends*, a survey of American society prepared for President Herbert Hoover that was published in 1933. There, economists envisioned employment opportunities for women, various racial and ethnic groups, and the population over age 16 "customarily employed." Contributors to *Recent Social Trends* did not specify the contributions employees past their prime might make to productivity; interestingly, they recognized that fueling consumption patterns among older Americans would spur growth in productivity (Mitchell 1933, 1:274, 1:332–34, 2:805). Neither was there any reference to the positive contributions older workers might make in the labor force in Edmund Vincent Cowdry's *Problems of Ageing* (1939), arguably the first handbook of gerontology published in the United States. That the first edition of the *Handbook of Aging and the Social Sciences* (Binstock and Shanas 1976), issued nearly four decades later, did not refer to "productive aging" offers proof that use of the concept was not yet very widespread by the 1970s.

PRODUCTIVE AGING AS A CONTEMPORARY GERONTOLOGICAL PARADIGM

Robert N. Butler, M.D., the first director of the National Institute of Aging, probably deserves the most credit for putting productive aging on the gerontological agenda. In his Pulitzer Prize–winning *Why Survive? Being Old in America*, Butler (1975) excoriated the "myth of unproductivity" in late life. He argued that it led to "dismal conclusions" about older people's creativity as well as their capacity to contribute to the national good. Seven years later, Butler and Herbert Gleason sponsored a conference on productive aging in Salzburg, Austria, which resulted in an edited volume by that title. Contributors argued that *Productive Aging* justified "the notion that we can, and must, express and facilitate our personal and social productivity as we grow older" (Hinterlong, Morrow-Howell, and Sherradan 2001, 5).

Thereafter, more and more researchers—mainly gerontologists—tried to define the scope and limits of the concept of productive aging. Most commentators agreed with Butler that deploying the term was a way to deflate stereotypes that characterized older men and women as useless, frail, and dependent. There was, moreover, an undeniable economic motif to analyses of productivity. Yet, scholars and federal bodies such as the National Research Council and the Panel to Review Productivity Statistics contended that monetary compensation alone did not embrace all of the dimensions of productive aging (Caro, Bass, and Chen 1993). There was consensus that formal and informal volunteer activities were important facets of productive aging. So was caregiving to the young, the old, and peers.

Still, disagreements over definitions of "productive aging" grew as the list of possible items for inclusion lengthened. Where, for instance, did adult learning fit in the scheme of things? (Re)training was often necessary if older workers were to remain productive in the marketplace. However, was taking a course on the Bible a productive use of elderly people's time in terms of building their capacity to serve? Or, to take an extreme case: meditating usually is meaningful to the person who sits silently in contemplation, but is silent prayer productive only insofar as it results in spiritual activity that benefits others? Some scholars worried that various notions of productive aging, with their emphasis on paid (part-time) work, ignored or marginalized the charitable services tirelessly performed by women and minorities (Hinterlong, Morrow-Howell, and Sherradan 2001, 7–8).

Not only did competing definitions of productive aging vie for pride of place, but other concepts emerging contemporaneously challenged its claim to being the premier way to rethink the meanings and experiences of growing older. H. R. Moody (2007), among others, proposed explorations into "conscious aging" as a "holistic line of development" representing "a new form of 'growth' in later adulthood." The National Council on the Aging advocated the idea of "vital aging" as a way to underline the capacity of every individual to celebrate and engage in the gift of life (Achenbaum 2005b). The most robust alternative to research on productive aging was *Successful Aging*, the MacArthur Foundation study spearheaded by John W. Rowe, M.D., and Robert L. Kahn. "Successful aging" emphasized "the *positive aspects of aging*" by moving "beyond the limited view of chronological age and to clarify the genetic, biomedical, behavioral, and social factors responsible for retaining—and even enhancing—people's ability to function in later life" (Rowe and Kahn 1998, 38). According to Rowe, Kahn, and their collaborators, three factors—avoiding disease and disease-related disability, maintaining high cognitive and physical functioning, and enjoying an active engagement with life—defined successful aging.

With MacArthur support and a splendid article in *Science*, one might have anticipated that successful aging would supplant productive aging as the focus of gerontological inquiry. "Once in a great while an outstanding health book comes along that should be featured on every radio and television talk show and in every major newspaper," observed Jane Brody, who writes on personal health for the *New York Times*, "yet it fails to attract the attention it deserves because it isn't 'sexy' enough" (Brody 1998, B15). Brody thought *Successful Aging* was such a book. Even gerontological lexicons had difficulty deciding where and how to catalog the concepts of "productive" and "successful" aging. The *Dictionary of Gerontology* (Harris 1988) discussed successful aging under its entry for "life satisfaction." Successful aging was allocated three pages in *Key Words in Sociocultural Gerontology* (Achenbaum, Weiland, and Haber 1996), but the compilers omitted productive aging.

Over time, the lines of convergence and divergence between productive aging and successful aging became clearer. Both sought to extol the potential of older adults to contribute to two mainstream values much esteemed in American culture. In debunking late-life stereotypes, proponents of productive aging and successful aging often broadened the boundaries ascribed to the middle decades of the life course. They did so by claiming that the constructive activities and positive outlooks of middle-aged men and women extended well into a period of life traditionally associated with obsolescence and decline. Yet, according to Scott Bass and his colleagues, there was a fundamental difference: "In productive aging, the emphasis is on the role older people can play in society; in successful aging, the emphasis is on individual physiological and psychological capacity and process" (Caro, Bass, and Chen 1993, 7). Others concurred. Successful aging focused on individual aging, particularly life satisfaction and efforts to prolong healthful aging longer in life. Productive aging, in contrast, dealt with the contributions older Americans can and do make to societal well-being through working, volunteering, and engaging in other paid and unpaid endeavors (Wykle, Whitehouse, and Morris 2005; Caro, Bruner-Canhoto, Burr, and Mutchler 2005).

There are clusters of researchers refining the notion of productive aging throughout the United States. A few examples suffice. Investigators at the Gerontology Institute at the University of Massachusetts–Boston are constructing instruments to measure motivation "for productive activity separately from motivation for activity generally" (Caro, Bruner-Canhoto, Burr, and Mutchler 2005, 21). In the Center for Social Development at the George Warren Brown School of Social Work at Washington University, as well as at the Urban Institute in Washington, D.C. (Morrow-Howell, Hinterlong, and Sherradan 2001), researchers have been designing schema for galvanizing productive behavior in later years. Marc Freedman adopted some applications of productive aging in operationalizing Civic Ventures. Denise Park's Productive Aging Laboratory at the University of Illinois focuses on cognitive and cultural differences in old age. Robert Butler (2000) at the International Longevity Center pursues his research agenda of seeking to promote productive aging and to extirpate ageism, one of the chief obstacles to recognizing the resources of late life. The University of Washington's de Tornyay Center for Healthy Aging (2007) collects videos related to productive aging.

Imaginative projects addressing the challenges and opportunities of productive aging are also under way beyond the academy and think tanks. To wit: Yad Sarah (Jewish Virtual Library) in Israel provides counseling and training programs to enable older volunteers to serve largely elderly clients. Corporate executives cite the work of scholars such as Nancy Morrow-Howell as they take steps to promote productive aging by offering greater options in the timing and types of retirement benefits, launching wellness programs, making job modifications to permit fuller worksite flexibility, and adjusting the corporate culture to create less devaluation of age and more opportunities for older workers (Mitchell 2006). The National Association of State Units on Aging (2007) has collected data on best practices, customized training and technical assistance, and facilitated peer-to-peer interactions through its Center for State Promotion of Productive Aging. The Reverend Jim Hughes has created Productive Aging Resources to educate "service-based" senior adult ministries.

This recent flurry of interest in productive aging (as well as "successful," "conscious," and "vital" aging) is no historical accident. As long as gerontology remains, in James Birren's memorable phrase, "data rich and theory poor," researchers on aging will embrace new paradigms and look for fresh ways of seeing the big picture. Advancing the idea of productive aging, H. R. Moody (2001) notes, serves many purposes. It provides a healthy antidote to the discredited "disengagement theory," as well as earlier images of elders as consumers of national resources rather than contributors to the commonweal. A more recent shibboleth impels intellectual engagement. Some of those engaged in basic and applied research on productive aging are reacting to stalwarts in the generational-equity debate of the 1980s who claimed that the elderly were "greedy geezers." Older Americans, it was argued, selfishly drained the economy, thereby shortchanging younger cohorts (especially minorities) to future claims on entitlements.

As a paradigm, productive aging might contribute to theory-building in the social sciences. We have already noted its complementarities with successful aging. It also intersects with various forms of the "political economy of aging" and the "moral economy of aging." Insofar as feminists criticize its implicit affirmation of a gendered Protestant work ethic, they demand revised concepts of productive aging that mesh with postmodern, gender-neutral notions of reflexivity and relativity.

From a historian's perspective, however, how is it possible for productive aging to be viewed as a modern, much less postmodern, concept? To cut to the chase: for virtually all of recorded history, older men and women were productive. Those who did not work did not survive very long. The historical treasure trove, moreover, is full of examples of elders as volunteers, pro bono public servants, caregivers, even contemplatives. After surveying the historical record, we must return to the question of what is potentially "new" about productive aging as a phenomenon and a paradigm.

PRODUCTIVE AGING, PAID AND UNPAID, IN PAST TIMES

Most historians believe that human civilization began in the Middle East sometime between 7000 and 35,000 B.C.E. Recent archeological findings, however, suggest earlier beginnings in Africa. In any event, the origins of humankind lie in hunter-gatherer societies. Given their limited natural and technological resources, probably few survived infancy and childhood diseases. Still, there is evidence suggesting that a small percentage lived to be at least fifty years old, some even reached their seventh decade (Robine et al. 2006). Productive aging in preagricultural societies meant participating in unpaid activities: sharing wisdom, performing domestic chores, and staying healthy. Doing otherwise was as risky for the very old as for the very young. Unproductive, often decrepit, elders were cannibalized in Africa, Oceania, and South America (Minois 1987).

The formation of agricultural communities did not affect the scope of productive aging, but it did alter generational stakes in controlling property. Elderly property owners who retained possession of their land usually worked; there are few instances of absentee landlords in ancient history. As in the Neolithic era, scarcity of food, inhospitable climates, and barren landscapes made older people vulnerable, especially if they were poor or ill. Aged women who ceased to be productive were given little assistance, though in places where female goddesses were venerated, older females benefited from their devotions to the Divine Feminine (Simmons 1945; Lerner 1986).

The Bible, one of our major sources of information about productive aging in the Classical era, offers bimodal evidence. Even if the longevity of the Patriarchs is grossly exaggerated, older men played critical roles in ritual, politics, and prophetic traditions. Elders represented the twelve tribes of Israel. Whereas Moses merely took advice from his Council of Seventy Elders, old men managed affairs in Jerusalem and during the Diaspora (Gottheil and Krauss 2007). Yet the Psalms record the plaint of those who felt abandoned on account of old age. Hebrew Scripture and the New Testament exhort the young to care for widows and orphans. Not all older women were marginal figures, however, as attested by the examples of Sarah giving birth to Isaac long past menopause and Anna, a widow for eight decades, praying daily in the Temple to see the Messiah.

The ancient Greeks honored older people with sufficient wealth and mental acuity to contribute to their city-states. Some heirs of the Muses produced their most creative work past the age of 60. Sparta had a *gerusia*, consisting of twenty-eight men and two kings over age 60. Rome, in contrast, was ruled mainly by men in their prime (40s and 50s) with the proper lineage (Parkin 2003; Beauvoir 1972). Negative evidence suggests that Romans were expected to remain productive as long as their health permitted. When they became obsolescent, they were subject to the death of *Sexagenarius de Ponte*—throwing the 60-somethings off a bridge. It is worth noting that this practice was embedded in the legend of the Hyperboreans and the Padeans of India and accounts of senicide from Central Asia and the isle of Ceos.

It is difficult to reconstruct a complete picture of productive aging in the Middle Ages. Renaissance Venice (1450–1630) provides the best case study. There, old age was thought to begin at age 40, but many of the elites lived at least thirty more years. Venice was a gerontocracy: the doge typically assumed office at age 72. (Renaissance popes, in contrast, were on average age 54 when they ascended to the throne of St. Peter and ruled for about a decade, assisted by cardinals of their cohort. Henry VIII died at 56, but he lived longer than all except one of the kings of England during the fifteenth and sixteenth centuries.) Though frail, most doges surrounded themselves with peers, who even in their 80s commanded the military and delegated responsibilities to men from influential families who from the age of 30 were rising from office to office to significant seats of power (Finlay 1980; Achenbaum 2003).

Britain offers the best glimpse of productive aging in the late medieval period among ordinary people. Here as elsewhere, men and women sometimes attained old age, but it was not a frequent phenomenon. Older men worked until death as common laborers or yeomen farmers. Retirement was uncommon, limited to a few privileged courtiers. Elderly women typically outlived their spouses; when incapable of making ends meet, they relied on family members for support. Expected to care for kin and perform domestic chores in return for food and lodging, theirs was unpaid productive aging (Kertzer and Laslett 1995; Rosenthal 1996).

Medieval demographic and socioeconomic patterns extended into the early modern period. Most elders worked until they died. Men were farmers or shopkeepers. Women performed domestic tasks. Mutual responsibilities to and with kin kept the aged productive in the household economy. Their efforts, in fact, made it possible for other family members to earn money outside the home.

With the dawn of the urban-industrial era, improvements in science, medicine, and public health increased life expectancy. As more and more people survived to 20, the incidence of disability and chronicity rose over the life course. In the eighteenth century, for instance, a 50-year-old manual laborer had half the work capacity of a 25-year-old. He had a third the capacity at 60 and 10 percent a decade later (Fogel 2004, 2, 8, 92). Accidents and chronic ailments curtailed production, paid and unpaid, for many in their prime. The deleterious impact of disability increased with the coming of advancing age.

In addition to demographic shifts, new modes of production began to change the economic productivity of older workers. Farming remained the primary source of employment for elderly men on both sides of the Atlantic until the late nineteenth and early twentieth centuries. Farming afforded an ideal setting for productive aging. Even farmers who were advanced in years could perform light tasks, supervise other laborers, manage the books, and share with others their knowledge of the seasons, crop rotation, horticulture, and animal husbandry. All this changed with the new industrial order. Clocks set the pace in factories. Quotas determined output. Experience mattered less than efficiency. Bureaucratic procedures replaced personal connections in obtaining and maintaining jobs. When the performance of older workers slackened, or they became injured or disabled (roughly a fifth of all employed by railroad and steel companies suffered a disabling accident within three years on the job), or when plants shut down, the aged were discharged as obsolescent (Achenbaum 1978; Haber and Gratton 1994).

During the early phases of industrialization, the superannuated were treated like the disabled: both groups were considered unproductive. They begged outside factory gates and in saloons. Some older workers on both sides of the Atlantic were given gratuities for faithful service in the last third of the nineteenth century. Economic historians contend that these early corporate and union pensions were actually a convenient way to improve the overall productivity of younger workers (Achenbaum 1983). The rate at which older workers voluntarily or (more likely) involuntarily left the labor force rose during the first third of the twentieth century. The exodus of older workers from business and manufacturing concerns increased economic dependency in late life, as it diminished their likelihood for being paid to be productive.

The work histories of aging women during the urban-industrial era differed from those of aging men. Most women did not work long outside the home, though percentages varied by ethnicity and race. Rarely did females' salaries exceed the earnings of males their age. Young women who secured paid employment became schoolteachers or nurses or worked as clerks in shops and commercial buildings. Upon marriage, young women by and large confined themselves to the household, engaging in unpaid but productive activities. In the prime of life, they raised children and performed domestic chores. Many widows, out of necessity, reentered the labor force: they opened their homes to boarders or ran saloons in ethnic neighborhoods (Bell 1944). Managers considered them too old to work as clerks or secretaries. Race and ethnicity were barriers for opportunities for employment, so black and immigrant older women generally settled for menial tasks and menial pay. Disability precluded productive aging at advanced ages.

Demographic and economic trends evident in the nineteenth century accelerated in the twentieth, changing the faces of productive aging. Life expectancy increased in advanced industrial nations as well as in developing countries. In many places, including the United States, men and women over the age of 85 constituted the fastest-growing segment of the population. At the same time, morbidity and mortality patterns altered. Chronic conditions were less widespread than a century earlier. Major causes of death changed in the United States. Tuberculosis accounted for a third of all deaths in 1860, to be surpassed forty years later by pneumonia. By 1970, a third of all deaths of older Americans were attributed to heart disease, double the percentage caused by cancer (Robine et al. 2006, 156; Fogel 2004, 111; Walford 1983, 8). The pool of healthy elders who putatively might engage in productive aging had grown enormously.

Yet most of the twentieth century witnessed the golden age of retirement. The introduction of social insurance systems around the world, often operating in concert with plans existing in the private sector, assured most workers of at least a minimal standard of living and access to health care in later years. Provisions varied by gender (women typically moved in and out of paid employment, were paid less for comparable work than men, and lived longer) and race (minorities generally had lower-paid jobs, less access to retirement and health care benefits, and a greater incidence of disabilities in midlife) (Achenbaum 2005a; Johnson 2005). That said, retirement packages generally were enough to entice many to spend their remaining years in pursuit of leisure, engaging more in consumption than production.

By the beginning of the current millennium, new trends in paid productive aging were taking shape. Several factors were at play. Some, who presumed that growing numbers of elders were a drag on the economy, felt that population aging was a time bomb; a nation of elders in the making threatened the solvency of social-insurance benefits for later cohorts. Others contended that increasing productivity was the key to economic prosperity and saw older people as a potential resource, not a burden. Meanwhile, the aged themselves adapted to new incentives to be productive. Growing numbers of older people were willing and able to return to the workforce on a part-time basis. Companies, realizing the experience and loyalty of elders, began to design flexible options that were mutually beneficial to employers and employees (Goldberg 2000; Riley, Kahn, and Foner 1994). And as we shall see, there were boundless opportunities for unpaid contributions in the voluntary sector. "Unretirement" paid off: increasing older people's productivity sustained prosperity.

A BRIEF HISTORY OF VOLUNTEERING AS PRODUCTIVE AGING

Examples from U.S. history demonstrate the important contributions older people make to their fellow citizens as unpaid volunteers in their local and national communities, religious institutions, and a host of civic organizations. French aristocrat Alexis de Tocqueville, touring the United States 170 years ago, understood that "voluntary associations" provided the social cohesion that made democracy in America possible:

> In no country in the world has the principle of association been more successfully used or applied to a greater multitude of objects than in America.... In the United States associations are established to promote the public safety, commerce, industry, morality, and religion. There is no end which the human will despairs of attaining through the combined power of individuals united in society. (1945, 1:198–99)

From the early days of the republic, older Americans volunteered their talents and energy to intergenerational and intragenerational endeavors. Every age group had to contribute to the public good, observed an orator at the opening of a canal on July 4, 1825, "all the vigor of youth, the strength and firmness of manhood, and the wisdom of age" (Achenbaum 1978, 9).

All sorts of voluntary associations enabled individuals to apply their talents through social-service agencies. Religious congregations and secular organizations in particular helped immigrants assimilate to urban-industrial America. The elderly were instrumental in establishing such institutions. Felix Adler, the head of the New York Society for Ethical Culture until he died at the age of 82, for instance, solicited his adherents to sponsor Visitor Nursing (a program absorbed by the city's public health network) and a free kindergarten for children of working parents (Achenbaum 2006/2007).

As documented elsewhere in this volume, older Americans participate in literally thousands of faith-based ventures and government-sponsored initiatives to help children, the sick, and the needy. Older volunteers are indispensable in attending to the needs of patients in hospitals. Elders typically organize neighborhood watches. They lead grassroots environmental interest groups, which in turn link to similar bodies around the world. Senior Corps oversees the Retired Senior Volunteer Program (RSVP), Foster Grandparents, and the Senior Companion Program, which attract more than 500,000 senior citizens to serve the commonweal (Senior Corps 2006).

Older Americans have been political activists since the colonial period. In the wake of the Glorious Revolution of 1688, mature males of property and standing served as judges, justices, and lawmakers, charged with adjusting political ties in their counties and provinces. Schoolchildren are taught to praise the virtues of the "Young Men of the Revolution," but sages such as Benjamin Franklin and Oneida chief Oskanondonha enunciated many of the issues debated as the Constitution was framed. Similarly, leaders of the abolitionist movement included elders such as Frederick Douglass, Harriet Tubman, and William Lloyd Garrison. The struggle to abolish slavery prompted the first feminist movement, which relied on the seasoned judgment of Lucretia Mott, Emma Willard, and Elizabeth Cady Stanton, among others. Another cohort of older women—including Susan B. Anthony and Charlotte Perkins Gilman—advanced the campaign for women's rights at the end of the century.

Older Americans have been advocates of social change throughout the twentieth century. Young men joined unions led by veterans of productivity such as Samuel Gompers and George Meany. Francis Townsend mobilized millions of senior citizens in the depths of the Great Depression to plead for relief from poverty. When forced to retire, Maggie Kuhn created the Gray Panthers, which resisted injustice and discrimination against the elderly, as well as against women and minorities.

Older people have also played a critical, productive role in promoting adult learning. Josiah Holbrook's Lyceum Movement in 1826 brought such venerable orators as Ralph Waldo Emerson and Oliver Wendell Holmes to rural communities. Aging leaders in urban centers and rural settlements took the initiative in establishing libraries, particularly after Andrew Carnegie, aged 67, earmarked generous funds for their construction. Originally designed for female Methodist Sunday School teachers, the Chautauqua Movement of 1874 became the prototype for modern-day Elderhostels.

Even this brief historical overview illustrates the range of volunteer activities that have engaged older Americans throughout our national experiences. "From the very beginning our people have markedly combined practical capacity for affairs with power of devotion to an ideal," observed President Theodore Roosevelt in 1902. "The lack of either quality would have rendered the possession of the other of small consequence." Older Americans who volunteer to lead or to participate in causes to advance social, political, educational, and community-based ideals engage in productive aging.

WHAT MAKES PRODUCTIVE AGING NOVEL?

So what makes "productive aging" novel? It cannot be that we are in the presence of the first cohort of older Americans engaged in productive activities. The historical record makes clear that from the beginning of human civilization the elderly have been productive out of self-interest: their very survival depended on the real and ascribed value of their contributions to others in their community. Self-interest, however altruistic in intent, motivated the aged to do unpaid work and to volunteer, and their efforts freed others to accomplish other tasks vital to the well-being of the community.

Researchers at Washington University contend that "productive aging, like most emergent policy concepts, has been characterized by advocacy and empirical work more than by theoretical development" (Morrow-Howell et al., 260). Marc Freedman's Experience Corps and Civic Ventures are perfect examples of what is possible when American pragmatism, social capital, and innovative risk-taking are combined under the banner of productive aging: "These efforts are part of the growing ferment of entrepreneurial efforts that are blending public and private financing and creating new roles for Americans in the last third of life" (Freedman 2001, 254). Gerontologists have been applying ideas from their own laboratories and the marketplace of ideas since research on aging emerged as a field of inquiry. Thanks to simple technological innovations, for instance, older Americans can live in barrier-free, safe homes (Achenbaum 1995). So what makes productive aging any different?

Crafting a concept of productive aging grounded in theory, in my opinion, would ensure the robustness and durability of the idea that older people have the capacity and experiences to produce distinctive contributions for the well-being of their environment (however broadly understood). Nancy Morrow-Howell and her associates at Washington University itemize six categories that must be part of any middle-level theory of productive aging (Morrow-Howell et al. 2001, 275–76):

- Sociodemographics
- Public policy
- Individual capacity

- Institutional capacity
- Productive behaviors
- Productivity outcomes

To this list I would add two other categories.

First, I would ask biomedical researchers to join the conversation. For far too long, the very investigators who advocate multidisciplinary research on aging have separated themselves into tribal cells. In an age of specialization, wherein disciplines are barely worthy of the designation, I fully acknowledge that I do not understand the mystifying details emanating from the Genome Project. But I also know that fundamental areas of the biological sciences—such as brain research—are truly frontiers that demand the attention of investigators and nonscientists alike. Science provides new grounds for claiming that "old dogs can learn new tricks." Incorporating the scientific basis for understanding self-interest and altruism, in addition to explicating how older brains process and assimilate new information, would benefit any theory of productive aging, particularly one meant to spur additional research and to attract public interest.

Second, any theory of productive aging must make it a priority to confront individual and institutional ageism. No decent human being would demean another person by making a racist, sexist, homophobic, religious, or ethnic slur. Laws protect people against discrimination on the basis of race, gender, sexual orientation, ethnicity, religion, and disability. Comparable laws also exist to prevent age-based disparities and prejudicial remarks, but they are less effective. Researchers have a choice to make. If they believe that demography is destiny, then they can perpetuate the notion that population aging is, in and of itself, a curse masquerading as a talisman of human progress. The countertactic is to begin with the premise that productivity is the engine of prosperity. In this scenario, a failure to provide opportunities, on theoretical and empirical grounds, for those older people willing and able to participate in paid work or as volunteers is a waste of social capital. Just as nineteenth-century canal builders needed the gifts of all age groups to serve the public good, so too can we ill afford to squander the resources of age.

The best way to build theories is to take theory-building seriously. Still reeling from the demise of many attempts to construct knowledge-based paradigms in gerontology, researchers feverishly grasp at the latest concept to come along. Productive aging offers more than a temporary guidepost for involving older Americans in paid and unpaid activities. It can be a way to knit much of the gerontological community together.

REFERENCES

Achenbaum, W. Andrew. 1978. *Old age in the new land.* Baltimore: Johns Hopkins University Press.
———. 1983. *Shades of gray.* Boston: Little, Brown.

———. 1995. *Crossing Frontiers*. New York: Cambridge University Press.

———. 2003. (When) Did the papacy become a gerontocracy? In *Societal impact on aging: Historical perspectives*, ed. K. Warner Schaie and W. Andrew Achenbaum. New York: Springer, 204–31.

———. 2005a. Aging and changing. In *The Cambridge handbook of age and ageing*, ed. Malcolm L. Johnson. Cambridge: Cambridge University Press, 21–30.

———. 2005b. *Older Americans, vital communities*. Baltimore: Johns Hopkins University Press.

———. 2006/2007. A history of civic engagement of older people. *Generations* 30 (Winter): 18–23.

Achenbaum, W. Andrew, Steven Weiland, and Carole Haber. 1996. *Key words in sociocultural gerontology*. New York: Springer.

Beauvoir, Simone de. 1972. *The coming of age*. New York: G. P. Putnam & Sons.

Bell, Thomas. 1944. *Out of this furnace*. Pittsburgh, PA: University of Pittsburgh Press.

Binstock, Robert H., and Ethel Shanas, eds. 1976. *Handbook of aging and the social sciences*. New York: Van Nostrand Reinhold.

Brody, Jane E. 1998. A valuable guide to successful aging. *New York Times*. April 14.

Butler, Robert N. 1975. *Why survive? Being old in America*. New York: Harper & Row.

———. 2000. Productive aging: Live longer, work longer. Paper presented to the World Congress on Medicine and Health, Hanover, Germany, September 21.

Caro, Francis A., Scott A. Bass, and Yung-Ping Chen. 1993. Introduction to *Achieving a productive aging society*, ed. Scott A. Bass, Francis Caro, and Yung-Ping Chen, 3–12. Westport, CT: Auburn House.

Caro, Francis A., Laney Bruner-Canhoto, Jeffrey Burr, and Jan Mutchler. 2005. Motivation for active aging: Results of a pilot study. Unpublished paper.

Committee on Economic Security. 1985. The report of the Committee on Economic Security. 50th anniv. ed. Washington, DC: National Conference on Social Welfare.

Cowdry, Edmund Vincent, ed. 1939. *Problems of ageing*. Baltimore: Williams & Wilkins.

De Tornyay Center for Healthy Aging, University of Washington. 2007. Resources: Video collection. Http://www.agingcenter.org/resources-video.asp.

Donadio, S., ed. 1988. *The New York Public Library book of 20th-century American quotations*. New York: Warner Books.

Finlay, Richard. 1980. *Politics in renaissance Venice*. New Brunswick, NJ: Rutgers University Press.

Fogel, Robert W. 2004. *The escape from hunger and premature death*. New York: Cambridge University Press.

Freedman, Marc. 2001. Structural lead: Building new institutions for aging America. In Morrow-Howell, Hinterlong, and Sherradan 2001, 214–22.

Goldberg, Beverly. 2000. *Age Works*. New York: Free Press.

Gottheil, Richard, and Samuel Krauss. 2007. Gerusia. *JewishEncyclopedia.com*, http://www.jewishencyclopedia.com/view.jsp?artid=190&letter=G.

Haber, Carole, and Brian Gratton. 1994. *Old age and the search for security*. Bloomington: Indiana University Press.

Harris, Diana K. 1988. *Dictionary of gerontology*. Westport, CT: Greenwood Press.

Hinterlong, James, Nancy Morrow-Howell, and Michael Sherradan. 2001. Productive aging: Principles and perspectives. In Morrow-Howell, Hinterlong, and Sherradan 2001, 3–18.

Johnson, M. L., ed. 2005. *The Cambridge handbook of age and aging*. Cambridge: Cambridge University Press.

Kertzer, David, and Peter Laslett. 1995. *Aging in the past*. Berkeley: University of California Press.

Lerner, Gerda. 1986. *The creation of patriarchy*. New York: Oxford University Press.

Minois, Georges. 1987. *History of old age*. Chicago: University of Chicago Press.

Mitchell, Kenneth. 2006. Productive aging: The new life stage. *World at Work Journal* vol 15, (2006, July): 62–72.

Mitchell, William, ed. 1933. *Recent trends in the United States*. 2 vols. New York: McGraw-Hill.

Moody, H. R. 2001. Productive aging and the ideology of old age. In Morrow-Howell, Hinterlong, and Sherradan 2001, 247–62.

———. 2002. Conscious aging: A new level of growth in later life. Http://www.wellnessgoods.com/consciousagingnewlevel.asp.

Morrow-Howell, Nancy, James Hinterlong, and Michael Sherradan, eds. 2001. *Productive aging: Concepts and challenges*. Baltimore: Johns Hopkins University Press.

National Association of State Units on Aging. 2007. State promotion of productive aging. http://nasua.org/productiveaging.cfm.

Parkin, Timothy G. 2003. *Old age in the Roman world*. Baltimore: Johns Hopkins University Press.

Riley, Matilda White, Robert L. Kahn, and Anne Foner. 1994. *Age and structural lag*. New York: John Wiley & Sons.

Robine, Jean-Marie, Elaine M. Crimmins, Sakao Horiuchi, and Zeng Yi. 2006. *Human longevity, individual life duration, and the growth of the oldest-old population*. Dordrecht, The Netherlands: Springer.

Rosenthal, Joel T. 1996. *Old age in late medieval England*. Philadelphia: University of Pennsylvania Press.

Rowe, John W., and Robert L. Kahn. 1998. *Successful aging*. New York: Pantheon.

Senior Corps. 2006. Senior Corps programs. Http://www.seniorcorps.gov/about/programs/index.asp.

Simmons, Leo W. 1945. *The role of the aged in primitive societies*. New Haven, CT: Yale University Press.

Tocqueville, Alexis de. 1945. *Democracy in America*. 2 vols. (1836–1840). Trans. Phillips Bradley. New York: Vintage.

Walford, Roy L. 1983. *Maximum life span*. New York: W. W. Norton.

Wykle, May L., Peter J. Whitehouse, and Diana L. Morris, eds. 2005. *Successful aging through the life span*. New York: Springer.

II
BOOMERS AND THE NEW ECONOMICS OF AGING

4

The Boomers and Their Economic Prospects

KAREN C. HOLDEN

L ittle economic news is reported these days without conclusions being drawn about the implications for the economic prospects of future retirees. Declines in the stock market lower the value of personal savings accounts and, potentially, jeopardize the funding status of defined benefit pension plans and the annuitized value of defined contribution plan accounts. Rising consumer prices threaten to reduce the real (consumption) value of current and potential retirement income that is not automatically adjusted for inflation. Slower wage growth threatens current income and future earnings prospects of families and individuals. Rising unemployment may lead to the loss of employer-provided pension coverage and the consequent cessation of employer contributions to defined contribution accounts or the freezing of service credits and earnings used to calculate defined benefit plan benefits. Rising unsecured consumer debt is taken as a signal of consumers' preferences for current over future consumption with the consequent shift of income (through borrowing) from the future (and retirement) to the present. Borrowing clearly reduces the potential for new savings, but it may also lead to borrowing against retirement savings already made.

The reverse of these economic events—a rising stock market, growth in employment and wages, reduced willingness to borrow by consumers—has had and would have beneficial effects on incomes of families and individuals, increasing their ability to save for retirement and growing their past savings for a more secure retirement. Legislation that offer new types of individual retirement accounts (IRAs) and raises limits on tax-deferred account contributions allow those in their peak earnings years to save more. Improved prescription drug benefits in public and private plans means retirement savings will not always have to fully cover those. Tighter regulations on insurance and on scams means that fewer will see their savings disappear.

THE BOOMERS' EARLY YEARS: A PERIOD OF PROSPERITY

The boomers, commonly defined as those born between 1946 and 1964, were born during a period of relative prosperity. Indeed, what became known as the "Easterlin hypothesis" argues that the boom in births was due in part to the relatively high incomes in the immediate post–World War II period of the relatively small cohort of young adults entering the workforce and forming families. The parents of the boomers were relatively well off compared to the economic status of the previous generation they observed when they themselves were young teens (Easterlin 1966). Postwar income growth and the higher consumption made possible by the lifting of war rationing encouraged family formation and larger families. The baby boomers were born in a period of relative prosperity, and from birth through to their current standing on the cusp of retirement, this larger generation has placed additional demands on public services.

Educational systems at all levels faced mounting pressure as this large cohort entered school and went on to college. Penner (1998) argues that the growth in educational expenditures "contributed disproportionately to the growth of total state and local government in the 1952–75 period, accounting for 46 percent of the increased share of GDP [gross domestic product], due to the need to educate the baby boomers." College enrollment expanded as the GI Bill enabled increased college enrollment among returning veterans, including the parents of boomers, and continued to do so as the next generation entered and completed college at rates higher than had their parents (Finberman and Dolbin-MacNab 2006). After 1975, education expenditures stabilized (Penner 1998) as the baby boomers had largely completed their education and moved into their working-age years (see figure 4-1).

On average, the baby boomers have enjoyed higher earnings and family incomes than did their parents (Poulos and Nightingale 1997), although this was in the face of higher unemployment rates (Russell 1982) and came about in part because of the earnings contributed by the higher labor force participation and earnings of wives (Blau, Ferber, and Winkler 1998). Homeownership rates grew among the baby-boom cohort and—perhaps in part because this large working-age cohort provided relatively low per-person financing for services to the smaller cohort of their retired parents—tax-favored retirement options and retirement services expanded during the 1980s and 1990s (Mitchell 2000).

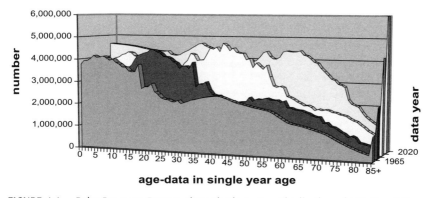

FIGURE 4-1.   Baby Boomers Passage through Time: Age Distribution of U.S. Population, 1965, 1979, 2000, 2020
Source: Author's calculation from U.S. Census Bureau data and projections.

Employer-provided pension coverage grew, reaching a peak of just less than 60 percent of the full-time workforce. Amendments to the Social Security Act in 1972 and 1977 instituted important automatic adjustments in benefit calculation and payouts of the Social Security system. Poverty rates fell among the elderly, and Social Security and employer-provided pensions accounted for an increasing share of the income received by the 65-and-over population. The labor force participation of men 60–69 declined steadily during the last three decades of the twentieth century, due to older workers choosing to take some of their greater prosperity as leisure (Quinn 2000). Greater retirement security for the baby-boom cohort compared to that of the previous generations seemed likely (Congressional Budget Office 1993).

EARLY AND LATER BABY BOOMERS: THEIR DIFFERENT EXPERIENCES

But there were early concerns that all would not be well in retirement—perhaps not even relatively well compared to their parents—for the baby-boom cohort. Having witnessed the effect of the larger cohort on the demand for education and employment-related services, it was apparent that their passage into retirement would present comparable challenges to public services, both to retirement income systems and to programs providing services to the elderly.

There was also early evidence that the economic experiences of the baby-boomer cohort had been and would continue to be different for the "early boomers" and the "later boomers." The first group is generally identified as those born from 1946 to about 1953, the second group as those born during the second half of the booming birth period. The first group, often also labeled the "leading edge" of the boomers to emphasize their role as the first to overload social services and economic institutions, entered schools as states and municipalities first began to expand and fund facilities to accommodate them as students. Subsequently, they were the leading edge of a larger cohort of workers, on average more highly educated than were members of the relatively small cohort of workers they followed.

The later boomers, by contrast, entered school systems that were already strained physically and fiscally by their older schoolmates and then entered the labor market, further expanding an already enlarged cohort of workers. This same distinction in the experience of these two subcohorts is reflected in the predictions about the baby boomers' retirement security. Once again the leading edge of the baby boomers will be the first of the cohort to interact with retirement systems that may be anticipating the large cohorts of retirees but have not yet felt the effects of the larger demand on retirement systems. The "trailing edge" will encounter retirement systems that have begun to face the retirement challenge presented by the earlier baby boomers and likely will encounter a system already modified by and because of the early boomers.

This difference in the retirement systems the two subcohorts will likely face as they approach and enter retirement is illustrated in figure 4-2, which shows for the Old Age and Survivors Insurance (OASI) system the estimated "actuarial balance" (annual income minus outgo of OASI) and the estimated trust fund ratio (the ratio of the fund to estimated expenses) at the age each birth-year cohort reaches age 62 (the early retirement age) and at their full retirement age (age 66 or 67, depending on year of birth). A fifth trend line shows the trust fund ratio at the age of full retirement plus life expectancy.

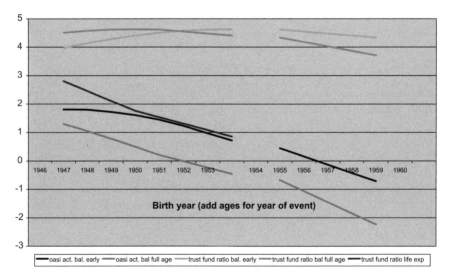

FIGURE 4-2. Social Security Ratios at Key Retirement Years: Baby Boomers Identified by Birth Year

When the first boomers reached age 62 in 2008, the OASI system was in surplus by all *annual* measures.[1] The Social Security actuarial balance was positive, and the trust fund stood at well over four times annual outgo. Based on the "Intermediate Assumptions," the system is projected to remain in surplus during the years this first subcohort becomes eligible for retired-worker benefits, although the actuarial ratios will steadily decline through much of their retired lives. Only in the later years of their lives (see the graph of trust fund ratio at life expectancy in figure 4-2) is the trust fund projected to be fully depleted.

The situation facing OASI during the retired lives of the later boomers will be markedly different. While it is no surprise to see the steady negative slope in all these lines, the graph visually shows the sharply different policy environment that is likely to prevail. As they first become eligible for Social Security retired-worker benefits, this trailing-end subcohort is projected (again based on the "Intermediate Assumptions") to confront a Social Security system that will, without changes in costs or benefits, continue its steady deterioration in financial health, including negative trust fund balances through most of their retired lives.

It is important to note that projections are of a scenario based on specific demographic and economic assumptions, including, in the case of Social Security, revenue and cost balances about benefits paid and FICA (Federal Insurance Contributions Act) tax levels. With benefit payments projected (without program changes) to persistently exceed system income over most of the lives of the earlier cohort, the later boomers will almost certainly face a less generous system. As the "pay-as-you-go" educational systems had to grapple with the questions of how to pay for the education of the baby boomers and what education would be necessary for economic growth and family well-being, so must this pay-as-you-go retirement income system grapple with the questions of what income is necessary for social and individual well-being in a world that will change over their retired lifetimes. The answers will likely affect the incomes and retirement behavior of the early and later boomers differently.

EARLY AND LATER BOOMERS: GROWING ECONOMIC AND DEMOGRAPHIC DIVERSITY

Arguably the most comprehensive projections of the economic well-being in retirement of the baby-boom generation come from the Social Security Administration's (SSA) MINT model, a simulation model developed by SSA's Office of Research, Evaluation, and Statistics in cooperation with the Brookings Institution, the RAND Corporation, and the Urban Institute (Toder et al. 1999). This model starts with a nationally representative sample from the 1990–1993 Survey of Income and Program Participation (SIPP), with individuals' records matched to SSA earnings and benefit data. It projects for each person over their remaining lifetime their marital status and changes; work patterns and earnings; asset holdings and growth; pension coverage, participation, and benefits; and Social Security receipt age and benefits.

Butrica, Iams, and Smith (2007) compare MINT projections for the two baby-boom subcohorts (as well as with projections for their parents' generation), and they project that on some key measures the two boomer subcohorts appear differently prepared for retirement, but that both groups are likely on average to have *higher retirement incomes* and experience *lower poverty rates* than did their parents.[2] This projected greater income security compared to previous generations reflects in part the growth in real wage earnings, the greater labor force participation and higher earnings of women in this generation compared to their mothers—either as sole workers or in dual-earning households—and the higher pension coverage and more generous benefit provisions for this compared to the previous generation. Likewise baby boomers are expected to have accumulated greater wealth compared to the previous generation (Congressional Budget Office 2004).

Differences between the two baby-boom subcohorts reflect the accumulating effects of retirement-related changes that took place over their working-age years—the slowing (though still positive) earnings growth, increasing rates of divorce, and declining importance of defined benefit pension plans. Health insurance coverage has also declined, leaving a slightly higher fraction of the baby boomers uninsured (Levy 2007) and vulnerable to higher out-of-pocket medical care costs. Likewise, baby boomers are estimated to face higher long-term care costs—with consequences for retirement savings adequacy—as fiscally constrained states and smaller families grapple with the tax consequences of a growing dependent and longer-lived population (Johnson et al. 2007). These trends become more evident among the trailing baby-boom subcohort.

While projected real retirement incomes are expected to be higher on average for more recent cohorts (among baby boomers and their parents), other economic well-being standards project a more complex picture. One frequently used standard of well-being is the extent to which retirees are able to maintain their preretirement consumption in retirement. This is a *relative* standard of well-being (in contrast to an *absolute* income measure) that is operationalized by comparing expected retirement income to preretirement income, with some percentage of preretirement income adopted as a measure of "sufficient" income or retirement savings.[3] The use of this relative (replacement rate) measure, rather than an absolute income measure, to judge the future well-being of retirees reflects an assumption that individuals wish to maintain preretirement consumption levels in retirement and that society should judge the adequacy of its retirement system by the degree to which retirees must (presumably unwillingly) alter their consumption and lifestyle when work ceases.[4]

Butrica, Iams, and Smith (2007) find that replacement rates have declined for the baby-boom cohort as a whole compared to earlier cohorts, though projected rates are identical (at 81 percent) for both the leading- and trailing-edge baby-boom subcohorts. Groups with the highest replacement rates reflect the progressive benefit formula of Social Security, which replaces a higher percentage of covered earnings of low earners, as well as access by low-income groups to means-tested benefits. Groups with projected higher replacement rates are disproportionately never-married women, those with fewer years of wage earnings, and those with the lower total lifetime earnings. Because the least advantaged economically are found to have higher replacement rates, Haveman and colleagues (2007a) argue that this standard has ambiguous social content. Using a replacement standard, policy makers would judge as worse off relative to their lower-income peers those with high preretirement income but low replacement rates, even if they are more able to cover expected postretirement consumption. Against this replacement standard of well-being, the baby-boom cohorts are worse off compared to their parents' generation despite higher real incomes.

In another study, Haveman and his colleagues (2007b) adopt a different standard, comparing the steady potential consumption stream obtainable from retirement resources with the poverty (or twice-poverty) threshold, asking whether expected income at retirement would be sufficient to maintain consumption above this social adequacy standard throughout every remaining year of expected life, including the years when only one spouse in a married-couple household survives. Individuals meeting the poverty standard of well-being are quite different from those meeting the replacement standard; those with less consistent labor market attachment and those with lower education levels are most likely to have insufficient retirement resources to maintain them above this poverty-level standard (or twice that standard) during all remaining years of retirement. In contrast to Butrica, Iams, and Smith (2007), Haveman and colleagues (2007b) estimate higher overall poverty rates for more recent retiree cohorts, although both estimate higher poverty rates for individuals with weak labor market attachments in younger than in older cohorts.[5] This is consistent with earlier speculation by Easterlin, Schaeffer, and Macunovich:

> On average, the boomers are currently doing considerably better than their parents did at the same point in the life cycle, and the prospect is that this will continue to be true into retirement. The possible exception is the poorest segment of the boomers, especially the trailing edge cohorts. Although they are currently somewhat better off than their counterparts in the parental generation, they may end up worse off. (1993, 518)

THE MOST VULNERABLE AMONG THE BABY BOOMERS

The probable higher poverty rates for some groups in more recent (including baby-boom) cohorts nearing retirement reflect labor market and demographic trends during the 1970s through the 1990s that increased economic risks for some and opportunities for others. While increased education among successive cohorts of boomers raised real earnings potential among both women and men, these gains were offset for some families by higher rates of divorce, single parenthood, and immigration and by declining employment in manufacturing jobs that generally had provided retirement and health benefits.

The baby boomers in many ways have led the way as the U.S. population became more diverse in terms of earnings capacity and economic security. From 1967 through the 1990s, income inequality grew among the nonelderly even as inequality fell among the then-elderly cohorts, the latter trend fueled in large part by improvements in Social Security benefits that favored lower income retirees (Bradbury 1996; Rubin, White-Means, and Daniel 2000).[6] Factors that have been identified as contributors to the growing inequality among workers include the widening gap in earnings by educational status, as the wages of high-school-graduates-only lagged; differences in family incomes of one- and two-earner families; and the increase in what is termed "assortative mating" by education and earning status.[7] This increase in working-age income inequality is expected to continue into retirement. Butrica, Iams, and Smith (2007) predict greater income inequality overall among baby-boomer cohorts than their parents' generation and also greater income inequality by education and ethnic group, especially for the trailing-edge boomers, who are characterized by increased demographic and economic diversity. It is this growing diversity in demographic composition and the behavioral responses to changing economic circumstances that make projections of baby boomers well-being an uncertain task.

One of the important demographic changes in which the baby boomers led is in ethnic composition. Lynch (2007, 851) contrasts the "largely white, aging baby boomers and a younger, far more ethnically diverse Global America." While it is true this generation is less ethnically diverse than will be later generations of retirees, the baby-boomer cohort consists of many more than just those born to post–World War II U.S. parents. It reflects the leading edge of ethnic diversity as well. Immigrants have increased the size of the early boomers' birth cohort by 14 percent and the later boomers' by 16.5 percent,[8] with more recent immigrants being increasingly Hispanic. This is thus already an ethnically diverse group, with immigrants adding to the productive capacity of a nation (and their cohort), though on average recording lower earnings and family income and higher poverty rates than their native-born peers (Butrica, Iams, and Smith 2007).

The economic security and vulnerability of members in this (or any) generation depend not just on the characteristics individuals bring to the labor market—their education and skills relative to the demand for workers—but also on the institutions with which they interact and how those institutions respond to this larger and more diverse cohort. Retirement institutions and savings vehicles have changed in important ways over the work-lives of this cohort. Amendments in 1978 to the Internal Revenue Code, effective in January 1980 when the oldest baby boomers were 34 and the youngest 20 years old, allowed for 401(k) accounts. While coverage by defined benefit pension plans has fallen for successively young boomers, increasing coverage by defined contribution pension plans and savings through 401(k) individual tax-deferred accounts and IRAs has most likely allowed for greater wealth accumulation by baby boomers, although this is most true for those with college educations (Bernheim and Scholz 1993).

Economic security also depends on the reaction of the baby boomers to changes in their economic circumstances. Easterlin et al. (1990) argued that the baby boomers would be better off than their parents in part because of their smaller families and more dual-earning households, and that the positive effect of these changes on family incomes for this cohort outweighs the adverse economic conditions many faced.[9] More recently, Plotnick (2008) documented the favorable economic position of childless married and single women and men. The implication of these findings is that behavioral responses by this cohort to socioeconomic conditions they confront as they approach retirement may cause divergence of actual economic status from projections due to behavioral adjustments.

Notably, the early retirement trend has slowed and perhaps reversed; Friedberg (2007) sees this is a likely response to increasing uncertainty about retirement security. Uncertainty about the future stability of retirement wealth holdings in the face of more recent mortgage crises and bank failures may also cause this cohort to further delay retirement, to save more for retirement, or to adjust consumption in retirement. Whether this makes individuals "worse off" in retirement than their parents were will be a matter of individual and social debate.

CONCLUSION

In a report for the Commonwealth Fund, a group of policy experts argued that (and titled the report) "demography is not destiny":[10]

> Society's future is not determined solely by demographic changes. Focusing on the anticipated growth in population by age group is just too simplistic an approach. Rather, the future is shaped by the choices made—or not made—individually and collectively, bounded by the limits in resources and, in particular, knowledge. Knowledge is at the heart of gains in productivity, economic growth, and the advances in medical care, agriculture, communication, transportation, and the environment. Population change must be considered in the context of other changes throughout the economy and society. Private markets and public policies are not only effective tools for encouraging individual behavior, but also for responding to the collective needs of consumers, workers, and employers. (Friedland and Summer 2005)

And so the economic well-being of the baby-boom cohort (and its subgroups) will depend on how it has been shaped by economic and social changes over time—both before and during retirement—as well as how institutions respond to the cohort, not just to its sheer size but also to other demographic and social changes.

The baby-boom cohort, especially its trailing edge, has been at the leading edge of changes that are not just limited in their effects to the social and economic well-being of this particular generation and to the retirement policies facing them as they age. Changes experienced by the baby-boom cohort will be mirrored in the smaller cohorts that follow. With more education, more women working, and more retirement savings options, many in the overall cohort will be better off than the early subcohort; the same will be true for the smaller subsequent cohorts. Higher rates of divorce, ethnic diversity, and immigration have contributed to growing inequality and probably higher rates of poverty in the future. The larger cohort approaching retirement, followed by a relatively small cohort of workers, is likely to increase employment opportunities for older individuals, delay retirement and the first receipt of retirement benefits, and change savings behavior at the end of life.

On the other hand, longer expected lives will increase potential years of retirement and disability, health care inflation may continue to raise health care and health insurance costs, and more older adults with fewer family caregivers may increase the demand for publicly financed custodial care. It is easy to use "simplistic" projections to project (usually) dire consequences for public and private retirement income programs from the "burden" of the larger baby-boom cohorts as well as for their children. Continued productive use of the human capital provided by the baby boomers is the challenge posed by the boomers to society and to themselves as well. The use of economic incentives to encourage their savings and wise use of those savings, including for investment in the economic future of their (or their neighbors') children, is the challenge.

NOTES

1. On February 12, 2008, the first baby boomer received a Social Security retirement benefit. Kathleen Casey-Kirschling was born one minute after midnight on January 1, 1946. See the Social Security Administration's press release at http://www.ssa.gov/pressoffice/pr/babyboomer-firstcheck-pr.htm.

2. This article and others on baby boom retirement behavior and well-being are available at the website of the Pension Research Council, which holds annual conferences with papers appearing in edited volumes. See http://www.pensionresearchcouncil.org/publications/papers.php?year=2007.

3. A standard of 70 percent of preretirement income has been used in the literature. The argument for less-than-100-percent replacement is usually that, when work ceases, there are declines in required work expenses, retirement income is tax favored, and retirees have more time to spend on activities that would have otherwise required

out-of-pocket expenditures (e.g., home maintenance, lower monetary but high time-cost travel). Others argue that their reduced mobility, loss of employer-provided benefits and services, and deteriorating health may increase income requirements. The 70 percent standard is used in Haveman et al. 2007a; Bernheim et al. 2001 provides evidence supporting the use of this percentage across income groups.

4. The degree to which consumption declines voluntarily is a complicated story. Lundberg, Startza, and Stillman (2002) find that consumption declines for couples but not for single individuals upon retirement. They hypothesize that wives bargain to preserve resources for their longer expected lifetimes, with their bargaining power increasing when husbands retire. In this scenario, consumption changes are due to couples' decisions about how to allocate resources over their remaining lifetimes. This suggests that changes in work and earnings patterns of husbands and wives and in the probability of marriage (and being married at retirement) will alter observed consumption patterns at retirement for the younger baby boomers, with those patterns being more consistent with longer life expectations and more favorable for the well-being of widowed men and women.

5. Higher predicted poverty rates for some vulnerable groups as overall poverty rates fall imply lower poverty rates predicted for others. This is where the two groups of researchers vary in their conclusions, with Haveman and colleagues (2007b) predicting less improvement in the economic circumstances of unmarried women.

6. Even if income increases for all groups, income inequality can grow if the growth is greater among higher-income groups. Inequality also increases if incomes at the lower end of the distribution grow more slowly than for most income groups. Both changes have contributed to the increase in income inequality in the United States. The share of resources going to the top 5 percent of the population in the income distribution has increased over time; the proportion who were poor grew in the 1980s, fell in the 1990s (Plotnick, Smolensky, and Evenhouse, 1998), and has risen slightly since 2000.

7. Assortative mating is the tendency to marry persons with like characteristics. This has increased over time, with more-educated (and therefore higher-earning) individuals increasingly likely to marry other well-educated individuals. The security once obtained through marriage to a more highly educated individual has diminished over time. See Holden and Fontes forthcoming.

8. Author's calculations from SIPP data.

9. The argument is that, as growth in earnings slowed, families in which total work hours increased—including due to additional family members entering the workforce—would be better off. If there were fewer children, resources could be diverted to retirement savings.

10. This report is a follow-up to a report issued in 1999 by the National Academy on an Aging Society by the same authors, and largely the same assembled experts, titled "Demography Is Not Destiny" (Friedland and Summer 1999).

REFERENCES

Bernheim, B. D., and J. K. Scholz. 1993. Private saving and public policy. *Tax Policy and the Economy* 7: 73–110.

Bernheim, B. D., J. Skinner, and S. Weinberg. 2001. What accounts for the variation in retirement wealth among U.S. households?" *American Economic Review* 91 (4): 832–57.

Blau, Francine D., Marianne A. Ferber, and Anne E. Winkler. 1998. *The economics of women, men and work*. 3rd ed. Upper Saddle River, NJ: Prentice Hall.

Bradbury, Katharine L. 1996. The growing inequality of family income: Changing families and changing wages *New England Economic Review*: 55–82.

Butrica, Barbara A., Howard M. Iams, and Karen E. Smith. 2007. Understanding baby boomers' retirement prospects. In *Redefining retirement: How will boomers fare?* ed. B. Madrian, O. S. Mitchell, and B. J. Soldo. Philadelphia: Wharton Pension Research Council/Oxford University Press.

Congressional Budget Office. 1993, September. Baby boomers in retirement: An early perspective. Washington, DC: Congressional Budget Office.

Congressional Budget Office. 2004. Retirement prospects of the baby boomers. Http://www.cbo.gov/ftpdoc.cfm?index=5195&type=0&sequence=0.

Easterlin, R. A. 1966. On the relation of economic factors to recent and projected fertility changes. *Demography* 3 (1): 131–51.

Easterlin, Richard A., Christine M. Schaeffer, and Diane J. Macunovich. 1993. Will the baby boomers be less well off than their parents? Income, wealth, and family circumstances over the life cycle in the United States. *Population and Development Review* 19 (3): 497–522.

———. Retirement prospects of the baby boom generation: A different perspective. *The Gerontologist* 30 (6): 776–83.

Finberman, Karen, and Megan Dolbin-MacNab. 2006. The baby boomers and their parents: Cohort influences and intergenerational ties. In *The baby boomers grow up: Contemporary perspectives on midlife*, ed. S. K. Whitbourne and S. L. Willis. London: Routledge.

Friedberg, Leora. 2007. The recent trend towards later retirement. Issues in Brief, Series 9. Boston: Boston College Retirement Research Center.

Friedland, Robert B., and Laura Summer. 1999. *Demography Is Not Destiny*. Washington, DC: National Academy on an Aging Society.

———. 2005. *Demography Is Not Destiny, Revisited*. New York: Commonwealth Fund.

Haveman, Robert, Karen Holden, Andrei Romanov, and Barbara Wolfe. 2007a. Assessing the maintenance of savings sufficiency over the first decade of retirement. *International Tax and Public Finance* 14:481–502.

Haveman, Robert, Karen Holden, Barbara Wolfe, and Andrei Romanov. 2007b. A comparison of two cohorts of retired workers at the time of retirement. In *Redefining retirement: How will boomers fare?* ed. B. Madrian, O. S. Mitchell, and B. J. Soldo. Philadelphia: Wharton Pension Research Council/Oxford University Press.

Holden, Karen, and Angela Fontes. Forthcoming. Economic security in retirement: How changes in employment and marriage have altered retirement-related economic risks for women. In *Women in the retirement years: New sources of diversity*, ed. Heidi Hartmann and Sunhwa Lee. New York: Russell Sage Foundation.

Johnson, Richard W., Desmond Toohey, and Joshua M. Wiener. 2007. Meeting the long-term care needs of the baby boomers: How changing families will affect paid helpers and institutions. The Retirement Project Discussion Paper 07-04. Urban Institute. Accessed at http://www.urban.org/url.cfm?ID=311451.

Levy, Helen. 2007. Health insurance coverage of the baby boomers approaching retirement. In *Redefining retirement: How will boomers fare?* ed. B. Madrian, O. S.

Mitchell, and B. J. Soldo. Philadelphia: Wharton Pension Research Council/ Oxford University Press, 159–75.

Lundberg, Shelly, Richard Startza, and Steven Stillman. 2003. The retirement-consumption puzzle: A marital bargaining approach. *Journal of Public Economics* 87 (5–6): 1199–1218.

Lynch, Frederick. 2007. Aging boomers and demographic change: New social contract or a *Blade Runner* society? *Gerontologist* 47 (6): 851–54.

Mitchell, Olivia S. 2000. New trends in pension benefit and retirement provisions: A report to the Pension and Welfare Benefits Administration of the U.S. Department of Labor. Available at http://www.dol.gov/ebsa/pdf/Mitchell020300.pdf.

Penner, Rudolph G. 1998. A brief history of state and local fiscal policy. New Federalism Series, No. A-27. Washington, DC: Urban Institute. Available at http://www.urban.org/url.cfm?ID=308018.

Plotnick, Robert D. 2008. Childlessness and the economic well-being of elders. Discussion Paper No. 1336-08. Madison, WI: Institute for Research on Poverty.

Plotnick, Robert D., Eugene Smolensky, and Eirik Evenhouse. 1998. The twentieth-century record of inequality and poverty in the United States. Discussion Paper No. 1166-98. Madison, WI: Institute for Research on Poverty.

Poulos, Stacy, and Demetra Smith Nightingale. 1997. Employment and training policy implications of the aging baby boom generation. Washington, DC: Urban Institute. Available at http://www.urban.org/url.cfm?ID=407145.

Quinn, Joseph. New paths to retirement. 2000. In *Forecasting Retirement Needs and Retirement Wealth*. ed. B. Hammond, O. Mitchell, and A. Rappaport. Philadelphia: University of Pennsylvania Press, 13–32.

Rubin, Rose M., Shelley I. White-Means, and Luojia Mao Daniel. 2000. Income distribution of older Americans. *Monthly Labor Review* (11): 19–30.

Russell, Louise B. 1982. *The baby boom generation and the economy*. Studies in Social Economics. Washington, DC: Brookings Institution Press.

Toder, Eric, Cori E. Uccello, John O'Hare, Melissa Favreault, Caroline Ratcliffe, and Karen E. Smith. 1999. Modeling income in the near term: Projections of retirement income through 2020 for the 1931-60 birth cohorts. Washington, DC: Urban Institute. Available at http://www.urban.org/url.cfm?ID=410315.

5

Will the Boomers Revolutionize Work and Retirement?

SARA E. RIX

On October 15, 2007, Kathleen Casey-Kirschling, less than three months shy of turning 62, applied for Social Security retired worker benefits. There was nothing unusual about her doing so—in recent years, nearly two million workers annually have been awarded benefits at age 62 (Social Security Administration 2007). But Casey-Kirschling is a boomer, celebrated as the first of 76 million babies born in the United States from 1946 through 1964, and boomers' retirement was going to be different from that of their parents and grandparents.

Casey-Kirschling may yet help redefine retirement for the millions of boomers marching inexorably toward Social Security eligibility age; however, she hardly sounded as if that were on her mind when she observed, "I'm going to take [Social Security] now because I *can* take it now. I'm thrilled to think that after all these years I'm getting paid back the money I put in" (Milbank 2007). In fact, Casey-Kirschling sounded much like her parents or other older relatives might have sounded when they reached the early benefit eligibility age. She would go on to receive her first check early in 2008.

A great deal seems to be expected of America's boomers as far as work and retirement are concerned. Boomers, it has been maintained, are going to reinvent and/or revolutionize retirement. Not for them is an early labor force exit to full and permanent retirement. Rather, they will work longer, perhaps *much* longer, than their parents and combine work and leisure in new and more rewarding ways. Assertions such as these are based in part on the observations of boomers themselves, 80 percent of whom have maintained that they plan to work in retirement (AARP 1998, 2004). Many boomers contend that they expect *never* to retire (AARP 2002b, 2004).

TRENDS IN LABOR FORCE PARTICIPATION

And millions of boomers might *not be able* to retire—at least not at the early ages typical for much of the past half-century. Estimates and conclusions about retirement preparation vary, but many boomers have relatively little in savings or projected retirement income beyond Social Security. For these workers, the options appear to be an early retirement with a reduced standard of living or working longer for the current income and the higher retirement benefits that longer work-lives make possible. The Congressional Budget Office (2004b), for example, has estimated that continuing to work and delaying receipt of Social Security benefits until age 70 would result in benefits up to 90 percent higher than they would be if taken at 62. Expecting most workers to remain on the job until age 70 may be unrealistic, yet even one additional year of continued beyond 62 means higher Social Security benefits.

Recent Trends

In recent decades, however, relatively few workers have opted to wait much beyond the age of early eligibility to collect Social Security (Social Security Administration 2007). But even before the age of eligibility for early benefits was lowered to 62 (in 1956 for women and 1961 for men), labor force participation rates at older ages were undergoing profound changes. Men were leaving the labor force in large numbers at relatively young ages. The labor force participation rate for men aged 55 to 64 fell sharply in the years following World War II, as did the rate for men aged 65 and over.

In contrast, the participation rate for women aged 55 to 64 rose markedly over the same period, while the rate for women aged 65 and older remained low and quite stable. Nonetheless, women's growing attachment to the labor force, although resulting in an increasingly female older workforce, was not enough to offset the withdrawal of men. As a result, the labor force participation rate for the 55-and-over population fell for several decades after World War II (see figure 5-1). By 1993, this age group comprised only 11.6 percent of the total workforce, down from a 1953 postwar high of 18.4 percent.

By the mid-1980s or so, things began to change for men. Labor force participation rates stabilized and then began to rise, most notably among men 65 and older. Rates continued to rise among women. Even women 65 and older have become increasingly likely to be working or looking for work. Indeed, growing numbers of older Americans have been bucking the retirement trend in recent years. In fact, some of the largest increases in labor

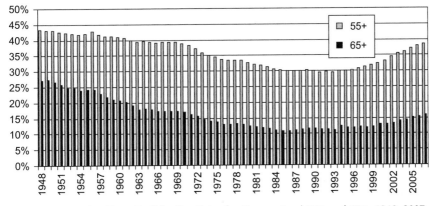

FIGURE 5-1.   Labor Force Participation Rates for Persons Aged 55+ and 65+, 1948–2007
Source: U.S. Bureau of Labor Statistics, labor force statistics from the Current Population Survey, available at http://data.bls.gov/PDQ/outside.jsp?survey=ln.

force participation rates over the past two decades have been among what has conventionally been thought of as the "retirement-age population," those aged 65 to 69. Increases in the 65-and-up group have been especially dramatic for women (see table 5-1 and figure 5-2).

Despite rising labor force participation at upper ages, receipt of Social Security at the early retirement age has remained the norm. With the passage of the Senior Citizens' Freedom to Work Act of 2000—which enabled workers above the full retirement age to collect Social Security and continue earning without any loss of benefits—one incentive to delay benefit receipt was eliminated. An uptick in benefits awarded at age 65 in 2000 indicates that some workers had been postponing collecting benefits due to the earnings penalty.[1]

TABLE 5-1.   Labor Force Participation Rates for Persons Aged 60–64, 65–69, and 70–74, 1985/1987–2007 (in percentages)

Age and Year	Both Sexes	Men	Women
60–64			
1985	43.8%	55.6%	33.4%
2007	53.3	59.2	47.9
65–69			
1985	18.4	24.4	13.5
2007	29.7	34.3	25.7
70–74			
1987	10.2	14.7	6.8
2007	17.2	21.2	14.0

Source: U.S. Bureau of Labor Statistics, labor force statistics from the Current Population Survey, available at http://data.bls.gov/PDQ/outside.jsp?survey=ln.

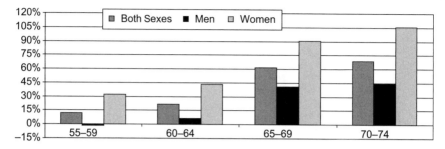

FIGURE 5-2. Percent Increase in Labor Force Participation Rates for Persons Aged 55+ by Age Group and Sex, 1985/1987–2007
Source: U.S. Bureau of Labor Statistics, labor force statistics from the Current Population Survey, available at http://data.bls.gov/PDQ/outside.jsp?survey=ln.

Although receipt of retirement benefits and continued employment are obviously not necessarily mutually exclusive, the benefit reduction for earnings above the taxable maximum—which remains for Social Security beneficiaries under the full eligibility age—has been viewed as a work disincentive (see Bartlett 2001). Private defined benefit pension plans may also discourage work after an often early normal retirement age when further accruals from continued employment fail to offset the loss of benefits not collected while working. Workers affected by such plans do not have to leave the labor force to collect their pensions, but until recently, if they were below a plan's normal retirement age, they had to switch employers, which is not always easy for an older worker. Or, they could retire and be rehired by their former employer. The Pension Protection Act of 2006 permits employers to pay benefits to workers at age 62 and thus alleviates this problem for workers whose employers agree to do so.

The Historical Pattern

As discussed below, there are many reasons to assume that the retirement timing of boomers will differ from that of their parents. However, it is worth keeping in mind that "retirement" as it is understood today is a relatively recent phenomenon. Not so long ago, few workers had any way of sustaining a nonworking old age unless they had accumulated sufficient savings or could depend on support from their families. Monthly Social Security payments were not available until 1940. In 1900, about two-thirds of men 65 and older were still in the labor force (U.S. Bureau of the Census 1975, table D 29-41). This figure fell gradually over the ensuing three decades and then took a sharp dive during the Great Depression. Participation increased somewhat as wartime labor shortages caused employers to turn to workers they would otherwise have bypassed in favor of prime-age males.[2]

By 1950, nearly 46 percent of men aged 65 and over were still in the labor force. As more workers found themselves covered by Social Security and private pensions and as Social Security benefits were enhanced, retirement became more economically feasible. Costa (1998) notes that, in addition, leisure activities were becoming more widespread and affordable. Retirement, in other words, no longer consigned someone to the proverbial rocking chair, but instead offered a growing choice of appealing leisure-time activities. Workers started to look forward to retirement, and men's participation rates began a fairly steady decline, not only for those 65 and over but for those between the ages of 55 and 64 as well.

By the mid-1980s, however, a change was becoming evident: the decline in the labor force participation rate for the 55-and-older population leveled off and then started to rise. The increase was once again more pronounced among women (22 percent in 1985 to 32.2 percent in 2007) than among men (41 percent to 43.7 percent).[3] Eventually, it seemed safe to conclude that the trend toward ever earlier retirement had reversed itself.

Future Projections

The Bureau of Labor Statistics projects a continued increase in labor force participation for this age group through 2016. The participation rate for men aged 55 and older is put at 48.3 percent in 2016 (still well below what it was a half-century ago); women are projected to have a participation rate of 38.1 percent (Toossi 2007). Nearly one in four workers will be 55 or older in 2016, up from about one in six in 2007.

Whether these potential developments mean a late, as opposed to a somewhat later, retirement remains to be seen. Boomers may expect to work in retirement, but not all of them want to, and some would like that working retirement to begin and end at relatively early ages. Over 40 percent of boomers say they cannot wait to retire (AARP 2004) and may opt to do so at the earliest opportunity. In 1998, the large majority of boomers, then aged 34 to 52, reported that they expected to work in retirement and anticipated stopping work completely at an average age of nearly 64.[4] Thus, for many, an early (pre-65) total retirement was still anticipated.

The age at which boomers would *prefer* to stop working completely, however, was considerably younger—59.7 years.[5] A preference for retirement at relatively early ages continues to characterize the American workers asked recently by Harris Interactive (2008) about their anticipated actual and preferred retirement ages. Workers in this survey—not all of whom were boomers—said that they expected to retire at an average age of 67.2 years but would like to retire at 59.7, exactly the age boomers preferred ten years earlier.[6]

WHY WORK?

Financial Considerations

People work for a variety of reasons, but financial ones tend to top the list, and boomers are no exception to this. Eighty percent of boomers in a 2002 survey noted that needing the money was a major factor in their decision to be working or looking for work (AARP 2002b). In fact, just over one-third strongly agreed that the *only* reason they continued work was because they needed the money. Nevertheless, work means more than money to boomers, nearly three-fourths of whom also reported that enjoying their work was a major reason they were working; in addition, majorities said that work makes them feel useful and that being productive is a way they can help others (AARP 2002b). These factors are likely to continue to be important as boomers make decisions about whether and when to retire. Although boomers who expect to work in retirement plan to do so for interest and enjoyment's sake as well as for the money, financial reasons seem to have become more salient with time (see AARP 1998, 2002, 2004).

Social Security's Role

Boomers should be concerned about whether their financial resources will last should they live well into their 80s or 90s. In all likelihood, Social Security will remain the dominant source of retirement income for boomers, as it has been for current retirees. Although replacement rates vary by work history and earnings, Munnell and Soto (2005) calculate a median replacement rate of only 44 percent for all households. Workers generally do not have to worry about replacing 100 percent of their preretirement earnings in order to maintain living standards after retiring, since some expenses fall; however, 44 percent will probably not be sufficient for most workers. Under the concept of the "three-legged stool" of retirement-income security, pensions and private savings are supposed to make up the difference between what Social Security provides and a replacement rate of perhaps 70–80 percent of preretirement earnings. Many workers have a long way to go to achieve that goal.

Private Pension Coverage

Pension coverage, for example, has stagnated since the late 1970s, and as of 2004, fewer than half (46 percent) of private-sector workers aged 25 to 64 participated in a pension plan at work (Center for Retirement Research 2008). A higher proportion of workers may eventually reach retirement age with access to pension benefits as a result of coverage on previous or subsequent jobs. However, without an expansion of coverage to workers (e.g., in small firms) who have typically lacked it, it is questionable just how great an increase will occur. Moreover, pension offerings themselves have changed dramatically. According to Munnell and Perun (2006), 62 percent of workers with pension coverage in 1983 had a defined benefit plan only and 12 percent had a defined contribution plan only. Twenty-one years later, only 20 percent of workers with coverage were covered by a defined benefit plan only; 63 percent were now covered by a defined contribution plan only.

Defined contribution plans shift the risk of retirement income preparation from employers to their employees, whose decisions about how much to save, where to invest, and how to disperse accumulations—as well as the returns to investments—determine what they will collect in the way of retirement benefits. This is in contrast to defined benefit pensions for which employers bear the risk and which generally pay out benefits in the form of guaranteed lifetime annuities. Given that the majority of workers with pension coverage are now in defined contribution plans, future retirees will have fewer assurances about pension plan payout. Furthermore, the majority of boomers lack much in the way of retirement savings beyond these pension plans. The Government Accountability Office (2006) finds that most of the money held by boomers in stocks, bonds, mutual funds, individual retirement accounts (IRAs), and other such retirement savings plans in 2004 was held by the wealthiest 10 percent of the population, concluding that "a large majority of boomers have few assets to sell" (2). For most, housing is the largest source of wealth.

Boomers may therefore increasingly face the tradeoff of working longer or making do with less. Some may opt for the latter, as many of today's retirees have apparently done. Fewer than half of the 65-and-older population—most of them retired—have private pension income. Despite the fact that a majority receive some income from assets, more than four in ten report no income from interest, dividends, rents, or royalties, and median amounts for those who do have assets tend to be low (Social Security Administration 2006).[7] Some retirees may have outlived their savings or pensions, but others may have concluded that they could afford to retire without much in the way of income to supplement Social Security, perhaps by voluntarily scaling back their expenditures. Baby boomers could always come to a similar conclusion, although from what they are saying in various surveys, working longer to boost replacement rates seems the way a larger number of them will go, if they can.

Market Uncertainty

Market uncertainty is another factor that may discourage workers from leaving the labor force quite as early as they might like to. It is easier for older workers to keep a job than to find a new one. This may be due in part to the Age Discrimination in Employment Act (ADEA), which Neumark (2001) suggests may have strengthened the long-term relationship between workers and firms and thus increased the employment of older workers, while at the same time having an adverse impact on hiring. Duration of unemployment tends to be substantially longer for older workers, and, during economic downturns, it can be expected to rise for workers of all ages. When the economy turned downward in 2001, older workers who had experienced stock losses could try to make up for those losses by working longer. About one-fifth of those aged 50 to 70 said they had pushed back the date of retirement; substantially fewer retirees, on the other hand, tried to find work (AARP 2002a). Uncertainties about the current market and economy may cause boomers (and other older workers) to think about adding an employment "leg" to their retirement-income stool.

Health Care Coverage

Other developments are likely to influence boomers' retirement decisions. Health care coverage in the United States is largely employer based. With cutbacks in retiree health benefits (Henry J. Kaiser Family Foundation and Hewitt Associates 2006), fewer workers can count on those benefits to serve as a bridge to Medicare eligibility. Workers who retire early, lose their jobs, move to employers who do not offer health insurance, or become self-employed and exhaust COBRA (Consolidated Omnibus Budget Reconciliation Act of 1986) coverage or lack a family member whose own health plan will cover them have few reasonably priced options for insurance but to remain with an employer who provides health insurance.

Considerations of Longevity and Health Status

Rising life expectancy may also give boomers pause when it comes to the retirement date. One might hypothesize that workers who expect to live long after retirement would delay claiming retirement benefits and perhaps even work longer before claiming. In fact, Hurd, Smith, and Zissimopoulos (2003) found that subjective probabilities of survival did have some impact on the claiming of Social Security benefits, with persons whose probabilities were very low claiming earlier than those with higher probabilities. But because most workers claim benefits as soon as they are eligible, the effects were not large.

Although it is hard to envisage boomers dwelling on their own life expectancy, the topic of possibly outliving one's resources is becoming somewhat more difficult to avoid in view of the burgeoning number of newspaper and magazine articles on retirement preparedness. A male at age 60 can expect to live another 20.8 years, on average, up by 4.8 years since 1969–1971; a female at that age has another 24 years to live on average, an increase of 3.4 years over the same period (Arias 2007). These are, of course, just averages, and many people will die at younger ages, but others will live well beyond them. Concern about resources lasting long enough, perhaps coupled with questions about how to spend decades of retirement, might prompt some workers to reassess the wisdom of early retirement.

Health status also influences the retirement decision, whether it is voluntary or involuntary. Workers in poor health are more likely than healthy workers to retire, especially at younger ages; retirees are also substantially more likely than their nonretired age peers to report fair or poor health and work-limiting conditions (Uccello 1998). These observations are hardly surprising. The key question is whether boomers are healthier than their parents or grandparents and so able to work longer.

Mortality rates at upper ages have fallen (National Center for Health Statistics 2006), and disability rates at upper ages have been declining (Manton and Gu 2001). It is commonly assumed that the overall health status of older Americans has changed for the better along with mortality and disability improvements. The percentage of persons over age 55 claiming to be in only fair or poor health fell by two to three percentage points between 1991 and 2004 (National Center for Health Statistics 2006). Crimmins (2001), however, observes that while people are living longer, they are not necessarily healthier and that the answer to the question of whether older persons are healthier today depends on the measure. Certain chronic conditions have been on the rise, while other indicators of health status have improved.

In an examination of respondents aged 51 to 56 from three different cohorts (1936–1941, 1942–1947, and 1948–1953) of the longitudinal Health and Retirement Study, Weir (2007) detected little evidence that the early boomers at this age were in better health on objective measures than those born twelve years earlier. Subjectively, however, boomers *felt* worse off. This analyses suggest a half-empty glass. Munnell and Libby (2007), on the other hand, seem to see a glass that is half full, concluding that the health of older workers today is at least as good as it was forty years ago. It would seem, therefore, that if a high percentage of Americans could work at older ages in the past, just as many and perhaps more should be able to do today. In a similar vein, Weir points out that most retirees in their 60s and 70s are healthy enough to work and that health conditions are being managed so "boomers could defer retirement several years" (2007, 109).

Factors Facilitating Longer Work Lives

The factors highlighted in the preceding paragraphs may discourage retirement and serve to keep workers in the labor force longer than they might prefer or would have done otherwise. Other factors, however, will likely encourage them to stay.

Rising Educational Attainment

One factor is rising educational attainment. Only 27 percent of persons 65 or older had not completed high school in 2004, compared to almost 45 percent in 1990 (U.S. Bureau of the Census 2006, table 38). Likewise, a higher proportion had a bachelor's or advanced degree. Educational improvements provide greater access to the types of jobs conductive to longer work-lives and make workers more attractive to employers, thus opening up employment opportunities not available to less well-educated workers. Haider and Loughran (2001) found that "elderly" workers, that is, those aged 65 or older, were better educated (as well as healthier and more affluent) than their nonworking age peers.

Less Physically Demanding Jobs

Also facilitating longer work-lives has been the decline in physically demanding jobs. Between 1950 and 1996, the proportion of workers in such jobs (i.e., those requiring frequent lifting or carrying objects weighing more than 25 pounds) fell from 20 percent to 7.5 percent (Steuerle, Spiro, and Johnson 1999). As of 2006, relatively few workers (7.3 percent) were in jobs imposing high physical demands (e.g., requiring exerting maximum muscle force to move objects) or the need to bend or twist, although about 46 percent were in jobs with *any* such demands (Johnson, Mermin, and Resseger 2007) To the extent that physically demanding work pushes people out of the workforce—and it does (Johnson, Mermin, and Resseger 2007; Uccello 1998)—these changes in the nature of work indicate that fewer workers are and will be leaving employment because their jobs are physically too demanding.

Workers may still face difficulties on the job as they age, although those difficulties are not necessarily age related. Johnson, Mermin, and Resseger (2007) have calculated, for example, that about one-fourth of all workers are in occupations with difficult working conditions, such as exposure to contaminants or high noise levels. More than 40 percent of jobs involve some stress, although fewer than 10 percent of workers are found in high-stress jobs. Johnson and colleagues note sharper declines in physically demanding jobs over time for workers aged 50 and older than for younger workers; however, the older group has experienced steeper increases in stressful, cognitively demanding work. Such working conditions might not be what workers want, but they are also not necessarily insurmountable barriers to later life employment, especially if coupled with the more flexible work options, including phased retirement, that older workers say they would like (AARP 1998, 2004; Watson Wyatt Worldwide 2004).

There would seem to be few significant physical reasons why most boomers could not work longer, although some will continue to retire due to health reasons. For instance, the Congressional Budget Office (2004a) reported in 2004—when the oldest boomer was only 58—that four million boomers had already left the labor force. The most common reason was disability, but even so, this was a very small proportion of the older population. Although the number of disabled boomers will rise with the aging of the population, most boomers are not likely to suffer work incapacitation at least through their 60s.

Appeal of Older Workers

A recent report of the European Agency for Safety and Health at Work (2007) highlights a variety of positive attributes of older employees that should make them appealing to employers. These include an ability to deal with complex organizational models, greater decision-making autonomy, highly developed quality perception, greater ability to estimate their own abilities and limitations, and more reliable judgment. The report said that older workers bring experience to the job and may "attain goals with less effort than younger employees" (69). Age is generally accompanied by declines in speed in physical and mental processes as well as in hearing and sight, although not necessarily to a degree that impedes functioning in most of the jobs characteristic of today's economy, especially if workforce modifications are introduced. In addition, many skills and attributes remain constant over the work-life.

EMPLOYER OPTIONS

One of the key factors that will influence older workers' employment options and decisions is employer demand. Even if the ADEA has helped workers remain on the job longer, if employers want to get rid of workers, they can usually find ways to do so, through, for example, restructuring or reorganization. If employers do not need older workers or if they fail to value them (and have sufficient alternative sources of labor), they are not likely to make the accommodations (flexible work arrangements, phased retirement options, job modification or redesign) that might encourage them to stay on and perhaps make their retention more productive. Nor will they be hiring many older workers.

Addressing Labor Shortages?

Employers facing skills or labor shortages, in contrast, will do what they have to do to acquire or retain the workers they need. This is already evident in the health care industry, where hospitals—desperate for nurses—have been flexible and creative in identifying ways to retain or hire members of this profession. If shortages are experienced elsewhere, comparable responses on the part of employers can be expected, as the pool of potential employees will have fewer young workers. To date, however, there is little evidence that employers in general are preparing for an aging workforce and boomer retirements (Buck Consultants 2007; General Accounting Office 2001).

Although there is considerable concern about potential labor and skills shortages (see Ellwood 2003)—and although shortages are apparent in some industries—consensus about the degree to which the country will face shortages is lacking. Some naysayers argue that growing numbers of older workers will remain in the workforce, which will help alleviate possible shortages (Cappelli 2003). Others point to the huge supply of labor available from elsewhere in the world, and some contend that even if there are shortages, they will not be the result of demographics (Freeman 2006a, 2006b). Outsourcing might also eliminate vastly more jobs than currently anticipated (Blinder 2005). If substantial labor shortages do materialize, the employment prospects of older workers should improve, just as they did during World War II. In addition to increasing employer interest in older workers, shortages would also presumably result in higher wages, better benefits, and employment policies that would likely entice more boomers to remain in the workforce longer.

Making Jobs Attractive

In addition to job vacancies, the attractiveness of available jobs will have an impact on whether boomers remain in the labor force and, if they do, for how long. Haider and Loughran's elderly workers may have been better educated and more affluent than their nonworking peers, but they also tended to be working for relatively low wages (Haider and Loughran 2001). This observation led to speculation that these workers may have made a tradeoff between wages and flexible work arrangements, perhaps opting for flexible arrangements in jobs that had lower wages rather than better-paying jobs with more traditional work arrangements.

"Flex Jobs"

Flexible work arrangements appear to be available more often on a case-by-case basis than as a workforce norm. About 30 percent of U.S. workers have arrangements that allow them to vary their work hours, a figure that more than doubled between 1985 and 1997 but that has remained stable since then (McMenamin 2007). Surprisingly, differences by sex are relatively minor. The same is generally true for age until the oldest ages. Of some interest is the fact that men aged 65 and older are substantially more likely than women of those ages to be able to vary their work hours (42 percent vs. 33 percent; see figure 5-3). Industry demand, according to McMenamin (2007) is the primary determinant of the availability of these schedules, and of shift work as well.

Phased Retirement

Phased retirement is another flexible work arrangement believed to be of particular appeal to older workers. Cahill, Gaindrea, and Quinn (2008) note that the majority of older workers (about two-thirds of those transitioning from a full-time career job) retire in stages rather than abruptly. Most workers do not, however, have access to formal phased retirement programs that enable them to scale back their work hours in jobs they know and presumably do well.[8] Most of the companies studied by Hutchens (2003) allow workers to reduce their work hours, but on an ad hoc basis rather than as company policy. A variety of barriers such as Employee Retirement Income Security Act (ERISA) regulations and the ADEA are believed to discourage employers from formalizing phased retirement policies; however, it may also be that ad hoc arrangements suit employers by giving them the flexibility they need to offer phased retirement to some workers and not others.

Despite professed boomer interest in scaling back work hours before full-time retirement (AARP 2004), full-time work has, somewhat surprisingly,

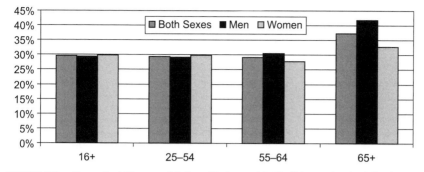

FIGURE 5-3. Percent of Wage and Salary Workers with Flexible Work Schedules by Age and Sex, May 2004
Source: Terence M. McMenamin, "A Time to Work: Recent Trends in Shift Work and Flexible Schedules," *Monthly Labor Review* 130 (12), table 3.

been on the increase among older workers. Gendell (2008) notes that, at 62.5 years, the average retirement age has been "essentially flat" for both sexes since the early 1990s.[9] However, the percentage of full-time workers has increased dramatically even at quite advanced ages, and among both men and women (see figure 5-4).

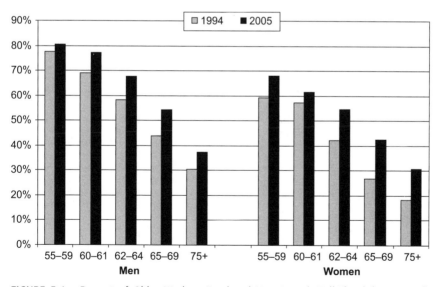

FIGURE 5-4. Percent of Older Workers Employed Year-Round, Full-Time* by Sex and Age, 1994 and 2005
*Full-time is a minimum of 50 weeks per year.
Source: Murray Gendell, "Older Workers: Increasing Their Labor Force Participation and Hours of Work," *Monthly Labor Review* 131 (1), table 4.

AND ARE BOOMERS WORKING MORE?

The oldest of the boomers began turning 62 only in 2008, so it is too early to know just what their later-life employment experiences will look like. Some insight into their labor force experiences can be obtained by examining single-year participation rates for boomers as they age. Table 5-2 reveals how participation changed as the oldest boomers aged from 55 in 2001 to 61 in 2007, the latest year for which data were available. As one moves along the diagonal in the upper and lower panels of the table, one observes a steady decline in rates (aside from a slight increase for women in 2003); the decline is about the same for both men and women (19 percent and 18 percent, respectively). At age 61, male and female boomers are substantially less likely to be in the labor force than they were just six years earlier. At age 55, for example, 82 percent of boomer men were in the workforce; by age 61, that was the case for only 66.4 percent. These do not appear to be the rates of persons about to revolutionize retirement via work. Women might, however, if their labor force attachment at older ages continues to grow.

Another way of assessing what of consequence may be happening is by examining how participation rates may be changing at each age in table 5-2. Rates for boomer men at *some* ages have risen, although not by much. Participation rates for boomer women aged 55 and older, however, have clearly

TABLE 5-2. Labor Force Participation Rates for Men and Women Aged 55–61, 2001–2007 (in percentages)

Sex and Age	2007	2006	2005	2004	2003	2002	2001
Men							
55	81.7	81.8	80.6	81.2	81.7	82.3	82.0
56	79.7	78.8	79.6	79.8	79.0	79.3	78.3
57	77.7	75.8	77.6	77.6	76.9	77.2	78.3
58	75.4	76.5	75.8	74.6	75.6	75.8	74.7
59	73.1	75.0	73.6	72.8	72.9	73.8	72.2
60	70.4	70.2	67.7	66.6	69.0	68.2	69.5
61	66.4	64.2	63.5	63.3	64.5	66.3	65.8
Women							
55	70.3	70.9	69.8	69.2	69.8	69.9	66.5
56	69.6	69.2	66.8	68.0	66.8	64.8	62.2
57	66.4	66.6	66.7	64.1	65.5	64.2	63.6
58	64.7	64.2	64.3	63.1	62.2	61.5	59.5
59	61.8	62.4	59.1	58.6	61.1	56.8	56.1
60	56.7	56.4	55.7	55.4	56.5	53.4	52.2
61	54.6	52.6	51.7	52.5	50.9	52.2	48.6

Source: U.S. Bureau of Labor Statistics, unpublished data.

trended upward. Whether this will continue remains to be seen. Women successful in their careers may find work more rewarding later in life, especially if family caregiving responsibilities have diminished. Women with discontinuous work histories and/or employment in low-wage, low-benefit, female-dominated occupations may need to prolong their work-lives. Or, it may be that, after decades in the labor force, growing numbers of boomer women will be financially and emotionally prepared for retirement and eager to leave the labor force at relatively young ages. In fact, all of these things are likely to characterize a population as diverse as that of the baby boom.

There are many reasons to anticipate that boomers, both male and female, will push back the date of retirement. They are likely to need to work longer; they say they want to work; and perhaps much of their image of themselves as ever-youthful boomers is tied to continued employment. Kathleen Casey-Kirschling, Boomer No. 1, may well still be working even though she is collecting Social Security. It would certainly enhance boomers' retirement-income security if they did work longer and postponed Social Security receipt in the meantime.

However, if boomers do remain longer in the labor force, it will not be as revolutionary a development as some pundits might lead us to believe. Boomers will, in fact, be following in the footsteps of even older workers, whose sharply rising participation rates (see table 5-1) would appear to be one of the more exciting and intriguing labor force developments of recent years. Boomers may yet end up doing something unusual in and with retirement, or it may be that they will just do what some even older persons are already doing, but in larger numbers. Workers older than boomers have already begun making their mark on participation rates at upper ages. More research may shed light on whether they—rather than the boomers—were really the harbingers of things to come.

NOTES

1. In 1999, 14.8 percent of men who were newly entitled Social Security beneficiaries were age 65; that figure rose to 20.3 percent in 2000 (Social Security Administration 2007, table 6.B5).

2. Decennial census figures put the labor force participation rate for men aged 65 and over at 63.1 percent in June 1900 and 41.8 percent in April 1940. The 47.1 percent participation rate for 1942 and the 46.8 percent for 1948 are annual estimates of average monthly figures and are not directly comparable to the decennial census figures. (See U.S. Bureau of the Census 1975.)

3. U.S. Bureau of Labor Statistics, unpublished data.

4. AARP unpublished data from the 1998 "Boomers Look toward Retirement" survey (AARP 1998).

5. Ibid.

6. This was a multicountry survey of adults ages 16–64 (18–64 in Italy) conducted online by Harris Interactive in partnership with France 24 and the

International Herald Tribune. The highest average expected retirement age was found for Americans.

7. Surprisingly, age does not seem to have much of an impact on receipt of retirement benefits other than Social Security, at least up until age 85. The percentage receiving such benefits was very similar for units aged 65–69, 70–74, 75–79, and 80–84 (Social Security Administration 2006, table 1.1).

8. Although there are undoubtedly exceptions, one assumes that poor performers would be weeded out before reaching retirement age.

9. If the average retirement age is defined as the age at which half of workers are out of the labor force, then the average retirement age for men as of 2007 was between 63 and 64 and for women between 61 and 62. These figures have been on the increase slightly in recent years (unpublished Bureau of Labor Statistics).

REFERENCES

AARP. 1998. *Boomers look toward retirement.* Washington, DC: AARP.

———. 2002a. *Impact of stock market decline on 50–70 year old investors.* Washington, DC: AARP.

———. 2002b. *Staying ahead of the curve: The AARP Work and Career Study.* Washington, DC: AARP.

———. 2004. *Baby boomers envision retirement II.* Washington, DC: AARP.

Arias, Elizabeth. 2007. United States life tables, 2004. *National Vital Statistics Reports* 56 (9). Hyattsville, MD: National Center for Health Statistics.

Bartlett, Bruce. 2001. *Why the Social Security earnings penalty should be repealed.* Policy Backgrounder No. 152. National Center for Policy Analysis. Available at http://www.ncpa.org/bg/bg152/bg152.html.

Blinder, A. S. 2005. Fear of offshoring. Working Paper No. 119. Princeton, NJ: Center for Economic Policy Studies. Available at http://www.princeton.edu/~ceps/workingpapers/119blinder.pdf.

Buck Consultants. 2007. *The real talent debate: Will aging boomers deplete the workforce?* San Francisco: Buck Consultants. Available at http://www.buckconsultants.com/buckconsultants/Portals/0/Documents/PUBLICATIONS/Press_Releases/2007/pr_06_11_07.pdf.

Cappelli, Peter. 2003. Will there *really* be a labor shortage? *Organizational Dynamics* 32 (3): 221–33.

Center for Retirement Research, Boston College. 2008. Pension sponsorship and participation nationwide, 1980–2002 [table]. http://crr.bc.edu/images/stories/Frequently_Requested_Data/table.xls.

Congressional Budget Office. 2004a. *Disability and retirement: The exit of baby boomers from the labor force.* Washington, DC: Congressional Budget Office.

———. 2004b. Retirement age and the need for saving. Washington, DC: Congressional Budget Office. Available at http://www.cbo.gov/ftpdocs/54xx/doc5419/05-12-RetireAgeSaving.pdf.

Costa, Dora L. 1998. *The evolution of retirement: An American economic history, 1880–1990.* Chicago: University of Chicago Press.

Crimmins, Elaine M. 2001. Americans living longer, not necessarily healthier, lives. *Population Today* 29 (2): 5, 8. Available at http://www.prb.org/Articles/2001/AmericansLivingLongerNotNecessarilyHealthierLives.aspx.

Ellwood, David. 2003. Grow faster together, or grow slowly apart: How will America work in the 21st century? Washington, DC: Aspen Institute Domestic Strategy Group. Available at http://www.aspeninstitute.org/atf/cf/%7BDEB6F227-659B-4EC8-8F84-8DF23CA704F5%7D/DSGBROCHURE_FINAL.PDF.

European Agency for Safety and Health at Work. 2007. *Expert forecast on emerging psychosocial risks related to occupational safety and health.* Luxembourg: Office for Official Publications of the European Community. Available at http://osha.europa.eu/publications/reports/7807118/7807118.pdf/at_download/file.

Freeman, Richard B. 2006a. Is a great labor shortage coming? Replacement demand in the global economy. National Bureau of Economic Research (NBER) Working Paper No. 12,541. Cambridge, MA: NBER.

———. 2006b. Labor market imbalances: Shortages, or surpluses, or fish stories? Paper prepared for the Boston Federal Reserve Economic Conference "Global Imbalances: As Giants Evolve," Chatham, MA, June 14–16. Available at http://www.bos.frb.org/economic/conf/conf51/papers/freeman.pdf.

Gendell, Murray. 2008. Older workers: Increasing their labor force participation and hours of work. *Monthly Labor Review* 131 (1): 41–54.

General Accounting Office. 2001. *Older workers: Demographic trends pose challenges for employers and workers.* Washington, DC: General Accounting Office.

Government Accountability Office. 2006. *Baby boom generation: Retirement of baby boomers is unlikely to precipitate dramatic decline in market returns, but broader risks threaten retirement security.* GAO-06-718. Washington, DC: Government Accountability Office.

Haider, Steven, and David Loughran. 2001. Elderly labor supply: Work or play? RAND Labor and Population Program Working Paper Series 01-09. Santa Monica, CA: RAND.

Harris Interactive. 2008. Views on retirement. http://www.harrisinteractive.fr/news/2008/HI_FR_F24-IHT_14mar2008-retirement-english.pdf.

Henry J. Kaiser Family Foundation and Hewitt Associates. 2006. Retiree health benefits examined: Findings from the Kaiser/Hewitt 2006 survey on retiree health benefits. Menlo Park, CA: Henry J. Kaiser Family Foundation. Available at http://www.kff.org/medicare/upload/7603.pdf.

Hurd, Michael D., James P. Smith, and Julie M. Zissimopoulos. 2003. The effects of subjective survival on retirement and Social Security claiming. Santa Monica, CA: RAND. Available at http://rand.org/labor/DRU/DRU3008.pdf.

Hutchens, Robert. 2003. The Cornell study of employer phased retirement policies: A report on key findings. Ithaca, NY: Cornell University, School of Industrial and Labor Relations. Available at http://www.ilr.cornell.edu/extension/files/20031219112155-pub1251.pdf.

Johnson, Richard W., Gordon B. T. Mermin, and Matthew Resseger. 2007. *Employment at older ages and the changing nature of work.* Issue Paper 2007-20. Washington, DC: AARP Public Policy Institute.

Manton, Kenneth, and S. Gu. 2001. Changes in the prevalence of chronic disability in the United States black and non-black population above age 65 from 1982 to 1999. *Proceedings of the National Academy of Sciences USA* 103 (48): 18374–79.

McMenamin, Terence M. 2007. A time to work: Recent trends in shift work and flexible schedules. *Monthly Labor Review* 130 (12): 3–15.

Milbank, Dana. 2007. Smile—you're on Social Security! *Washington Post*. October 16. Available at http://www.washingtonpost.com/wp-dyn/content/article/2007/10/15/AR2007101501359_pf.html.

Munnell, Alicia H., and Jerilyn Libby. 2007. *Will people be healthy enough to work longer?* Issue in Brief, No. 2007-33. Chestnut Hill, MA: Center for Retirement Research.

Munnell, Alicia H., and Pamela Perun. 2006. *An update on private pensions*. Issue in Brief, No. 50. Chestnut Hill, MA: Center for Retirement Research.

Munnell, Alicia H., and Mauricio Soto. 2005. *How much pre-retirement income does Social Security replace?* Issue in Brief, No. 36. Chestnut Hill, MA: Center for Retirement Research.

National Center for Health Statistics. 2006. *Health, United States, 2006, with chartbook on trends in the health of Americans*. Hyattsville, MD: National Center for Health Statistics. Available at http://www.ncbi.nlm.nih.gov/books/bv.fcgi?rid=healthus06.

Neumark, David. 2001. *Age discrimination legislation in the United States*. NBER Working Paper No. 8152. Cambridge, MA: NBER.

Social Security Administration, Office of Policy. 2006. *Income of the Population 55 or Older, 2004*. Washington, DC: GPO.

———. 2007. *Annual statistical supplement to the Social Security Bulletin, 2006*. Washington, DC: GPO.

Steuerle, Eugene, Christopher Spiro, and Richard W. Johnson. 1999. *Can Americans work longer?* Straight Talk on Social Security and Retirement Policy Brief No. 5. Washington, DC: Urban Institute. Available at http://urbaninstitute.org/Uploaded PDF/Straight5.pdf.

Toossi, Mitra. 2007. Employment projections to 2016: More workers in their golden years. *Monthly Labor Review* 130 (11): 33–54.

Uccello, Cori. 1998. *Factors influencing retirement: Their implications for raising retirement age*. Washington, DC: AARP.

U.S. Bureau of the Census. 1975. *Historical statistics of the United States, Colonial times to 1979, Part 1*. Washington, DC: GPO.

———. 2006. *Statistical abstract of the United States, 2007*. Washington, DC: GPO.

Watson Wyatt Worldwide. 2004. *Phased retirement: Aligning employer programs with worker preferences*. Washington, DC: Watson Wyatt Worldwide.

Weir, David R. 2007. Are baby boomers living well longer? In *Redefining retirement: How will boomers fare?* ed. Brigitte Madrian, Olivia S. Mitchell, and Beth J. Soldo, 95–111. Oxford: Oxford University Press.

6

The Looming Economics of Boomer Health Care

CHRISTINE BISHOP

W ill the nation's health system withstand the baby boomers' health costs? The answer is surprising. Despite the fact that health spending tends to increase with age, the relative size of the generation born just after World War II has had very little impact on past growth in health expenditures, nor will it be directly responsible for much of the increase that experts forecast for the coming years. Indirectly, the boomers' demands for improved technology to address the illnesses and conditions of aging will continue to fuel the technological advances that drive much of health expenditure growth, but they are only part of the general demand for new treatments and procedures. The concentration of older adults in publicly funded programs, especially Medicare and Medicaid, will exert exceptional pressure on these vital portions of the nation's health financing system—certainly a matter for concern. But overall, the aging of the population will not in itself have a major impact on the growth of total health expenditures—the blame for uncontrolled health sector growth falls elsewhere.

However, as we think about demographic change and health care costs, there is a second question: Even if the nation's health system is expected to take on the boomers in stride, are the boomers prepared to afford the health care they need? Here the relentless growth of health expenditures, linked to expanding capacity of the health system to treat illness in new ways, becomes the culprit. We all want to benefit from future health advances, which have the potential to mitigate or cure disease and grant years of vital activity into old age. But if elders do not set aside funds for future increases in Medicare and health insurance premiums and increasing obligations to pay out-of-pocket for health services, they will find their basic well-being in retirement eroded by health expenses.

IMPACT OF AGING ON HEALTH EXPENDITURES

Increases Directly Due to Population Aging Are a Small Proportion of Total Health Expenditure Growth Because Technological Advances Are So Expensive

Per-capita personal health expenditures for adults aged 65 and older reached $14,797 in 2004, 3.3 times the per-capita amount spent on working-age adults and 5.6 times the amount for children and adolescents (Hartman et al. 2007). As the U.S. population aged 65 and older grows from 35 million persons in 2000 to a projected 87 million in 2050, multiplying current per-capita expenditure for the aged by the number of aged suggests that the onslaught of the baby boom will be responsible for huge increases in health care expenditures. The future elderly are expected to live more years after age 65, further increasing their numbers and the number at advanced ages. Applying current per-capita health expenditures at each post-65 age to the specific life-years the boomers are expected to live past 65 would further increase our back-of-the-envelope estimate of future health expenditures.

However, projections of future health expenditures show surprisingly little impact of population aging on the demand for health services. The impact of the boomer aging wave is dwarfed by a rising tide for all health expenditures, driven by technological change and markets with few internal checks on rising costs.

Models projecting future health expenditures can expose the moving parts that drive health expenditure growth and show policy makers ways to change future outcomes. The projections themselves are only as good as the relationships built into the models and their assumptions about future trends in the factors that affect health spending. Simple extrapolation of past trends leads to the impossible conclusion that health services will soon commandeer the entire productive capacity of our economy. The model used for the all-important task of projecting the impact of health expenditures on federal spending for Medicare and Medicaid under current law is developed by the Medicare Trustees[1] (Boards of Trustees 2007). Projections of spending for these public programs are used as inputs into the model used by the Office of the Actuary to project total health spending (Keehan, Sisko, et al. 2008). The Congressional Budget Office (CBO) has developed a model of health expenditures that assumes that if total health spending growth begins to cause an absolute reduction in real consumption, economic decision makers (including Congress) will change their behavior to avoid this outcome (CBO 2007). All of these projection models include the impact on total health expenditures of the expected increase in the number of Americans aged 65 and older as the large numbers in the baby-boom generation cross that threshold. In all of them, the contribution to total expenditure of growth in the age-adjusted cost of services per person (which wraps together both utilization of services and the resource inputs needed for increasingly sophisticated services) far outweighs the contribution of the aging of our society. For example, the Office of the Actuary model finds that the changing age mix of the population will add between 0.4 percent and 0.6 percent to growth over the next decade, with population growth adding 0.8 percent annually—both small in comparison to annual growth rates expected to exceed 6.5 percent (see also Keehan, Lazenby, et al. 2004; Keehan, Sisko, et al. 2008).

Population Aging Will Increase Health Spending, But Less Than Might Be Expected, Because Rates of Disability Are Falling and Lifespans Are Lengthening

In addition, simple calculations based on the higher costs of current elders would overshoot the mark. Future elders are expected to live longer but also to experience lower rates of disability at each age. Health expenditures in each year of life vary with an individual's disability status: elders without functional impairments use fewer health resources than those with disabilities. Although there is not a firm consensus, most scholars agree that age-adjusted disability rates have been steadily declining for the over-65 population and that the baby-boomer cohort is approaching retirement age with lower levels of disability (Freedman, Crimmins, et al. 2004; Manton, Gu, and Lamb 2006; Freedman, Schoeni, et al. 2007). The idea is that lifestyle changes and better medical care are postponing the effects of illness, so that both morbidity (clinical illness, functional limitations) and mortality are occurring later in life. With a greater proportion of years disability-free, per-capita annual health expenditures should stabilize or even fall (but see Chernew et al. 2005 for a different view).

Further, health expenditures in the last year of life represent a substantial proportion of total post-65 spending. Because the amount spent in the last year is lower for older as opposed to younger decedents, this proportion, around 0.3 for cumulative Medicare expenditures, is relatively constant (Lubitz and Riley 1993). Recent studies have reached the surprising conclusion that cumulative post-65 health costs are similar in magnitude regardless of the number of years lived past 65 (Spillman and Lubitz 2000; Lubitz et al. 2003). Thus it appears that older adults with lower prevalence rates for disability at every age and living longer will have annual health costs averaged over remaining life-years that are not much higher, and may even be lower, than current elders (Cutler and Sheiner 1999). This trend is already appearing in current data: between 1987 and 2004, the rate of growth of per-capita expenditures for elders aged 85 and older was 20 percent lower than the growth for all persons aged 65 and older (Hartman et al. 2007).

Clouding this picture for the longer run is another set of trends, such as the prevalence of diabetes and obesity increase in the younger working-age population (Lakdawalla, Goldman, and Shang 2005; Bhattacharya, Choudhry, and Lakdawalla 2008). Findings of a recent study suggest that the baby-boom generation may be entering retirement years with slightly more chronic illness and lower functional status than previous generations at the same point in the life cycle (Soldo et al. 2006). But the stability of cumulative expenditures should hold even if the next generations of older adults reach 65 with greater rates of disability and mortality risk—cost per year of life would be higher but would be paid for fewer years.

Population Aging May Not Play a Large Role in Health Expenditure Growth. But Growth in Expenditures for Everyone Is Driven by Insurance and Technological Advances, and the Path of Future Health Advances Will Likely Be Shaped by Boomers' Demands

Health economists have concluded that at least half of past growth of health expenditures is due to technological advances (Newhouse 1992). Over recent decades, medical knowledge has expanded so that diseases and conditions that previously could not be treated can now be addressed. And when treatments are available, they are used. Resources used per episode of illness increase when health services providers can do more to help patients, who are able to pay for expanded care thanks to growing incomes and insurance.

Treatment for heart disease is a good example of the pattern of technological advances. Even by the mid-twentieth century, there was little that medical care could do beyond bed rest and pain relief to treat or prevent heart disease (CBO 2008). Development of coronary angiography allowed physicians to pinpoint the location of disease, and heart-lung machines enabled heart bypass operations. Less invasive angioplasty was developed to open blocked vessels, and its use spread to patients who were not considered candidates for open heart surgery. Stents are now implanted in an effort to keep vessels open, and thrombolytic therapy is used to dissolve clots. All of the interventions that have been added to the medical armamentarium are continually subject to improvement, from the contrast medium used in angiography to the new and improved stents developed each year to new generations of clot-busters. The result has been substantial increases in health care spending, in exchange for substantial improvement in the prognosis of heart disease and many life-years saved; most would agree that the benefits are worth the costs (Cutler and McClellan 2001; Cutler 2007).

These advances are available to old and young alike, so per-capita health expenditures rise for everyone. A health sector serving an aging population without this technology-driven expansion in per-capita expenditures would experience a much lower rate of growth than we actually expect to see. This is why analysts can say that population aging is not responsible for much of future growth—aging would be important if it were the *only* source of growth, but in comparison to technological advances, aging is the least of our worries.

However, the baby-boom cohort represents a large market for goods and services of all kinds. When they reach age 65, they will be nearly universally insured by Medicare, which will provide the buying power to respond to many of the health needs of aging. An expanding market for aging health services can be expected to continue the drive toward technological advances that address conditions prevalent among the aging. Advances in basic science form the foundation for all new medical technology, but insurance coverage for diagnostic tests and treatments tilts technological advances toward new approaches that use covered or insurable health services (Weisbrod 1991). For example, the development and refinement of surgical techniques has made surgical interventions safer and more effective, while increasing the number of older adults (and others) benefiting from gall bladder surgery, cataract surgery, joint replacement, and heart surgery (Escarce, Bloom, and Hillman 1995; Lavernia, Lee, and Hernandez 2006). These procedures have become old news, an accepted part of medicine's armamentarium, with new developments ahead.

In the area of pharmaceutical interventions, we have seen an array of medical discoveries that result in lifetime drug treatment once a chronic condition is diagnosed. Physicians are now able to treat high cholesterol before the patient has symptoms of heart disease or any adverse effects. Hypertension can be addressed before the patient experiences a stroke. Some cancers are no longer acute, life-ending illnesses, but rather have become chronic diseases, requiring lifetime treatment. Drug treatments are attractive targets for research and development in part because increasing numbers of people hold insurance for prescription drugs and thus can pay for lifetime treatment. There is not as much impetus for research on lifestyle modifications and alternative remedies that cannot be patented. Further, health insurance has developed to pay for definable, expensive health interventions for illness, and tends not to encourage the health awareness, lifestyle coaching, and watchful waiting that may also support healthy living and conservative treatment.

On the whole, though, it can be exhilarating to gaze into the crystal ball of future medical innovations, even though costs may seem overwhelming. Knowledge of our genome opens many possibilities: if the drug likely to work best for each patient could be selected based on his or her own genetic markers, time to effective treatment and negative side effects would be reduced. So-called biologics, produced using biotechnological methods, are being developed to treat currently untreatable conditions, but are so difficult to produce and so narrowly targeted to small numbers of individuals that they will cost thousands of dollars for a course of treatment. Benefits could be many times costs—but costs will rise.

Americans value sophisticated health services, and analysts argue that advances in health services and the high spending that brings these advances to patients are exactly how we want to spend a rising portion of our growing national income (Cutler and McClellan 2001). There has been little political will to rein in health costs—even those that appear to be wasteful—and even less determination to slow the development of new diagnostic techniques, surgical procedures, and medicines (CBO 2008).

The RAND Corporation developed a microsimulation model that used the actual health status for current elders by age to model transitions among health and disability states, yielding the rates at which the elder population acquires chronic illness diagnoses and functional disabilities (Goldman, Shekelle, et al. 2004). Health services use was then estimated for each disease/disability state, both under the current state of medical knowledge technology and with advances in medical treatment. The microsimulation approach builds up end results by running simulated individuals through many lifetimes. This gives simulation models the ability to account for the fact that even if a medical breakthrough prevents, cures, or ameliorates a given disease or chronic condition, elders who would have suffered from the conquered disease in 2015 or 2030 will still be subject to all the remaining causes of disability and mortality. The RAND model focused specifically on the possibilities of new medical advances, which might work so well that they return ill patients to good health or, as has happened in the past, may provide continuing treatment for ongoing diseases that previously have not been as well addressed.

Advances that prevent or cure disease (Thomas's [1971, 1974] "full" technologies) can be very costly and still be preferable to treatments that ameliorate disease states ("halfway" technologies). Cancer vaccines are one example of a "full technology" on the horizon; the RAND team estimated that if cancer vaccines were developed and available to Medicare beneficiaries, treatment cost would increase health spending over the status quo by 0.1 percent in 2015 and 0.4 percent in 2030—with a cost per additional life-year of about $18,000. In contrast, development and use of pacemakers for atrial fibrillation would increase health spending by 2.2 percent and were projected to cost $1.4 million per life-year saved. Development and use of anti-angiogenesis drugs to treat solid tumor cancers would increase health costs between 8 percent and 9 percent and result in benefits projected to cost about half a million dollars per life-year saved. The engines of technological change are fueled by science and by the waiting market, and our society has been willing to pay their price.

The recent expansion of the indications for approved use of Avastin, a drug developed to treat colon cancer, shows these trends at work today (as predicted by Goldman, Shang, et al. 2005; Pollack 2008). The Food and Drug Administration (FDA) has now approved Avastin for use in treating breast cancer, where it is typically added to an already expensive and demanding chemotherapy regimen at an additional cost of approximately $7,700 per month. A clinical trial demonstrated that inclusion of Avastin in chemotherapy lengthened the time to worsening of cancer or death, from 5.8 months with the standard treatment to 11.3 months with the combination. However, the women receiving Avastin had no significant improvement in survival. FDA approval carries with it coverage under drug insurance plans, including Medicare Part D, reducing the hesitation of physicians to prescribe and patients to accept a treatment that appears to offer marginal benefits at great cost. The costs will soon be shared by everyone paying drug insurance premiums, as well as by patients subject to copayments for their treatment.

Aging of the Population Will Shift Expenditures to Medicare and Medicaid

Although the aging of the population is not projected to overwhelm total health spending growth in itself, as the baby-boom generation begins to stream over the 65-year age threshold, their impact will be felt in Medicare and Medicaid, the two major government programs that finance health care. But again, the impact of their aging numbers will be dwarfed by overall growth in per-capita spending due to other causes.

Enrollment in Medicare has already started to grow. Over most of its history, Medicare has added an average of about 600,000 net beneficiaries a year (Boards of Trustees 2007, table III.A.3, p. 34). As the postwar babies reach 65 over the next few years, that number will rise, growing to over a million starting in 2011 and averaging 1.5 million over the next twenty years. By 2040, enrollment will be almost double what it is today. But the CBO estimates that, like its impact on overall health spending, population aging alone will have a relatively small impact on federal spending on Medicare. It assesses that the increased numbers of the baby boomers will be responsible for only about a quarter of the projected increase in federal Medicare and Medicaid spending (net of beneficiary premiums) relative to gross domestic product (GDP) (CBO 2007, 14; see also Potetz 2008). In the next decades, the influx of baby boomers will actually skew the age distribution of Medicare enrollees toward younger ages. When combined with falling age-specific rates of disability, this should reduce per-capita Medicare expenditures below what they otherwise would have been (Bhattacharya, Cutler, et al. 2004). Of course, over time the per-capita spending increases that afflict all health spending will be magnified by the growing number of enrollees, so the CBO projects that Medicare spending net of premiums will grow from 3 percent of GDP in 2006 to 6 percent by 2030 and will reach 15 percent in fifty years under current law (computed by Potetz 2008).[2]

Medicaid, the state-federal program aimed at covering health services for specified categories of the poor, will also feel the age wave. Elders 65 and older form one of the categories of persons that Medicaid serves when they meet a means test, so Medicaid enrollment will grow. In 2006, elders were 9.6 percent of Medicaid beneficiaries, but used 22.6 percent of benefits, mostly for long-term care services, which are not covered by Medicare or private health insurance (Gleckman 2007). If the baby-boom generation reaches old age even less well prepared to meet long-term care expenses than current elders, the proportion of elders eligible for Medicaid could increase. Further, Medicaid-eligible elders with a strong preference for remaining in their own homes rather than entering a nursing home have avoided seeking Medicaid-funded services, because many state Medicaid programs formerly paid for long-term care only when a beneficiary was using nursing home care. In the past decade, state Medicaid programs have been expanding the options for services provided at home, a policy likely to address many unmet needs of eligible elders, at lower cost per person served than nursing home care. But by making Medicaid services more palatable, this policy will likely expand total Medicaid long-term care expenditures.

There are some mitigating factors, however. Although the cost of serving long-term care recipients will grow with wage growth throughout the economy, the long-term care sector offers fewer opportunities for quality-increasing high-tech advances than the acute health sector. In addition, prescription drugs, a category of health services very much a vehicle for expensive technological advances, have been shifted from Medicaid to Medicare. These factors, and falling rates of age-adjusted disability, suggest that Medicaid spending for elders will not explode out of control. Recent projections show Medicaid spending rising from 2.6 percent of GDP in 2006 to 4.1 percent in 2025 and 6.5 percent by 2045, but most of this growth is focused on other populations that Medicaid serves, with little due directly to increased spending on the aged population (Kronick and Rousseau 2006; CBO 2006).

IMPACT OF RISING HEALTH EXPENDITURES ON THE BOOMERS

Americans apparently are unwilling to slow the growth of health expenditures by slowing technological advances or reining in possibly wasteful spending. But this means that even older adults, who are better insured than younger populations for many health needs, will find personal health costs increasingly burdensome. Retired boomers may be less prepared than they expect to meet health and related needs.

Many Older Adults Currently Spend a Substantial Proportion of Income on Health Insurance Premiums, Copayments, and Uncovered Health Services

Medicare does not cover all health costs, and elders can face substantial out-of-pocket expenses. Some Medicare beneficiaries currently spend substantial amounts out-of-pocket on Medicare and private health insurance premiums, deductibles and copayments that are part of insurance plan design, and on services, such as long-term care, that are not covered by insurance. And retirees are in a difficult situation—they cannot rely on future earnings growth or adjustments in work behavior to meet unexpected health spending needs.

Median out-of-pocket health care spending for community-dwelling older households was almost $2,300 in 2002; over three-fifths of this went to pay Medicare and private premiums (Johnson 2006). The median elderly household spent 11.8 percent of income on health care. Out-of-pocket spending as a proportion of income was highest for those without additional insurance and those relying on individually purchased Medigap insurance, lower for those covered by employer-sponsored insurance plans, and lowest for Medicaid beneficiaries, who pay neither premiums nor copayments.

If they were steady and predictable, even expenditures of this magnitude relative to income could be part of retirement planning. But health expenditures are not evenly distributed: almost one-sixth of community-dwelling households spent more than a third of their income on health care (Johnson 2006, table A-22). And of course it is the oldest and sickest elders who have the largest out-of-pocket bills in relation to their incomes (Johnson 2006, table A-22; Schoenberg et al. 2007).

By examining spending in relation to income for community-resident elders only, we can understand the extent to which the out-of-pocket health costs reduce their ability to pay for other necessities (housing and food, for example) and thus reduce quality of life. Elders who have moved into a nursing home generally do not have so many other spending needs, and so may be considered able to devote a larger proportion of income to health services, which then cover their room and board. However, an overall evaluation of the risks to retirement security posed by rising health costs should also include long-term care expenditures, which are not covered by private insurance or Medicare and thus may be catastrophic for elders not eligible for Medicaid. A study using the Medicare Current Beneficiary Survey was able to calculate the portion of income spent on health services and premiums for all beneficiaries, including institutional residents (Desmond et al. 2007; Neuman et al. 2007). Because income tends to fall and out-of-pocket health expenditures to increase with age, the median percentage of income spent on health was 13.8 percent for all adults aged 65 to 74, rising to 22.2 percent for beneficiaries 85 and older; the top decile of the spending distribution spent more than 58 percent of their income on health insurance premiums, copayments, and uncovered health services, including long-term care.[3]

The medians and average health expenditure figures, even when expressed as a proportion of income, hide a particular vulnerability of couples: if one member of a couple experiences a typically expensive last illness, the surviving spouse may find herself or himself in much-reduced economic circumstances. Income falls after widowhood due to provisions in Social Security and private pensions, and the impact of a spouse's terminal-year health expenditures on the economic well-being of the survivor can compound these losses (McGarry and Schoeni 2005a, 2005b).

The Burden of Uncovered Health Expenditures Is Likely to Be Heavier for Future Elders

With many Medicare beneficiaries already facing substantial out-of-pocket costs, the future increases in health expenditures do not bode well for the baby boomers. First, this generation will have less help from employers in paying premiums for insurance to supplement Medicare. Already Medicare beneficiaries covered by employer-provided supplementary insurance have seen their median mandatory premium contributions more than triple between 1998 and 2002 (Johnson 2006). And corporate commitments to postretirement health insurance coverage, which have been eroding for many years, are becoming increasingly uncertain as costs rise, Part D subsidies for corporate insurance continuation play out, and rules change. A recent analysis attempts to put a number on the uninsured liability represented by uncovered costs, rising premiums, and disappearing coverage, estimating that a couple would need to save an additional $550,000 to cover these costs through age 95 (Fronstin 2006). Such an estimate is useful to call attention to the threat that relatively predictable rising health costs pose to retirement wealth, but even this large figure cannot be guaranteed to protect elders from the variability of expenditure needs and the possibility of expenditure catastrophe.

Medicare itself has design features that will place financial burdens on future elders. Premiums for Part B and Part D are required by statute to rise with costs, because no more than a fixed proportion of program costs can be funded out of general revenues. Copayments set at a percentage of costs (for example, 20 percent for the ambulatory care services covered by Medicare Part B and 5 percent for prescription drug expenses over Part D's catastrophic limit) will rise with physician and pharmacy prices. Prices for drugs that are heavily used by Medicare beneficiaries are already experiencing large increases, suggesting that current estimates of future Part D premiums may be too low (Frank and Newhouse 2008). In addition, elders will pay increasing taxes along with all taxpayers as an increasing amount of Medicare costs is financed by general revenues (Munnell 2007). Out-of-pocket health expenditures as a share of after-tax income will only increase.

Long-term care costs, discussed elsewhere in this volume, are not covered by Medicare or private health insurance and thus can represent a substantial portion of uncovered health services, especially for the oldest elderly with incomes and assets above Medicaid eligibility thresholds. Long-term care services assist persons with disabilities in carrying out daily activities and by definition require time from another human being—these tasks cannot be accomplished by a device, a computer, or a drug. This means that techno-logical advances will probably not push the prices of paid long-term care services higher, but as productivity increases throughout the economy drives general wages higher, the wages of personal care labor employed in this service industry must follow, because workers must be paid enough to keep them in carework (Baumol 1967). In addition, we can hope that the quality of care and quality of life available to future elders will exceed what is cur-rently on offer, and improvements are likely to add to the cost of care. Most important, future elders will need to pay for more of the services they need, because unpaid care from family is expected to become less available (Johnson, Toohey, and Wiener 2007).

Finally, retirement income prospects for the baby boomers are not all rosy, especially for those surviving to the oldest ages when out-of-pocket health expenses are expected to be greatest (Butrica, Smith, and Toder 2002; Butrica, Iams, and Smith 2004; Butrica, Cashin, and Uccello 2005; Butrica, Goldwyn, and Johnson 2005). There is substantial variability in the net worth of the boomers as they approach retirement, and a large proportion of this genera-tion's wealth is in housing wealth, which may become more uncertain in the near term (Lusardi and Mitchell 2007). Bringing together trends in retirement income and the relentless increase in health costs that drives insurance cover-age, premium costs, out-of-pocket spending, and taxes, Johnson and Penner (2004) use the Urban Institute's microsimulation model to assess the impact of these forces on future elders. The news is not good: they conclude that although the income of older adults is poised to keep pace with income growth throughout the economy, their spending power will be curtailed by the rise in out-of-pocket health spending, for both premiums and health service, and by the tax increases required by current law as Medicare expenses rise. They estimate that elders' after-tax income net of health spending will do no more than stay steady in real terms, as older couples spend 35 percent of their after-tax income on health services by 2030, and unmarried older adults, with lower incomes and more help from Medicaid, spend three-tenths of after-tax income on health. If health spending trends cannot be altered, the boomers will find the gains of productivity growth and lifetime saving obliterated.

CONCLUSION

If we can see a disaster coming, we can prepare for it. The baby boomers' age wave has been predictable since their births between 1946 and 1964. But it turns out that within the larger trends of overall health expenditure growth, the impact of population aging on health resource use will be more a pop than a boom. However, as technological advances drive health expen-ditures' growth, the amount that households must budget for premium pay-ments and both expected and unexpected out-of-pocket spending will increase, causing special burdens for retirees with little room to maneuver financially. The real challenge, for both the boomers and society as a whole, will be finding a way to contain health expenditure growth itself, so that we can sustain health and garner the health benefits of scientific advances while still maintaining or even increasing resources for other desired goods and services.

NOTES

1. Formally the Trustees of the Federal Hospital Insurance and Federal Supplementary Medical Insurance Trust Funds.

2. The Trustees' estimates were made on a slightly different basis and differ somewhat, but are still very large: they estimate that federal spending on Medicare will grow from 3.1 percent of GDP in 2006 to 6.3 percent in 2030 and 11.3 percent fifty years later (Boards of Trustees 2007).

3. In these studies based on the Medicare Current Beneficiary Survey, income was computed per person by dividing household income among household members. Other studies attempting to estimate the amount and distribution of elders' out-of-pocket health costs, providing evidence on the impact of health costs on their well-being, include Crystal et al. 2000; Maxwell, Moon, and Segal 2001; Goldman and Zissimopoulos 2003; Caplan and Brangan 2004; Butrica, Goldwyn, and Johnson 2005; Burham 2007; and Social Security Administration 2007.

REFERENCES

Baumol, W. J. 1967. The macroeconomics of unbalanced growth: The anatomy of urban crisis. *American Economic Review* 57:415–26.

Bhattacharya, J., K. Choudhry, and D. Lakdawalla. 2008. Chronic disease and severe disability among working-age populations. *Medical Care* 46 (1): 92–100.

Bhattacharya, J., D. M. Cutler, D. P. Goldman, M. D. Hurd, G. F. Joyce, D. N. Lakdawalla, C. W. Panis, and B. Shang. 2004. Disability forecasts and future Medicare costs. *Front Health Policy Research* 7:75–94.

Boards of Trustees, Federal Hospital Insurance and Federal Supplementary Medical Insurance Trust Funds. 2007. *2007 annual report of the Boards of the Trustees of the Federal Hospital Insurance and Federal Supplementary Medical Insurance trust funds.* Available at http://www.cms.hhs.gov/ReportsTrustFunds/downloads/tr2007.pdf.

Burham, K. 2007. Expenditures of the aged. *Social Security Bulletin* 67 (1): 45.

Butrica, B. A., D. B. Cashin, and C. E. Uccello. 2005. Projections of economic well-being for Social Security beneficiaries in 2022 and 2062. *Social Security Bulletin* 66 (4): 1.

Butrica, B. A., J. H. Goldwyn, and R. W. Johnson. 2005. Understanding expenditure patterns in retirement. Center for Retirement Research Working Paper No. 2005-03. Available at http://crr.bc.edu/images/stories/Working_Papers/wp_2005-03.pdf.

Butrica, B. A., H. M. Iams, and K. E. Smith. 2004. It's all relative: Understanding the retirement prospects of baby boomers. Paper prepared for the National Academy of Social Insurance Annual Conference.

Butrica, B. A., K. Smith, and E. Toder. 2002. Projecting poverty rates in 2020 for the 62 and older population: What changes can we expect and why? Center for

Retirement Research Working Paper No. 2002-03. Available at http://crr.bc.edu/working_papers/projecting_poverty_rates_in_2020_for_the_62_and_older_population_what_changes_can_we_expect_an.html.

Caplan, C., and N. Brangan. 2004. Out-of-pocket spending on health care by Medicare beneficiaries age 65 and older in 2003. AARP Public Policy Institute Data Digest No. 101. Available at http://assets.aarp.org/rgcenter/health/dd101_spending.pdf.

CBO (Congressional Budget Office). 2006. Medicaid spending growth and options for controlling costs. Statement of Donald B. Marron, Acting Director, before the Special Committee on Aging, U.S. Senate, July 13, 2006.

———. 2007. The long-term outlook for health care spending. Available at http://www.cbo.gov/ftpdocs/87xx/doc8758/11-13-LT-Health.pdf.

———. 2008. Technological change and the growth of health care spending. Pub. No. 2764. Available at http://www.cbo.gov/ftpdocs/89xx/doc8947/01-31-Tech Health.pdf.

Chernew, M. E., D. P. Goldman, F. Pan, and B. P. Shang. 2005. Disability and health care spending among Medicare beneficiaries. *Health Affairs* 24 (6): W5R42–W5R52.

Crystal, S., R. W. Johnson, J. Harman, U. Sambamoorthi, and R. Kumar. 2000. Out-of-pocket health care costs among older Americans. *Journals of Gerontology Series B: Psychological Sciences and Social Sciences* 55 (1): S51–S62.

Cutler, D. M. 2007. The lifetime costs and benefits of medical technology. *Journal of Health Economics* 26 (6): 1081–1100.

Cutler, D. M., and M. McClellan. 2001. Is technological change in medicine worth it? *Health Affairs* (Millwood) 20 (5): 11–29.

Cutler, D. M., and L. Sheiner. 1999. Demographics and medical care spending: Standard and non-standard effects. In *Demographic change and fiscal policy*, ed. A. Auerbach and R. Lee, 253–91. Cambridge: Cambridge University Press.

Desmond, K. A., T. Rice, J. Cubanski, and P. Neuman. 2007. The burden of out-of-pocket health spending among older versus younger adults: Analysis from the Consumer Expenditure Survey, 1998–2003. Kaiser Family Foundation Issue Brief. Available at http://www.kff.org/medicare/upload/7686.pdf.

Escarce, J., B. Bloom, and A. Hillman. 1995. Diffusion of laparoscopic cholecystectomy among general surgeons in the United States. *Medical Care* 33 (3): 256–71.

Frank, R. G., and J. P. Newhouse. 2008. Should drug prices be negotiated under part D of Medicare? And if so, how? *Health Affairs* (Millwood) 27 (1): 33–43.

Freedman, V. A., E. Crimmins, R. F. Schoeni, B. C. Spillman, H. Aykan, E. Kramarow, K. Land, et al. 2004. Resolving inconsistencies in trends in old-age disability: Report from a technical working group. *Demography* 41 (3): 417–41.

Freedman, V. A., R. F. Schoeni, L. G. Martin, and J. C. Cornman. 2007. Chronic conditions and the decline in late-life disability. *Demography* 44 (3): 459–77.

Fronstin, P. 2006. Savings needed to fund health insurance and health care expenses in retirement. Employment Benefits Research Institute Issue Brief No. 295. Available at http://www.ebri.org/pdf/briefspdf/EBRI_IB_07-20061.pdf.

Gleckman, H. 2007. Medicaid and long-term care: How will rising costs affect services for an aging population? Issue in Brief, No. 7-4. Chestnut Hill, MA: Center of Retirement Research. Available at http://crr.bc.edu/images/stories/Briefs/ib_2007-4.pdf.

Goldman, D. P., B. P. Shang, J. Battacharya, A. M. Garber, M. Hurd, G. F. Joyce, D. N. Lakdawalla, C. Panis, and P. G. Shekelle. 2005. Consequences of health trends and medical innovation for the future elderly. *Health Affairs* 24 (6): W5R5–W5R17.

Goldman, D. P., P. G. Shekelle, J. Bhattacharya, M. Hurd, G. F. Joyce, D. N. Lakdawalla, D. H. Matsui, S. J. Newberry, C. W. A. Panis, and B. Shang. 2004. Health status and medical treatment of the future elderly. Final Report TR-169-CMS. Prepared for the Centers for Medicare and Medicaid Services by the RAND Corporation.

Goldman, D. P., and J. M. Zissimopoulos. 2003. High out-of-pocket health care spending by the elderly. *Health Affairs* (Millwood) 22 (3): 194–202.

Hartman, M., A. Catlin, D. Lassman, J. Cylus, and S. Heffler. 2007. U.S. health spending by age, selected years through 2004. *Health Affairs* (Millwood).

Johnson, R. W. 2006. *Health insurance coverage and costs at older ages: Evidence from the health and retirement study.* AARP Public Policy Institute Research Report No. 2006-20.

Johnson, R. W., and R. G. Penner. 2004. Will health care costs erode retirement security? Issue in Brief, No. 23. Chestnut Hill, MA: Center of Retirement Research. Available at http://crr.bc.edu/images/stories/Briefs/ib_23.pdf.

Johnson, R. W., D. Toohey, and J. M. Wiener. 2007. Meeting the long-term care needs of the baby boomers: How changing families will affect paid helpers and institutions. Retirement Project Discussion Paper No. 07-04. Available at http://www.urban.org/UploadedPDF/311451_Meeting_Care.pdf.

Keehan, S. P., H. C. Lazenby, M. A. Zezza, and A. C. Catlin. 2004. Age estimates in the national health accounts. *Health Care Financing Review Web Exclusive* 1 (1): 1–16.

Keehan, S., A. Sisko, C. Truffer, S. Smith, C. Cowan, J. Poisal, M. K. Clemens, and N.H. Accounts Projections Team. 2008. Health spending projections through 2017: The baby-boom generation is coming to Medicare. *Health Affairs* (Millwood).

Kronick, R., and D. Rousseau. 2006. Is Medicaid sustainable? Spending projections for the program's second forty years. *Health Affairs* (Millwood) 26:W271.

Lakdawalla, D. N., D. P. Goldman, and B. Shang. 2005. The health and cost consequences of obesity among the future elderly. *Health Affairs* (Millwood) 24, suppl. 2: W5R30–W5R41.

Lavernia, C., D. J. Lee, and, V. H. Hernandez. 2006. The increasing financial burden of knee revision surgery in the United States. *Clinical Orthopaedics and Related Research* 446:221–26.

Lubitz, J., L. M. Cai, E. Kramarow, and H. Lentzner. 2003. Health, life expectancy, and health care spending among the elderly. *New England Journal of Medicine* 349 (11): 1048–55.

Lubitz, J. D., and G. F. Riley. 1993. Trends in Medicare payments in the last year of life. *New England Journal of Medicine* 328 (15): 1092–96.

Lusardi, A., and O. S. Mitchell. 2007. Baby boomer retirement security: The roles of planning, financial literacy, and housing wealth. *Journal of Monetary Economics* 54 (1): 205.

Manton, K. G., X. Gu, and V. L. Lamb. 2006. Change in chronic disability from 1982 to 2004/2005 as measured by long-term changes in function and health in the

U.S. elderly population. *Proceedings of the National Academy of Science USA* 103 (48): 18374–79.

Maxwell, S., M. Moon, and M. Segal. 2001. Growth in Medicare and out-of-pocket spending: Impact on vulnerable beneficiaries. Urban Institute. Available at http://www.commonwealthfund.org/usr_doc/ maxwell_increases_430.pdf?section=4039.

McGarry, K., and R. F. Schoeni. 2005a. Medicare gaps and widow poverty. *Social Security Bulletin* 66 (1): 58.

———. 2005b. Widow(er) poverty and out-of-pocket medical expenditures near the end of life. *Journals of Gerontology Series B: Psychological Sciences and Social Sciences* 60B (3): S160.

Munnell, A. H. 2007. Medicare costs and retirement security. Issue in Brief, No. 7-14. Chestnut Hill, MA: Center of Retirement Research. Available at http://crr.bc.edu/images/stories/Briefs/ib_7-14.pdf.

Neuman, P., J. Cubanski, K. A. Desmond, and T. H. Rice. 2007. How much "skin in the game" do Medicare beneficiaries have? The increasing financial burden of health care spending, 1997–2003. *Health Affairs* (Millwood) 26 (6): 1692–1701.

Newhouse, J. P. 1992. Medical care costs: How much welfare loss? *Journal of Economic Perspectives* 6 (3): 3–21.

Pollack, A. 2008. F.D.A. extends Avastin's use to breast cancer. *New York Times*. February 23.

Potetz, L. 2008. Financing Medicare: An issue brief. Kaiser Family Foundation Pub. No. 7731. Available at http://www.kff.org/medicare/upload/7731.pdf.

Schoenberg, N. E., H. Kim, W. Edwards, and S. T. Fleming. 2007. Burden of common multiple-morbidity constellations on out-of-pocket medical expenditures among older adults. *Gerontologist* 47 (4): 423–37.

Social Security Administration. 2007. Expenditures of the aged chartbook. Available at http://www.socialsecurity.gov/policy/docs/chartbooks/expenditures_aged/index.html.

Soldo, B. J., O. S. Mitchell, R. Tfaily, and J. F. McCabe. 2006. Cross-cohort differences in health on the verge of retirement. National Bureau of Economic Research (NBER) Working Paper No. 12,762. Cambridge, MA: NBER.

Spillman, B. C., and J. Lubitz. 2000. The effect of longevity on spending for acute and long-term care. *New England Journal of Medicine* 342 (19): 1409–15.

Thomas, L. 1971. The technology of medicine. *New England Journal of Medicine* 285 (24): 1366–68.

———. 1974. *The lives of a cell: Notes of a biology watcher.* New York: Viking.

Weisbrod, B. A. 1991. The health care quadrilemma: An essay on technological change, insurance, quality of care, and cost containment. *Journal of Economic Literature* 29 (2): 523–52.

III
BOOMERS AND THE NEW POLITICS OF AGING

7

Public Policy and the Boomers: An Expanding Scope of Conflict

ROBERT B. HUDSON

B aby boomers about to enter old age will encounter a public policy landscape that would have been virtually unrecognizable to their grandparents. Programs that either did not exist or were only in their infancy are now enormous and entrenched. Older people, who were once little more than a residual demographic category, have now developed a political self-identity that has made them a formidable presence in national politics. And this combination of large public programs and growing political identity has led to the creation of more than fifty age-related interest groups in Washington, an assemblage so large that the groups have had to form their own organization.

This chapter explores the world of public policy that the boomers are likely to experience and the political role they may play in helping to shape that world. As we are repeatedly informed, the boomers in old age will make a profound impact on institutions of all kinds, political ones included. In the following chapter, Robert Binstock reviews the potential presence the boomers may have in American political life. Here, we review the current public policy arena on aging, how it developed, and what accounts for the particular dimensions it has assumed. As we will see, both the prominence and understanding of policies on aging have undergone a profound reassessment in recent decades, and the boomers will enter into a more contested aging-policy arena than that experienced by earlier generations.

During the period 2010–2030, the boomers will surely assume a very prominent public role, but they will do so in an environment where economic and political pressures are bearing down on the major age-related programs, notably Social Security and Medicare. Ironically, the pressures building on these programs result, in part, from the very successes that they have had in improving the well-being of older people. Thus, the boomers will face a policy world in which a growing chorus of critics asks whether the programs are affordable and if they are all necessary. For their part, the boomers will be well positioned to defend the programs because, while older people were once singularly needy (and thus seen as especially deserving), they are now significantly better off (and thus able to mobilize impressive political resources on their own behalf). Thus, the growing pressures both to curtail and to preserve current benefits for the rising elder boomer cohort represent something of a political "perfect storm."

THE DEVELOPMENT OF SOCIAL POLICY FOR OLDER AMERICANS

Social policies were slow to develop in the United States, initially including those directed at older Americans. Frequently noting a pattern of "American exceptionalism" (Lipset 1996) in comparison to developments in other countries, analysts have referred to the United States as being a "welfare laggard" (Orloff 1988) or as having created "a reluctant welfare state" (Wilensky and Lebeaux 1958). Yet, within this generally delayed framework, policies for older Americans generally came sooner, were funded more generously, and grew faster than programs directed at other populations or problems.

With the notable exception of Civil War pensions (Skocpol 1993), the federal government had very little presence in social welfare prior to the twentieth century. Local and state governments played limited and often punitive roles through such institutions as asylums, sanitariums, poorhouses, reform schools, and state mental hospitals (Katz 1996). Charity offered in community settings (so-called outdoor relief) was exclusively the province of private philanthropy. Modest expansion of public activity took place during the early twentieth century through the efforts of the Progressive movement, which focused attention on child labor and "mothers' pension" legislation assisting young widows with children.

Aging Policy Development: The Expansionary Period

The New Deal of the 1930s brought the national government into the business of social welfare on an unprecedented scale, and the needs of older Americans were prominently featured in these efforts. The Social Security Act was the crowning achievement of these efforts, with Title I of the Act establishing Old Age Assistance for the poor aged, and Title II establishing Old Age Insurance, the cornerstone of today's Social Security system.

The salience of these two programs was based on the dire and unquestioned needs of the elderly during the Depression, bringing into stark relief the great historical fear associated with old age, namely, that of outliving one's income. In the absence of individual wealth or family supports, individuals in old age were left largely to the mercies of private charity or public alms. At the time of Social Security's enactment, it is estimated that just over half of all cash income that older people received came from their adult children (Upp 1982). Today, thanks largely to Social Security, that figure is down to less than 3 percent (Federal Interagency Forum on Aging-Related Statistics 2007).

The New Frontier/Great Society era of presidents John Kennedy and Lyndon Johnson was the next watershed period in social policy. Scores of mainly small services programs were initiated on behalf of a variety of groups, such as the unemployed, welfare recipients, residents of both inner-city and rural areas, and the sick. What ultimately emerged as the two largest programs passed at the time were health care programs directed either exclusively (Medicare) or significantly (Medicaid) to seniors. After income needs, health care concerns were the biggest worry of older people and their families, and this concern was widely recognized at the time. Advocates for national health insurance settled on the elderly to be sole beneficiaries in order to assure passage of some form of governmentally financed health care. As for Medicaid—a means-tested public assistance program—it has become the largest payer in the country of older people's long-term care needs.

The expansion of public programs for the aged continued into the 1970s, making the 1965–1974 period something of a "golden decade" for older people. In addition to Medicare and Medicaid, this ten-year period saw the passage of the Older Americans Act in 1965 (and creation of the "aging network" of social service agencies), the Age Discrimination in Employment Act in 1967, the Supplemental Security Income (SSI) program in 1972, and the Employee Retirement Income Security Act (ERISA) in 1974. The decade also witnessed creation of the National Institute on Aging within the National Institutes of Health, a cumulative 70 percent increase in Social Security benefits between 1967 and 1972, and inflation protection for beneficiaries through a provision tying future benefit increases to increases in the cost-of-living index.

The mid-1970s represented the high-water mark for enacting programs on behalf of older Americans and other social policy constituencies as well. Indeed, analyses covering a number of Western nations find the mid-1970s to be a breakpoint between expansionary and retrenching phases of welfare state development (Pierson 1995; Myles and Quadagno 2002). In the United States, events pressuring programs across the board included the Vietnam War, the residual effects of the Watergate scandal, the economic shocks produced by the oil embargo of the early 1970s, a period of economic "stagflation" that lasted most of the decade, and a malaise about the ability of the federal government during the presidencies of Gerald Ford and Jimmy Carter to address rising economic and social concerns.

Yet additional factors weighed in particular on aging-related programs during this period. First, expenditures under the big entitlement programs—Social Security and Medicare—were now growing faster than had historically been the case and, at least in the near term, were outpacing the payroll tax revenues used to sustain the programs (Greenspan Commission 1983). Second, there was a growing awareness that longer-run demographic trends were going to increase these fiscal pressures over time. So long as the baby boomers were in the active labor force—which would extend from the mid-1960s when the early boomers hit adulthood until the 2010s when they would begin retiring—these pressures would be manageable. But it was realized as inevitable that the retirement of the baby boomers and the attainment of adulthood by a much smaller "Generation X" cohort (born between 1965 and 1981) would dramatically transform the fiscal underpinnings of Social Security and Medicare. Third, it was also becoming clear that health care inflation and the costs of new medical technology were leading to much faster expenditure growth under Medicare than had been anticipated when the program was enacted. After growing only marginally in its early years, Medicare expenditures grew at an annual rate of 17 percent between 1970 and 1980, and continued to grow at an annual rate of more than 11 percent during the 1980s (Center for Medicare and Medicaid Services 2007). Concerns about future expenditure growth have certainly been borne out since, Medicare costs having risen from $109 billion in 1990 to $401 billion in 2006.

As a result of these combined pressures, the next wave of aging-related legislation was restrictive rather than expansionary. In 1977, President Carter signed a bill that increased the payroll tax rather than liberalized benefits, representing the first restrictive legislation in Social Security's history. In 1983, the so-called Greenspan Commission (1983) designed a package, subsequently enacted by Congress, whereby Social Security payroll tax increases were accelerated, new state and local workers were brought into the system, the cost-of-living adjustment was delayed for six months, and taxation of Social Security benefits of higher-income beneficiaries was introduced for the first time. At roughly the same time, a new "prospective payment" reimbursement system for hospitals was introduced into Medicare, again designed to rein in costs.

In the late 1980s, an attempt was made to add new catastrophic coverage, long-term care protections, and spousal safeguards as part of the Medicare Catastrophic Coverage Act (MCCA) (Himelfarb 1995). While adding these benefits would clearly be expansionary, the financing requirement built into the law—insisted upon by President Ronald Reagan—was that older people themselves would have pay for these added benefits through income tax surcharges to be levied on upper-income seniors. Insisting on *intra*generational financing, rather than continuing to rely on *inter*generational financing through the payroll tax, proved to be both conceptually and politically controversial. While analysts debated the former concern, older people and their advocacy groups mounted a ferocious mobilization against the proposed tax. They created such a firestorm that the MCCA was repealed less than a year into its existence. The MCCA episode illustrated the political muscle older people were capable of exercising around issues of direct concern to them. It also represents a first chapter in the more contentious politics of aging that have now emerged and which will very much mark the coming experience that older boomers will have in the political arena.

The next major aging-policy episode took place in the mid-1990s, when the "Republican Class of 1994" attempted to cut the future growth of Medicare and Medicaid by a total of $400 billion over a ten-year period (Smith 2002). This led to a drawn-out battle with President Bill Clinton, resulting in the temporary shutdown of the federal government in 1997. In the end, the Clinton position prevailed, but again the newly contested politics of aging were in full view. Victory here meant avoiding expenditure cuts, not expanding enrollee benefits.

The growing politicization of aging-related policy was seen in the debate leading to passage of Medicare Part D, the prescription drug legislation that has been the biggest expansion in Medicare since its inception. Eager to make inroads into the older voting constituency, Republicans had been promoting drug legislation and made it a major issue in the 2000 and 2002 elections. Because of the Republican sponsorship and particular aspects of the plan, Democrats found themselves in the awkward position of opposing this major addition to the program. But there were tensions on both sides of the aisle: conservative Republicans was opposed to such a massive entitlement expansion, regardless of the political benefits, and Democrats found reason to oppose the legislation because of the central role private managed-care firms would play in program implementation (Pear 2003). To further complicate matters, the aging-based interest groups were divided on the issue, with AARP famously supporting the legislation while most other groups opposed it. The legislation passed in 2003 and has greatly expanded drug coverage for elders, but, as both sets of critics warned, it has proven to be very expensive and has encouraged the expansion of so-called Medicare Advantage plans to attract a growing proportion of Medicare beneficiaries into the quasi-private market.

The most contentious episode yet seen in aging politics took place in 2004–2005 as President George W. Bush made the partial privatization of Social Security the initial cornerstone of his second-term agenda. While an actual bill was never introduced, the president's proposal would have diverted a portion of workers' Social Security payroll tax payments into mandatory private retirement accounts akin to 401(k) defined contribution plans. The president argued that this approach offered greater choice and control for plan participants.

The baby boomers figured centrally into the political calculations made by the White House. Boomers were seen by many Republicans and business executives as a new generation that had grown up comfortable with equities and other private investment vehicles (Weisberg 2005). In this way, they were seen as more of a "take-charge" generation than the so-called silent generation that had preceded them, and certainly more so than the yet-earlier Depression generation, which had grown up leery of the stock market in light of their disastrous exposure to it. The boomers were to be key players in the president's "ownership society" (Allen 2005).

These generalizations were true of many well-off boomers, but they did not extend to many present-day older Americans nor to many younger family members—including many boomers—aware that lower Social Security benefits might affect them as well as their aging parents. The view that the Bush plan was more about undermining the existing system than creating new investment opportunities for future beneficiaries ultimately carried the day. After months of heated debate, it was clear by the end of 2005 that the president's ideas had failed in the court of public opinion and within much of the "policy elite" community in Washington. The proposals were withdrawn without enabling legislation having ever been introduced in Congress.

ACCOUNTING FOR THE GROWTH AND DEVELOPMENT OF OLD-AGE POLICY

A clear result of these various twists and turns in aging policy development is that public programs and expenditures on behalf of the aged today represent an enormous investment by the federal government. Social Security and Medicare alone accounted for 30 percent of all federal spending in 2004. When another dozen or so small programs benefiting the aged are added to the list, this proportion increases to 37 percent. The question here becomes how these efforts became so substantial, again remembering that the United States trails most other industrialized nations in terms of the proportion of its overall economic output devoted to public social programs.

We first look at the factors that help explain both the absolute and relative growth of programs for the old in the United States and then at an emergent set of factors that are now accounting for heightened levels of conflict around aging policy. These discussions set the stage for considering what policy landscape awaits the boomers in old age.

The Political Appeal of Old Age in American Social Policy

A number of factors account for the policy appeal of old age. The most prominent of these has been that advanced age has long been seen as a close proxy for demonstrated need. Until the very recent past and with very rare exceptions, to be old was to be poor, ill, frail, and dependent. Old age was a time of decline; indeed, it was the last of the many "bad things" that could happen to people in an industrial society (Rubinow 1934). Nor were older people to be blamed for this state of events; their situation, in Franklin Roosevelt's words, "is not a result of a lack of thrift or energy ... it is a mere byproduct of modern industrial life" (Rimlinger 1971, 212).

The long-accepted inability of the old to work took on a special place in the American political culture where work and self-sufficiency are the hallmarks of the complete citizen. It is in this sense that American social policies have long been understood to be largely "residual," that is, providing modest benefits to individuals when economic supports of the private market and/or social supports of the family have somehow failed those individuals. Only then would government intervene, and then presumably on a temporary and needs-tested basis. In short, most Americans were expected to find an economic home in the market and a social home in the family, and those who did not were routinely looked upon unfavorably.

Because the old were no longer expected to succeed in the market and were known to often be without adequate family supports, they developed a relatively privileged place in the social policy arena. In the words of political scientists Anne Schneider and Helen Ingram (1993), the elderly have enjoyed "a positive political construction." Put somewhat differently, seniors have possessed a high level of political legitimacy (Hudson 1978), with legitimacy's key ingredient being a broad-based belief that one *should* receive government benefits. This was critical to their early policy success, because legitimacy obviated the need for power, which the aged did not then possess.

Certainly, this legitimacy has been a central ingredient to their policy success, but that status had to be actualized for it to result in tangible programmatic enactments. That catalyst was added over the years by policy entrepreneurs and advocates seizing on the positive standing of the aged to try to extend social policies to other groups in the harsh American climate. Pleased to see the needs of older people addressed, these advocates also sought to use older people as something of "an ideological loss leader" (Hudson 1978), strategizing that bringing benefits to the old could be a critical first step in extending benefits to others, as well.

Acting on the Appeal of Old Age: From Standing to Statutes

The twin workings of the aged's political standing and others' desire to capitalize on it can be seen in three important legislative episodes. These are important both in how they help explain major policy expansions on behalf of older people and because they shed light on the difficulties of extending social welfare benefits more widely to the U.S. population.

The Aged and the Birth of Social Insurance

In the depths of the Depression, no group was more destitute than the old. Partly as a result, President Roosevelt designated Old Age Assistance (OAA) as Title I of the Social Security Act of 1935. OAA was a classic residual program, and it drew no opposition other than from those opposing any federal government social policy activity at all (Gordon 1994).

Roosevelt and his advisors were also hoping that the popularity of Title I would extend to the much more controversial Title II: Old Age Insurance (OAI), the cornerstone of today's Social Security program. While centered on the old, OAI was a policy of a far different stripe than OAA. Old Age Insurance was not a residual program; it was to be an institutional one, that is, permanent, ongoing, routinized, and funded by a new tax dedicated solely to it. OAA was about responding to temporary need; OAI was about protecting against permanent risks, in this case the undisputed likelihood that old age would result in loss of income. In his "fireside chats" selling this seemingly revolutionary policy model to the American public, Roosevelt emphasized that it simply acknowledged the support required when one could no longer work.

Initially, Title II was limited to retirees themselves; it would be another few years before it was extended, with some controversy, to the dependents of retired and deceased workers, that is, people who were in need and were related to a worker but who themselves had not worked. Nonetheless, this redubbed OASI (Old Age and Survivors Insurance) program struggled to gain legitimacy vis-à-vis OAA until the early-1950s, when its gradual expansion gave it firm and, soon thereafter, dominant footing (Skocpol and Ikenberry 1987).

Medicare as a Step toward National Health Insurance

The second major policy episode featuring the aged centers on Medicare. Presidents Roosevelt and Truman had each hoped to develop a national health program that would cover a broad range of Americans. Roosevelt never submitted such a plan to Congress, having more than enough controversy swirling around what he was already attempting. Truman attempted repeatedly to move a bill forward in the late 1940s, but Republicans using Communist-scare tactics and Southern Democrats using racist tactics doomed these efforts to defeat (Quadagno 2005).

In the wake of Truman's failure, health care advocates in Washington sought a new strategy to try to bring life back to the health insurance idea. By the late 1950s, they had settled on the one group about whom "one could not say that members should have taken care of their financial-medical problems by earning or saving more money" (Marmor 1970, 17). For the better part of a decade, these advocates pushed for a hospital-based insurance proposal directed to older persons. In 1965, in the wake of President Kennedy's assassination and President Johnson's landslide victory in the 1964 election, Medicare for the old (and later, the disabled) became law.

Once again, the singular legitimacy of the old carried the day. And, again, it stands as a uniquely American way of doing social policy business: No other country in the world targeted the elderly alone in enacting national health programs; certainly, older people were included, but it was current workers more than the old that tended to be the center of attention.

Supplemental Security Income: From Single Mothers to the Poor Elderly

A third and final episode featuring the elderly's favorable political standing originated, oddly enough, from a proposal to radically reform the Aid to Families with Dependent Children program (AFDC, aka "welfare") supporting low-income single mothers. In 1970, President Richard Nixon proposed a Family Assistance Program (FAP) to Congress in which a range of social services enacted during the 1960s would be eliminated and the existing cash grant would be standardized across the country, representing a very modest guaranteed income for these women and their children (Moynihan 1973). The idea of a guaranteed income was essentially unheard-of in American social policy circles, and its sponsorship by Nixon made it seem more unlikely yet.

After much discussion and passage by the House of Representatives, FAP finally went down to defeat in the Senate Finance Committee. Republicans and Southern Democrats could not abide the idea of an income guarantee, and liberal Democrats found the guarantee amount—$1,600 per year—woefully inadequate. In the wake of this defeat, advocates and analysts once again tried to see if anything could be salvaged from all the time and effort that had been devoted to the proposal. Realizing that AFDC was a highly controversial program—being about work and often illegitimacy and desertion—it occurred to these reformers that focusing instead on the "adult categories" programs might prove a safer bet.

Thus, it was proposed that the administration and financing of the Old Age Assistance, Aid to the Blind, and Aid to the Totally and Permanently Disabled programs be nationalized and contain a national income guarantee regardless of where recipients lived. Seen as a needed supplement to these individuals' Social Security benefits, the Supplemental Security Income program was enacted quickly and without great fanfare in the wake of the FAP failure (Burke and Burke 1974). Here, again focusing on older people helped snatch victory from the jaws of defeat.

The Growing Presence of Seniors in American Life

These legislative episodes, now dating back thirty years or more, took place when older people were both demographically and sociologically a relatively minor segment of the U.S. population. Their lack of recognition was captured by a feature in the U.S. Senate Committee on Aging's annual publication *Developments in Aging*, which was labeled "Every Eleventh American" in the 1960s editions and "Every Tenth American" in the early 1970s (Senate Committee on Aging 1972), hoping to highlight the growing presence of older people in the American population.

By some time in the late 1970s, the point was made, and the ensuing years have seen growing awareness and, more recently, even alarm at the rising presence of the old in American life. Demographically, seniors now account for 12 percent of the population, a figure which is expected to rise to 20 percent by 2030 as the boomers complete their entry into old age. Sociologically, old age has become "a distinct phase of life" (Kohli 1988) or, in Peter Laslett's (1987, 134) words, has emerged as "a third age" which by the 1980s "had became a settled feature of the industrial nations." Economically, the aged are no longer almost universally poor. Due largely to the growth of Social Security, between 1960 and 2004, poverty among the elderly decreased from just under 40 percent to a fraction over 10 percent. From 1967 to 1992, the median income of those aged 65 and above (in 1992 dollars) rose from $8,940 to $15,143, or 69 percent, compared to an increase of only 26 percent among those 64 and younger, from $16,994 to $21,330 (Radner 1996).

By the late twentieth century, the most notable culmination of these trends was the emergence of retirement as a distinctive and institutionalized stage of life (Atchley 1982). Largely unknown early in the last century, by its end, retirement had become an established expectation of most workers. Between 1950 and 1990, the percentage of men aged 65 and above in the labor force fell from 45.8 percent to 16.3 percent (Purcell 2000). Once a dreaded event—being given a gold watch and ushered out the door—retirement came to be eagerly anticipated by most workers a few decades later. As noted by labor organizer Jerry Flint:

> There used to be a stigma to going out. He was over the hill. But now it's a looked-for status. Those retirement parties, they used to be sad affairs. They are darn happy affairs now. The peer pressure is for early retirement. (Schulz 1984, 84)

Recently, however, a notable countertrend has emerged, requiring nothing less than "reconsidering retirement" (Morris and Bass 1988). Most notably, labor force participation rates among older men appear to have at least partially reversed, rising from 1990's 16.3 percent to an estimated 17.8 percent in 2008. Pressures on retirement are coming from a number of directions: older workers facing the prospect of inadequate retirement incomes (Munnell, Sass, and Aubry 2006); employers contemplating possible labor shortages given the low growth rates of young and middle-aged populations (and actually negative for those aged 35 to 44) (Dychtwald, Erickson, and Morison 2004); and the government worried about escalating public pension and health care costs (Walker 2007).

Importantly, these pressures are coming to a head just as the boomers attain old age. Their road to retirement will be noticeably different than that of their parents, and it stands as one of the major challenges that the boomers and society will face in the decades ahead.

The New Political Standing of Older Americans

Not surprisingly, the growing social and economic presence of the elderly now extends to the world of politics and policy. Once a relatively small, needy, and residual population, older people have now come to command a very prominent position in American public life. Their heightened role in politics is seen most directly through increasing levels of political participation. Their place in policy is seen through growing expenditures under public income and health care programs, notably Social Security and Medicare. Indeed, an almost synergistic interplay between political participation and policy outcomes has been shown by recent scholarship to centrally account for the dramatic increase in seniors' new political standing.

On the political side of this equation, the most notable indicator of new senior involvement is found through their voting behavior. Looking at the percentages of different age groups voting from 1964 to 2004 (see table 7-1), seniors emerge as the only voting age population group whose rate of electoral participation has actually increased. Senior participation has slightly risen over this period, while it has notably decreased for all three younger groups, especially among those aged 18–44. As a result of these countertrends, seniors today have higher voting rates than all other age

TABLE 7-1. Percentage of Voting Age Persons, by Age Group, Who Voted in Presidential Elections, 1964–2004

Year	Age Group			
	18–24	25–44	45–64	65+
1964	51	69	76	66
1968	50	67	75	66
1972	50	63	71	64
1976	42	59	69	62
1980	40	59	69	65
1984	41	58	70	68
1988	36	54	68	69
1992	43	58	70	70
1996	32	49	64	68
2000	32	50	64	67
2004	42	52	67	69

Source: U.S. Census Bureau, Current Population Survey, November 2004 and earlier reports.

groups, whereas in 1964, they exceeded only the youngest group. The lament most usually drawn from data such as these follows from their strong suggestion that Americans are becoming increasingly disconnected and even alienated from politics. Certainly, the drop in the voting percentage of the two younger groups, by 18 percent and 25 percent, respectively, is certainly a cause for alarm. For purposes here, however, the critical finding is that, being the only age group whose participation is increasing, seniors are finding reasons to participate while others are not.

There are additional measures documenting seniors' new interest in politics. As carefully documented by Campbell (2003), other forms of political participation—being informed, letter-writing, campaigning, contributing—also show absolute and relative increases among senior citizens over the past half-century. The establishment of retirement as a defined role, increasing economic well-being, and more leisure time have each given seniors a heightened political identity that has been translated into political behaviors such as these.

The role of older people in politics has also expanded through interest group representation, a relatively recent phenomenon. With the fleeting exception of the Townsend Movement (Holtzman 1963; Amenta 2006) of the Depression years, older people had no organized political presence until the 1960s. Indeed, Henry Pratt (1976) refers to the period from the early 1940s to the mid-1950s as the "dismal years" for senior political organizations. The most well-known of the groups—the American Association of Retired Persons (renamed AARP in the mid-1990s to formalize its interest in issues beyond "retirement")—was formed in 1958. It, in turn, was an outgrowth of a predecessor organization (the National Retired Teachers Association), which had been formed as an organizational consequence of a life insurance company identifying and selling policies to retired teachers beginning in the late 1940s.

A second mass-membership organization—the National Council of Senior Citizens (NCSC)—emerged from the "Senior Citizens for Kennedy" movement formed around the 1960 presidential election; NCSC continued to lobby for Medicare's enactment after the election and then to lobby on behalf of issues of concern to retired blue-collar workers. In this expansive period, circa 1960–1975, numerous other groups appeared, most of them made up of largely nonelderly professionals working on behalf of older people (and, critics argued, themselves), including service providers, advocates, academic researchers, and public officials running public programs directed at seniors (Binstock 1972). In the ensuing years, the number of such groups continued to grow. Their new presence was formalized through the creation of the Leadership Council of Aging Organization (LCAO), an organization itself made up of other aging-related organizations.

As if further evidence were needed, LCAO's creation symbolized that older people had arrived in Washington in a big way. As detailed in table 7-2, LCAO now counts 54 organizations as its members. There is debate

TABLE 7-2. Members of the Leadership Council of Aging Organizations

•AARP	•National Adult Day Services Association (NADSA)
•AFL-CIO Department of Public Policy (AFL-CIO)	•National Asian Pacific Center on Aging (NAPCA)
•AFSCME Retiree Program (AFSCME)	•National Association for Home Care (NAHC)
•Alliance for Aging Research (AAR)	•National Association of Area Agencies on Aging (N4A)
•Alliance for Retired Americans	•National Association of Foster Grandparent Program Directors (NAFGPD)
•Alzheimer's Association	•National Association of Nutrition and Aging Services Programs (NANASP)
•American Association for International Aging (AAIA)	•National Association of Professional Geriatric Care Managers (NAPGCM)
•American Association of Homes and Services for the Aging (AAHSA)	•National Association of Retired and Senior Volunteer Program Directors, Inc. (NARSVPD)
•American Federation of Teachers Program on Retirement & Retirees (AFT)	•National Active and Retired Federal Employees Association (NARFE)
•American Foundation for the Blind	•National Senior Corps Association
•American Geriatrics Society (AGS)	•National Association of Social Workers (NASW)
•American Postal Workers Union Retirees	•National Association of State Long Term Care Ombudsman Programs (NASOP)
•American Public Health Association	•National Association of State Units on Aging (NASUA)
•American Society of Consultant Pharmacists (ASCP)	•National Caucus and Center on Black Aged, Inc. (NCBA)
•American Society on Aging (ASA)	•National Committee to Preserve Social Security and Medicare (NCPSSM)
•Asociacion Nacional pro Personas Mayores (ANPPM) (National Association For Hispanic Elderly)	•National Citizens Coalition on Nursing Home Reform
•Association for Gerontology and Human Development in Historically Black Colleges and Universities (AGHDHBCU)	•National Council on the Aging, Inc. (NCOA)
•Association of Jewish Aging Services (AJAS)	•National Hispanic Council on Aging (NHCOA)
•B'nai B'rith International	•National Indian Council on Aging, Inc. (NICOA)
•Catholic Health Association of the United States (CHA)	•National Osteoporosis Foundation (NOF)

(Continued)

•Eldercare America, Inc.

•Experience Works, Inc.

•Families USA

•The Gerontological Society of America (GSA)

•Gray Panthers

•International Union, United Auto Workers

•Meals On Wheels Association Of America (MOWAA)

•Military Officers Association of America (MOAA)

•National Academy of Elder Law Attorneys (NAELA)

•National Senior Citizens Law Center (NSCLC)

•Older Women's League (OWL)

•Service Employees International Union Retired Members Program (SEIU)

•United Jewish Communities

•Volunteers of America

Source: Leadership Council of Aging Organizations, http://www.lcao.org/membership.htm.

among observers about how effectively LCAO and these groups actually represent the elderly in Washington, but doing so is clearly their formal intent: LCAO is "concerned with the well-being of America's older population and is committed to representing their interests in the policy-making arena" (LCAO 2006). The mass membership groups can most clearly make that claim, but a literature on the "professionalization" of citizen representation in the form of paid staffs and a growing bureaucracy argues that even these claims may be suspect (Skocpol 1996). The activities of the provider groups tend to be focused more directly on legislation directly affecting that provision.

The New Policy Standing of Older Americans

These aging-related demographic, social, economic, and political trends have been accompanied by major policy developments. Since the 1970s, this has been seen less in new authorizations (i.e., new legislation on behalf of the old) than in greatly expanded appropriations under existing authorizations. The only new major legislation enacted since the late 1970s has been the Medicare Part D prescription drug program passed in 2003. Modest expansions have taken place under the Older Americans Act, new financing and delivery provisions have been added to Medicare, and potentially expansionary waivers have been introduced under Medicaid, but nothing approximating the floodgate of new legislation of the 1965–1974 period has been seen since.

Expenditures on behalf of seniors have been an entirely different story. Because the three largest programs affecting the old (and three of the largest items in the entire federal budget)—Social Security, Medicare, and Medicaid—are "entitlement programs," the government is required to provide benefits to all individuals meeting eligibility requirements. Put differently, the money must be made available independent of the annual appropriations process associated with most other programs (Weaver 1988). Because the older population is growing, because Old Age and Survivors benefits under Social Security are indexed to current wages and adjusted for future cost-of-living increases, and because medical inflation and technology are driving health care costs higher (including those under Medicare and Medicaid), federal expenditures on behalf of the old are rising rapidly. Table 7-3 makes clear both the sizable nature of these expenditures and the degree to which they are increasing over time.

The Critical Relationship between Aging Policy and Politics

Beyond noting the dramatic rise in the standing of the old in the world of politics, it is important to say a word about how this has come about or, more exactly, what is driving what. This is not just of interest for academic purposes; rather, it is important because it says a great deal about the public-sector prospects of the baby-boom generation. As we will note in the chapter's concluding section, the boomers are about to face a political arena that will be both more inclusive and more contentious than any that older people have faced to this point. The respective roles of aging-related policies and politics will say much about how these future events play out.

It has long been conventional wisdom that the rise of aging-based policy was the result of large numbers of increasingly well-organized older people voting, organizing, and lobbying for such benefits. This understanding was found in both scholarly (Pratt 1976; Price 1997) and popular treatments (Thurow 1996; Peterson, 1999). While there can be no question of the aged's growing presence in politics, the question remains as to whether our major public policies on aging in fact owe their existence to this newfound presence.

Recent scholarship suggests that this is probably not the case. Indeed, the causal connection may be the other way around: it is the policies themselves that have helped create the political identity and organization that older people unquestionably enjoy today. A simple chronology hints at this possibility when one notes that significant policy enactments and expansions appear to have *preceded* rather than followed group developments. Thus, AARP had virtually no political presence until the 1970s, and one of its first political statements was to oppose as inflationary a 1972 Democratic proposal to raise Social Security benefits by 20 percent (Pratt 1976).

In his now-classic treatment "The Origins and Maintenance of Interest Groups in America," political scientist Jack Walker (1983) highlighted the interplay of aging-related groups and policies, noting that more than half of

TABLE 7-3. Estimated Federal Spending for the Elderly under Selected Programs, 1971–2010 (by fiscal year, in billions of dollars)

	1971	1980	1990	2000	Projected 2010
Mandatory Programs					
Social Security	29	85	196	307	471
Federal Civilian Retirement	2	8	21	33	50
Military Retirement	1	2	7	14	21
Annuitants' Health Benefits	*	1	2	4	9
Benefits for Coal Miners/ Black Lung	*	1	1	1	1
Supplemental Security Income	1	2	4	6	10
Veterans' Compensation & Pensions	1	7	4	9	14
Medicare	8	29	96	189	377
Medicaid	2	5	14	33	77
Food Stamps	*	1	1	1	1
Total	*44*	*137*	*349*	*597*	*1,026*
Discretionary Programs					
Housing	*	2	4	7	10
Veterans' Medical Care	1	3	6	9	13
Administration on Aging Programs	*	1	1	1	1
Low Income Energy Assistance	n.a.	*	*	*	1
Total	*1*	*6*	*11*	*17*	*24*
Federal Spending on People 65 and Over					
Total, all federal spending	46	144	360	615	1,050
As a % of the Budget	21.7	24.3	28.7	34.8	42.8
As a % of GDP	4.2	5.3	6.3	6.4	7.1
Per elderly person (in 2000 $)	8,896	11,839	15,192	17,688	21,122

* = less than $500 million; n.a. = not applicable

Source: Congressional Budget Office (2002).

the 43 aging interest groups in his study came into existence after 1965, the touchstone year that saw the enactment of Medicare, Medicaid, and the Older Americans Act. In Walker's words:

> In all of these cases, the formation of new groups was one of the *consequences* of major new legislation, not one of the *causes* of its passage. A pressure model of the policymaking process in which an essentially passive legislature

responds to petitions from groups of citizens who have spontaneously organized because of common social or economic concerns must yield to a model in which influences for change come as much from inside the government as from beyond its institutional boundaries. (403)

Being entirely about service provision rather than direct benefits to seniors, the Older Americans Act provides a concrete example of this process. The state agencies charged with administering the program formalized their trade association, the National Association of State Units on Aging, in the years after 1965, and the sub-state agencies brought into existence through amendments in 1972 created their trade association, the National Association of Area Agencies on Aging, in the wake of that authorization. Groups of nutrition, transportation, and legal-service providers were also formed subsequent to the legislative events.

Yet more compelling evidence of the policy-to-politics chain is seen in the realization of seniors themselves as a self-identified political constituency. In her pathbreaking book *How Policies Make Citizens: Senior Political Activism and the American Welfare State*, Andrea Campbell (2003) documents how the now imposing political presence of older people owes much of its existence to the expansion of Social Security. In carefully crafted research juxtaposing public opinion and voting data with Social Security program expansion, Campbell shows how levels of political consciousness, participation, and salience followed in the wake of Social Security's growth. She goes on to argue that the program, in dramatically improving the economic well-being of older people, created both time and interest for seniors to involve themselves in political matters more heavily than had ever been the case.

> Senior mass membership groups did not create Social Security policy. Rather, the policy helped create the groups. Social Security's effects on individual—the increases in income, free time due to retirement, and political interest—enhance the likelihood of group membership. Social Security created a constituency for interest group entrepreneurs to organize, just as it defined a group for political parties to mobilize. (77)

While the causal role of policy is the principal contribution of this analysis, the secondary effects of policy's role are equally important. Thus, at "Time 1," public policy may have been critical in the creation and institutionalization of the organized aging, but at "Time 2," the groups became critical in efforts to expand or—more recently—to defend the policies against outside encroachment. Put differently, the Walker/Campbell argument does not dismiss the role of interest groups; rather, it helps explain both their origins and the dynamic—namely, benefit protection—that keeps formal members or informal adherents tuned in to their messages. In short, "AARP may be the biggest lobby in Washington," but AARP would not be where it is if (1) Social Security had not helped galvanize the elderly and (2) Social

Security and other programs were not there as a policy fulcrum around which AARP could rally the membership.

AGING BOOMERS AND PUBLIC POLICY

The baby boomers entering old age in 2011 are facing a far different policy world than did their grandparents and parents. For the thirty-year period following the passage of Social Security, the aged were a marginal population being served by extremely modest programs. For those entering old age about the time of Medicare's enactment in 1965, new programs and program benefits were to bring with them levels of well-being and opportunity unequaled by any previous older generation. For the boomers about to enter old age, there is good news and bad news: the benefits are still there, but a host of pressures will be brought to bear on their future size and direction.

The list of factors behind these pressures is well known (and reviewed in detail elsewhere in these volumes). The growth in aging-related expenditures for retirement income and especially health care programs will surely be reined in from what current policy would otherwise allow. Pressures for older boomers to remain in the labor force are certain to build as they contemplate retirement in the face of smaller succeeding generations being potentially unable to meet the demand for workers, skilled and unskilled alike. Finally, the improved well-being of the older boomer generation— brought about in part by the very programs being brought under pressure— will lead to questions of relative need and equity in the face of growing cost and competing budgetary pressures. These costs and pressures might focus on "young versus old" or perhaps on the "well-off versus the less well-off," or even on "younger, less well-off populations of color versus relatively well-off non-Hispanic whites." These are some of the potential political fault lines older boomers could confront.

Yet, the evidence presents a far from certain picture that major fissures will open along age and generational lines. The "politics" evidence, as reviewed in the next two chapters by Robert Binstock, John Williamson, and Diane Watts-Roy, does not point to sharp intergenerational (or inter-ethnic) polarization, although efforts to frame issues in those terms are certain to persist. In the face of the various pressures that are building, it is important to note that there is no sociological or anthropological literature suggesting deep-seated animosity among older and younger people (Bengtson, Marti, and Roberts 1991). Moreover, myriad surveys centered on the enormous Social Security program find, if anything, that younger people are more supportive of the program than are older ones, with over 90 percent of all age groups favoring the program's maintenance at either current or expanded levels (Cook 2002).

More likely will be policy initiatives centered on "deconstructing" the older population, acknowledging increasing levels of intragenerational diversity in well-being among older boomers. This could lead to more means-testing or, for the well-off, "affluence-testing" being introduced into the major entitlement programs. Such means-testing might not only be confined to questions of income. So-called functional means-testing has been selectively introduced into health and social service programs, signifying that one must be frail as well as poor (and perhaps without a relative or other "informal" caregiver to lend assistance) in order to receive public benefits.

Another widely discussed idea among those wishing to curtail age-related benefits on both political and administrative grounds is raising the age of eligibility for various age-based programs. Raising the normal retirement age for Old Age Insurance benefits not only is an administratively efficient way of cutting future benefits but also reasserts (a now higher) advanced age as a reasonably proxy for being in need of social protection. Public pension policy has always been central to defining old age (Otto von Bismarck was the first to "create" the threshold of old age as 65 in German legislation in the late 1880s). It is nonetheless a matter of great controversy whether we wish to essentially "re-residualize" old age by postponing the retirement age in light of strides that have been made in recent decades to improve the well-being of the "current" older population, that is, those aged 65 and above (Hudson 1999). With the age for full benefits already scheduled to rise to 66 in 2009, a step in this direction has already been taken.

Nor will pressures to raise eligibility levels derive from cost-cutting concerns alone. The very considerable growth of the "old-old" population of boomers beginning around 2020 will mean added long-term care expenditures, an area where the federal government's response long has been seen as inadequate when compared to acute health care expenditures under Medicare, a program designed for a notably different older population than the one rising now (see chapter 12 in this volume). Chronic illnesses of the very old constitute the looming health care crisis facing the long-lived boomers. A report commissioned by the Alzheimer's Association (2008), finds that Medicare spent $91 billion on people with Alzheimer's and other dementias in 2005, and that number is expected to climb to $160 billion by 2010 and $189 billion by 2015.

In the face of these pressures, the remaining question is how the boomers will respond. Ideologically, the boomers are somewhat to the right of the Depression-era generation that preceded them, but probably not to such a degree that their "interest-specific" concerns around Social Security and Medicare would lead them to abandon their vested interest in such programs. Yet, many boomers themselves realize that they are better off and have the potential to make greater societal contributions than did predecessor generations. Whether it be through extended work years, voluntarism, civic engagement, or family caregiving, there is some reason to believe that the ratio of boomers' "contributions" to their "drawdowns" will be higher than those who came before. Indeed, the literature on intergenerational transfers finds considerably more movement of resources from the old to the middle-aged and young than the reverse. Nonetheless, it is hard to argue that private and informal transfers from old to young will politically offset public and formal ones from young to old. Ultimately, in the words of Williamson and Watts-Roy, it will make an enormous difference whether these inevitable tensions get played out using an "intergenerational equity" frame or an "intergenerational reciprocity" one.

It is conceivable but unlikely that the fiscal pressures may prove to be such that most observers, including the boomers, will agree that reforms must be made. European experience suggests that this can be done, though not without considerable controversy. Because age is a less salient feature of both politics and policy in the European nations and because their decision-making structures have historically been more centralized than those in the United States, it is far from certain that the U.S. system could pull off inclusive and redistributive allocations around these issues. It is also the case that the U.S. demographic profile is more "favorable," in that higher fertility rates and patterns of immigration mean that the country will continue to have relatively fewer older people than is the case in Europe. It thus seems that, in policy terms, we may limp along, broadly understanding that something must be done. Absent a real (or manufactured) crisis atmosphere, it seems likely that the contending forces will be at loggerheads, and such stalemate may well put off the day of reckoning.

For old-age income supports and Social Security, this would not be the worst of all outcomes. A reasonable case can be made that older people will work and contribute longer, and adjustments can be made in the program to maintain its viability well into the future. However, health care costs and Medicare/Medicaid are a different story. But here the issue is less about aging and older people than it is about medical inflation and technological/pharmaceutical innovation. Meeting this health care challenge will be extraordinarily difficult, but it is not principally about the boomers and should not be cast in that light.

REFERENCES

Allen, M. 2005. Congressional Republicans agree to launch Social Security campaign. *Washington Post.* January 31.

Alzheimer's Association. 2008. *2008 Alzheimer's disease facts and figures.* Chicago: Alzheimer's Association.

Amenta, E. 2006. *When movements matter: The Townsend movement and the rise of Social Security.* Princeton, NJ: Princeton University Press.

Atchley, R. 1982. Retirement as a social institution. *Review of Sociology* 8:263–87.

Bengtson, V., G. Marti, and R. E. L. Roberts. 1989. Age-group relationships: Generational equity and inequity. In *Parent–child relationships throughout life,* ed. K. Pillemer and K. McCartney, 253–78. London: Routledge.

Binstock, R. H. 1972. Interest-group liberalism and the politics of aging. *Gerontologist* 12:265–80.

Burke, V. J., and V. Burke. 1974. *Nixon's good deed: Welfare reform*. New York: Columbia University Press.

Campbell, A. L. 2003. *How policies make citizens: Senior political activism and the American welfare state*. Princeton, NJ: Princeton University Press.

Center for Medicare and Medicaid Services. 2007. *National health expenditures*. Washington, DC: Office of the Actuary, Center for Medicare and Medicaid Services.

Cook, F. L., with L. Jacobs. 2002. Assessing assumptions about Americans' attitudes about Social Security: Popular claims meet hard data. In *The future of social insurance*, ed. P. Edelman and D. L. Salisbury, 82–110. Washington, DC: Brookings Institution Press.

Dychtwald, K., T. Erickson, and B. Morison. 2004. It's time to retire retirement. *Public Policy & Aging Report* 14 (3): 1, 23–27.

Federal Interagency Forum on Aging-Related Statistics. 2007. *Older Americans update, 2006: Key indicators of well-being*. Washington, DC: U.S. Administration on Aging. Available at http://agingstats.gov/agingstatsdotnet/Main_Site/Data/2006_Documents/slides/OA_2006.ppt.

Gordon, L. 1994. *Pitied but not entitled: Single mothers and the history of welfare*. Cambridge, MA: Harvard University Press.

Greenspan Commission. 1983. *Report of the National Commission on Social Security Reform*. Available at http://www.ssa.gov/history/reports/gspan.html.

Himelfarb, R. 1995. *Catastrophic politics: The rise and fall of the Medicare Catastrophic Care Coverage Act of 1988*. University Park: Pennsylvania State University Press.

Holtzman, A. 1963. *The Townsend Movement: A political study*. New York: Bookman Associates.

Hudson, R. B. 1978. The graying of the federal budget and its consequences for old-age policy. *Gerontologist* 18:428–40.

———. 1999. Conflict in today's aging policy: New population encounters old ideology. *Social Service Review* 73 (3): 358–79.

Katz, M. 1996. *In the shadow of the poorhouse*. New York: Basic Books.

Kohli, M. 1988. Ageing as a challenge for sociological theory. *Ageing and Society* 8:367–94.

Laslett, P. 1987. The emergence of "the third age." *Ageing and Society* 7:133–66.

LCAO (Leadership Council of Aging Organization). 2006. Our mission. http://www.lcao.org/our_mission.htm.

Lipset, S. M. 1996. *American exceptionalism: A double-edged sword*. New York: W. W. Norton.

Marmor, T. 1970. *The politics of Medicare*. Chicago: Aldine.

Morris, R., and S. Bass. 1988. *Retirement Reconsidered*. New York: Springer.

Moynihan, D. P. 1973. *The politics of a guaranteed income: The Nixon administration and the Family Assistance Plan*. New York: Vintage.

Munnell, A., S. A. Sass, and J. P. Aubry. 2006. *Employer survey: 1 of 4 boomers won't retire because they can't*. Issue Brief, Series 6. Chestnut Hill, MA: Center for Retirement Research.

Myles, J., and J. Quadagno. 2002. Political theories of the welfare state. *Social Service Review* 75 (1): 34–58.

Orloff, A. S. 1988. The political origins of America's belated welfare state. In *The politics of social policy in the United States*, ed. M. Weir, A. S. Orloff, and T. Skocpol. Princeton, NJ: Princeton University Press.

Pear, R. 2003. Medicare plan covering drugs backed by AARP. *New York Times*. November 18.

Peterson, P. G. 1999. *Gray dawn: How the coming age wave will transform America —and the world*. New York: Times Books.

Pierson, P. 1995. *Dismantling the welfare state? Reagan, Thatcher, and the politics of retrenchment*. New York: Cambridge University Press.

Pratt, H. 1976. *The gray lobby*. Chicago: University of Chicago Press.

Price, M. C. 1997. *Justice between generations: The growing power of the elderly in America*. Westport, CT: Greenwood Press.

Purcell, P. 2000. Older workers: Employment and retirement trends. *Monthly Labor Review* (10): 19–30.

Quadagno, J. 2005. *One nation, uninsured*. New York: Oxford University Press.

Radner, D. 1996. Incomes of the elderly and non-elderly. *Social Security Bulletin* 58:82–97.

Rimlinger, G. 1971. *Welfare policy and industrialization in Europe, America, and Russia*. New York: John Wiley.

Rubinow, I. 1934. *The quest for security*. New York: Henry Holt.

Schneider, A., and H. Ingram. 1993. Social construction of target populations. *American Political Science Review* 87 (2): 334–47.

Schulz, J. S. 1984. *The Economics of Aging*. 4th ed. New York: Auburn House.

Senate Committee on Aging. 1972. *Developments in Aging, 1972*. Report 93-147. Washington, DC: GPO.

Skocpol, T. 1993. *Protecting soldiers and mothers*. Cambridge, MA: Belknap Press of Harvard University Press.

———. 1996. Advocates without members: The recent transformation of American civic life. In *Civic engagement in American democracy*, ed. T. Skocpol and M. Fiorina. Washington, DC: Brookings Institution Press, 461–509.

Skocpol, T., and J. Ikenberry. 1987. Expanding social benefits: The role of Social Security. *Political Science Quarterly* 102 (3): 389–417.

Smith, D. 2002. *Entitlement politics: Medicare and Medicaid, 1995–2001*. New York: Aldine de Gruyter.

Thurow, L. C. 1996. The birth of a revolutionary class. *New York Times Magazine*, May 19, 46–47.

Upp, M. 1982. A look at the economic status of the aged then and now. *Social Security Bulletin* 45:16–20.

Walker, D. 2007. Testimony before Senate Budget Committee by the Comptroller General of the United States. January 11.

Walker, J. 1983. The origins and maintenance of interest groups in America. *American Political Science Review* 77:390–406.

Weaver, J. 1988. *Automatic government: The politics of indexation*. Washington, DC: Brookings Institution.

Weisberg, J. 2005. Bush's first defeat: The President has lost on Social Security. *Slate*, March 31, http://www.slate.com/id/2115141/.

Wilensky, H., and C. Lebeaux. 1958. *Industrial society and social welfare*. New York: Free Press.

8

The Boomers in Politics: Impact and Consequences

ROBERT H. BINSTOCK*

More than three decades ago (in 1974), the prestigious American Association for the Advancement of Science (AAAS) sponsored a symposium entitled "The 1990s and Beyond: A Gerontocracy?" It raised and seriously addressed the question of whether the United States would become a country dominated and ruled by elders. Although many members of Congress and other political leaders are of advanced age, they were not the focus of the AAAS discussion. Rather, the symposium focused on the political consequences of population aging and presented different views regarding the likely effects of demographic change on the outcome of national elections. The general answer from the panelists was that an America with a much larger population of elders would see only a modest change in American politics in the twenty-first century.

But in recent years, a number of prominent opinion makers believe that older people will soon play a much stronger role in politics than in the past because of the 76 million baby boomers now beginning to join the ranks of old age and becoming eligible for Social Security and Medicare. Some of these opinion makers envision such a powerful role for the boomers in politics that they have virtually become prophets of doom. Among them is Peter

*Some portions of this chapter are adapted from *Aging Nation: The Economics and Politics of Growing Older in America*, by James H. Schulz and Robert H. Binstock, copyright 2006, with the permission of Greenwood Publishing Group, Inc., Westport, CT.

G. Peterson, a Wall Street financier and former secretary of commerce. For years, he has argued that government obligations under these old-age entitlement programs must be drastically reduced and has warned that the political power of boomers may make these reforms difficult, if not impossible:

> Will global aging enthrone organized elders as an invincible political titan? ... Picture retiring boomers, with inflated economic expectations and inadequate nest eggs, voting down school budgets, cannibalizing the nation's infrastructure, and demanding ever-steeper hikes in payroll taxes. (1999, 209)

Peterson is so concerned about the impact of boomers on politics that he has established a foundation, to be funded by a billion dollars of his personal assets, to carry forward his message. According to a report in the *New York Times*, one of his specific objectives "is organizing a youthful equivalent to the powerful lobby group for seniors, AARP" (Thomas 2008, C4).

Similarly, MIT economist Lester Thurow has depicted aging boomers as a dominant bloc of voters whose self-interested pursuit of government benefits will pose a fundamental threat to our democracy:

> No one knows how the growth of entitlements can be held in check in democratic societies.... Will democratic governments be able to cut benefits when the elderly are approaching a voting majority? Universal suffrage ... is going to meet the ultimate test in the elderly. If democratic governments cannot cut benefits that go to a majority of their voters, then they have no long-term future.... In the years ahead, class warfare is apt to be redefined as the young against the old, rather than the poor against the rich. (1996, 47)

Are Peterson and Thurow—and the many pundits, think tank analysts, journalists, and public academicians who share their perspective—correct in their view that elderly boomers will dominate American politics as they strive to maintain and enhance their old-age benefits? Will boomers band together with other elders to engage in generational conflict over taxes and spending? Or will the politics of aging be much as is it is today?

A good place to start in answering these questions is by considering what we know about participation in politics by cohorts of older persons in recent decades. Then we can consider whether and how the broader arena of politics may change in the years ahead, perhaps leading older boomers to behave politically in a fashion different from their predecessor cohorts.

POLITICAL PARTICIPATION BY OLDER PERSONS

There is little doubt that older Americans are highly engaged in political participation today. They vote, contribute to and work in political campaigns, contact public officials, serve on local public advisory boards and councils on aging, and participate in political processes created especially for them such as White House Conferences on Aging and, at the state level, "Silver-Haired

Legislatures." In addition, millions of them belong to mass membership organizations that engage in political activity. As MIT political scientist Andrea Campbell (2003, 65) has observed, older persons "are indeed *senior citizens*, fully incorporated into social and political citizenship."

Voting

Voting is the type of political activity by older persons that is most amenable to nationwide, ongoing documentation (through U.S. Census data and election exit polls). It is also the arena of activity that is most widely publicized. As elections approach, especially presidential elections, journalists, pollsters, and campaign strategists mobilize a perennial cliché: *Senior voters are a key battleground in this election.*

One reason for this cliché is that older persons are a readily identifiable program constituency that has been created by old-age public policies such as Social Security and Medicare. Therefore, seniors are a tempting campaign target, particularly because they are potentially "swing voters," not committed heavily as a bloc to either Democrats or Republicans.

A second reason why older people are viewed as an important electoral target is that they turn out to vote at a higher rate than do members of other age groups. As table 8-1 shows, in the past seven U.S. presidential elections individuals aged 65 and older voted at a substantially higher rate than those in the 18–24 and 25–44 age groups, and (except in 1980 and 1984) as high as or higher than the 45–64 age group. The same general pattern of age group turnouts has occurred in the last seven midterm elections.

As a consequence of their comparatively high voting rate, older Americans have typically constituted a larger share of those who actually vote than they are of the voting-age population. For instance, in the 2004 presidential election, voters aged 65 and older cast 19 percent of the votes, even though they were only 16 percent of the voting-age population (U.S. Census Bureau 2005).

Reasons for High Participation Rates

Why do older persons vote at a higher rate than younger persons? This is a difficult question to answer, because the various age brackets for which

TABLE 8-1.   Percentage of Voting-Age Persons Who Voted in U.S. Presidential Elections, by Age Groups, 1980–2004

Age Group	1980	1984	1988	1992	1996	2000	2004
18–24	40%	41%	36%	43%	32%	32%	42%
25–44	59	58	54	58	49	50	52
45–64	69	70	68	70	64	64	67
65+	65	68	69	70	68	67	69

Source: U. S. Census Bureau, 2005.

voting is reported have comprised different birth cohorts over time, and the political context of each election is somewhat unique. Moreover, although the connection between age and voting participation has been investigated a great deal, overall the reasons for the relationship remain rather controversial.

One factor that contributes to the relatively high turnout rates in old age is age group differences in voting *registration*, an essential precursor to voting. Table 8-2 shows that in the presidential elections from 1980 through 2004, the rate of registration among persons aged 65 and older was usually the highest among age groups, and substantially higher than the youngest groups.

A two-stage study of voter registration and turnout in national elections (Timpone 1998) found that increased age (from age 18 to 88) is monotonically related to being registered (as generally reflected in table 8-2). It also found that age was the second most influential factor (among twenty-one variables) in distinguishing between registrants and nonregistrants. Another aging-related factor, length of residence in one's home, also had a substantial influence on registration.

An additional phenomenon that may contribute to the high voting rates among older people is that persons who are comparatively well informed about politics and public affairs are more likely to register and vote. As McManus (1996, 35) observes, "Older persons are more likely to pay attention to the news and to rely upon a wider array of news sources to follow public affairs." More specifically, older people tend to be more generally knowledgeable about politics than younger people. In studies and surveys of different cohorts over the years, older persons report the highest level of interest in political campaigns and public affairs generally, and their level of political knowledge shows no sign of decline as they reach advanced old age. Campbell (2003) argues that the very existence of Social Security has fostered seniors' interest in public affairs and enhanced their feelings of political efficacy as they have achieved the notice of public officials.

Still another contributing factor to the high voting rate of older persons is the well-established connection between the strength of political party identification and higher rates of voting participation. Strong partisans are most likely to vote. And older persons identify with the major political parties more strongly than younger persons because their partisan attachments have been reinforced over a long period of time (McManus 1996).

TABLE 8-2. Percentage of Persons Registered to Vote in U.S. Presidential Elections, by Age Groups, 1980–2004

Age Group	1980	1984	1988	1992	1996	2000	2004
18–24	49%	51%	48%	53%	49%	45%	52%
25–44	66	67	63	65	62	60	60
45–64	76	77	76	74	74	71	73
65+	75	77	78	77	77	76	77

Source: U.S. Census Bureau, 1998.

Electoral Impact

What impact does the high rate of voting participation by older Americans have on elections?

One definite effect is that candidates for office make an effort to court the "senior vote" with policy statements and appear during election campaigns at many senior centers and other settings where older persons congregate. In 2000, for example, both Al Gore and George W. Bush widely promised they would establish prescription drug coverage under Medicare. In 2004, President Bush, while promoting his proposal for partially privatizing Social Security, took pains to repeatedly assert that current seniors and near-seniors would be protected from benefit reductions. Senator John Kerry wooed senior voters by implying that Bush's proposal would lead to benefit cuts for these same older groups and vowed that he would make feasible the importation of relatively inexpensive prescription drugs from Canada in order to make up for poor drug coverage under Medicare.

On the other hand, the high voting participation rate of older persons *does not* have a distinctive impact on the *outcome* of elections. *To date, older Americans have not shown any tendency to vote as a bloc.*

Over the years, voters aged 60 and older (the oldest age range consistently reported in exit polls throughout recent decades) have tended to distribute their votes among candidates in presidential elections[1] roughly in the same proportions as other age groups (except 18- to 29-year-olds) and the electorate as a whole. As can be seen in figure 8-1, for example, in the vote for Republican presidential candidates from 1980 through 2004, the gap in votes between older voters and the overall electorate ranged from

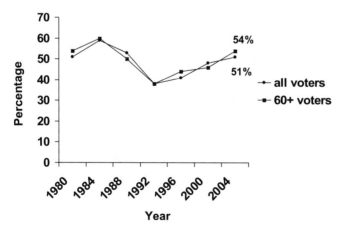

FIGURE 8-1.   Percent of All Voters and Voters Aged 60+ Voting for Republican Presidential Candidates, 1980–2004

Source: Connelly, M. 2004. "How Americans Voted: A political Portrait." *New York Times*, Nov. 7: 4wk.

three percentage points in several elections to nonexistent in the 1992 election. In those instances when the gap reached three percentage points, the difference has not been enough to affect the outcome of the popular vote. In the 2004 election, for instance, if the ballots of voters aged 60 and older had been distributed in the same proportions as the overall national tally—51 percent for Bush and 48 percent for Kerry (rather than the actual 54 percent for Bush and 46 percent for Kerry)—Bush's margin would have been smaller by 1.4 million votes. Nevertheless, Bush still would have had 1.9 million more votes than Kerry (author's calculations, based on data from the Edison/Mitofsky [2004] exit poll).

In addition, there are specific examples that clearly contradict the concept that older persons automatically vote against candidates that don't support old-age entitlements and seek to reduce them. Consider the case of Ronald Reagan. When he ran for president the first time in 1980 he received 54 percent of the elderly vote. After he was elected, he froze an annual cost-of-living increase in Social Security benefits, and he also proposed a more permanent cut in benefits. Yet, when he ran for reelection in 1984, his share of the elderly vote increased to 60 percent—a figure right in line with the 59 percent Reagan received overall (Connelly 2004).

So, despite the fact that older Americans participate in elections at a high rate, there is little indication that they participate *as older persons, per se.* To be sure, they have self-interests in Social Security, Medicare, and other old-age benefit programs. Yet, there are many reasons why older persons do not vote as a self-interested bloc in response to old-age policy issues.

To begin with, there is no sound reason to expect that a birth cohort—diverse in economic and social status, labor force participation, gender, race, ethnicity, religion, education, health status, family status, residential locale, political attitudes, partisan attachments, and every other characteristic in American society—would suddenly become homogenized in self-interests and political behavior when it reaches the old-age category. Old age is only one of many personal characteristics of aged people, and only one with which they may identify themselves.

Moreover, if some older voters primarily identify themselves in terms of their age status, this does not mean that their self-interests in old-age policy issues are the most important factors in their electoral decisions. Of greater importance may be partisan attachments, the characteristics of candidates, policies unrelated to old-age interests (e.g., foreign policy), altruism, and many other campaign stimuli. Even if one assumes that rational self-interest is the major determinant of voting behavior (for voters of all ages), the voter's vision of his or her self-interest may not be the same as the political analyst's. The analyst's "objective" characterization of what is at stake for the voter may not correspond to the voters' subjective judgment. As Nobel Laureate Herbert Simon has described the situation of an individual voter:

Differences in the kind of evidence you respond to may have nothing to do with your utility function. Instead, they may reflect the model you have of the world, the beliefs you have formed about the meanings and predictive value of different kinds of available information, and what information has come to your attention. (1985, 300)

Finally, the self-interests of older people in relation to old-age policy issues, and the intensity of their interests, may vary substantially. Consider, for example, the relative importance of Social Security as a source of income for aged persons who are in the lowest and highest income quintiles. Social Security provides 83 percent of income for those in the lowest quintile, but only 18 percent for those in the highest (Federal Interagency Forum on Aging-Related Statistics 2008). Some older persons have much more at stake than others do in policy proposals that would reduce, maintain, or enhance Social Security benefit payments.

Other Forms of Political Participation

The political engagement of older Americans is hardly confined to Election Day. Campbell's (2003) research on political participation by seniors, summarized below, documents their involvement in other arenas. Their participation rates in these various activities do not match their roughly 70 percent rate of voting. But their engagement is at least comparable to that of other age groups and in some cases greater.

Contributing to Campaigns

Elders make campaign contributions at higher rates than younger persons. In the 2000 presidential campaign, for instance, 13.7 percent of persons aged 65 and older contributed to a campaign; the proportion for 35- to 64-year-olds was 10.5 percent, and for 18- to 34-year-olds it was less than 3 percent. As a consequence, seniors were 28 percent of all contributors. A much smaller proportion of seniors, just 2 percent, work in election campaigns, but this rate of participation is comparable to those in middle-aged and younger groups. In 2000, older persons were 12 percent of campaign workers.

Contacting Representatives

By all accounts from congressional staff members, many older persons are not reticent about contacting their representatives regarding old-age policy issues. This is confirmed by Campbell's analysis of data from the Roper Social and Political Trends Archive, which covers the period from 1973 to 1993. Ten surveys were taken in 1993 that included the following sequence of statement and questions: "Here is a list of things some people do about government or politics. Have you happened to have done any of those things in the past year? Written your Congressman or Senator?" (Campbell 2003, 127). The responses indicated that older persons wrote letters to their senators and representatives at about the same rate as middle-aged persons (13 and 14 percent, respectively) and at about twice the rate of the youngest group (6 percent). However, as Campbell notes, the rate at which older persons contact their representatives can be much higher in response to specific policy events. In 1983, for example, the outlook for sustaining Social Security benefits looked bleak until remedial amendments to the program were enacted. During that year, the rate at which seniors contacted their representatives peaked at 20 percent.

Membership in Politically Active Organizations

Still another avenue of political engagement by older Americans is through membership in a variety of politically active organizations. The political activity of such an organization, however, may or may not be the primary reason that an older person joins it.

The National Committee to Preserve Social Security and Medicare (NCPSSM)—founded in 1982 in the midst of a funding crisis in Social Security—has over a million dues-paying members, most of whom are older persons. There is little question why people join NCPSSM. The general outline of its mission is clear enough from its name, and in fact its primary organizational activity is lobbying Congress regarding old-age benefit programs. Similarly, the Gray Panthers, with a multigenerational membership, was founded in the 1970s explicitly as a political action group to lobby and protest for social justice (including old-age policy issues) for persons of all ages. Members have joined the Gray Panthers because they subscribe to its mission and enjoy solidarity with likeminded fellow members.

In contrast, the incentives that attract some 39 million members to join AARP (formerly the American Association of Retired Persons) are primarily material and solidary, not political. To be sure, AARP engages substantially in lobbying the federal and state governments regarding policies affecting older persons. In 2006, it spent $67 million, about 6.5 percent of its $1.04 billion budget, on public policy research and legislative lobbying (AARP 2008). In addition, it sponsors a number of volunteer programs. But—unlike NCPSSM and the Gray Panthers—much of the organization is engaged in a large business operation that offers to its members auto, health, prescription drug, and long-term care insurance; mutual funds; credit cards; and support for travel (including hotel and automobile discounts). The largest portion ($403 million) of AARP's revenue comes from "royalties and service provider relationship fees" on the products and services that it markets to its members.

However, even if most AARP members may initially join the organization for nonpolitical reasons, a by-product is that the organization heightens political awareness among its members. The monthly *AARP Bulletin* features stories on Social Security, Medicare, other old-age policies, and the organization's stances, thereby engendering and maintaining the interest of members in politics. In turn, this interest can trigger various forms of individual political activity by its members.

Enrollment by older persons in mass-membership old-age organizations also has some major indirect political effects. Public officials are willing to listen to the views of these "representatives of the elderly" and often find it useful to invite such organizations to participate in policy activities. A brief meeting with the leaders of AARP and other old-age organizations enables an official to demonstrate that he or she has been "in touch" (symbolically) with tens of millions of older persons.

This symbolic legitimacy of old-age organizations affords them several types of power. First, they have easy informal access to public officials. Second, their legitimacy enables them to obtain public platforms in the national media, congressional hearings, and other age-related policy forums. And third, old-age interest groups can mobilize their members when changes are being contemplated in old-age programs.

Perhaps the most important form of power available to the old-age interest groups is the "electoral bluff." Although these organizations have not demonstrated a capacity to swing a decisive bloc of older voters, incumbent members of Congress are hardly inclined to risk upsetting the existing distribution of votes that puts them and keeps them in office. The perception of being powerful is, in itself, a source of political influence for these organizations. Hence, when congressional offices are flooded with letters, e-mail messages, faxes, and phone calls expressing the (not necessarily representative) views of older persons, members of Congress do take heed.

In the case of AARP, the electoral bluff has been exploited during the 2000s in relation to major policy decisions regarding Medicare and Social Security (see Schulz and Binstock 2008). The organization's support for the Medicare Prescription Drug Improvement and Modernization Act at a strategic moment in the 2003 legislative process may have been decisive in establishing the program's coverage for prescription drugs, the largest benefit expansion in Medicare since it was originally enacted in 1965. And the strong distaste among all age groups for President Bush's 2005 proposal to privatize Social Security may have been fueled considerably by AARP's public relations campaign against it.

BOOMERS AND THE POLITICS OF AGING

This review of what we know about the modern politics of aging puts us in position to undertake informed speculation regarding what the political milieu will be like when boomers have joined the ranks of older voters. On the one hand, present and past cohorts of older persons have shown no signs of bloc voting as a response to self-interests in old-age benefit programs.

On the other hand, politicians do perceive older voters as an electoral constituency, attempt to appeal to them, and fear retribution from them. This, in turn, gives various types of old-age interest groups opportunities for exercising some degrees of influence regarding a variety of minor old-age policies.

How will these patterns in the politics of aging play out in the decades immediately ahead? Will the political characteristics and behavior of elderly boomers be different from today's and yesterday's elders? Will they band together as an electoral force? Will politicians pander to them—voluntarily or in response to pressures from old-age-based interest groups—by increasing government old-age benefits? Is intergenerational political warfare likely? What broader social forces may shape the future politics of aging?

In general, a reading of the modern history of the politics of aging would support the view that Social Security old-age benefits will be maintained for boomers in a form and level roughly comparable to today's benefits. In no small part, such an outcome would be due to politicians' concerns about the old-age vote and the strong political presence that AARP has established in the early years of this century. Moreover, despite the revenue demands necessary to do this, history as well as current age group attitudes and studies (e.g., Levy and Schlesinger 2005) suggests that there will not be severe intergenerational warfare.

But extrapolation from past and current trends is often a poor mode of prediction in the public policy arena (see, e.g., Aaron 2002), especially when anticipating the state of affairs several decades hence. The prevailing economic and political contexts could be radically different from those of today, giving rise to new forms of age group politics. Some are predicting just such a change.

Boomers and Voting Participation

How accurate is Lester Thurow's suggestion that older persons will become a "voting majority"? When all boomers are age 65 and older in 2030, they will still be only about 27 percent of voting-age American residents, and some of them will not be able to vote because they aren't citizens (cf. U.S. Census Bureau, 1998, 2004).[2] But the share of votes cast by older Americans will probably be even higher than 27 percent.

As noted above, older voters have tended to turn out to vote at a higher rate than younger voters. This pattern will likely continue, even though the various age brackets of voters in the future will be composed of different birth cohorts than in the past. Although some scholars (e.g., Miller and Shanks 1996) have hypothesized that the different age group turnout rates can be explained by cohort replacement, various analyses (e.g., Rosenstone and Hansen 1993; Teixera 1992) have pretty well established that life-cycle factors are at work rather than cohort replacement. This conclusion is reinforced by a study of age-group voting turnout over four decades in Sweden and Germany (Myers and Agree 1993). The age-bracket differences in those countries were similar to those in the United States, despite the fact that cohorts in these three nations experienced different political events distinctive to their own countries. All this suggests that boomers will at least continue the pattern of high turnout when they are old, especially given that they have conformed to participation rates of various age-brackets as they have moved through the life course (see table 8-1).

Sociologist John Williamson (1998) suggests that the participation rate for boomers when they reach old age may even be greater than those of previous old-age cohorts because, on average, they will have better health and higher levels of education and income than their elderly predecessors. Another factor that may increase the participation rate of boomers in old age is that specific steps are being taken to enhance voting accessibility for elderly voters by improving election procedures and practices (GAO 2008).

The factor that is most likely to substantially increase the voting rate of older boomers is their eligibility for old-age entitlement benefits—starting right now for relatively few of them, but eventually swelling to include nearly all boomers—with its consequence that national politicians will increasingly propose (and oppose) significant changes in Social Security and Medicare. Over the next twenty years, the number of individuals eligible for Social Security retirement benefits and Medicare health insurance will essentially double. Projections based on this simple fact as applied to the financing of these benefits, together with the sharply increasing costs of health care, have brought the issues of substantially reforming these entitlement programs to the national policy agenda. They will stay there until Congress and the president deal with them. Between now and then, boomers may increasingly become conscious constituents of these programs.

As the trustees of the Social Security system made clear in their latest annual report (Social Security Administration 2007), the longer that reforms in Social Security and Medicare are delayed, the more "disruptive" (read *drastic*) will be the changes in the programs. Over time, one can easily imagine a presidential election campaign that is highly focused on age-related issues, with the candidates taking starkly opposed policy positions regarding the future of Social Security and Medicare. Depending on the details—for instance, sharp reductions in benefits or new taxes to help sustain the old-age entitlements—such a political context might substantially increase the turnout rate of older boomers. But then, it might also have a similar effect on the turnout among younger groups. So the net effect in terms of the percentage of votes cast by older boomers is impossible to estimate.

In short, all that one can confidently predict regarding voting participation is that when all members of the baby-boom cohort are aged 65 and older, the proportion of the total vote that is cast by older people in national elections will probably be significantly higher than it is today. But even so, it is highly unlikely to approach Thurow's "majority."

Will Aged Boomers Be Politically Cohesive?

Unlike preceding cohorts of older Americans, will aged boomers cast a notably cohesive "senior vote"? Is it conceivable that Thurow's specter of class warfare between the old and the young will materialize?

During the late 1960s and early 1970s, the baby-boom cohort was popularly characterized as a monolithic political group, notable for its liberal activism. As political scientist Paul Light notes, its members had much in common:

> They shared the great economic expectations of the 1950s and the fears that came with Sputnik and the dawn of the nuclear era. They shared the hopes of John F. Kennedy's New Frontier and Lyndon Johnson's Great Society, and the disillusionment that came with the assassinations, Vietnam, Watergate, and the resignations. (1988, 10)

Yet, as Light also notes, far from all of the boomers were liberal protesters on college campuses. Some went to Vietnam instead, and others went straight from high school to work.

Regardless of stereotypes of the baby boom in this earlier period, it is clear that its members are not homogenous. Members of the boomer cohort are diverse in numerous characteristics relevant to voting behavior, just like members of the cohorts that have preceded them and followed them. Among the sources of diversity, of course, are socioeconomic status, gender, race, ethnicity, religion, immigration, cultural mores, education, health status, geography, and family structure. A MetLife profile of boomers (MetLife Mature Market Institute 2007), compiled from a variety of governmental sources, provides some interesting snapshots of this diversity. For instance, the percentage of boomers who have never married is 12.6 percent, and 14.2 percent of them are divorced. People of Hispanic origin (of any race) constitute 9 percent of boomers, blacks 10 percent, Asians and Pacific Islanders 4 percent, and Native Americans almost 1 percent.

In addition, age differences within the boomer cohort have significance. As Williamson (1998) notes, boomers are made up of two subcohorts, those born between 1946 and 1954 and those born between 1955 and 1964. He points out that the economic experiences of these two groups have been different. The demand for jobs and housing was not exceptional when the older boomers entered those markets. But both markets were tight and difficult for the younger boomers.

Given the diverse individual characteristics of the boomers, it should not be surprising that collectively they have shown no signs of being or becoming a cohesive voting bloc during the past thirty years. Tracking their votes starting with the 1976 presidential election (the first in which the earliest boomers were old enough to vote) and following them as they have moved into various older age groups in the elections since then, they have tended to split their votes for president between the Democratic and Republican parties in harmony with the splits of the electorate as a whole. In 2004, for example, when most of the boomers were in the 45–59 age bracket reported in exit polls, 51 percent of their votes went to President Bush and 48 percent went to Senator Kerry. This exactly matched the figures for the electorate as a whole (Connelly 2004).

When boomers reach old age, they are likely to continue splitting their votes among candidates in patterns similar to those of younger age groups, unless the political context of election campaigns is radically different from what it has been over the last three decades. Although boomers will come to share characteristics of old age, this will only be one set of characteristics that members of the group will have.

Yet it is possible, under certain circumstances, that old age could become the most important characteristic influencing electoral decisions of boomers. As national politicians come to grips more fully with the fiscal challenges of sustaining Social Security and Medicare, Republican and Democratic candidates might espouse drastically different positions regarding government benefits for older persons. Such a development might especially emerge in the broader context of a prevalent pessimistic viewpoint regarding the country's economic future. For ultimately, the challenge of sustaining our large governmental expenditures on old-age benefits will depend on whether our nation has enough wealth to do so, as well as on its political will to transfer a significant amount of that wealth to older boomers.

In the context of a gloomy economic outlook, for instance, one party might propose substantial cuts in Social Security benefits. In addition, or alternatively, it might endorse retrenchments in existing Medicare coverage for expensive diagnostic tests and medical procedures, as has been urged by prominent opinion makers for many years (e.g., Callahan 1987; Lamm 2002). The platform of the other party could be to preserve Social Security with minor changes and to oppose the notion that Medicare recipients should be denied coverage for the fruits of advances in medical technology and procedures. In such circumstances, the votes of boomers might tend to coalesce as never before, in favor of the latter party, as the self-interest of depending on old-age benefits might well transcend other issues and partisan attachments for a great many (if not all) of them.

The coalescence of older boomers as a powerful political force could also be enhanced if AARP succeeds in its efforts to recruit boomers during the next two decades. This possibility, no doubt, is what led *Washington Post* columnist Robert Samuelson to declaim:

> Among AARP's 36 million members, there must be many decent people.... But I won't be joining, because AARP has become America's most dangerous lobby. If left unchecked, its agenda will plunder our children and grandchildren. Massive outlays for the elderly threaten huge tax increases and other

government spending. Both may weaken the economy and the social fabric. (2005, A19)

At the turn of the century, the American Association of Retired Persons (as it was known then) had the foresight to recognize that it needed to enroll boomers as members if it wanted to survive over the long run. Part of its marketing effort was to drop "retired persons" from its name in 1998 and officially become simply AARP. And in 2001, the organization launched a new magazine, *My Generation*, targeted to boomers. Apparently this new publication did not prove to be a successful recruiting tool because it stopped publication after a short period of time. By all accounts, recruitment of boomers to AARP has been disappointing so far, but the organization is persistent in its efforts. In early 2008, it launched AARP-TV, joining forces with Retirement Living TV, a Columbia, Maryland–based seniors network (White 2008). Among its two weekly shows is *My Generation*, resurrecting the title of the defunct magazine that AARP had targeted to boomers seven years earlier.

AARP's campaign to enroll boomers could be successful in the long run because the material incentives the organization offers to members may very well appeal to boomers as they increasingly enter the old-age category. Alternatively, however, a new organization, say, an American Association of Baby Boomers, might be created and successfully capitalize on the existing moniker for the birth cohort, preempt AARP's recruitment efforts, and become a political force itself.

Will There Be Intergenerational Warfare?

If an overriding "old-age political consciousness" develops among boomers—provoked by drastic proposed changes in old-age policies and/or nurtured by AARP or a similar mass membership organization—it might even be built on and magnified by the creation of a political party to protect the interests of older persons. To be sure, no major old-age parties have yet developed in Western democracies. But a minor precursor of what could develop occurred in the Netherlands in the early 1990s. Controversial Dutch national policies relevant to older people led to the establishment of two national parties, the General Senior Citizen's Union and Union 55+. Together, in 1994, they won 7 of the 150 seats in parliament (Schuyt, García, and Knipscheer 1999). If radical proposals for revising Social Security and Medicare are seriously entertained or implemented—and supported by both the Democratic and Republican parties—one could imagine the creation of a Seniors' Rights party in the United States and the development of the type of intergenerational warfare envisioned by Thurow, Peterson, and some of the many other prophets of doom.

Such warfare is possible, but not very likely. Barring a seriously negative economic situation, the policy reforms proposed and acted upon to affect the old-age benefits available to boomers are unlikely to involve radical changes. The prime reason is that the political parties and candidates are well aware of the very large latent constituency of older voters that boomers will comprise. And they are likely to both court them and be wary of making enemies of them. Because of this, the likelihood of intergenerational political clashes will be minimized.

The experiences of pension reform throughout Europe reinforce this assessment that intergenerational conflict will be minimal when the bulk of U.S. boomers have reached old age. The proportions of European populations that are aged 65 and older have been considerably higher in recent decades than in the United States. In 2005, for instance, the proportion was 19.2 percent in Italy and 18.6 percent in Germany, compared with 12.4 percent in the United States (Berghammer et al. 2006); the average for the European Union (EU) was 16.6 percent. Moreover, the projections for 2030 are much higher: Italy and Germany, 27.5 percent, and the EU 24.7 percent, compared with a U.S. projection of 19.6 percent. These high proportions of older people in European nations are due to "baby busts" rather than baby booms. (The average fertility rate for the EU is 1.5 children per woman, well below the 2.3 rate that is needed to maintain a stable population size.)

Facing such proportions of older persons, European nations undertook fifty-five pension reforms between 1986 and 2002 in order to deal with potential fiscal and economic growth problems (Arza and Kohli 2007). Kohli (2007) notes that the politics of these reforms did not provide much evidence of a generational cleavage and conflict. On the basis of their comprehensive book on European pensions reforms, Arza and Kohli (2007, 16) conclude: "The prediction (or fear) that the political agenda will increasingly be dominated by narrowly conceived old-age interests is thus not warranted."

The European experiences also indicate a key factor that helps to minimize the chances of intergenerational conflict, as well as the domination of national politics by old-age interests. It is the design of reforms that have long transition periods, thereby reducing the visibility of benefit cutbacks and rendering them politically viable (Natali and Rhodes 2007). A prime example of such a policy in the United States was the Social Security Reform Act of 1983. It cut back benefits by increasing the "normal retirement age" in the program from age 65 to age 67. But the transition from 65 to 67 was not scheduled to begin until twenty years later, in 2003, and not scheduled to be completed for another twenty-five years, by the end of 2027. In 1983, literally no one was provoked politically by this reform.

Today, there is still sufficient time to craft U.S. reforms in old-age entitlements (whether through tax increases, benefit cuts, or both) that employ such a strategy of advance planning, semidistant startup, and gradualism. If such policies are devised, the odds that boomers will unite or be coalesced as a major political force in old age will be substantially reduced. And so will the likelihood of intergenerational political warfare.

NOTES

1. Although candidates for Congress often stake out positions on old-age policy issues in their campaigns and incumbents have voting records on such issues, congressional elections are excluded from this discussion. In any given election, the circumstances affecting voting participation can vary substantially from one congressional district to another and from one state to another. Such circumstances include, for example, legal and other local practices that facilitate or hinder voter registration; whether a congressional candidate's seat is "safe" or "hotly contested"; scandals or prominent issues that are local in nature; electoral contests for statewide office that may elicit higher-than-usual participation or that may be of less-than-usual interest to potential voters; and many others. For an appropriate analysis of age-group voting participation, factors of this kind would have to be explored in 535 electoral contests—435 for the U.S. House of Representatives and 100 for the U.S. Senate (involving a different third of the states in each of the three senatorial elections that take place during a six-year period). Although these circumstances are also relevant to presidential elections and are worth exploring (see Binstock 1997), their impact on analyses of data from a single nationwide election contest is more diffuse than in the many separate congressional contests.

2. The most recent (2004) Census Bureau projections regarding the age distribution of American residents in 2030 does not break down information on 18- and 19-year-olds from the larger category of ages 5–19. Consequently, the 1998 projections, which do include a category that begins with age 18, are relied on for the total number of voting-age residents.

REFERENCES

Aaron, H. J. 2002. Budget estimates: What we know, what we can't know, and why it matters. In *Policies for an aging society*, ed. S. H. Altman and D. I. Schactman, 63–80. Baltimore: Johns Hopkins University Press.

AARP. 2008. *AARP 2006 annual report*. Retrieved on February 28, 2008, from http://assets.aarp.org/www.aarp.org_/build/common/pdf/aarp_2006_annual_report.pdf.

Arza C., and M. Kohli. 2007. Introduction: The political economy of pensions reform. In *Pension reform in Europe: Politics, policies and outcomes*, ed. C. Arza and M. Kohli, 1–21. London: Routledge.

Berghammer, C., R. Gisser, W. Lutz, M. Mamolo, D. Phillipov, S. Scherbov, and T. Sobotka. 2006. European demographic data sheet: 2006. Vienna: Austrian Academy of Sciences; Washington, DC: Population Reference Bureau.

Binstock, R. H. 1997. The 1996 election: Older voters and implications for policies on aging. *The Gerontologist* 37(1): 25–39.

Callahan, D. 1987. *Setting limits: Medical goals in an aging society*. New York: Simon & Schuster.

Campbell, A. L. 2003. *How policies make citizens: Senior political activism and the American welfare state*. Princeton, NJ: Princeton University Press.

Connelly, M. 2004. How Americans voted: A political portrait. *New York Times*. November 7.

Edison/Mitofsky. 2004. *U.S. President/national/exit poll*. Retrieved on November 4, 2004, from http://www.cnn.com/ELECTION/2004/pages/results/president/?TTFUID=NSELCT3.

Federal Interagency Forum on Aging-Related Statistics. 2008. *Older Americans update, 2006: Key indicators of well-being.* Washington, DC: U.S. Administration on Aging.

GAO (United States Government Accountability Office). 2008. Elderly voters: Some improvements in voting accessibility from 2000 to 2004 elections, but gaps in policy and implementation remain. Testimony by Bovbjerg, B. D., and Jenkins, W. O., before the Special Committee on Aging, United States Senate, January 31, 2008. Retrieved on January 31, 2008, from http://www.gao.gov/highlights/d08209high.pdf.

Kohli, M. 2007. Generational equity: Concepts and attitudes. In *Pension reform in Europe: Politics, policies and outcomes,* ed. C. Arza and M. Kohli, 196–214. London: Routledge.

Lamm, R. D. 2002. The moral imperative of limiting elderly health entitlements. In *Policies for an aging society,* ed. S. H. Altman and D. I. Shactman, 196–216. Baltimore: Johns Hopkins University Press.

Levy, B. R., and M. J. Schlesinger. 2005. When self-interest and age stereotypes collide: Elders opposing increased funds for programs benefiting themselves. *Journal of Aging and Social Policy* 17 (2): 25–39.

Light, P. C. 1988. *Baby boomers.* New York: W. W. Norton.

McManus, S. A. 1996. *Young v. old: Generational combat in the 21st century.* Boulder, CO: Westview Press.

MetLife Mature Market Institute. 2007. A profile of American baby boomers. Retrieved on February 29, 2008, from http://www.metlife.com/WPSAssets/86451660901172586182V1FBoomerProfile2007.pdf.

Miller, W. E., and J. M. Shanks. 1996. *The new American voter.* Cambridge, MA: Harvard University Press.

Myers, G. C., and E. M. Agree. 1993. Social and political implications of population aging: Aging of the electorate. In *Proceedings of the International Population Conference, Montreal 1993,* 3:37–49. Liege, Belgium: International Union for the Scientific Study of Population.

Natali, D., and M. Rhodes. 2007. The "new politics" of pension reforms in Continental Europe. In *Pension reform in Europe: Politics, policies and outcomes,* ed. C. Arza and M. Kohli, 25–46. London: Routledge.

Peterson, P. G. 1999. *Gray dawn: How the coming age wave will transform America—and the world.* New York: Times Books.

Rosenstone, S. J., and J. M. Hansen. 1993. *Mobilization, participation, and democracy.* New York: Macmillan.

Samuelson, R. J. 2005. AARP's America is a mirage. *Washington Post.* November 16.

Schulz, J. H., and R. H. Binstock. 2008. *Aging nation: The economics and politics of growing older in America.* Baltimore: Johns Hopkins University Press.

Schuyt, T., L. L. García, and K. Knipscheer. 1999. The politics of old age in the Netherlands. In *The politics of old age in Europe,* ed. A. Walker and G. Naegele, 123–34. Buckingham, PA: Open University Press.

Simon, H. A. 1985. Human nature in politics: The dialogue of psychology with political science. *American Political Science Review* 79:293–304.

Social Security Administration. 2007. *Status of the Social Security and Medicare programs: A summary of the 2007 annual reports.* Retrieved on February 25, 2008, from http://www.ssa.gov/OACT/TRSUM/trsummary.html.

Teixera, R. A. 1992. *The disappearing American voter.* Washington, DC: Brookings Institution.

Thomas, L., Jr. 2008. Reconciling opposites: A crusade against cozy tax breaks, led by one who benefited. *New York Times.* February 15.

Thurow, L. C. 1996. The birth of a revolutionary class. *New York Times Magazine,* May 19, 46–47.

Timpone, R. J. 1998. Structure, behavior, and voter turnout in the United States. *American Political Science Review* 92:145–58.

U.S. Census Bureau. 1998. *Current population reports, series P2* (Middle Series Projections). Washington, DC: GPO.

———. 2004. U.S. interim projections by age, sex, race, and Hispanic origin. Retrieved on February 24, 2008, from http://www.census.gov/ipc/www/usinterimproj/.

———. 2005. Reported voting and registration by race, Hispanic origin, sex, and age groups: 1964 to 2004 Retrieved July 7, 2005, from http://www.census.gov/population/www/socdemo/voting.html.

White, T. 2008. AARP is launching foray into TV aimed at seniors: Group joining forces with Columbia network. Retrieved on March 7, 2008, from www.baltimoresun.com/business/bal-bz.md.seniortv07/mar07,0,2088137.story.

Williamson, J. B. 1998. Political activism and the aging of the baby boom. *Generations* 22 (1): 55–59.

———— 9 ————

Aging Boomers, Generational Equity, and the Framing of the Debate over Social Security

JOHN B. WILLIAMSON AND DIANE M. WATTS-ROY*

O ver the next few decades, the United States (and many other nations around the world) will be contending with the burden of financing the retirement of the baby-boomer generation. With the retirement of these very large cohorts will come pressures to substantially increase government spending on old-age pensions and health care. For the United States, one consequence of this projected demographic shift, and the associated increase in number of people eligible for pension and health insurance benefits, is the projected depletion of the Social Security and Medicare trust funds in the not-too-distant future. Current projections suggest that if no policy changes were to be made in the years ahead, the Social Security trust fund would be depleted by 2041. This does not mean that there would be no money to pay Social Security pensions, as billions of dollars would continue to be collected each year, but that benefits would have to be reduced by about 25 percent or that payroll taxes would have to be increased, at that point, by about 32 percent (i.e., four percentage points, with half of this increase paid by employers) (Board of Trustees 2007).

---

*Portions of this material have been adapted from Williamson, J. B., T. K. McNamara, and S. A. Howling, "Generational Equity, Generational Interdependence, and the Framing of the Debate over Social Security Reform." *Journal of Sociology & Social Welfare* 30 (2003): 3–14. Used with permission.

Few analysts believe that this scenario will be played out; most expect that changes will be made long before 2041. However, such projections do suggest that some changes will be needed to deal with the retirement of the boomers, and they will be the type most politicians try to avoid. Most likely, the changes will involve a combination of direct and indirect benefit cuts and tax increases. Such projections have led to much discussion about how best to bring projected pension benefits and revenues into balance. Central to this debate are the explicit and implicit discussions about whom to ask to contribute more taxes and whom to ask to accept lower benefits. Many analysts are also asking about race, class, gender, age, and cohort (generation) differences with respect to how the burden should be shared (Kohli 2006; Kingson 2007; Baker and Weisbrot 1999).

In this chapter, we will be analyzing the ideological contest between two major frameworks for thinking about the share of societal resources that ought to go to elder members of American society. One framework is often referred to as the *generational equity perspective* and the other as the *generational interdependence perspective* (Williamson 2007; Williamson and Watts-Roy 1999). This discourse goes by various names, but the most common is the "generational equity debate." This debate emerged between the late 1970s and the mid-1980s as part of an ideological swing to the right in American society. The debate's emergence was linked to a confluence of several economic, political, and demographic forces.

Due to a combination of falling birth rates, increasing life expectancy, the declining age of retirement, and the size of the boomer cohorts, demographic projections began pointing to a dramatic drop in the future ratio of workers to retirees, particularly once the boomers started to retire. These trends raised questions about the projected economic burden future retirees would place on the Social Security program and the associated increases in payroll taxes on future workers. Changing economic conditions during the 1970s, including two major oil embargoes, the associated declines in the rate of economic growth, and the combination of high inflation and high unemployment referred to as "stagflation," all taken together, made Americans increasingly pessimistic about their economic future (Kuttner 1980). Political problems such as the war in Vietnam, the Watergate scandal, the failure of most "War on Poverty" programs, and the Iranian hostage crisis contributed to a decline in public confidence in the government's ability to effectively deal with societal problems. The combination of all the above factors made the American public increasingly reluctant to support social programs designed to help various vulnerable groups, including retirees (Powell, Williamson, and Branco 1996).

Concurrently, increasingly well-funded conservative think tanks and foundations such as the Cato Institute, the American Enterprise Institute, and the Heritage Foundation helped to catalyze a sharp shift to the political right. The resulting ascendancy of the conservative wing of the Republican Party was capped by the 1980 election of Ronald Reagan as president. Soon many social programs, including even the nation's single most popular government program, Social Security, were coming under intense criticism (Béland 2005; Williamson, McNamara, and Howling 2003).

Social Security was subjected to intense scrutiny for several reasons. First, of all the old-age policies, Social Security was by far the most costly. Second, demographic projections pointed to the impending retirement of the very large cohorts associated with the boomer generation. A third factor was Social Security's first short-term financing shortfall in the late 1970s—due in part to a combination of high inflation, high unemployment rates, and low wage increases, as well as a rising number of people receiving pension and disability benefits (Berkowitz 1997). In addition to unfavorable demographic trends, a faulty cost-of-living formula enacted in 1972 also contributed to the projected long-term financing shortfall.

While conservatives attempted to define the financing problem as a "crisis," liberals tried to depict it as a relatively easy-to-manage short-term funding problem. Conservative efforts to frame the Social Security financing problem as a crisis represented a deliberate effort to undermine public confidence in the program as part of a broader effort to reduce government spending and ultimately the size of the American welfare state (Béland 2005; Powell, Williamson, and Branco 1996; Butler and Germanis 1983). In response to these funding problems, the Social Security program was amended first in 1977 and then again in 1983. Although these reforms ensured that Social Security would take in more revenues than it paid out as pension benefits, at least for the next few decades, the process sparked an enduring debate over Social Security, and, as we shall see, the issue of generational equity became central to that debate.

FRAME ANALYSIS OF THE GENERATIONAL EQUITY DEBATE

What eventually came to be referred to as the generational equity perspective began to emerge as a subtext of the Social Security "crisis" frame in the early 1980s. Conservative critics of the Social Security program argued that it was a pyramid scheme in which younger working-age adults were paying into a system from which they would get little or nothing in return; this argument is still being repeated today (Longman 1982; Lamm 2007). In part, this argument is premised on the idea that the Social Security system will go bankrupt before younger workers reach retirement age. Some conservative commentators began to use terms such as "justice between generations" and "generational equity" to describe the projected conflict of financial interests between different age groups (Longman 1985).

While conservative policy analysts found it very effective to use the term *generational equity* when writing about old-age policy, most liberal analysts and commentators were much more comfortable with such terms as *generational interdependence* or *intragenerational equity* (Kingson, Hirshorn, and Cornman 1986). However, in the end it was the proponents of the generational equity frame who were most successful in marketing their catch phrase to refer to, and thus help frame the debate over, distributional aspects of old-age policy reform. This has become the term most often used, even by many liberal commentators, when referring to this set of issues.

The debate is as much a symbolic contest as a disagreement over specific policies. The competing advocacy networks, representing the "generational equity" and "generational interdependence" frames, attempt to depict their respective interpretative packages in ways that resonate with larger cultural themes. Below, we outline the core elements of each interpretative package and the strategies that each advocacy network has used to promote its views. The way in which an advocacy network promotes its interpretative package affects the extent to which a frame becomes accepted. Consequently, each group adopts rhetorical strategies in an effort to make its interpretative package appear more appealing and credible than the alternative frame. (For discussions of how to do frame analysis, see Gamson 1992 and Lakoff 2004.)

The Generational Equity Perspective

At the heart of the generational equity interpretative package is the idea that each generation should provide for itself. Proponents of generational equity generally offer ways to view old-age policy that lead to proposals to cut back on entitlement programs, such as Social Security, or would at least partially privatize such schemes.

Beginning in the mid-1980s, advocates of the generational equity perspective argued that there was a conflict of interest between elders and the working-age population. These advocates included several well-known conservative journalists, such as William F. Buckley Jr., as well as other commentators linked to conservative think tanks such as the Cato Institute and conservative foundations such as the Olin Foundation. The advocacy network also included organizations that explicitly focused on promoting generational equity. For instance, Senator David Durenberger founded Americans for Generational Equity (AGE), an organization that was funded largely by conservative foundations and businesses (Binstock 1999; Quadagno 1989). Both AGE and other advocates of the generational equity perspective repeatedly cited the work of well-respected demographer Samuel Preston (1984), who presented evidence that the economic status of elders had been improving while that of children had been deteriorating. He interpreted his data in such a way as to suggest that the improved conditions of elders had been achieved, at least partially, at the expense of children. Advocates for the generational equity perspective often argued that due to overly generous spending on programs for elders, young adults and children were being shortchanged.

The generational equity frame combines claims of fairness and of affordability (Marmor, Cook, and Scher 1999). Specifically, the advocates of this frame argue that most of today's elders are financially secure. This claim is partly based on statistics showing that, in the aggregate, the well-being of elders has improved over the past several decades. For instance, between 1959 and 1987, the percentage of those age 65 and over living below the poverty line fell from 35 percent to 12 percent (Clark 1990). By 2005, it had fallen further to 10 percent, considerably below the 18 percent rate for those under age 18 (DeNavas-Walt, Proctor, and Lee 2006).

The claim that elders are for the most part economically secure is based to some extent on fact, but it downplays the diverse economic conditions among different subgroups of elders. While poverty rates for those age 65 and older have declined, the incomes of many continue to hover close to the official poverty line. For example, in the late 1990s, while only 11 percent of elders were below the poverty line, more than 25 percent of elders were "near poor," defined as having incomes less than 150 percent of the poverty level. In addition, poverty rates for some subgroups, such as minority elders and those over the age of 85, were far higher than the data for the average senior. In 1998, approximately 27 percent of elder blacks, 21 percent of elder Hispanics, and 49 percent of elder black women living alone had incomes below the poverty line (Crown 2001). Poverty rates are high not just among elder black and Hispanic women but also among elder white women, particularly those who are divorced or widowed (Estes 2004; Williamson and Rix 2000).

Another claim by advocates of the generational equity frame is that elders are getting more than their fair share of government resources, often at the expense of young adults and children (Chakravarty and Weisman 1988; Farlie 1988). They contend that high federal spending on elders has contributed to the poverty rate of children. Reducing spending on Social Security and Medicare, they argue, would free up money for programs for children and young adults (Silverstein et al. 2000). Advocates of the generational equity frame often base their claims on data about the proportion of government social spending that is directed toward elders. The lion's share of the nation's social welfare spending is, in fact, for programs that benefit elders. In 2004, about one-third of the federal budget was spent on Social Security, Medicare, and Medicaid, as has been the case for more than a decade (Binstock 2007; Congressional Budget Office 2004).

However, there is very little evidence that current old-age policies are directly or indirectly harmful to the welfare of children and young adults. Critics of the generational equity frame point out that the modest increase in the poverty rate among children, from 16 percent in 1979 to 18 percent in 2005 (DeNavas-Walt, Proctor, and Lee 2006), is most likely due to other factors such as increases in single-parent households and declining wage rates. In addition, the claim that elders are getting more than their fair share of resources is premised in part on the idea that elders are affluent and need the benefits of public social programs less than children. However, as discussed above, there is much diversity among this population. While some elders are affluent, many are not.

The advocates of the generational equity frame claim that policies unfair to working-age adults have thrived in part due to the political influence of old-age interest groups such as AARP (Farlie 1988; Longman 1989). The argument that elders use their political power to promote their own economic interests is loosely rooted in the fact that elders do form a larger percentage of the electorate today than do families with children (Binstock 2000). However, the advocates of the generational equity framework ignore two related facts about the voting behavior of elders.

First, elders tend to carry ideological orientations from midlife into old age, and they seldom vote as a monolithic block (Binstock 2000). For instance, a small, unrepresentative group of comparatively affluent older persons voted for the repeal of the Medicare Catastrophic Coverage Act of 1988 (Binstock 1995). This act benefited economically vulnerable elders, but much of the tax burden was borne by the smaller group of affluent elders. Thus, the interests of different subgroups of elders do not always converge.

Second, the interests of elders do not always diverge from those of children and working-age adults. True, there is evidence that elders sometimes do use their voting power to support policies that benefit their age group at the expense of young adults and children (Rosenbaum and Button 1989). However, there is also evidence that both younger and older Americans often oppose cutting spending on education, student loans, and health programs for women and children (Minkler 1991). In fact, during the 1980s, while advocates of the generational equity frame warned against the disproportionate power of elders, spending on schools rose more than 2.4 percent faster than inflation (Moody 1992). Thus, the claim that elders use their political power to promote policies advantageous to them and disadvantageous to other age groups is often overstated.

Another claim associated with the generational equity frame is that current old-age policies are unsustainable due to the nation's changing demographic structure. As the population ages, the argument goes, these policies will become unaffordable (Concord Coalition 1993; Peterson 1996). This claim is often supported with data about dependency ratios. The dependency ratio is a measure of the economic burden of the population *not* in the paid labor force to those who *are* in the paid labor force. In the decades ahead, the ratio of elders to the working-age population will increase in all industrialized nations. While the claim that policies such as Social Security and Medicare are unsustainable are to a degree based on demographic trends, old-age dependency ratios are only part of the story. For instance, while it is true that the old-age dependency ratio has increased, the child-dependency ratio has decreased (Marmor, Cook, and Scher 1999). In addition, the relative number of people in different age categories is used as a proxy to estimate the burden of elders on the working-age population. This approach does not take into account the many elders who remain in the labor force (Binstock 1999). Thus, while population aging is a demographic reality, an emphasis on projected changes in the old-age dependency ratio tends to overstate the severity of the problem.

Finally, advocates of the generational equity frame argue that because old-age policies are unsustainable, it is unfair to expect each generation to support the one that precedes it (Kotlikoff and Burns 2004; Borden 1995). They argue that the pay-as-you-go system by which current workers support current retirees presumes that each generation can and should be supported by the generation that follows. However, if today's working-age adults cannot count on the same level of Social Security, Medicare, and Medicaid benefits when they retire as their parents' generation is receiving today, the pay-as-you-go system is unfair. The argument is that while many current retirees are receiving more in benefits than can be justified based on their payroll contributions, today's young adults will generally receive much less than they have contributed. Rather than assuming that each generation should support the generation that precedes it, advocates of the generational equity frame typically believe that each generation should be responsible for itself (Kotlikoff 1992; Longman 1989).

In general, advocates of the generational equity perspective make claims based loosely on fact, but overlook other important factors. However, the frame has appeal to many Americans because it resonates with individualism, a dominant value in American culture. Individualism is linked to values of autonomy, personal ownership, liberty, individual responsibility, and personal freedom. Although advocates of the generational equity framework are not opposed to redistribution within families or voluntary redistribution by charitable organizations, they oppose "mandatory" redistribution through government programs. Social Security and Medicare, by this argument, infringe on individual freedoms and make people less likely to rely on themselves to plan their retirement. Those who favor the generational equity frame suggest that people who oppose the partial privatization of Social Security or cutbacks on entitlement programs lack an ethic of work and individual responsibility. According to this frame, we need to ensure an equitable distribution of resources across generations, both today and in the future. At the same time, we need to emphasize deeply held American values such as thrift, self-reliance, and limited government. Reducing government spending on elders is one way to encourage self-reliance and to discourage an entitlement ethic.

Generational Interdependence Perspective

Critics of the generational equity frame have proposed an alternative interpretative package often referred to as the generational interdependence frame. This frame arose largely out of the criticisms of the generational equity frame (Williamson and Watts-Roy 1999). In addition to the various arguments offered so far that question the claims of the generational equity frame, this alternative interpretative package makes several more assertions.

The first is that different generations have much to offer one other. For instance, the authors of *Ties That Bind*, a report commissioned by the Gerontological Society of America, argue for a perspective on social policy that focuses on the interdependence between generations (Kingson, Hirshorn, and Cornman 1986). The gains of one generation are not necessarily achieved at the expense of others. Economic changes, increases in single-parent households, and cutbacks on social spending for the poor, they argue, are more directly linked to the increase in poverty rates for children than is federal spending on elders. Generations United is one of the most active advocacy organizations with a focus on promoting and celebrating interdependence among generations (Kingson 2007; Rother 2007).

Advocates of the generational interdependence frame point to the ways in which policies that benefit elders often also indirectly benefit young adults. For instance, Kuttner (1982) argues that critics of the Social Security system, focusing on the economic drawbacks of the system for the working-age population, underestimate the benefits to the adult children of elders. Even with Social Security and Medicare, the adult children of elders often take their parents into their homes or provide them with financial assistance (Foner 2000). Reducing Social Security and Medicare benefits, rather than lessening the burden on the working-age population, would put millions of families under pressure to provide economic support for their aging parents.

Advocates of the generational interdependence frame also argue that elders have a stake in policies targeting young adults and children. Kingson, Hirshorn, and Cornman (1986), for instance, argue that elders benefit from programs directed toward the young in several ways. They note that the economic interests of elders are tied to the productivity of future workers. Thus, elders indirectly benefit from education spending that makes future workers more productive. Advocates for elders often have a stake in policies that benefit both elders and children. These policies include income maintenance policies such as unemployment insurance, health care programs such as Medicaid, and other programs such as transportation and caregiving services. Social Security itself provides direct benefits to millions of people who are not elders, including 3.8 million children (of disabled, retired, or deceased workers), 4.9 million disabled workers, and 4.7 million spouses of deceased workers (Congressional Budget Office 2001). Many of these people would be economically dependent upon their elder parents, or in some cases their adult children, were it not for these Social Security benefits (Kingson and Williamson 2001).

Proponents of the generational interdependence frame point to the two-way flow of services and support between different generations. While many working-age Americans act as caregivers for elders, there are also many ways in which elders contribute to the welfare of the working-age population. Elder parents are often caregivers for grandchildren and functionally disabled family members. More than one in ten elders has been responsible for at least one grandchild for at least six months. In 1994, some 3.7 million grandchildren lived in the homes of their grandparents (Saluter 1996). Additionally, a substantial portion of the financial support provided to family members is provided by elders (Rubinstein 1993). Finally, many elders provide psychological and financial support to their adult children. By focusing on several different fronts, the advocates of the generational interdependence perspective emphasize what each generation has to offer other generations rather than accentuating conflict between generations.

Another claim of the generational interdependence frame is that elders must be viewed as heterogeneous, not homogeneous. Some critics of the generational equity frame note that it focuses on equity between generations at the expense of other kinds of equity, such as those linked to race, class, and gender. A core disagreement between the generational equity and generational interdependence frames is how public policy ought to treat equity between generations compared to equity between other groups, such as the haves and the have-nots (Kingson 2007). While some elders are affluent, others need substantial financial assistance. Economically vulnerable groups tend to be overlooked in the generational equity perspective (Kingson and Williamson 1993). Proponents of the generational interdependence frame view the generational equity frame as overly simplistic, neglecting economic needs related to inequality within a generation (or age cohort) in the name of reducing inequality in federal spending levels between cohorts.

The generational interdependence perspective has generally been less successful than the generational equity perspective in framing debates about old-age policy in the American mass media. In part, this is because the generational interdependence frame focuses on the community obligation to provide for vulnerable populations. In this context, critics of proposals to privatize Social Security argue that the more privileged members of society have an obligation to protect low-wage and vulnerable workers in retirement (Ball and Bethell 2000; Quadagno 1996). Historically, except under very special circumstances such as the Great Depression, the countertheme of community obligation has been less powerful than the dominant theme (or value) of individualism. Thus, advocates of the generational interdependence perspective often find themselves at a disadvantage, as their interpretative package generally resonates less strongly with dominant American cultural values.

GENERATIONAL EQUITY AND SOCIAL SECURITY REFORM

Over time, the focus of the generational equity debate has shifted. At the outset, the focus was on the fairness of what was perceived as overly generous Social Security pension benefits during the 1980s. Subsequently it evolved into a debate over the projected growth in entitlement spending. Proponents of the "entitlement crisis" thesis draw on ideas about equity between generations to call for cuts in spending, particularly projected future spending on such entitlement programs as Social Security and Medicare (Peterson 1996). Advocates of the entitlement crisis argument are among those who have pushed for the means-testing or income-testing of Social Security benefits (Howe and Longman 1992). Supporters of the generational interdependence frame tend to be critical of this proposed means-testing because it would undermine the political support for Social Security, which in turn would very likely lead to an erosion of benefits over time (Kingson and Schulz 1997).

Another form the generational equity debate has taken has been the discourse concerning "generational accounting," first proposed by economist Laurence Kotlikoff and his associates (Kotlikoff 1992; Kotlikoff and Burns 2004). Kotlikoff's complex economic models purport to present a precise—some would say more scientific—formulation of the generational equity arguments. His models lead to the conclusion that under current legislation each generation can expect to pay a heavier tax burden than the generation before it. Critics of generational accounting affiliated with the generational interdependence advocacy network call into question a number of the economic assumptions built into Kotlikoff's models, including the neglect of the nonmarket reproductive labor of women (Estes 2004; Baker and Weisbrot 1999; Binstock 1993).

PARTIAL PRIVATIZATION OF SOCIAL SECURITY?

Of the many proposals for reform that have been made in recent years, the press has given the most attention to those calling for the partial privatization of Social Security through the introduction of individual accounts. Some see the introduction of these individual accounts as an end goal; others see such a reform as a first step toward what they hope will eventually become the full privatization of Social Security (Ferrara and Tanner 1998; Peterson 1999). This issue has been at the core of the generational equity debate in the United States in recent years. Proponents of generational equity are on record in support of introducing individual Social Security accounts (partial privatization), while advocates of the generational interdependence frame have opposed the various proposals to partially privatize the scheme.

Why are such accounts opposed? There are many reasons (Williamson 1997). One major reason is that they tend to be associated with schemes that will shrink the traditional defined benefit component of Social Security, the component that is guaranteed by the government. Another is that such accounts would expose many of the most economically vulnerable to unacceptable levels of risk due to fluctuations in financial markets (Szinovacz 2003; Munnell 2001; Ginn and Arber 2000).

Policy analysts linked to the libertarian Cato Institute have been making proposals along these lines since the early 1980s (Ferrara 1985). Prior to the mid-1990s, such proposals were associated with the radical right and not taken very seriously by mainstream Social Security policy analysts. This changed in the mid-1990s due to the attention given to such proposals by the Bipartisan Commission on Entitlement and Tax Reform (1995) and the Advisory Council on Social Security (1997). More recently, three alternative privatization proposals were outlined by President Bush's commission on Social Security released at the end of 2001 (President's Commission to Strengthen Social Security 2001). The report of this commission was yet another effort to build support for the partial privatization of Social Security.

While this report did not get much attention between 2002 and the end of 2004, after Bush won reelection in 2004, he made one last push to build the political support that would be needed to enact the legislation that would partially privatize Social Security. He made the idea of introducing individual accounts a central theme in his 2005 State of the Union Address and then went on to spend much of the next six months traveling around the country giving talks designed to build support for the idea. His goal seems to have been to make this one of the major policy legacies of his presidency. In the end, the effort failed. Democrats were unified in opposition, and many Republicans, particularly those who would be up for election in 2006, made it a point to distance themselves from what had become a very unpopular proposal. It seems that the more the public learned about what such a scheme would look like, the less they liked it.

Between the mid-1990s and about 2005 there was relatively little mention of the concept of generational equity in connection with the debate over Social Security reform. Advocates of partial privatization for the most part shifted to arguments emphasizing the ownership and personal economic self-interest aspect of the personal accounts (Svihula and Estes 2007), the ability to pass assets in those accounts to friends and relatives, and what some referred to as the potential for class warfare (a dramatic way of referring to the potential increase in the tax burden on the affluent due to some of the reforms that were being suggested, such as a sharp increase in the cap on earnings subject to the payroll tax) in the future to cover the projected gap between revenues collected and benefits promised (Hewitt 2007). On the left, the response was to emphasize the risk associated with assets invested in equity markets and the huge profits investment banks stood to make (White 2001; Baker and Weisbrot 1999)

THE FUTURE OF THE DEBATE

The first wave of the boomer generation is now starting to draw Social Security pensions. In the years ahead, the number of recipients and the cost of paying those pensions will both be increasing sharply. Relatively soon after the 2008 election, we expect the issue of Social Security reform to again become central to the nation's policy agenda and, with it, debates that evoke themes of generational equity and generational interdependence.

There is every reason to believe that as the boomers continue to age and more of them retire, there will be an ever-increasing pressure to make some of the hard choices about Social Security reform that politicians have been putting off for many years. In large measure, the advocacy networks that have dominated the debates and shaped old-age policy in recent decades will be back at work attempting to frame these debates in ways that are advantageous to their respective constituencies.

Modern telecommunication technologies tend to emphasize sound-bite messages and to deemphasize nuanced, fine-grained analyses calling for a careful weighing of the potential benefits and risks associated with alternative policy alternatives. As a result, it is likely that many consumers of the information that will be put out in connection with these policy debates will not be fully informed about the long-term risks and distributional consequences associated with the proposed changes. Most likely, these debates will be dominated by advocacy organizations focusing on oversimplified arguments involving easily digested catch phrases and metaphors. In such an environment, skill in framing the issues will become increasingly relevant to the success of the competing advocacy networks.

While the broad outline of the generational equity debate is likely to parallel what we have seen over the past twenty years or so, there is evidence that some important changes are taking place. The rhetoric of the environmental movement is, interestingly enough, being mixed with the rhetoric of both generational equity and generational interdependence interpretative packages. Discussions of generational equity are being linked to discourse about ecological issues and concepts such as sustainability, thrift, conservation, efficiency, and waste reduction (Kohli 2006; Schor 2004). From organizations such as Americans for Generational Equity, we will be seeing more references to "sustainability," a term that is being used more and more often, in part due to its positive connotations to environmentalism—the argument being that the current levels of Social Security pension benefits and Medicare reimbursements will not be sustainable in the decades ahead.

Those supporting the generational interdependence perspective will continue to make the argument that policy makers should not be narrowly focused on how to reduce the gap in government pension spending between different generations (or more precisely age cohorts), but instead should focus on dealing with other forms of inequality such as the pension income gaps between men and women, blacks and whites, the affluent and poor. A new theme that we anticipate hearing more about in connection with the generational interdependence frame is how to combine concerns about generational justice and environmental justice. There is going to be more focus in the decades ahead on increasing spending on environmental issues such as global warming so as not to leave a huge ecological burden on the post-boomer generations (Kingson 2007).

While there was a period between about 1995 and 2005 when there was a drop in explicit mention of generational equity, recently we have started to see more references to themes linked to this debate in discussions of aging policy. One reason is the recognition that, as each year passes, the number of boomers who are retired, retiring, or approaching retirement is increasing. There is acknowledgment by many on the political right that this demographic trend is going to make it increasingly difficult to get the political support needed to enact the partial privatization of Social Security.

One reflection of the resurgence of the contest between those advocating policies consistent with the two competing frames is the emergence in 2006 of an organization called Americans for Generational Equity (AGE). This is the same name and includes many of the same leaders and sources of funding as the earlier AGE organization that debuted in 1985 but closed in 1990 (Kingson 2007). Another organization has emerged with the name "For Our Grandchildren." As with other conservative organizations that focus on the generational equity frame and policy agenda, it does not push for more spending on programs for children, but rather on efforts to partially privatize Social Security in the name of helping today's children when they become taxpayers and eventually Social Security recipients. Other organizations, such as Generations United and AARP, are also trying to influence policy, but in ways that are consistent with generational interdependence themes. In the case of Generations United, the concern with the social welfare of both children and elders, with particular attention to finding ways to bring these groups together for mutual benefit, is particularly transparent.

Within the next few years, it is likely that some important changes will be made in Social Security policy in an effort to bring projected long-term revenues and pension expenditures into balance. Quite possibly the changes will be based on policies proposed by a truly bipartisan commission on Social Security policy along the lines of the commission that proposed the changes made in 1983. If done under a Democratic administration, the reformed system will probably be very similar to the current system, which has proven to be the nation's most popular social program for many decades.

It is not at all clear at this point that reforms will be seriously entertained by any such commission that would attempt to make a more systematic effort to balance the burden of dealing with future financing problems between the workers who are paying the payroll taxes used to finance pensions and retirees who are living on those pensions. However, there are countries that are exploring such alternatives. Some of the reforms being considered could, at least in theory, be adapted for use in the United States with the goal of increasing equity between age cohorts (generations) without subjecting economically vulnerable segments of the population to the vicissitudes of financial markets. Any future bipartisan commission dealing with Social Security reform in the United States would do well to take a close look at the pros and cons of some of these schemes, most notably the notional (unfunded) defined contribution (NDC) models that have already been introduced in countries such as Sweden, Poland, and Latvia, as well as an even newer idea referred to as the fixed relative position (FRP) model (Williamson 2004; Myles 2002). Closer to home, Diamond and Orszag (2004) offer a number of innovative ideas that deserve serious consideration, including their concept of "legacy debt," which could help with burden sharing between age cohorts without the typical regressive consequences.

REFERENCES

Advisory Council on Social Security. 1997. *Report of the 1994–1996 Advisory Council on Social Security*. Vol. 1, *Findings and recommendations*. Washington, DC: GPO.

Baker, D., and M. Weisbrot. 1999. *Social Security: The phony crisis*. Chicago: University of Chicago Press.

Ball, R. M., and T. N. Bethell. 2000. *Insuring the essentials: Bob Ball on Social Security*. New York: Century Foundation.

Béland, D. 2005. *Social Security: History and politics from the New Deal to the privatization debate*. Lawrence: University Press of Kansas.

Berkowitz, E. D. 1997. The historical development of Social Security in the United States. In *Social Security in the 21st century*, ed. E. R. Kingson and J. H. Schulz, 22–38. New York: Oxford University Press.

Binstock, R. H. 1993. Will "generational accounting" doom the welfare state? *Gerontologist* 33:812–16.

———. 1995. The oldest old and "intergenerational equity." In *The oldest old*, ed. R. M. Suzman, K. G. Manton, and D. P. Willis, 394–417. New York: Oxford University Press.

———. 1999. Scapegoating the old: Intergenerational equity and age-based health care rationing. In *The generational equity debate*, ed. J. B. Williamson, E. R. Kingson, and D. M. Watts-Roy, 185–203. New York: Columbia University Press.

———. 2000. Older people and voting participation: Past and future. *Gerontologist* 40:18–31.

———. 2007. Is responsibility across generations politically feasible? In *Challenges of an aging society: Ethical dilemmas, political issues*, ed. R. A. Pruchno and M. A. Smyer, 311–31. Baltimore: Johns Hopkins University Press.

Bipartisan Commission on Entitlement and Tax Reform. 1995. *Bipartisan Commission on Entitlement and Tax Reform: Final report*. Washington, DC: GPO.

Board of Trustees, Federal Old Age and Survivors Insurance and Disability Insurance Trust Funds. 2007. *2007 annual report of the Board of Trustees of the Federal Old Age and Survivors Insurance and Disability Insurance trust funds*. Washington, DC: GPO.

Borden, K. 1995. *Dismantling the pyramid: The why and how of privatizing Social Security*. Cato Project on Social Security Privatization SSP No. 1. Washington, DC: Cato Institute.

Butler, S., and P. Germanis. 1983. Achieving Social Security reform: A Leninist strategy. *Cato Journal* 3:547–56.

Chakravarty, S. N., and K. Weisman. 1988. Consuming our children. *Forbes*, November 14, 222–32.

Clark, R. L. 1990. Income maintenance policies in the United States. In *Handbook of Aging and the Social Sciences* (3rd ed.), ed. R. H. Binstock and L. K. George, 382–97. San Diego: Academic Press.

Concord Coalition. 1993. *The zero deficit plan.* Washington, DC: Concord Coalition.

Congressional Budget Office. 2001. *Social Security: A primer.* Washington, DC: GPO.

———. 2004. The budget and economic outlook: Fiscal years 2005 to 2014. Washington, DC: Congressional Budget Office.

Crown, W. 2001. Economic status of the elderly. In *Handbook of aging and the social sciences* (5th ed.), ed. R. H. Binstock and L. K. George, 352–68. San Diego: Academic Press.

DeNavas-Walt, C., B. D. Proctor, and C. Hill Lee. 2006. *Income, poverty, and health insurance coverage in the United States: 2005.* U.S. Census Bureau, Current Population Reports, P60-231. Washington, DC: GPO. Available at http://www.census.gov/prod/2006pubs/p60-231.pdf.

Diamond, P., and P. Orszag. 2004. *Saving Social Security: A balanced approach.* Washington, DC: Brookings Institution Press.

Estes, C. L. 2004. Social Security privatization and older women: A feminist political economy perspective. *Journal of Aging Studies* 18:9–26.

Farlie, H. 1988. Talkin' 'bout my generation. *New Republic* 198:19–22.

Ferrara, P. J. 1985. Social Security and the super IRA: A populist proposal. In *Social Security: Prospects for real reform,* ed. P. Ferrara, 193–220. Washington, DC: Cato Institute.

Ferrara, P. J., and M. Tanner. 1998. *A new deal for Social Security.* Washington, DC: Cato Institute.

Foner, A. 2000. Age integration or age conflict as society ages? *Gerontologist* 40:272–76.

Gamson, W. A. 1992. *Talking politics.* New York: Cambridge University Press.

Ginn, J., and S. Arber. 2000. Gender, the generational contract and pension privatization. In *The myth of generational conflict: The family and state in ageing societies,* ed. S. Arber and C. Attian-Donfut, 133–53. London: Routledge.

Hewitt, P. S. 2007. A conflict of generational interests. *Together* 12 (2): 4, 27.

Howe, H., and P. Longman. 1992. The next new deal. *Atlantic Monthly,* April, 88–99.

Kingson, E. R. 2007. Generations at war: The sequel. *Together* 14 (2): 5–6.

Kingson, E. R., B. A. Hirshorn, and J. M. Cornman. 1986. *Ties that bind.* Washington, DC: Seven Locks Press.

Kingson, E. R., and J. H. Schulz. 1997. Should Social Security be means-tested? In *Social Security in the 21st century,* ed. E. R. Kingson and J. H. Schulz, 41–61. New York: Oxford University Press.

Kingson, E. R., and J. B. Williamson. 1993. The generational equity debate: A progressive framing of a conservative issue. *Journal of Aging and Social Policy* 5:31–53.

———. 2001. Economic security policies. In *Handbook of aging and the social sciences* (5th ed.), ed. R. H. Binstock and L. K. George, 369–86. San Diego: Academic Press.

Kohli, M. 2006. Aging and justice. In *Handbook of Aging and the Social Sciences* (6th ed.), ed. R. H. Binstock and L. K. George, 456–78. San Diego: Academic Press.

Kotlikoff, L. J. 1992. *Generational accounting: Knowing who pays, and when, for what we spend.* New York: Free Press.

Kotlikoff, L. J., and S. Burns. 2004. *The coming generational storm: What you need to know about America's economic future.* Boston: MIT Press.

Kuttner, R. 1980. *The revolt of the haves: Tax rebellions and hard times.* New York: Simon & Schuster.

———. 1982. The Social Security hysteria. *New Republic*, December 27, 17–21.

Lakoff, G. 2004. *Don't think of an elephant!* White River Junction, VT: Chelsea Green.

Lamm, R. D. 2007. Crime of the century. July 13. Retrieved March 1, 2008, from www.age-usa.org/articles/

Longman, P. 1982. Taking America to the cleaners. *Washington Monthly*, November, 25–30.

———. 1985. Justice between generations. *Atlantic Monthly*, June, 73–81.

———. 1989. Elderly, affluent—and selfish. *New York Times.* October 10.

Marmor, T. R., F. L. Cook, and S. Scher. 1999. Social Security and the politics of generational conflict. In *The generational equity debate*, ed. J. B. Williamson, E. R. Kingson, and D. M. Watts-Roy, 185–203. New York: Columbia University Press.

Minkler, M. 1991. "Generational equity" and the new victim blaming. In *Critical perspectives in aging*, ed. M. Minkler and C. Estes, 67–79. Amityville, NY: Baywood Press.

Moody, H. R. 1992. *Ethics in an aging society.* Baltimore: Johns Hopkins University Press.

Munnell, A. H. 2001. Individual accounts versus social insurance: A United States perspective. In *Building Social Security: The challenge of privatization*, ed. X. Scheil-Adlung, 63–82. New Brunswick, NJ: Transaction.

Myles, J. 2002. A new social contract for the elderly? In *Why we need a new welfare state*, ed. G. Esping-Andersen, 130–72. Oxford: Oxford University Press.

Peterson, P. G. 1996. *Will America grow up before it grows old?* New York: Random House.

———. 1999. How will America pay for the retirement of the baby boom generation? In *The generational equity debate*, ed. J. B. Williamson, E. R. Kingson, and D. M. Watts-Roy, 41–57. New York: Columbia University Press.

Powell L. A., J. B. Williamson, and K. Branco. 1996. *The senior rights movement: Framing the policy debate in America.* New York: Twayne.

President's Commission to Strengthen Social Security. 2001. *Strengthening Social Security and creating personal wealth for all Americans: Report of the President's Commission.* Available at http://www.csss.gov/reports/Final_report.pdf.

Preston, S. H. 1984. Children and the elderly: Divergent paths for America's dependents. *Demography* 21:81–86.

Quadagno, J. S. 1989. Generational equity and the politics of the welfare state. *Politics and Society* 17:353–76.

———. 1996. Social security and the myth of the entitlement "crisis." *Gerontologist* 36:391–99.

Rosenbaum, W. A., and J. W. Button. 1989. Is there a gray peril? Retirement politics in Florida. *Gerontologist* 29:300–306.

Rother, J. 2007. Beyond intergenerational conflict. *Together* 12 (2): 5, 12.

Rubinstein, R. L. 1993. Cultural frameworks and values in intergenerational justice. In *Justice across generations: What does it mean?* ed. L. M. Cohen, 139–52. Washington, DC: American Association of Retired Persons.

Saluter, A. F. 1996. Marital status and living arrangements: March 1994. In *Current population reports* (Series P-20, no. 484). Washington, DC: U.S. Department of Commerce, Bureau of the Census.

Schor, J. 2004. Older consumers and the ecological dilemma. *Harvard Generations Policy Journal* 1 (Winter): 79–90.

Silverstein, M., T. M. Parrott, J. J. Angelelli, and F. L. Cook. 2000. Solidarity and tension between age groups in the United States: Challenge for an aging America in the 21st century. *International Journal of Social Welfare* 9:270–84.

Svihula, J., and C. L. Estes. 2007. Social Security politics: Ideology and reform. *Journal of Gerontology: Social Sciences* 62B (2): S79–S89.

Szinovacz, M. E. 2003. Contexts and pathways: Retirement as institution, process and experience. In *Retirement: Reasons, process and results*, ed. G. A. Adams and T. A. Beehr, 6–52. New York: Springer.

U.S. Census Bureau. 2006. Income, poverty, and health insurance coverage in the United States: 2005. Current Population Reports, P60-231. Retrieved February 25, 2008 from www.census.gov/rod/2006pubs/p60-231.pdf.

White, J. 2001. *False alarm*. Baltimore: Johns Hopkins University Press.

Williamson, J. B. 1997. A critique of the case for privatizing Social Security. *Gerontologist* 37:561–71.

———. 2004. Assessing the pension reform potential of a notional defined contribution pillar. *International Social Security Review* 57 (1): 47–64.

———. 2007. Social Security reform and responsibility across the generations: Framing the debate. In *Challenges of an aging society: Ethical dilemmas, political issues*, ed. R. A. Pruchno and M. A. Smyer, 311–31. Baltimore: Johns Hopkins University Press.

Williamson, J. B., T. K. McNamara, and S. A. Howling. 2003. Generational equity, generational interdependence, and the framing of the debate over social security reform. *Journal of Sociology & Social Welfare* 30:3–14.

Williamson, J. B., and S. E. Rix. 2000. Social Security reform: Implications for women. *Journal of Aging & Social Policy* 11:41–68.

Williamson, J. B., and D. M. Watts-Roy. 1999. Framing the generational equity debate. In *The generational equity debate*, ed. J. B. Williamson, E. R. Kingson, and D. M. Watts-Roy, 3–37. New York: Columbia University Press.

IV
BOOMERS AND PUBLIC POLICY

10

Population Aging, Entitlement Growth, and the Economy

JOHN GIST

The aging of the baby-boom generation and increasing longevity will, in the view of many experts, not only transform the demographic composition of the U.S. population but also cause federal spending and budget deficits to rise rapidly, driving up federal debt at a rate beyond our capacity to sustain it. In the worst-case scenario, the United States would be like a family living on credit cards and paying off debt with one card while running up spending faster with another, with insufficient income to ever pay down or get control of its debt.

This growing debt, if not checked or reversed, would absorb available capital to pay debt service rather than be used for investment, stifling economic growth. Projections by the Congressional Budget Office (CBO) of gross domestic product (GDP) growth over the forty-four years from 2006 to 2050 average only 2.2 percent per year, compared with 3.4 percent over the forty-four years 1962–2006. To illustrate the significance of the difference, in fifty years the lower growth rate would triple the size of the economy, but the higher rate would quintuple it.

A stagnant economy would also affect the standard of living of American families. As overall economic growth slows, family income growth would be ratcheted down as well. The income stagnation that middle-class families have experienced in recent years would likely become routine, and families would face the additional burdens of reductions in employer-arranged benefits, increased private health insurance premiums, and increased taxes and Medicare premiums intended to offset the effects of rising deficits.

In this chapter, I examine the role of population aging in our long-term budgetary problems. The first section discusses entitlements and their historical and projected growth patterns, and the following section shows that aging plays only a minor role in the growth of entitlement programs. I then review some of the beneficial effects of entitlement spending and compare spending entitlement programs with tax programs that confer similar entitlement benefits on their beneficiaries. The last two sections discuss several factors that may mitigate future budgetary pressures and offer a plausible scenario for addressing future budgetary challenges.

WHAT ARE ENTITLEMENTS?

The term *entitlements* is shorthand for a category of benefits defined in the Congressional Budget Reform and Impoundment Control Act of 1974 that are conferred directly by legislation on any person or unit of government that meets the eligibility requirements established by such legislation.[1] In budgetary terms, entitlements are programs that generally carry permanent authorizations and are not subject to annual appropriations, thereby insulating them from congressional appropriations scrutiny.

Although there are more than four hundred entitlements (General Accounting Office 1994), they are often thought of as synonymous with the three largest of those programs—Social Security, Medicare, and Medicaid—because the three compose more than 75 percent of entitlement outlays. The measure most often used to gauge the size of entitlement spending is its ratio to GDP, the total output of the economy. This measure provides a rough index of the burden of entitlement spending on the overall economy. Figure 10-1 shows the ratio of total entitlement spending and the three largest entitlement programs (Social Security, Medicare, and Medicaid) to GDP from 1962 to the present and projected out to 2050.[2]

Numerous experts have characterized entitlement growth as "unsustainable." The CBO has provided a succinct definition for sustainability: "[F]or any path of spending and revenues to be sustainable, the resulting debt must eventually grow no faster than the economy"—that is, debt must represent a constant or declining ratio to GDP (CBO 1998).

Although entitlement spending has grown faster than GDP when measured over the past four decades (5 percent vs. 3.5 percent), the difference is entirely attributable to a period of growth in spending from 1967 through 1983 that was spurred by new programs, expansions of existing programs, and three recessions. During that period, entitlement spending increased more than twice as fast as GDP (7 percent vs. 2.8 percent) and doubled as a share of GDP, at a time when two oil shocks, a deep recession, and record-high interest rates were roiling the U.S. economy.

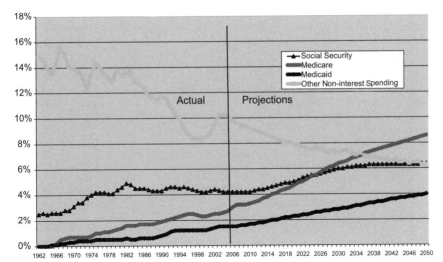

FIGURE 10-1. Spending for Largest Three Entitlements and All Other Noninterest Spending as a Percentage of GDP, 1962–2050
Source: CBO 2005, Supplemental Data (Intermediate projections)

Since its high point in 1983, however, entitlement spending has been a picture of stability, growing at virtually the same rate as the economy (3.37 vs. 3.31 percent). It has also shown a slight countercyclical pattern, increasing during every economic recession in the past thirty years (1973–75, 1980–82, and 1990–91) and declining relative to GDP in every economic expansion over the same period (see figure 10-2). The lines in figure 10-2 generally move in opposite directions, except for the 1999–2004 period. Compared with the more volatile 1970s, this countercyclical pattern has become more muted in recent years, but it illustrates that sustained and strong economic expansions are still contributing factors to containing entitlement spending—they slow the rate of growth of populations in need and they cause income tax revenue, due to graduated rates, to grow faster than the economy. The past stability of entitlement spending may be at an end, however, judging from CBO projections.

In this chapter, I use CBO's "mandatory spending" budget category as synonymous with entitlement spending, which it virtually is. This category excludes another item of required spending in the budget—net interest payments. Net interest is not typically considered an entitlement because it is not a benefit program.[3] I follow the CBO practice and do not treat net interest as an entitlement in this analysis.

Some entitlements are "non-means-tested," meaning there are income or wealth tests to determine who is eligible for benefits. These include Social Security, Medicare, unemployment insurance, and civilian and military

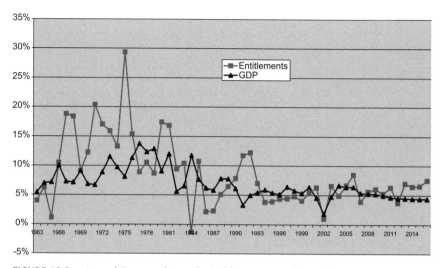

FIGURE 10-2. Annual Percent Change in Entitlement Spending and GDP, 1962–2016
Source: CBO 2006, appendix F, Historical Budget Data

retirement programs, which all provide benefits based on work histories rather than need. Means-tested entitlements include Supplemental Security Income (SSI), food stamps, Medicaid, and many smaller programs. Non-means-tested programs are more than three times as large as means-tested benefits, and the difference is likely to increase in future years with the growth in Social Security and Medicare.

Besides these familiar spending programs, entitlements also include the outlay portion of the Earned Income and Child Tax credits. Although these are tax provisions, they result in direct spending because they are "refundable" credits. If a tax filer's credit exceeds his or her income tax liability, the Internal Revenue Service pays a cash refund. The refundable amount is the entitlement outlay. In truth, however, the entire amount of the tax reduction, not just the direct outlay, represents a benefit to the taxpayer, so it is conceptually equivalent to an entitlement. In the language of tax policy, these are commonly known as "tax expenditures,"[4] and they bear a striking resemblance to spending entitlements. Like spending entitlements, they confer direct benefits automatically under the law to those individuals who meet the legal requirements without any advance appropriation, and they have the same effect on the budget deficit as spending programs do.[5] We will return to these tax provisions later in the chapter.

WHAT DRIVES ENTITLEMENT SPENDING?

Demographic aging is not a sufficient explanation for the projected future growth in entitlement spending. If it were, we ought to see similarities in the projected growth of those programs that primarily target older

Americans—namely, Social Security and Medicare.[6] Instead, there are very distinct differences in the past and future growth patterns of these two social insurance programs, which illustrates that demography as an explanation misses much of the story.

Differences in Entitlement Growth Rates

As figure 10-3 shows, different types of entitlements have had very different growth histories and will have very different growth futures. *Retirement* programs—Social Security and federal civilian and military pensions—have had a far more stable pattern than federal *health* spending, which is dominated by Medicare and Medicaid.[7] A third "safety net" category consists of mostly means-tested programs. This category includes those entitlements—such as SSI, food stamps, and unemployment compensation—that are targeted at individuals who are in economic need. We place all other entitlements into a residual category.

Health spending is the only category of entitlement spending that has grown without interruption, a virtually unbroken string of increases in health spending over forty years, with one notable exception in the last three years of the Clinton administration. Retirement spending, which peaked at 6.1 percent of GDP in 1983, has since drifted down to 5.5 percent and is projected to reach only 5.7 percent of GDP in 2016, eight years after the first boomer receives early Social Security benefits. Safety net spending has fluctuated between 1 and 2 percent of GDP, after peaking in 1976 at 2.3 percent of GDP. It has since declined slowly to about 1.5 percent today and is

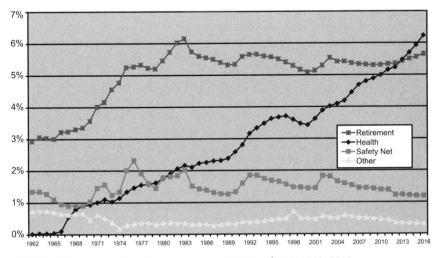

FIGURE 10-3. Types of Entitlements as a Percentage of GDP, 1962–2016
Source: CBO 2006, appendix F, Historical Budget Data

projected to decline further by 2016. "Other" entitlement spending has never exceeded 1 percent of GDP, and it is projected to be 0.3 percent in 2016.

The CBO projects Social Security, Medicare, and Medicaid separately to 2050 based on size of beneficiary populations and average per-capita cost. It forecasts that Social Security will drift upward from about 4 percent to about 6 percent of GDP between 2010 and 2030, then remain virtually flat, whereas the health spending share will continue its rise, reaching roughly double the size of Social Security by 2050. Social Security's growth "bump" from 2010 to 2035 is due almost entirely to the retirement of the boomer cohort, while the steep health spending trajectory is largely due to nondemographic factors, especially medical technology.

Is Aging the Cause of Increases in Health Entitlements?

If health spending is the primary driver of past and future total entitlement spending, does aging explain that growth?[8] According to estimates from the CBO, Medicare cost growth is not primarily due to population aging but rather to other factors. The CBO has estimated that about one-sixth of Medicare's cost growth since 1970 was due to increases in the size of the older population, with the rest attributed to other causes (see figure 10-4).

Other studies have demonstrated that lifetime health care costs are not much different for Americans with average life expectancies than for those with much longer life spans (Lubitz et al. 1995, 2003; Spillman and Lubitz 2000; Joyce et al. 2005). Elderly persons in better health have longer life

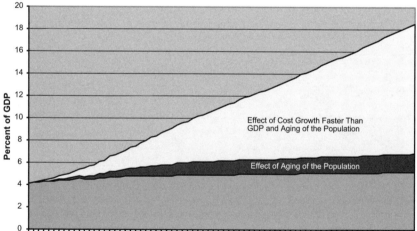

FIGURE 10-4.   Effect of Aging and Excess Cost Growth on Medicare and Medicaid Spending, 2007–2082

Source: CBO 2007, supplementary data

expectancies than those in poorer health, but they have similar cumulative health care expenditures until death for those health services that are covered by Medicare (Lubitz et al. 2003). Medicare expenditures will be affected much more by the absolute increase in the numbers of the elderly, which will surge between 2010 and 2030, than by longevity increases.

On the other hand, nursing home care costs (which, for the most part, are not covered by Medicare) and to a smaller extent home care costs climb steeply with advanced age. These costs mainly affect the Medicaid program (see below).

Is the Rise in National Health Spending Due to Health Entitlements?

Although health spending across the board has proven difficult to restrain, Medicare spending overall has been contained more effectively than has private-sector health spending for decades. Medicare has actually led the nation in the effort to control health care costs through innovations in reimbursement for hospitals and physicians. These innovations, which have been copied by many private-sector insurers, have proven effective, as seen in the differences in the rates of growth of public and private health care costs over the past three decades (Boccuti and Moon 2003) (see figure 10-5 below).

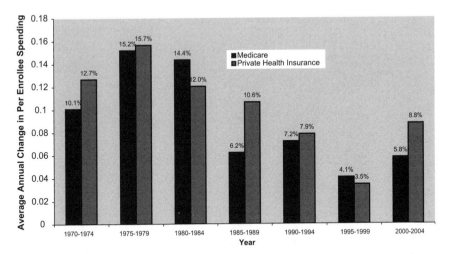

FIGURE 10-5. Average Annual Change in Per-Enrollee Medicare Spending and Private Health Insurance Premiums (for Common Benefits), 1969–2004

Note: Annual change is calculated from previous year. "Common benefits" refers to benefits commonly covered by Medicare and private health insurance: hospital services, physician and clinical services, other professional services, and durable medical products.

Source: Centers for Medicare and Medicaid Services, Office of the Actuary, National Health Statistics Group, table 13, http://www.cms.hhs.gov/NationalHealthExpendData/downloads/tables.pdf.

As a federal-state program, Medicaid has much greater spending variation than Medicare because it pays for health care for a variety of low-income persons. The average growth in costs per Medicaid beneficiary was highest among aged beneficiaries between 1975 and 2002 (5.3 percent per year) (see figure 10-6). Yet because the growth rate in the number of aged beneficiaries was far below that of any other beneficiary group (0.3 percent per year between 1975 and 2002), the growth in the total cost of aged Medicaid beneficiaries was below that of both disabled and child beneficiaries, and only slightly higher than that for adult beneficiaries. Aged beneficiaries accounted for 37 percent of all Medicaid program expenditures in 1975, but by 2002 that share had dipped to 25 percent (Boccuti and Moon 2003, 8, table 2).

The consensus among health experts is that a small number of factors accounts for the bulk of the increases in health spending. The most important of these is technological change, which affects both the public and private health sectors. As the CBO has noted, "In the health care field, unlike in many sectors of the economy, technological advances have generally raised costs rather than lowered them" (2005, 6). Another factor is the use or intensity of services, and a third is the sharp increases in the cost of prescription drugs. While they contribute to the growth in the costs of Medicare and Medicaid, these factors also drive up the cost of health care nationally, affecting all payers, both public and private, including individuals, employers, and state and federal governments.

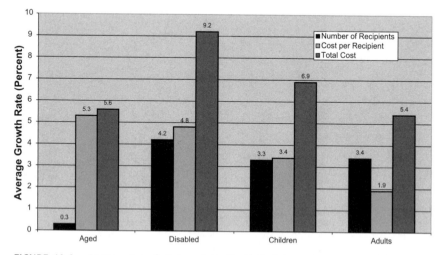

FIGURE 10-6. Average Growth Rates of Medicaid Recipients, Costs per Recipient, and Total Costs by Eligibility Category, Fiscal Years 1975–2002
Source: Congressional Budget Office, "Medicaid Spending Growth and Options for Controlling Costs," testimony of Donald B. Marron before the Special Committee on Aging, United States Senate, July 13, 2006.

ECONOMIC AND DISTRIBUTIONAL EFFECTS OF ENTITLEMENTS

Entitlement spending programs represent the most visible part of our nation's social welfare system. The "big three" entitlement programs have had significant impacts on the economic and health status of older Americans. Social Security has brought about sharp decreases in elderly poverty since the early 1960s (Beedon and Wu 2005) and has had important impacts on income levels and income inequality, although such comparisons should acknowledge that in the absence of Social Security, people would likely behave quite differently. The incomes of seniors would be less than half as large without social insurance cash transfers (U.S. Bureau of the Census 2006), and these transfers have increased the share of income going to the top three-fifths of the population.[9] Social Security has allowed older Americans to have much greater independence than they did a half-century ago (McGarry and Schoeni 1998). Medicare was responsible for bringing health insurance coverage to nearly all older Americans, only a little more than half of whom had coverage in 1963 before Medicare was created (Moon 2000; AARP 2005). The introduction of Medicare has been estimated to reduce by 40 percent the out-of-pocket costs for the quarter of beneficiaries with the highest out-of-pocket costs (Finkelstein and McKnight 2005).

Although most Americans are familiar with the part of our social welfare system represented by these spending programs, an entirely distinct and more "hidden" part of our social welfare system operates through the tax code (Howard 1997; Hacker 2002). It provides more than $100 billion for retirement savings and more than $90 billion each for health insurance and the purchase of homes. The tax code contains hundreds of such provisions, including deductions, preferential rates, exclusions from income, and credits against tax liability that confer substantial but far less visible benefits that are for all practical purposes another category of entitlements—"tax entitlements." After the Tax Reform Act of 1986 took effect, tax entitlements increased as a percentage of total spending entitlements from just over 50 percent in 1988 to nearly 60 percent of spending entitlements today. To put the size of tax entitlements into proper perspective, the total estimated revenue loss from individual tax expenditures was 6.4 percent of GDP in 2006, more than three times the federal budget deficit (Hungerford 2006b).[10]

Distribution of Spending Entitlements by Income

The argument is occasionally heard that spending entitlements should be means-tested, on the grounds that they provide excessive benefits to the affluent. Such arguments are rarely heard about tax benefits. Spending entitlements have contributed to a much-reduced poverty rate and a more equal distribution of income; tax entitlements, with certain obvious exceptions like the Earned Income Credit, have not.

Direct spending entitlement programs have been well targeted at lower- and middle-income and vulnerable populations, bringing about dramatic changes in economic and social well-being for Americans of all ages. Social Security and Medicare are relatively progressive programs, because younger workers redistribute income toward lower-income retirees. Figure 10-7 shows that the seven largest entitlement spending programs, which total more than three-fourths of all spending entitlement dollars, are fairly evenly distributed by income, with the bottom half and top half each receiving roughly 50 percent of all benefits.[11]

Distribution of Tax Entitlements by Income

Tax entitlement benefits have in some cases also brought about dramatic economic changes, such as high rates of homeownership and broad health insurance coverage. But in marked contrast to spending entitlement programs, tax entitlements disproportionately benefit the highest income classes. Figure 10-8 shows the distribution of nine tax entitlements, including the seven largest, representing more than half of all tax entitlement dollars. Using the same income framework as with spending entitlements, tax entitlements are overwhelmingly concentrated in the top two income deciles, which receive almost two-thirds of all the tax benefits for these nine items.

Even those tax entitlements that are fairly widely received, such as the mortgage interest or state and local tax deductions, are highly skewed.

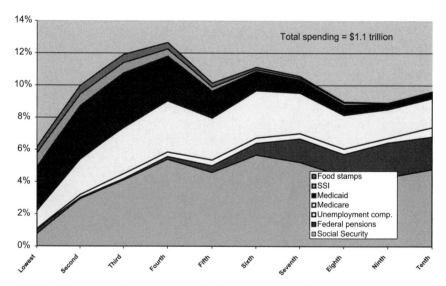

FIGURE 10-7. Cumulative Percent Distribution of Selected Major Spending Entitlements, All Ages, by Income Decile
Source: Estimates by Chainbridge Software using its Individual Income Tax Model

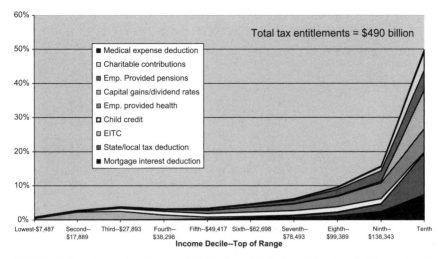

FIGURE 10-8. Cumulative Percent Distribution of Selected Major Tax Entitlements, All Ages, by Income Decile, 2006
Source: Estimates by Chainbridge Software using its Individual Income Tax Model

Nearly 80 percent of mortgage interest deduction benefits go to the top 20 percent of households. An even larger percentage of state and local tax deductions—nearly 90 percent—goes to households in the top 20 percent.[12]

Distribution of Entitlements by Age

Entitlement critics have argued that the benefits of spending entitlements are excessively skewed toward the older population. Tax entitlements are rarely subjected to the same analysis. Figure 10-9 compares the age distribution of the seven spending and nine tax entitlements discussed above. Of all spending entitlements (a total of more than $1.1 trillion included here), about six in ten federal dollars went to the older population, while nearly seven of eight federal tax benefit dollars (of nearly $500 billion included here) went to those under age 65.[13] Tax experts might point out that older citizens are less likely to pay income taxes and therefore cannot realize tax benefits, which they would have received as younger workers. But the same can be said of Social Security and Medicare—these benefits are received by older citizens, but they will also enjoy these benefits when they reach eligibility age.

Joint Distribution of Spending and Tax Entitlements by Age and Income

Figure 10-10 combines the distribution of both spending and tax entitlements by age and income. Overall, about 54 percent of all entitlement dollars are received by the under-65 population, represented by the top two areas.

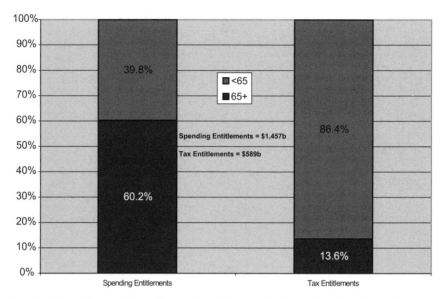

FIGURE 10-9.   Shares of Spending and Tax Entitlements Received, by Age Group, 2006

The 54 percent is divided roughly equally between spending ($450 billion) and tax ($424 billion) entitlements. Only 46 percent of all the entitlement benefits represented in figure 10-10 are received by the 65-and-older population, 42 percent coming from spending and 4 percent from tax entitlements.[14]

The share of entitlements received by older Americans tends to be more concentrated in the middle of the income distribution. By contrast, the entitlement benefits received by the under-65 age group occur at the two extremes of the income distribution. The low-income group is due to means-tested benefits primarily, whereas the high-income group is mainly due to tax benefits for the affluent. Although this suggests nothing about the individual lifetime distribution of entitlement benefits, collectively these benefits are spread fairly evenly across the life cycle, not concentrated on those in retirement.

SOME MITIGATING FACTORS

Several factors may warrant a more optimistic perspective on long-term budgetary trends.

Future Dependency Ratios Stay below Their 1960s Levels

One overlooked factor is that we have had larger dependent populations in our history than we have today or will have in the distant future. Although slow growth in the labor force and rapid growth in the retired population are projected to cause the *aged* dependency ratio—the ratio of

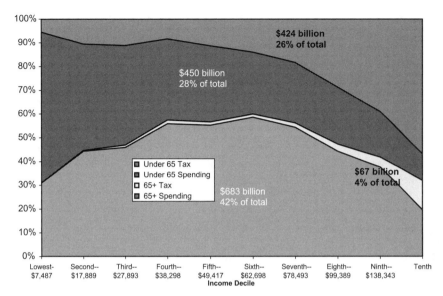

FIGURE 10-10. Shares of Combined Spending and Tax Entitlements Received by 65+ and Under 65 Age Groups, by Income Decile (in thousands of 2006 dollars)
Source: Estimates by Chainbridge Software using its Individual Income Tax Model.

elderly persons to working-age persons—to rise from 0.203 in 2005 (or about four workers to every elderly person) to 0.431 in 2080 (or slightly more than two workers to every elderly person), the *total* dependency ratio—the ratio of the retirees *plus* youth to people of working age—will be lower in 2010 (0.66) than it was in the 1960s (0.95) and will remain below 0.9 through 2080 (Board of Trustees 2005, table V.A.2.)

The increasing need to spend on the old is partially offset by the shrinking need to provide for the young through schools. The total dependency ratio reached its peak in the mid-1960s, with nearly one worker for each child or elderly person. It fell steadily from the late 1960s through 2005, and it has not yet bottomed out. By 2010, it is expected to hit its low point and start rising again, although it will not return to its 1965 peak during the seventy-five-year forecast horizon. Even as late as 2080, the ratio is projected to stand at 0.859—lower than it was in 1960 (Board of Trustees 2005, table V.A.2). As noted earlier, the costs of younger dependents are approximately 40 percent those of older dependents (CBO 2000; Cutler et al. 1990).

Lengthening Work Lives

It is often suggested that it will be necessary to raise the Social Security normal retirement age to make Social Security solvent. Yet important shifts have already taken place in labor force participation rates among older workers, and the trends show signs of continuing (see figure 10-11). There has been a perceptible and steady increase over time in the labor force participation of people in their late 50s, 60s, and 70s (Quinn 1999). Labor force participation rose in the late 1990s, undoubtedly in part to the robust economy, but the trend continued during the 2001 recession and after.

Previous projections of labor force participation rates for workers age 55 and older (Fullerton 1999) may underestimate the increase (Verma and Rix 2002). Four-fifths of boomers report that they expect to work at least part-time in retirement (AARP 1999), and the age at which people can receive full Social Security benefits is increasing to 67, reducing benefits accordingly and encouraging more people to work longer.

Although total Social Security program costs are little affected if people delay Social Security benefit receipt because of actuarial adjustments,[15] working longer and opting for later benefits increases monthly Social Security benefit payments and reduces the number of years workers need to cover with their private savings. For example, the oldest boomers will be eligible to receive only 75 percent of their normal Social Security benefit if they apply at age 62 (70 percent for younger boomers), 100 percent if they wait until age 66, and 132 percent if they wait until age 70 (CBO 2004). Working longer also gives a worker fewer years of retirement to finance and more time to accumulate additional savings. Furthermore, it helps the Social Security trust fund by adding payroll tax revenues. A CBO report has shown that a working couple at the median income level could, by working until

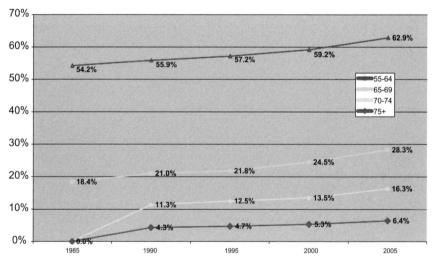

FIGURE 10-11. Labor Force Participation Rates of Persons Aged 55 and Older, by Age Group, 1985–2005
Source: U.S. Bureau of Labor Statistics, *Labor Force Statistics from the Current Population Survey, 1985–2005,* http://data.bls.gov/PDQ/outside.jsp?survey=ln.

age 70 rather than retiring at age 62, reduce by *90 percent* (from $510,000 to $51,000) the amount of assets they would need *at age 62* to produce a desired replacement rate of 80 percent in retirement.

Declining Disability Rates

A study of changing disability patterns found that the prevalence of disability among older Americans is declining at an accelerating pace (Manton and Gu 2001). Singer and Manton (1998) have argued that if a 1.5 percent annual decline (comparable to 1989–1994 and slower than 1994–1999; see figure 10-12) in chronic disability continued indefinitely, it would substantially bolster the long-term fiscal solvency of *both* the Medicare and Social Security programs. Since then, that rate of disability decline has not only continued but has accelerated. However, others have suggested that, despite savings from reductions in the prevalence of disability, the increases in technology-driven costs are still likely to exceed those savings (Cutler 2001).

Although they did not estimate impacts on the Medicaid program, Manton and Gu (2001) found that the relative decline in nursing home use between 1994 and 1999 was larger (3.5 percent per year) than the decline in disability, suggesting the potential for significant savings in the Medicaid program as well. Nursing home utilization occupancy rates declined by 41 percent between 1973 and 2004 for the 65-and-older population. Health improvements have shrunk the long-term care market directly by reducing the base of people who need care, and they have shrunk the market

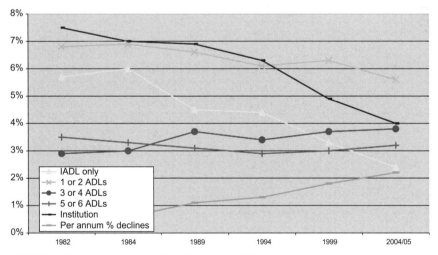

FIGURE 10-12. Percentage of Disability Group Estimates, National Long-Term Care Survey, 1982–2004/2005
Source: Manton et al. 2006.

indirectly by increasing the supply of healthy elderly people who can provide care at home (Lakdawalla and Philipson 2002).

MAKING ENTITLEMENTS SUSTAINABLE: POLICY SOLUTIONS

A Plausible Future Scenario

In the CBO's long-term budget scenarios, the most important spending factor is the rate of growth of health care costs, and the most important revenue factor is the assumption made regarding congressional action on taxes. The CBO's intermediate assumption about health care costs was that Medicare and Medicaid would grow in the future by one percentage point faster than the rate of growth of per-capita GDP. This "excess cost growth" assumption is consistent with declining costs for both Medicare and Medicaid since 1970, and evidence that the rate of excess cost growth in Medicare dropped to 0.9 percent from 1992 to 2003 (White 2006).

Using the intermediate assumption, the CBO projected that Medicare and Medicaid spending would triple to 12.6 percent of GDP by 2050, that the three largest entitlements would increase from 8.4 percent to 19 percent of GDP by 2050, and that total federal spending would rise by 50 percent, from 20.1 percent to 30 percent of GDP. However, primary spending (i.e., excluding net interest) would rise by somewhat less, from 18.5 percent to 25.3 percent, or by 37 percent.

On the revenue side, the CBO's future revenue scenarios followed one of two simple rules of thumb: (1) continue current law, allowing tax revenues automatically to rise as a percentage of GDP, or (2) hold tax revenues at the same ratio to GDP that they have been for the past thirty years (i.e., about 18.3 percent) via periodic tax *cuts*. Assuming the former, revenues would grow to 23.7 percent of GDP by 2050.[16] Assuming current law revenue policy coupled with intermediate health spending growth would yield a primary deficit (i.e., the gap between revenues and noninterest, or primary, spending) of 1.6 percent of GDP by 2050. This figure is smaller than the primary deficit in the federal budgets of 2003 and 2004, and only slightly higher than the 2005 deficit. This scenario's revenue, primary spending, and primary and total deficit projections are shown in figure 10-13.

This plausible scenario shows that, with health spending restraint comparable to that of the past decade and with a "hands-off" revenue policy[17]—we can at least *approach* a solution to our long-term fiscal problem.[18] This scenario still does not achieve sustainability, though, because annual deficits would cumulate over time (notice the bottom light line in figure 10-13), resulting in debt levels nearly equal to GDP by 2050 and rising faster than the economy—an unsustainable outcome.[19] Additional fiscal actions would be needed to either moderate the rate of spending growth or further boost federal revenues in order to achieve a sustainable debt-to-GDP ratio. Some of those actions are discussed briefly below.

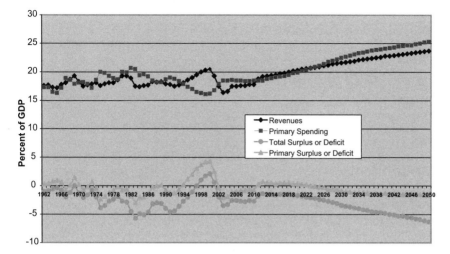

FIGURE 10-13. Federal Revenues, Primary Spending, and Surpluses/Deficits as a Percentage of GDP under CBO Long-Term Budget Scenarios, 2006–2050
Source: CBO 2005.

Make Social Security Solvent

The reforms needed to bring Social Security into long-term actuarial balance are far from radical. To put the funding gap in perspective, between 1967 and 1983, Social Security nearly doubled as a percentage of GDP, from 2.6 percent to 4.9 percent, in *fifteen years*. By contrast, Social Security will grow by about the same amount (smaller in percentage terms), from 4.2 percent to 6.6 percent of GDP, over the next *twenty-five years*.

Expressed as a percentage of payroll, Social Security's financing gap is about 1.95 percent of covered payroll over the next seventy-five years. It is unlikely that solvency will be achieved with revenue-only or spending-only solutions. Raising the taxable wage base to 90 percent of covered wages would restore the Old-Age, Survivors, and Disability Insurance (OASDI) taxable wage base to historical levels and close nearly half of the funding gap. Other proposals would bring in additional revenues, such as including all newly hired state and local workers in Social Security.

Benefit reductions are also likely. Adjusting the Social Security benefit formula to scale total benefits back while protecting the lowest-income workers and indexing benefits for longevity could achieve sufficient benefit reductions, coupled with the above revenue increases, to achieve solvency.

Expand the Federal Revenue Base

Although federal revenues have returned to their long-run average relative to GDP after deep tax cuts in 2001 and 2003, the level of federal revenues is simply too low to finance our increasing domestic and global commitments. The U.S. federal tax burden is one of the lowest in the industrialized world. Allowing revenues to rise automatically with economic growth would be a simple way to bolster federal revenues, but it would gradually raise effective marginal tax rates on all Americans. Higher tax rates are said to reduce the incentives to work, save, and invest, lowering labor supply and capital investment and threatening economic growth. Despite the theoretical reasoning behind this position, the historical and current evidence for it is weak (Lindert 2004; Hungerford 2006a).

The CBO's examination of two long-term budget scenarios provides further evidence that higher revenues will not seriously damage the economy. Either scenario would achieve long-term growth while roughly balancing revenues and outlays. In one option, balance would be achieved by allowing revenues to rise by 6.2 percent of GDP; in the other, by cutting spending by that amount. The CBO found that the revenue-increase option would result in an economy in 2050 of $31.5 trillion, compared with $32.8 trillion with the lower-spending option. This difference in 2050 represented an annual growth difference of 0.09 percentage points—for example, a rate of 2.91 percent per year rather than 3 percent, which is hardly a doomsday scenario (CBO 2005). Choosing some *combination* of increased revenues and spending rate reductions would presumably produce an even smaller reduction in future GDP.

Increase Personal and National Savings

The long-term growth of the economy depends on adequate saving to finance capital investment. The personal saving rate in the United States, as measured by the Federal Reserve's measure of personal savings in the Flow of Funds Accounts, has steadily declined since the 1980s, dropping below zero for the first time since the 1930s at the end of 2005 and remaining negative in 2006. The structure of savings incentives in the tax code mainly benefits higher-income taxpayers and is poorly designed to increase savings. Tax incentives that target lower-income households, which are most likely to be saving below their desired and optimal levels, are likely to be more efficient. The best way to target those who are in the bottom tier of income is through employer-based salary reduction plans that are structured in ways to take advantage of the inertia and the "path of least resistance" that workers frequently exhibit. Plans that have automatic enrollment as the default option or a mandated contribution rate dedicated to personal retirement saving, an employer (or government) match for those with lower incomes, a moderate-risk default investment portfolio, and sharply limited opportunities for cashing out accounts are more likely to increase saving among lower-income workers. Plans that require employees to opt in, do not offer a match, allow workers to invest too conservatively, and make cash-outs relatively easy are not likely to successfully increase saving (Choi et al. 2001a, 2001b).

For those fortunate enough to have access to a 401(k) plan through their employer, introducing these automatic features has proven effective as a way to boost participation. For those less fortunate, pending legislative proposals to introduce an "auto-IRA" via payroll deduction would use the same method proven effective with 401(k)s to boost savings among those who have no pension at all.

The Saver's Credit is the only vehicle that targets saving incentives to those with low and moderate income, whose saving is more likely to represent net additions to national saving rather than asset shifting. This provision was recently made permanent by Congress and its income thresholds indexed for inflation. The maximum credit is $1,000, but the average credit actually claimed in tax year 2002 was about $200. The Saver's Credit could be an even more effective saving incentive if it were expanded and made refundable, so that a greater benefit would flow to lower-income households. Its perverse income phaseout rates could also be modified to avoid creating excessively high effective marginal tax rates on individuals who pass from the lowest income-eligibility category (about twice the poverty line) to the next (Southworth and Gist 2008).

Restore Fiscal Discipline

Personal saving is not the only saving that counts. Declines in private saving were offset in the 1990s by *public* saving due mostly to federal budget surpluses. Fiscal experts have said for years that the best way to increase national saving was to eliminate the federal budget deficit. What once seemed impossible—a balanced federal budget—was achieved by 1998, followed by three more surplus years. As recently as 2001, surpluses were forecast to continue into the era of boomers' retirement, permitting the elimination of the entire public debt by fiscal year 2010.

An important step toward rectifying our fiscal shortfalls is to increase our revenue base to a level that is adequate to meet our domestic and global commitments. Federal spending in 2007 was 20.0 percent of GDP, while revenues were at 18.8 percent, a large disparity for a period of economic expansion. Any new spending or tax measure should be weighed against its impact on the deficit. Important and desirable policy changes, such as reform of the individual alternative minimum tax, should be undertaken with the goal that they should not worsen the overall budget deficit. A serious commitment to fiscal discipline requires that we retain the pay-as-you-go (paygo) rules that require equal offsets for any increase in entitlement spending or reduction in taxes.

CONCLUSION

The "graying" of America has caused alarm among many experts that the future cost of federal health and retirement programs will create huge federal deficits, dry up capital for investment, and jeopardize long-term economic growth. Spending entitlements—specifically Social Security, Medicare, and Medicaid—are generally seen as the main factor driving this scenario. But the data show that an aging population actually explains relatively little of the long-term growth in spending. The most important factor is the growth in health care costs, and health spending has been contained even more effectively in the Medicare program than in private health insurance plans.

Spending entitlements represent only one portion of our social welfare programs—tax preferences represent nearly another trillion dollars in social welfare benefits. And although critics often claim that older Americans benefit disproportionately from entitlement spending, when tax entitlements and spending entitlements are cumulated, a majority of combined entitlement benefits are actually received by people under age 65.

Certain hopeful trends may portend a more sustainable economic future. Older workers have been staying in the labor force longer, a trend that means higher Social Security taxes to improve the system's finances. In addition, disability rates appear to have declined steadily for the past decade or more, and nursing home utilization rates have also declined. The productivity of workers has surged in recent years and, if sustained, could help offset the future expected decline in the size of the labor force.

A plausible long-term scenario suggests that a future "train wreck" can be averted if we are able to maintain the same level of spending restraint in our health programs that we have already achieved in the past decade *and* we allow revenues to rise automatically without legislating additional tax cuts. In such a scenario, the primary deficit would be no larger in 2050 than it is today. Because debt would still be rising in this scenario, additional policy solutions would be needed to keep debt from growing faster than GDP—making Social Security solvent, increasing federal revenues, boosting national saving, imposing tighter fiscal discipline, and improving control of health care costs.

NOTES

1. The Congressional Budget Act defined *entitlement authority* as "authority to make payments (including loans and grants), the budget authority for which is not provided for in advance by appropriations Acts, to any person or government if, under the provisions of the law containing such authority, the United States is obligated to make such payments to persons or governments who meet the requirements established by such law" (P.L. 93-344, 88 Stat. 297, July 12, 1974).

2. The CBO projects spending for Social Security, Medicare, and Medicaid through 2050 based on growth in beneficiary populations as well as other programmatic assumptions. Other entitlements are simply assumed to grow at the same rate as GDP.

3. Interest on the debt is a contractual agreement and not technically an entitlement, but it should be included in any discussion of budget items not *controllable* through the normal congressional appropriations process.

4. Tax expenditures are defined in the Congressional Budget Reform and Impoundment Control Act of 1974 as "revenue losses attributable to provisions of the Federal tax laws which allow a special exclusion, exemption, or deduction from gross income or which provide a special credit, a preferential rate of tax, or a deferral of tax liability" (P.L. 93-344, sec. 3[3]).

5. To quote the congressional Joint Committee on Taxation: "Special income tax provisions are referred to as tax expenditures because they may be considered to be analogous to direct outlay programs, and the two can be considered as alternative means of accomplishing similar budget policy objectives. Tax expenditures are similar to those direct spending programs that are available as entitlements to those who meet the statutory criteria established for the programs" (U.S. Congress, Joint Committee on Taxation 2006, 2).

6. Both programs have a substantial share of beneficiaries who are under 65 but disabled.

7. Medicaid is a federal-state program that pays for health care for certain categories of very low-income people, as well as being the chief source of spending for long-term care services. It could be regarded as the single largest safety net program, but for analytical purposes, we include it with health entitlements.

8. Although Medicare is typically thought of as a program for the population age 65 and older, in 2003 about 14.3 percent of enrollees were under age 65, including 13.9 percent who were eligible for Medicare because of a disability and 0.4 percent who were eligible because they had end-stage renal disease (ESRD).

9. Based on the Current Population Survey's pretax, post-transfer income definition and not adjusted for family size. When incomes are adjusted for the lower taxes and smaller household size of older households, income differentials are much smaller. Retirement income among U.S. retirees is, with the exception of Social Security, not indexed for inflation. As a consequence, other income categories decline in real terms over the course of retirement in the United States, while Social Security does not (Hungerford 2003).

10. Strictly speaking, tax entitlements are not additive. Each one is estimated separately as though all the others are in place. They interact, and the sum of all tax entitlements would not precisely equal the amount of revenue gained if they were all repealed. However, many experts have added them together to provide a rough approximation of their combined effect (Hungerford 2006b).

11. The estimates were provided by Chainbridge Software, an economic consulting firm. The income definition used to classify individuals starts with adjusted gross income and adds tax-exempt interest, the employer share of Medicare and Social Security payroll taxes, workers' compensation, and untaxed Social Security benefits. The cutting points for the ten deciles, which are for the entire population, are $7,487 (between the first and second deciles), $17,889, $27,893, $38,298, $49,417, $62,698, $78,493, $99,389, and $138,343.

12. Some experts question whether tax entitlements are really like entitlement spending, arguing that they are not "exceptions" to the "normal" tax code but rather part of lawmakers' intent, so that the code with all its exceptions should be regarded as the baseline for comparison. That argument would be more persuasive if the special provisions were all part of the original code, but most provisions have not been. Furthermore, because some types of income, such as pension contributions, receive "consumption tax treatment" (taxes deferred until income is consumed), they are explicitly treated

differently from the way they would be treated under a pure income tax. This preferential treatment suggests that these provisions are exceptions.

13. In this analysis, we have apportioned Social Security, Medicare, and Medicaid benefits to those under age 65 and those aged 65 and older.

14. It is true that a smaller percentage of the population age 65 and older pays income taxes compared with younger age groups, and therefore they have less likelihood of benefiting from tax entitlements. But the reason they do not pay income taxes is that a higher percentage of elderly households have incomes too low to be taxable and therefore are not *able* to receive tax benefits.

15. Some cost reduction occurs if people die prior to receiving benefits.

16. That scenario would cause revenues to increase due to real bracket creep and to increases in the number of taxpayers subject to the alternative minimum tax (AMT). Although the AMT and real bracket creep reflect the current law baseline, they would entail noticeable tax increases, and a shift in policy to a revenue level substantially higher, at 23.7 percent of GDP, than its previous historic high at 20.9 percent.

17. Some, perhaps many, would dispute whether this is a plausible assumption, but it has the advantage of requiring no congressional action and, as current law, at least of being consistent with the assumptions made about spending.

18. It would also assume retention of the individual AMT, which is a high priority for reform. There is general agreement on the need for reform of the AMT, but given the costliness of repeal or reform, it should be accomplished in a revenue-neutral manner or as near to it as possible.

19. This scenario entails a federal sector that is nearly 40 percent larger than today's and a federal budget composition that has shifted substantially more to spending on entitlements.

REFERENCES

AARP. 1999. Baby boomers envision their retirement: An AARP segmentation analysis. Washington, DC: AARP.
———. 2005. Medicare at 40: Past accomplishments and future challenges. Press release, July 28. Available at http://www.aarp.org/research/press-center/presscurrentnews/medicare_at_40.html.
Beedon, L., and K. Wu. 2005. *Women age 65 and older: Their sources of income.* Data Digest No. 126. Washington, DC: AARP Public Policy Institute. Available at http://www.aarp.org/research/socialsecurity/benefits/dd126_women.html.
Board of Trustees, Federal Old Age and Survivors Insurance and Disability Insurance Trust Funds. 2006. *2006 annual report of the Board of Trustees of the Old Age and Survivors Insurance and Federal Disability Insurance trust funds.* Washington, DC: GPO. Available at http://www.ssa.gov/OACT/TR/TR06/tr06.pdf.
Boccuti, C., and M. Moon. 2003. Comparing Medicare and private insurers: Growth rates in spending over three decades. *Health Affairs* 22 (2): 230–37.
CBO (Congressional Budget Office). 1998. *Long-term budgetary pressures and policy options.* Washington, DC: GPO. Available at http://www.cbo.gov/ftpdocs/4xx/doc492/ltbudg98.pdf.
———. 2000. Federal spending on the elderly and children. Http://www.cbo.gov/ftpdocs/23xx/doc2300/fsec.pdf.

———. 2004. *Retirement age and the need for saving*. Washington, DC: GPO.

———. 2005. *The long-term budget outlook*. Washington, DC: GPO. Available at http://www.cbo.gov/ftpdocs/69xx/doc6982/12-15-LongTermOutlook.pdf.

———. 2006. *The budget and economic outlook, fiscal years 2007 to 2016*. Washington, DC: GPO.

———. 2007. *The long-term outlook for health care spending*. Washington, DC: GPO.

Choi, J., D. Laibson, B. Madrian, and A. Metrick. 2001a. Defined contribution pensions: Plan rules, participant decisions, and the path of least resistance. National Bureau of Economic Research (NBER) Working Paper No. 8,655. Washington, DC: NBER.

———. 2001b. For better or for worse: Default effects and 401(k) savings behavior. NBER Working Paper No. 8,651. Washington, DC: NBER.

Cutler, D. 2001. Declining disability among the elderly. *Health Affairs* 20 (6): 11–27.

Cutler, D., J. Poterba, L. Sheiner, and L. Summers. 1990. An aging society: Opportunity or challenge? *Brookings Papers on Economic Activity* 1:1–73.

Finkelstein, A., and R. McKnight. 2005. *What did Medicare do (and was it worth it?)*. NBER Working Paper No. 11,609. Washington, DC: NBER. Available at http://www.nber.org/papers/w11609.

Fullerton, H. 1999. Labor force projections to 2008: Steady growth and changing composition. *Monthly Labor Review* 122 (11): 19–32.

General Accounting Office. 1994. *Budget policy: Issues in capping mandatory spending*. GAO/AIMD-94-155. Washington, DC: GAO.

Hacker, J. 2002. *The divided welfare state: The battle over public and private social benefits in the United States*. Cambridge: Cambridge University Press.

Howard, C. 1997. *The hidden welfare state: Tax expenditures and social policy in the United States*. Princeton, NJ: Princeton University Press.

Hungerford, T. 2003. Is there an American way of aging? Income dynamics of the elderly in the United States and Germany. *Research on Aging* 25 (5): 435–55.

———. 2006a. *The effect of government expenditures and revenues on the economy and economic well-being: A cross-national analysis*. Congressional Research Service. April 5.

———. 2006b. *Tax expenditures: Trends and critiques*. Congressional Research Service. September 13.

Joyce, G. F., E. B. Keeler, B. Shang, and D. P. Goldman. 2005. The lifetime burden of chronic disease among the elderly. *Health Affairs* 24, Suppl. 2: W5R18–29.

Lakdawalla, D., and T. Philipson. 2002. The rise in old-age longevity and the market for long-term care. *American Economic Review* 92 (1): 295–306.

Lindert, P. 2004. *Growing public: Social spending and economic growth since the eighteenth century*. Cambridge: Cambridge University Press.

Lubitz, J., et al. 1995. Longevity and Medicare expenditures. *New England Journal of Medicine* 332 (15): 999–1003.

———. 2003. Health, life expectancy, and health care spending among the elderly. *New England Journal of Medicine* 349 (11): 48–55.

Manton et al. 2006. Change in chronic disability from 1982 to 2004/05 as measured by long-term changes in function and health in the U.S. elderly population. *Proceedings of the National Academy of Sciences* 103 (48): 18374–79.

Manton, K., and X. Gu. 2001. Changes in the prevalence of chronic disability in the United States black and nonblack population above age 65 from 1982 to 1999. *Proceedings of the National Academy of Sciences* 98 (11): 6354–59.

McGarry, K., and R. Schoeni. 1998. Social Security, economic growth, and the rise in independence of elderly widows in the 20th century. NBER Working Paper No. 6,511. Washington, DC: NBER.

Moon, M. 2000. Medicare matters: Building on a record of accomplishments. *Health Care Financing Review* 22 (1): 9–22.

Quinn, J. 1999. Retirement patterns and bridge jobs in the 1990s. Employee Benefit Research Institute (EBRI) Issue Brief No. 206. Washington, DC: EBRI.

Singer, B., and K. Manton. 1998. The effects of health changes on projections of health service needs for the elderly population of the United States. *Proceedings of the National Academy of Sciences* 95 (26): 15618–22.

Southworth, L., and J. Gist. 2008. The saver's credit: What does it do for saving? AARP Public Policy Institute Insight on the Issues No. 1.

Spillman, B., and J. Lubitz. 2000. The effect of longevity on spending for acute and long-term care. *New England Journal of Medicine* 342 (19): 1409–15.

U.S. Bureau of the Census. 2006. The effects of government taxes and transfers on income and poverty: 2004. Available at http://www.census.gov/hhes/www/poverty/effect2004/effectofgovtandt2004.pdf.

U.S. Congress. Joint Committee on Taxation. 2006. *Estimates of Federal Tax Expenditures for Fiscal Years 2006–2010.* Washington, DC: GPO.

Verma, S., and S. Rix. 2002. Retirement age and Social Security reform: The macroeconomic effects of working longer. AARP Public Policy Institute Issue Brief No. 59.

White, C. 2006. *The slowdown in Medicare spending growth.* Congressional Budget Office Working Paper 2006-08. Available at http://www.cbo.gov/ftpdocs/74xx/doc7453/2006-08.pdf.

11

Private Pensions and the Boomers: How Much Is Enough?

JACK L. VANDERHEI AND CRAIG COPELAND

The approaching retirement of the post–World War II baby-boom generation has increased public scrutiny of whether this cohort is likely to achieve an "acceptable" standard of living in retirement. Unfortunately, there have been several answers to this question, depending on the type of model adopted, income threshold used, sample analyzed, and assumptions chosen. This chapter attempts to sort through some of these variations and assist the reader in formulating an opinion on this important public policy issue.

The chapter begins with a brief overview of the major types of retirement plans (e.g., defined benefit vs. defined contribution). Recent statistics with respect to retirement plan participation are then provided, along with a summary of the work effects of retirement plans. At that point, the concept of retirement income adequacy is explored by defining the metric most commonly used (a replacement rate), examining the various economic risks faced by most retirees, and then summarizing recent research into how high the replacement rate needs to be to provide various levels of confidence that the retiree will have "adequate" retirement income for the remainder of his or her life.

We then distill years of research on retirement income adequacy for boomers into a series of scenarios. Under the baseline scenario (originally modeled in 2003), we find vast pockets of the overall population of boomers that will be at risk of not having sufficient resources to pay for "basic" retirement expenses with even a 75 percent probability. In the second scenario, we attempt to control for a recent phenomenon among many defined benefit plan sponsors: freezing future accruals for new employees and—in some cases—existing employees also.

Finally, we focus on a relatively recent plan design development that will be extremely important with respect to the expansion of future retirement wealth among the boomers in the private sector—the 401(k) plan. We show that this plan provides the potential for substantial retirement wealth—for those employees who choose to participate in the plan and make prudent decisions with respect to contribution and investment behavior. Unfortunately, a significant percentage of employees have not maximized the value of this type of retirement plan, and legislation was recently passed (the Pension Protection Act of 2006) to increase the likelihood that 401(k) sponsors would provide plans with certain default provisions (automatic enrollment plans) that would use the employees' inertia to work in their favor to increase retirement wealth.

We conclude the chapter by summarizing recent research that suggests that those 401(k) participants with several years remaining in the workforce (including some of the younger boomers) will likely have significant increases in their retirement income as the 2006 legislation is implemented.

RETIREMENT PLAN PARTICIPATION

Private pensions are typically provided on a voluntary basis by the employer and are of one of two types: defined benefit or defined contribution. In a *defined benefit* plan, the employer typically provides a formula that is based on years of participation and/or average compensation. For example, a defined benefit formula might provide that, starting at age 65, an employee will have a nominal annuity provided for the remainder of his or her life equal to 2 percent of average compensation times the number of years of participation. Under this formula, an employee with average compensation of $100,000 and twenty-five years of participation would be entitled to an annual benefit of $50,000 starting at age 65.[1] It is important to note that neither investment risk nor longevity risk is borne by the employee under this arrangement.

In contrast, a *defined contribution* plan will typically have a provision under which the employer's annual contribution to the employee's account balance is determined. This amount may be supplemented by employee contributions (this may be provided on a pretax or post-tax basis, or a combination of the two, depending on the type of defined contribution plan). Investment income will be generated based on the investments selected for the employee's account balance and the market return for those investments. There is no specific guarantee with respect to the amount that will be generated by the employee's retirement age, and in most cases the employee is allowed to determine how much of the remaining balance will be spent each year in retirement (subject to certain tax limitations). In other words, both the investment risk and the longevity risk are borne by the employee in this arrangement.

Among all baby-boomer workers (45–64 years old) in 2006, approximately 57 percent worked for an employer or union that sponsored a retirement plan (either a defined benefit or defined contribution plan) and nearly 50 percent participated in such a plan (Copeland 2007a). This level surpassed those of younger workers, with those aged 35–44 participating at the next highest rate, 46 percent. Focusing only on wage and salary workers, as the youngest baby boomers have moved into the 45- to 54-year-old age group, the percentage of this age bracket of workers participating in a retirement plan has steadily declined. In 1998, nearly 63 percent of 45- to 54-year-old wage and salary workers participated in an employment-based retirement plan. By 2006, this number had declined to 54.0 percent. A smaller decline has occurred in recent years among workers aged 55–64, from 57.7 percent in 2004 to 53.6 percent in 2006.

On a family basis, a somewhat different trend emerges. Among families headed by an individual aged 55–64 in 2001, 42.2 percent had a participant in an employment-based retirement plan (Copeland 2006). By 2004, this number had increased 47.1 percent. However, for families headed by younger boomers (ages 45–54), the percentage with a participant decreased from 58.4 percent in 2001 to 56.9 percent in 2004. In 2004, of those families with heads aged 55–64 who were retirement plan participants, 22.6 percent had a defined benefit plan only, 48.9 percent had a defined contribution plan only, and 28.5 percent had both. Furthermore, 74 percent had a 401(k)-type plan. In 1992, more than 40 percent of these retirement plan participant families had a defined benefit plan only, with approximately 25 percent having both a defined benefit and defined contribution plan.

The 401(k)-type plan participation rate for baby-boomer family heads has been in the 75–85 percent range, with heads aged 45–54 having a participation rate of nearly 77 percent and those aged 55–64 at 85 percent in 2004 (Copeland 2006). While the participation rates held relatively steady from 1992 to 2004, the percentage of those who were eligible to participate but did not and who also had a defined benefit plan plummeted. In 1992, 60.3 percent of 55- to 64-year-old family heads who were eligible but chose not to participate in a defined contribution plan participated in a defined benefit plan; by 2004, this number had dropped to 24.4 percent.

Consequently, boomers are rapidly approaching retirement with a lower likelihood of being retirement plan participants than that of the immediately preceding generation of retirees. Those who *were* retirement plan participants were more likely to have a defined contribution plan only. Furthermore, while participation rates among those in the 45–64 age bracket have held steady as the baby-boom generation reached those ages, the percentage eligible to participate but are not doing so who have a defined benefit plan declined dramatically. Therefore, if boomers are not taking advantage of an offered defined contribution plan, then they are not likely to have any retirement savings through an employer.

WORK EFFECTS

The benefits available to boomers will influence their decision to remain in the workforce into later ages. The availability of health insurance for retirees has been on the decline, and among those who have it, a significant number are being required to contribute a larger share of the costs. Therefore, the lack of access to health insurance will lead some boomers to remain in the workforce. However, as shown above, a larger proportion of boomers will have only a defined contribution plan, which will also have the effect of keeping workers in the workforce longer, either to continue to build up their account balance or to delay tapping into the account. These two factors will force boomers to remain in the workforce, particularly as they become aware, or are already aware, that they have not prepared well enough for retirement and/or will not have access to affordable health care insurance.

The trend toward a higher percentage of individuals age 55 or older being in the labor force has been established, as the oldest baby boomers are becoming a large proportion of that group. In 1993, 29.4 percent of Americans 55 or older were in the labor force. This grew to 38.0 percent by 2006 (Copeland 2007c). Not only are a larger percentage of workers that age in the labor force, but of those working, the percentage working full-time year-round also significantly increased, from 54.5 percent in 1990 to 65.5 percent in 2006 (Copeland 2007b). This increase in full-time, full-year work was at the expense of part-year workers, as the part-time, full-year workers' percentage over this same time remained flat. Furthermore, the trend of more older workers in the labor force is projected to continue, with the group of workers age 55 or over expected to increase by almost 50 percent by 2016, making up nearly one-quarter of the workforce, compared with 17 percent in 2006 (Toossi 2007). Consequently, more boomers will be in the workforce into older ages than previous generations—increasingly out of necessity, not choice.

WHAT IS RETIREMENT INCOME ADEQUACY?

A traditional way of determining retirement income adequacy in a relatively easy-to-understand number is the *replacement rate*. This attempts to quantify the gross retirement income that must be received as a percentage of the employee's gross income prior to retirement in order to provide the same after-tax income, after adjusting for differences in savings, age, and work-related expenditures in the two periods (VanDerhei 2004).

While the concept of a replacement rate remains the standard for assessing retirement income adequacy, it does suffer from some well-known limitations, especially as defined contribution plans become a larger proportion of employees' retirement wealth and the likelihood of the traditional type of employer-provided retiree health coverage continues to decrease. Recently, a new generation of retirement models has been developed to include such crucial factors as longevity, investment, and health care risk into their retirement planning process.

The huge variation in the range of replacement rate targets—depending on the individual's income, the degree of annuitization for initial retirement wealth, and the asset allocation of the postretirement investments—calls into question whether a *single* rule-of-thumb measure is realistic to use in the retirement planning process. Given the wide differences in individual circumstances (such as age, health, and income) and the complexity of retirement risks that need to be dealt with—such as longevity (addressed through annuitization of assets), old-age infirmity (addressed through long-term care insurance), and asset preservation (addressed through investment allocation)—a simple one-size-fits-all replacement rate will not work for most Americans.

The results published in VanDerhei 2006 show the sobering (if not staggering) amounts of money needed to provide a reasonably high chance of being able to afford retirement if the retiree self-insures one or more of the three key risks of retirement planning (investment risk; longevity risk; and the risk of catastrophic retiree health costs, including nursing home costs). However, the results also show the positive impact that can be obtained by annuitizing assets in retirement to protect against the risk of longevity. In this regard, the model points not only to a more realistic size of the retirement income problem but also to ways that individuals can begin to deal with it.

How much of a difference will this process make in the initial determination of a target replacement rate? If it is assumed that there is no equity allocation of assets nor is any of the initial retirement wealth annuitized, a stylized high-income male would need a 52 percent replacement rate in order to have a 50 percent chance of covering his retirement expenses if he retires at age 65. If he is not comfortable with a 50–50 prospect of "running out" of retirement income, he could increase his chances of success to 75 percent by raising his income replacement rate to 78 percent; if he wants a 90 percent chance of success, he would have to raise his replacement rate to 119 percent.[2]

What would it mean if this high-income male took early retirement as soon as he is eligible for Social Security (at age 62)? The replacement rates jump considerably: For a 50–50 chance of success, his income replacement rate would be 64 percent; for a 75 percent chance of success, 97 percent; and for a 90 percent chance, 149 percent. If, on the other hand, he decides to delay retirement until age 68, he can decrease the figures to 43, 66, and 97 percent, respectively.

WILL THE BOOMERS HAVE SUFFICIENT RETIREMENT INCOME?
BASELINE RESULTS

Whether a significant percentage of boomers will be able to accumulate sufficient retirement wealth to achieve these replacement rate targets is a question that requires separate modeling. In VanDerhei and Copeland 2003, we
combined simulated retirement income and wealth with simulated retiree
expenditures to determine how much each family unit would need to save
today (as a percentage of their current wages) to maintain a prespecified
"comfort level" (i.e., confidence level) that they will be able to afford the
simulated expenses for the remainder of the lifetime of the family unit
(i.e., death of second spouse in a family).[3] Below, we report these savings
rates by age cohort, family status (at retirement), and gender. Six five-year
birth cohorts were simulated. The oldest group was born in the period 1936
to 1940, inclusive, while the youngest group was born in 1961 to 1965, inclusive. Three combinations of gender/family status at retirement are
reported: family, single male, and single female. In addition, the relative
income is reported by estimating lifetime income quartiles (from 2002
though retirement age) for each of the eighteen combinations of birth cohort
and gender/family status at retirement.

It is important to note that within each of the groups modeled there will
undoubtedly be significant percentages in the zero category as well as those at
levels beyond which anyone could reasonably assume more than a de minimis
number of individuals could possibly save. We account for these situations in
two ways. First, we report medians for each of the groups. In other words, the
numbers presented in the first two charts represent the estimate for the 75th
and 90th percentiles, respectively, when ranked by percentage of compensation.
Second, we limit the reported values to 25 percent of compensation, under the
assumption that few, if any, family units would be able to contribute in excess
of this percentage on a continuous basis until retirement age.

It is also important to note that these percentages merely represent savings that need to be generated *in addition to* what retirement income and/or
wealth is simulated by the model. Therefore, if the family unit is already
generating savings for retirement that is not included in defined benefit or
defined contribution plans, individual retirement accounts (IRAs), Social Security, and/or net housing equity, that value needs to be deducted from the
estimated percentages.

Figure 11-1 shows the median percentage of compensation that must be
saved each year until retirement for a 75 percent confidence level when combined with simulated retirement wealth, assuming current Social Security benefits and assuming that housing equity is never liquidated. For example, all
gender/family combinations in the first two income quartiles for the oldest
birth cohort are at the 25 percent of compensation threshold. For those in the
highest income quartile for this birth cohort, the percentages of compensation

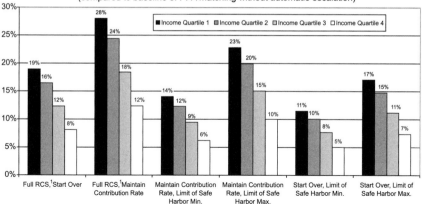

FIGURE 11-1. Percentage of Added Compensation That Must Be Saved Annually Until Retirement for a 75% Chance of Covering Basic Retirement Expenses (assumes current Social Security and housing equity is never liquidated)
Source: EBRI-ERF Retirement Security Projection Model.

needed to be saved are 23.8 percent for single females, 13.9 percent for single males, and 6.1 percent for families.

Figure 11-2 shows the additional savings required to provide retirement adequacy in nine out of ten simulated life paths. In this case, nearly all of the combinations of gender/family status at retirement for the first three income quartiles are at the threshold (the median for families in the third quartile is estimated at 24.8 percent of compensation). Those in the highest income quartile of this birth cohort all have requirements that would prove difficult if not impossible to implement: single females are estimated to now need to save more than 25 percent of compensation, single males 22.1 percent of compensation, and families 10.1 percent of compensation. Given that most individuals would be unlikely to choose a situation that would provide them with adequate retirement income only 50 percent of the time, this analysis focuses on the 75 percent and 90 percent confidence levels.

We have purposely structured many of our assumptions to provide conservative estimates of the amounts that would be needed to be saved while employees are working to alleviate any deficits. For example, we have assumed in this version of the model that all employees continue to work until age 65, even though there has been a long-term trend toward earlier retirement (albeit one that seems to be reversing in recent years). We have also assumed that individual account balances are "self-annuitized" over a period of time that expands the individual and/or family life expectancy by five years, even though there appears to be limited evidence that this type of buffer is actually contemplated by retirees as a risk-reduction device.

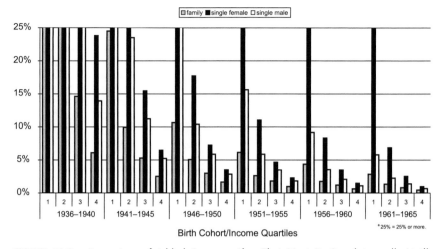

FIGURE 11-2. Percentage of Added Compensation That Must Be Saved Annually Until Retirement for a 90% Chance of Covering Basic Retirement Expenses (assumes current Social Security and housing equity is never liquidated)
Source: EBRI-ERF Retirement Security Projection Model.

Even with these conservative biases built in, the numbers appear troubling for some age cohorts and almost fatalistic for others. The good news is that if many of the younger cohorts begin saving a reasonable amount to supplement their Social Security and qualified retirement plans now, they have a good chance of providing themselves with reasonable assurance that they will at least be able to cover basic retirement expenditures. However, changes in public policy and additional resources from families and charities would be required to provide adequate retirement income for retirees with greater longevity who suffer serious and persistent chronic disease.[4]

HOW WILL DEFINED BENEFIT PLAN FREEZES IMPACT RETIREMENT INCOME ADEQUACY?

Although the analysis described in the previous section assumed that employers will continue to provide defined benefit coverage at the same rates that were provided at the time the model was constructed (2003), there have been major changes in recent years with respect to the likelihood that workers will be covered by defined benefit plans in the future.

The dawn of the new year in 2006 began with a flood of news reports about the supposedly new trend among private defined benefit plan sponsors of "freezing" their pension plans for current or new workers. In reality, these decisions have been quite prevalent in recent years and are part of the well-documented and long-term decline of "traditional" pension plans;

what's unusual is the large size of some of the employers that have recently announced pension freezes and the frequency of the announcements.

While it is obvious that pension plan freezes affect some workers negatively, it is *not* obvious *which* workers are affected nor *to what degree* they are affected by a pension freeze. There are many reasons for this, most importantly the unique characteristics and terms of each pension plan and each freeze, along with the age and characteristics of the workers. This section summarizes how pension freezes are likely to impact existing employees as a function of plan type and employee demographics. However, a detailed analysis of how this trend will impact retirement income adequacy must wait for additional data on the number of plan sponsors undertaking this activity, as well as information on the amount of additional employer contributions that tend to be provided as a quid pro quo for the termination of additional accruals for the defined benefit plan.

Although it is too early to quantify the expected impact of this trend on retirement income adequacy, it is possible to model the additional employer contribution (expressed as a percentage of employee compensation) that would need to be provided to the employee subjected to a pension freeze to indemnify him or her in an expected-value sense for the reduction in defined benefit accruals. This additional amount is referred to as the *indemnification contribution rate*. If the employer increases the amounts contributed to the defined contribution plan by at least this amount, the employee is not likely to suffer with respect to retirement income adequacy. If the employer provides an increase to the defined contribution plan of less than this amount, the employee is likely to end up with less retirement income unless he or she chooses to make up the differential through increased contributions.

The amount needed to indemnify the employee will obviously depend on a number of factors. Besides the key assumptions of future rates of return on various asset classes and future salary growth, the indemnification contribution rate will depend upon:

- *The type of defined benefit plan that was previously sponsored.* Final-average plans[5] (and to a lesser extent, career-average plans) tend to grow faster toward the end of the employee's active working career than the other plan types and (all else being equal) should have a larger indemnification contribution rate for older and/or longer-tenured employees; the bigger the potential pension benefit, the more would have to be made up through defined contribution plan contributions. Cash-balance pension plans[6] tend to accumulate benefits in a fashion that is similar to defined contribution plans, and the indemnification contribution rate will be determined by the relative size of the cash-balance pay credits and the spread between the assumed interest credit for the cash-balance plans and the assumed rate of return for the 401(k) plans.
- *Generosity parameters of the defined benefit plan.* Within any plan type, there are a variety of plan design considerations that may make the plan more or

less valuable to the employee. For example, one plan may provide 1 percent of final-average, three-year compensation, while another might provide 2 percent. Alternatively, the averaging period might have been five years, or the plan benefits might have been integrated with Social Security. As described above, the higher the relative value of the defined benefit pension plan, the higher the indemnification contribution rate.

The additional contribution needed from the employer to financially indemnify the employee for the loss in expected retirement benefits as a result of the defined benefit freeze will depend on both the individual's asset allocation and the future rates of return in each asset class. In an attempt to simplify the presentation of the results, only two alternatives scenarios are presented: one in which the employee is assumed to earn a constant 4 percent nominal rate of return each year until retirement age and a second in which the employee is assumed to earn a constant 8 percent rate of return.

Overall Results by Plan Type

- *4 percent rate of return:* The median indemnification contribution rate for a career-average defined benefit pension plan is 11.6 percent, assuming a 4 percent rate of return. An indemnification contribution rate of 18.8 percent would be sufficient to cover 75 percent of the employees covered by this type of plan. The median rate for a final-average plan is larger, as expected, at 13.5 percent, and the threshold rate for the 75th percentile increases to 21.0 percent. Cash-balance plans have a median indemnification contribution rate of 4.6 percent, with a 75th-percentile threshold rate of 6.3 percent using the current interest credits.[7]
- *8 percent rate of return:* If the rate of return assumption is increased to 8 percent nominal, the median indemnification contribution rate for a career-average defined benefit plan is 6.6 percent. An indemnification contribution rate of 14.8 percent would be sufficient to cover 75 percent of the employees covered by this type of plan. The median for a final-average plan is 8.1 percent and the 75th-percentile threshold increases to 16.0 percent. Cash-balance plans have a median indemnification contribution rate of 2.7 percent, with a 75th-percentile threshold of 4.5 percent using the current interest credits.[8]

Results by Age and Plan Type

Although the median indemnification contribution rates for career- and final-average plans at a 4 percent rate of return were 11.6 percent and 13.5 percent, respectively, these values ignore the impact of the employee's age on the rates. Figure 11-3 shows that the median rates increase substantially with the age of the employee. For career-average plans, the medians increase from 5.1 percent for those currently aged 30–34 to 20.1 percent when they are 60–64. Final-average plans have an even larger increase: from 3.9 percent to 22.4 percent. Cash-balance plans display little variation by age regardless of the interest credit chosen.

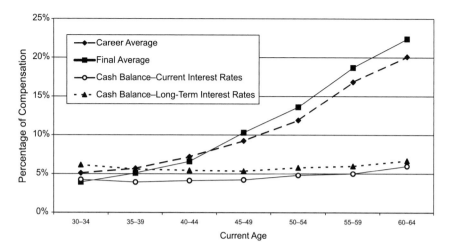

FIGURE 11-3. Median Percentage of a Worker's Annual Pay Needed to Offset the Impact of a Pension Freeze in 2006, by Pension Plan Type and Current Age (assumes 4% annual rate of return)
Source: Author's tabulations from the EBRI/ERF Retirement Income Projection Model.

Figure 11-4 shows similar results when an 8 percent rate of return is chosen: the indemnification contribution rates for career-average plans increase from 1.4 percent for the youngest workers analyzed to 16.6 percent for the oldest cohort, while the rates for final-average plans increase from 1.1 percent to 18.6 percent for the respective age cohorts. Cash-balance plans remain much flatter than the other two types but no longer appear age-invariant: the rates increase from 1.1 percent to 4.8 percent for the young/old age cohorts when current interest credits are used, and 1.7 percent to 5.4 percent when long-term rates are assumed.

As defined benefit pension sponsors continue to freeze benefit accruals for new and/or current employees and substitute either new or enhanced 401(k) plans, many observers will be concerned whether the total *expected* retirement income from the combination of the frozen defined benefit and the new/additional 401(k) balances will equal or exceed what the employees might have thought they would receive from the original defined benefit plan, assuming it continued without modifications.

As figures 11-3 and 11-4 show, there is tremendous variability regarding what it would take to financially indemnify an employee for such a freeze. Because workers affected by a pension freeze vary greatly by age, salary, and job tenure; by the specific provisions and formula in the types of retirement plans they are covered by (both pension and 401(k)); and by the underlying economic assumptions that are used to estimate the effects of a pension freeze, there is fundamentally no simple answer to the question. However, these data illustrate the general impact of age and tenure: Older, longer-tenure workers

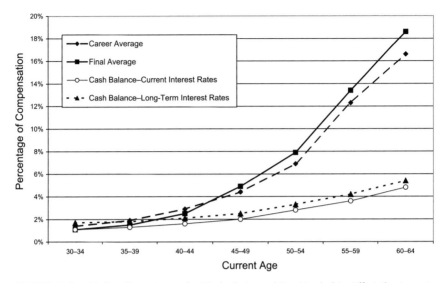

FIGURE 11-4. Median Percentage of a Worker's Annual Pay Needed to Offset the Impact of a Pension Freeze in 2006, by Pension Plan Type and Current Age (assumes 8% annual rate of return)
Source: Author's tabulations from the EBRI/ERF Retirement Income Projection Model.

tend to be affected by a pension freeze more than younger workers because they do not have as much time left in their working careers to accumulate funds in a 401(k) plan to offset the accrual loss from a pension freeze.

HOW WILL AUTOMATIC ENROLLMENT PROVISIONS FOR 401(K) PLANS IMPACT RETIREMENT INCOME ADEQUACY?

The retirement income prospects for future generations of retirees have been modeled by the Employee Benefit Research Institute (EBRI) extensively in recent years, in an attempt to more accurately predict how various cohorts of Americans will likely fare in retirement. Results have ranged from very bleak for substantial portions of the U.S. population to fairly positive for 401(k) participants with continuous coverage throughout their working careers: Results suggest a significant portion of these workers' preretirement income could be replaced by 401(k) accumulations when combined with Social Security (at the least Social Security benefits projected under current statutory provisions).

Assuming that 401(k) accumulations are used to purchase nominal annuities at age 65, the EBRI/ICI 401(k) Accumulation Projection Model predicts baseline median replacement rates at retirement ranging from 51 to 69 percent, by quartile, based on final five-year average salary ("replacement rate" meaning the percentage of a worker's final salary that is replaced in retirement by a nominal annuity purchased by 401(k) assets). However, these

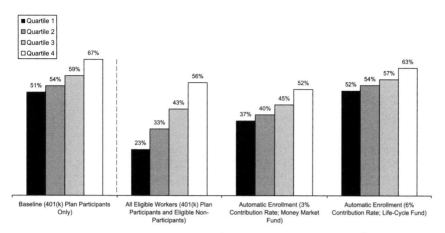

FIGURE 11-5. Median Replacement Rates[1] from 401(k) Accumulations[2] for Workers Turning 65 between 2030 and 2039, by Income Quartile at Age 65 (percentage of final five-year average salary)

Source: EBRI/ICI 401(k) Accumulation Projection Model.

[1]In all four simulations presented in this figure, workers experience continuous employment, continuous 401(k) plan coverage, and investment returns based on historical returns from 1926 to 2001. In the baseline, only 401(k) participants with account balances at year-end 2000 are considered. In the other three scenarios, all eligible workers are considered.

[2]The 401(k) accumulation includes 401(k) balances at employer(s) and rollover IRA balances.

baseline results were predicated on the assumption that any worker currently participating in a 401(k) plan would continue to be offered a 401(k) plan for each future job. If it is assumed that the worker would have only an average chance of being offered a 401(k) plan at future jobs, the income replacement rates decrease to a range of 21–26 percent. While this scenario is certainly far too pessimistic to be correct, the disparity between the two sets of results demonstrates the importance of continued participation in a 401(k) plan throughout an employee's working career.

A year prior to the enactment of the Pension Protection Act of 2006 (PPA), the EBRI/ICI 401(k) Accumulation Projection Model was used to simulate the impact of universal adoption of automatic enrollment features under a combination of default contribution rates and default investment allocations (Holden and VanDerhei 2005). In order that the beneficial effect of the expected increase in participation rates could be included in simulation results, "synthetic" employees were generated in the model to include eligible workers who chose *not to participate* in the 401(k). When these employees were added to the model, the median replacement rates under the baseline assumption mentioned above decreased significantly for the lowest-income quartile (23 percent, down from 51 percent) but only mildly for the highest-income quartile (56 percent, down from 67 percent).

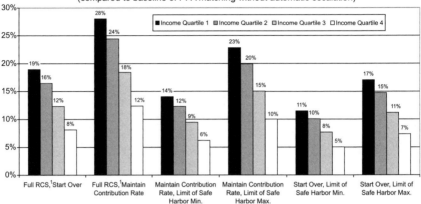

FIGURE 11-6. Impact of Automatic Escalation: Percentage Increase in Median Replacement Rates from 401(k) Accumulations for Workers Turning 65 between 2030–2039, by Income Quartile at Age 65 (compared to baseline of PPA matching without automatic escalation)

Source: Author's simulations from the EBRI/ICI 401(k) Accumulation Projection Model.
[1]Retirement Confidence Survey.

Assuming that *all* 401(k) plan sponsors would adopt automatic enrollment immediately (in 2005), the median replacement rates for the lowest-income quartile increased to 37 percent (from the 23 percent baseline) even under the conservative assumptions of a 3 percent default contribution rate and a money market default investment (see figure 11-5). When the default contribution rate was increased to 6 percent and the default investment was changed to a life-cycle fund, the median replacement rate for this group increased further to 52 percent. These results illustrate the very strong improvements that can result from automatic enrollment of workers in a 401(k) plan—especially for the lowest-income workers.

VanDerhei 2007a reports data from the 2007 Retirement Confidence Survey (RCS), fielded several months after the enactment of the PPA to estimate the additional retirement income likely to arise from the implementation of automatic escalation of contributions in 401(k) plans.

One of the extremely important plan design decisions a 401(k) plan sponsor must make because of the PPA is whether to introduce automatic enrollment features. There is extensive literature on the potential benefits of automatic enrollment on participation rates, especially for young employees and those with low incomes. However, there is also a recognition that the introduction of these programs has a tendency to "anchor" participants' contribution rates and asset allocation to the defaults chosen by the sponsor; hence, the overall increase in expected account balances from adopting these plans will be a function of both the employee's relative wage level and the employer's default decisions.[9]

Figure 11-6 summarizes the results in VanDerhei 2007a by comparing the median replacement rates against the baseline in each of six scenarios by whether the contribution is constrained by the safe harbor minimum or maximum, or whether the full RCS distribution can be used. Not surprisingly, the maximum impact is seen when the full RCS distribution is used (without constraints) and the scenario in which employees maintain the contribution rate from the previous employer when they change jobs is assumed. In that case, the median replacement rate for the lowest-income quartile increases by 28 percent, while the rate for the highest-income quartile increases by 12 percent. Even for the scenario with the smallest expected impact, the lowest-income quartile still experiences an income replacement rate increase of 11 percent and the highest-income quartile increases by 5 percent.

CONCLUSION

The process of projecting which individuals are likely to have adequate retirement income has always been problematic. This has undoubtedly become more difficult in the last two decades, as the private retirement system in the United States has gradually evolved from one that was, for many employees, focused primarily on defined benefit plans to one that is more of a hybrid between defined benefit (pensions) *and* defined contribution (401(k)-type) plans.[10]

The reason for the increased modeling difficulties stems largely from the introduction of employee choice as a major determinant of the eventual retirement income for a retiree. In a *defined benefit* plan, the employer makes most (if not all) of the decisions, and an employee is either covered or not. Once the likelihood of coverage and the generosity parameters of the plans are modeled, the only major uncertainty is the employee's participation in the labor market, relative wage growth, and job change behavior. *Defined contribution* plans offer several additional modeling challenges, in addition to the need to project future investment income, at least as currently designed. In many defined contribution plans, employees must make the decision to participate and, if they do, how much to contribute and where to invest their own employee contributions and (if offered) often the employer contributions. Job turnover presents another modeling challenge, as the probability of cashing out (as opposed to retaining the amounts in the current employer's plan or rolling them over to the new employer's plans and/or an IRA) must be estimated. Another problem arises at the time of retirement, given the increased probability that employees will need to deal with longevity risk, as opposed to purchasing an immediate annuity or otherwise shifting at least some of this risk to another entity similar to the annuity options inherent in a defined benefit plan.

Any accurate analysis must pay careful attention to the likely structural changes in defined contribution plans by sponsors that modify their defined benefit plans. VanDerhei (2007b) demonstrates that a much larger percentage of defined benefit sponsors that have either closed or frozen their pension plans in the last two years, or plan to do so in the next two years, will end up with automatic enrollment provisions in their defined contribution (401(k)-type) plans than their counterparts who do *not* adopt these changes to their defined benefit plan pensions. The ability to establish defined benefit–type provisions (such as automatically enrolling employees in the plan and making default contribution and asset allocation decisions for them) in the defined contribution plan has extremely important public policy implications.

As is typically true in the private retirement universe, plan sponsors' reaction to influences such as the Pension Protection Act of 2006 and the Financial Accounting Standards Board's modifications of pension accounting requirements will likely be quite varied. Projection models will need to reflect employer modifications to their retirement plans and employees' responses to those changes to evaluate the likely impact of these changes on overall retirement income adequacy for future retirees.

NOTES

1. Plans often allow retirement at an earlier age subject to a permanent reduction in the annual benefit.

2. The same simulations for stylized lower-income retirees would require significantly larger replacement rates, since non–health care retirement expenditures are not reduced proportionally with retirement income, nor is the health care expense typically a function of income.

3. After the retirement income and wealth was simulated for each family unit, we simulated 1,000 observations (from retirement age until death of the individual for single males and single females or the second person to die for families) and computed the present value of the aggregated deficits at retirement age. At that point, we rank-ordered the observations in terms of the present value of the deficits and determined the 75th and 90th percentiles of the distribution. Next we determined the future simulated retirement income accumulated to retirement age and used this information to determine the percentage of compensation that would need to be saved to have sufficient additional income to offset the present value of accumulated deficits for the 75th and 90th percentiles of the distribution.

4. Additional estimates in VanDerhei and Copeland 2003 include both the status quo for Social Security benefits as well as two reform scenarios that would decrease benefits for future generations.

5. Final-average defined benefit plans base the annual retirement benefit on average compensation near the end of the employee's tenure with the plan sponsor, whereas benefits paid by career-average defined benefit plans are a function of compensation over the employee's entire tenure with the plan sponsor.

6. Cash-balance plans are defined benefit plans in which the benefit formula resembles a defined contribution plan: a notional account balance is maintained based on annual pay credits and interest credits. Unlike defined contribution plans, cash-balance plans are not participant directed and employers guarantee the investment income that will be provided during a specific period.

7. These values increase to 5.7 percent and 7.3 percent if, instead, the cash-balance plans are assumed to credit interest at the intermediate long-term assumption for the interest rate of the Treasury special public-debt obligation bonds issuable to the Old-Age, Survivors, and Disability Insurance (OASDI) trust funds, as specified in the 2005 Trustees of the OASDI Trust Funds Report (5.8 percent).

8. These values increase to 3.1 percent and 5.2 percent if the cash balance plans are assumed to credit interest at 5.8 percent.

9. The PPA provided a significant incentive for employers that had not already adopted automatic enrollment to reconsider their decision. The PPA preempts state laws that might affect plans adopting automatic enrollment provisions and provides additional nondiscrimination safe harbor protections for them. To qualify for the automatic enrollment safe harbor, the contribution rate for automatic enrollees must be at least 3 percent of salary during the first year of participation, 4 percent during the second year, 5 percent during the third year, and 6 percent thereafter. The plan may specify a higher contribution up to a maximum of 10 percent.

10. Although the explosion of 401(k) plans following the release of the proposed regulations in November 1981 is often cited as the catalyst of the defined contribution plan expansion, other types of defined contribution plans were already quite prevalent, and indeed defined contribution plans already accounted for 69 percent of the total number of private defined retirement plans in 1981 (albeit that many of these were small plans, and in terms of active participants, defined contribution plans only accounted for 41 percent of the total). See Olsen and VanDerhei 1997 for more detail.

REFERENCES

Copeland, Craig. 2006. Individual account retirement plans: An analysis of the 2004 Survey of Consumer Finances. Employee Benefit Research Institute (EBRI) Issue Brief No. 293. Washington, DC: Employee Benefit Research Institute.

———. 2007a. Employment-based retirement plan participation: Geographic differences and trends, 2006. EBRI Issue Brief No. 311. Washington, DC: Employee Benefit Research Institute.

———. 2007b. Employment status of workers age 55 or older. EBRI Notes 28 (8): 1–7.

———. 2007c. Labor-force participation: The population age 55 or older. EBRI Notes 28 (6): 1–8.

Holden, Sarah, and Jack VanDerhei. 2005. The influence of automatic enrollment, catch-up, and IRA contributions on 401(k) contributions at retirement. EBRI Issue Brief No. 283. Washington, DC: Employee Benefit Research Institute.

Olsen, Kelly, and Jack VanDerhei. 1997. Defined contribution plan dominance grows across sectors and employer sizes, while mega defined benefit plans remain strong: Where we are and where we are going? In Retirement prospects in a defined contribution world, ed. Dallas Salisbury, 55–92. Washington, DC: Employee Benefit Research Institute.

Toossi, Mitra. 2007. Labor force projections to 2016: More workers in their golden years. *Monthly Labor Review* 130 (11): 33–52.

VanDerhei, Jack. 2004. Measuring retirement income adequacy, part one: Traditional replacement ratios and results for workers at large companies. *EBRI Notes* 25 (9): 1–14.

———. 2006. Measuring retirement income adequacy: Calculating realistic income replacement rates. EBRI Issue Brief No. 297. Washington, DC: Employee Benefit Research Institute.

———. 2007a. The expected impact of automatic escalation of 401(k) contributions on retirement income. *EBRI Notes* 28 (9):1–8.

———. 2007b. Retirement income adequacy after PPA and FAS 158: part one—Plan sponsors' reactions. EBRI Issue Brief No. 307. Washington, DC: Employee Benefit Research Institute.

VanDerhei, Jack, and Craig Copeland. 2003. Can America afford tomorrow's retirees? Results from the EBRI-ERF Retirement Security Projection Model. EBRI Issue Brief No. 263. Washington, DC: Employee Benefit Research Institute.

12

Medicare in the Image of the Baby-Boom Generation

EDWARD F. LAWLOR

The imminent march of the baby-boom generation into old age begs for a rethinking of the philosophy, coverage, and incentives in Medicare policy to assure a good fit between the health circumstances of the population and the delivery of health care services. Much has changed since Medicare's implementation in 1965, not the least being the epidemiology and major health circumstances of a population that has grown older under profoundly different conditions than the first generation of beneficiaries some fifty years ago.

All of the recent tumult over the Medicare Modernization and Prescription Drug Act (MMA)—the doughnut hole, state financing of Medicaid—has effectively crowded out "big think" and discussion of Medicare's future vision and appropriate policy design for coverage and benefits of the baby-boom generation.

Behind the scenes of these Medicare Part D controversies, however, has been a steady accretion of literature and futuristic policy thinking about the broader coverage and design of the Medicare program. Spread out over a variety of disciplines, journals, and the Web are ideas and proposals to enhance Medicare's prevention and health promotion orientation, better map coverage to chronic and long-term care, better extend the Medicare franchise to mental health and disabilities, introduce evidence-based models of disease management, and upgrade the geriatric and gerontology workforce to produce more appropriate and cost-effective care. Taken together, this literature envisions a Medicare program that puts much greater emphasis on social functioning, community-based care, continuity of care, and reallocation of resources from high technology to health promotion, primary care, and social support.

Of course, many of these ideas have been described and advocated for a long time in the literature on successful aging, productive aging, public health, and geriatric medicine; and some of these priorities have even been piloted or demonstrated in small ways in the existing Medicare program. The MMA itself made some modest advances to promote this agenda of care: The Chronic Care Improvement Program (now called Medicare Health Support), for example, pilots and then presumably will cover new services for beneficiaries with diabetes, congestive heart failure, and chronic obstructive pulmonary disease (COPD). The Case Management for High Cost Beneficiaries program attempts to get physicians, hospitals, and other providers to implement new forms of disease management.

But the politics and economics of "body part" medicine, as well as the constituencies and money that surround particular conditions or treatments, have effectively militated against significant change in the overall philosophy or design of the program along these lines. Indeed, the very notion that we are adding "parts," now Part D, to the Medicare program signals that the fundamental constructs of hospital and medical coverage in Medicare have been largely retained since 1965.

This chapter sketches a set of alternative purposes, design contours, and potential politics for a next-generation Medicare, one that anticipates the new epidemiology and vision of aging in the next fifty years of the program. However, the policy, political, and economic obstacles in the way of such a vision are daunting,

PURPOSES

There is no doubt that Medicare has been extremely successful in realizing its initial policy vision. The program dramatically improved access to medical care, provided substantial financial protection to the elderly and disabled, supported the unprecedented advancement of the health care industry, and enjoyed enormous popular and political support. Coverage and reimbursement emphasized acute and episodic care provided by physicians and hospitals, with other covered services triggered by medical decision making. Medicare skilled nursing home and home health care coverage, for example, were triggered by an acute hospital episode and were largely conceptualized as lower-cost substitutes for inpatient care, not social or supportive services in their own right. On the professional side, Medicare reimbursement is generally restricted to physician services or those services that are conditional on physician services or orders. This places heavy restrictions on the role and contribution that allied health professionals can play in care and effectively eliminates a host of potentially valuable (and potentially cost-effective) case management, counseling, and educational functions in geriatric health services.

While this acute, medical, and episodic model of Medicare grew out of the policy of 1965 and its subsequent politics, much has changed in the social and economic circumstances, as well as the medical and health demands, of Medicare beneficiaries. The paradigmatic conditions that shaped the "old" Medicare were heart disease, cancer, and stroke. The paradigmatic conditions of the next generation of Medicare will be chronic conditions such as diabetes, mental health conditions such as depression, dementia, and the interactions of such conditions as osteoporosis with falls or other life shocks.

Consider these epidemiologic facts, generally well known to students of public health and aging:

1. *Chronic conditions:* More than 80 percent of Medicare beneficiaries have a chronic condition; the quarter of beneficiaries who have five or more chronic conditions account for 68 percent of Medicare expenditures (Anderson 2005). As Gerald Anderson (2005) has documented, use of the health system by this group of beneficiaries with multiple chronic conditions is extraordinary: averaging thirteen different physicians (ambulatory and inpatient) and filling fifty prescriptions per year.

2. *Dementia:* Estimates of the prevalence of dementia in the population age 65 and over range from 5 to 10 percent of the population, with the absolute numbers of Medicare beneficiaries with Alzheimer's and other dementias expected to triple in the next fifty years. Kenneth Langa and his colleagues (2001) at the University of Michigan estimate that the additional yearly cost of informal care for each case amounted to $3,630 for mild dementia, $7,420 for moderate dementia, and $17,700 for severe cases.

3. *Mental health:* Best estimates of the prevalence of significant depression in old age place rates between 15 and 33 percent of the population at a moment in time (Gallo and Lebowitz 1999; Cole, Bellavance, and Mansour 1999). Depression by itself has important implications for functional and cognitive decline and has complex interactions with alcohol and substance abuse, anxiety disorders, suicide, and dementia. Just the informal caregiving provided to older persons with depression accounts for more than $9 billion annually (Langa et al. 2004).

4. *Obesity and diabetes:* Already, diabetes affects 12 percent of the elderly population. The dramatically increasing rates of obesity and diabetes in younger cohorts mean that this condition and its comorbidities will affect a large proportion of Medicare beneficiaries and account for increasing costs in the program. By 2010, the prevalence of obesity is expected to increase to 37 percent of persons age 60 and older (Arterburn, Crane, and Sullivan 2004). The costs of these cases are tremendous. A recent study by Lakdawalla, Goldman, and Shang (2005) estimates that obese 70-year-olds will spend

about $39,000 more on health care than persons of normal weight. These persons will experience higher rates of diabetes, hypertension, and heart disease. Although these beneficiaries will cost Medicare an average of 34 percent more, they will not necessarily experience shorter life expectancies, but will experience fewer disability-free life years.

5. *Orthopedics, arthritis, pain, and the rehabilitative disciplines:* With the aging of the baby-boom population comes a shift in the physical and functional limitations of the older population. Some of this is a result of different life experiences and exposure (such as life courses of physical activity), and some of it follows from increasing life expectancies and attendant falls; prevalence of arthritis, osteoporosis, and back pain; and advances in joint replacement, orthopedic surgery, and rehabilitative science. This changing priority for a rehabilitative orientation for Medicare is already evident in prevalence rates for the older population. Arthritis, for example, is the most prevalent chronic condition among older persons in general and for each ethnic and racial minority group. It is projected to increase from 15 percent of the over-65 population in 1990 to 18.2 percent (59.4 million persons) in 2020 (Dunlop et al. 2001).

Of course, none of these conditions are mutually exclusive in populations, nor do they represent distinct classes of beneficiaries, which makes the traditional policy approach of "carving out" these conditions and treatments all the more counterproductive. Patients (and families) with dementia tend to have high rates of depression and other chronic conditions. Patients with diabetes tend to exhibit high rates of depression, heart disease, kidney disease, hypertension, strokes, and visual and other impairments. Acute episodes of care disproportionately affect all of these groups.

There are many ways to think about the costs and larger significance of these interactions among prevention and health promotion, chronic care, mental health, and long-term care. An analysis by James Lubitz and his colleagues (2003) and an accompanying editorial by David Cutler (2003) suggests an intriguing hypothesis: systematically tying medical advances to "nonmedical" approaches such as behavior change, cognitive stimulation, and education could produce the policy equivalent of a "win-win," improving life expectancy and functioning with no net increase in lifetime costs.

INGREDIENTS OF A TRULY MODERN MEDICARE SYSTEM

Prevention and Promotion

A large body of recent scientific evidence has established the feasibility, efficacy, and cost-effectiveness of pursuing prevention and health promotion strategies in old age (Rowe 1999; Russell 1998). Modern thinking about the process of aging itself—particularly the plasticity and behavioral change that occurs into very old ages—provides the basis for thinking very differently about the possibilities and efficacy of prevention and health promotion in Medicare.

While some demonstrations and selected programs have promoted screening (e.g., mammography), behavioral changes (e.g., quitting smoking), injury reduction (e.g., prevention of falls), and appropriate medications use (e.g., antihypertensives), the Medicare-related promotion-and-prevention enterprise is still extremely limited. Mobilizing a vigorous health promotion-and-prevention approach would require a substantial research and development (R&D) effort (to identify the battery of cost-effective approaches), incentives and supports for beneficiaries to engage in such behaviors, the careful targeting of prevention and promotion, and engagement of a set of organizations such as senior centers that have acted outside the orbit of traditional Medicare policy and payment.

Disease Management

Although disease management approaches have been embraced by Congress and the Centers for Medicare and Medicaid Services (CMS) as promising strategies, particularly for high-cost chronic conditions, the early evaluation returns have been mixed. However, sophisticated and prospective models of care for chronic conditions will require much more scale, time, innovation in delivery systems, and resources than have been deployed in the demonstrations to date. In particular, these approaches need to be tailored to the reality that many, if not most, candidates for disease management present with multiple chronic conditions with high degrees of social complexity and high-cost trajectories of care.

Beneficiary-centric, Patient-centric

It is possible that a convergence of some ideological forces and some applied innovations in the organization and financing of health services in old age will produce a significant shift in the payment and control of services. On the ideological side, the recent and not-so-recent push to increase consumer control and choice in health care has produced ripples in design and incentives across the Medicare program. On the innovation side, the early results from experiments in "cash and counseling" and other demonstrations of consumer-directed chronic and long-term care have established the feasibility and some of the benefits that arise from greater individual and family responsibility over care. Most intriguing is the early evidence about the potential benefits of so-called self-management approaches in chronic care. As Edward Wagner and his colleagues have summarized in their review of evidence-based approaches to chronic illness, "There is now considerable evidence that individual and group interventions that emphasize patient empowerment and the acquisition of self-management skills are effective in diabetes, asthma and other chronic conditions" (Wagner et al. 2001, 74).

Compensation for Socioeconomic Status

Health care providers know that life histories of poverty, poor access to medical care, environmental exposure, and other socioeconomic determinants of health status in old age compound the challenge of delivering Medicare-financed services, especially for chronic conditions. The chief executive officer of a large health system once complained to me that his hospitals had "a Medicaid population grown old" in its Medicare services, and he believed that coverage, reimbursement, and support systems were woefully inadequate for compensating the life histories of many of his system's poor and minority patients. In health services research, this problem has been framed largely as inadequate risk adjustment, where the comorbidities and complications that arise for disadvantaged populations do not capture the full extent of risk and expense in care. But when a broader conception of Medicare—one that takes full account of chronic and long-term care needs—is contemplated, disadvantages in social supports, the built environment, and allied health services take on increased significance. Systematic differences in access to these supports and services by socioeconomic status would require a broad rethinking of coverage and payment for Medicare to assure equity across beneficiaries.

Delivery System Reform

Just as the epidemiology of chronic and long-term conditions highlights the prevalence of many chronic conditions, so too the delivery systems for the next generation of care will need to be much more variegated and flexible. Some of the most interesting new models of geriatric and chronic care seamlessly mix such diverse disciplines as nutrition counseling, vision care or dentistry, physical therapy, and mental health. Moreover, they support medical services with appropriate phone follow-up, transportation services, and patient education so as to increase the likelihood of behavior change or adherence to treatment.

Recent Medicare reform has recognized the importance of chronic conditions and the salience of quality improvement for this population (Daaleman 2006). Section 231 of the MMA provides encouragement and incentives for managed care plans to develop innovative and specialized plans to address the needs of beneficiaries with disabilities or chronic conditions. The development of these alternatives may be an important testing ground for larger payment and delivery system reforms to address disabilities and chronic conditions.

Agents and Support Systems

Much of the challenge for beneficiaries—especially the kinds of beneficiaries with disabilities, chronic conditions, mental illness, dementias, and other vulnerabilities—lies in navigating the complex array of Medicare coverage, medical providers, and social supports. In practice, the medical decisions are inextricably linked with the support systems of families and communities, housing, home care, transportation, and so forth. Typically, these decisions need to be made under duress, when a beneficiary is sick, confused, or experiencing a crisis of housing or care.

Missing in this system is a solution to the agency problem that most beneficiaries face in organizing care and supports, making medical and related decisions, and managing the complexities posed by Medicare's particular structure of coverage (Lawlor 2003). While much of the national discussion has implied that physicians need to take a stronger role in care management, it is not at all obvious that the professional orientation of doctors is appropriate to the task, or that the basic approach should not be more interdisciplinary (Sommers et al. 2000). The private market has produced some modest examples of agents; public and nonprofit organizations such as Area Agencies on Aging provide some of these agency functions (particularly information and referral), and the medical system has some experiments (such as the National Cancer Institute's Patient Navigators) in patient decision making and care support. While these examples are notable, they represent a tiny intervention in the scale of complexity and frequency of decisions that Medicare beneficiaries are asked to make.

An Appropriate Workforce

Almost any careful analysis of community-based, chronic, or long-term care highlights the fundamental problem of workforce training and supply to respond to the demands of an aging society. Even in the medical sphere, the failure of geriatrics to grow as a discipline in numbers and stature illustrates the disconnect between national need and professional response. Outside of medicine, the relatively small numbers of nurses, social workers, physical therapists, occupational therapists, and other allied disciplines who have been specifically trained and reimbursed to provide continuity of care in aging is a serious constraint to building an appropriate delivery system. Already, 91 percent of nursing homes report that they do not have sufficient staff to provide basic care. Even paraprofessional or nonprofessional responses to this national need are missing. Closely tied to our inability to publicly pay for services that are not intrinsically connected to a Medicare-reimbursed physician visit or procedure is the lack of a market response that provides low-tech and community-based supportive services in old age.

The Technology Quid pro Quo

The ability to manage technology in the acute sector is the quid pro quo of building a modern policy approach to preventative, chronic, and long-term care. Technology is the single largest mutable long-term driver of Medicare costs and effectiveness. Because Medicare has never developed a rigorous approach to technology assessment and coverage decisions, instead loosely relying on the "reasonable and necessary" criteria of the original legislation, new acute medical technology is the tail wagging the dog in program coverage and cost. One of the major obstacles to overcome in implementing more formal technology assessment is the historic political opposition to the use of cost-effectiveness criteria and the explicit consideration of costs in Medicare coverage decisions.

If better management of technology in Medicare coverage decisions were not a big enough policy challenge, an additional analytic and policy hurdle is the adoption of quality-of-life and functional outcomes as explicit criteria for all Medicare coverage services. The hypothesis of this chapter is that if quality-of-life and functional outcomes were given true standing in the Medicare coverage process, then a variety of low-tech supportive services would be justifiable on cost-effectiveness grounds, and some of the most expensive acute interventions would not. At a minimum, effective behavioral approaches for diet or physical rehabilitation would be put on equal footing for coverage with left ventricular assist devices or lung volume reduction surgery. In order to move this agenda without the fear of uncontrollable costs and coverage, tough-minded approaches to intervention (Freedman et al. 2006b) and cost-effectiveness analysis in Medicare (Neumann, Rosen, and Weinstein 2005) will be necessary.

Complications

Would this reorientation of Medicare imply an abandonment of Medicare's acute coverage tradition or a retreat from the success of medical advancement and care that have been the hallmark of Medicare's first forty years? Not really. This change would move the center of gravity of Medicare's coverage and payment policy from the acute setting to chronic and long-term care, effectively shifting the conceptualization of care from episodic to longitudinal. Instead of treating and paying for care one episode at a time, providers and payment would be restructured to move with the patient along the journey of home, community, chronic, acute, and long-term care. Instead of preventive, chronic, and long-term care being seen as appendages to an acute episode, these become the fundamentals of a social and health care plan, with acute episodes interspersed. The easiest place to start would be the Medicare Advantage Program, where payment and mandate to managed care providers could be feasibly adapted to promote prevention, social functioning, and quality-of-life outcomes. Some of this is already occurring. Indeed, this approach would bring managed care back to the prevention-and-promotion vision of the early prepaid health care movement in the United States.

The fear that mushrooming costs would accompany a move to a more community-based, public health–oriented, and social approach to Medicare policy has effectively chilled serious discussion of ways in which this might happen in a cost-effective and fiscally prudent way. The principal fear is the "woodwork effect," where millions of beneficiaries and their families would come out of the woodwork to take advantage of community-based and social services under a chronic or long-term care regime. A government official once complained to me that community-based approaches to long-term care would cost "kazillions of dollars" because so many households would shift the responsibility for care and support over to the public sector.

There is also no natural or substantial political constituency for such reform, and powerful interests are invested in protecting the status quo. Many years ago, Carroll Estes (1983) described the "aging enterprise," a version of the medical-industrial complex that attaches to medical and social services in aging. In the current day, this political economy might be better described as the Medicare-industrial complex, where large interests representing pharmaceuticals, medical suppliers, academic medicine, hospitals, and specialty societies are politically organized and well financed to protect a strongly biomedical version of Medicare coverage.

GETTING FROM HERE TO THERE

This chapter has made the argument that Medicare needs a fundamental, not incremental, shift in its philosophy of care and social support to address the changing epidemiology and life circumstances of beneficiaries in the twenty-first century. In effect, Medicare needs to adopt a new *gestalt* of policy that embraces the reality of chronic and mental health conditions in the population and promotes allied health professionals, payment incentives, delivery systems, and agents to better support vulnerable beneficiaries as they navigate the complexities of cognitive declines, multiple diagnoses, and misfits in their housing and social supports. Imagine a Medicare program that supports the careful and ongoing assessment of the health and social needs of beneficiaries, supports a delivery system that provides the metaphorical continuum of care and social support, and is disciplined by cost-effective approaches to improving quality of life and social functioning.

Such a program would depart significantly from the original policy architecture of Part A (Hospital Care) and Part B (Supplemental Medical Insurance), and its successors in Parts C and D. Such a program would anticipate the epidemiological realities of health behavior, mental health, chronic conditions, long-term care, and social functioning as primary, not secondary, constructs for policy design. Such a program would anticipate and respond to the challenges of diabetes, Alzheimer's, and osteoporosis in an aging population. A modern Medicare program would be specifically configured to deal with a beneficiary population (and their families) dealing with these complex bundles of cognitive, behavioral, mental health, physical, and medical conditions.

A recent framework by the Assistant Secretary for Planning and Evaluation of the Department of Health and Human Services, for example, emphasizes the following interventions for reducing and addressing the prevalence of disability in the older population:

1. implementing smoking cessation
2. improving exercise
3. implementing good chronic disease care
4. implementing depression screening, treatment, and follow-up
5. implementing fall prevention systems for frail elderly persons
6. modifying homes and providing assistive devices
7. implementing widespread care planning for seriously ill people (Friedman et al. 2006b)

It is interesting how closely this overall framework for high-impact interventions for late-life disability reflects the discussion of a priority agenda for Medicare itself in this chapter.

To take this agenda seriously, a different paradigm of services R&D, financing and payment reform, and workforce development will be necessary. Indeed, some of the recent reforms have had the effect of diminishing rather than enhancing the capacity of the system to respond to complex bundles of beneficiary and caregiver needs that span the acute, chronic, and long-term care spectrum. For example, the recent extension of prospective payment for long-term and post-acute care facilities had the effect of reinforcing the "silos" of care for Medicare beneficiaries, not necessarily encouraging the selection of the most appropriate and cost-effective environment for services across provider types.

Reframing the agenda would require significant political push and champions, both from within the Congress and without. Without leadership in Congress and a dedicated effort by the large membership organizations such as AARP (who have not shown an appetite to pursue this vision aggressively), it is still hard to imagine a reframing of the Medicare agenda that truly embraces health prevention and promotion and the chronic, mental health, disability, rehabilitation, dementia, and long-term care for an aging population.

REFERENCES

Anderson, G. F. 2005. Medicare and chronic conditions. *New England Journal of Medicine* 353 (3): 305–9.

Arterburn, D. E., P. K. Crane, and S. D. Sullivan. 2004. The coming epidemic of obesity in elderly Americans. *Journal of the American Geriatrics Society* 52 (11): 1907–12.

Cole, G. C., F. Bellavance, and A. Mansour. 1999. Prognosis of depression in elderly community and primary care populations: A systematic review and meta-analysis. *American Journal of Psychiatry* 156 (8): 1182–89.

Cutler, D. M. 2003. Disability and the future of Medicare. *New England Journal of Medicine* 349 (11): 1084–85.

Daaleman, T. P. 2006. Reorganizing Medicare for older adults with chronic illness. *The Journal of the American Board of Family Medicine,* 19: 303–9.

Dunlop, D., L. M. Manheim, J. Song, and R. W. Chang. 2001. Arthritis prevalence and activity limitations in older adults. *Arthritis & Rheumatism* 44 (1): 212–21.

Estes, C. 1983. *The aging enterprise.* San Francisco: Jossey-Bass.

Freedman, V. A., N. Hodgson, J. Lynn, B. C. Spillman, T. A. Waidmann, A. M. Wilkinson, and D. A. Wolf. 2006a. A framework for identifying high-impact interventions to promote reductions in late-life disability. Prepared for the Office of Disability, Aging and Long-Term Care Policy, Office of the Assistant Secretary for Planning and Evaluation, U.S. Department of Health and Human Services. Available at http://aspe.hhs.gov/daltcp/reports/2006/prodecl.pdf.

———. 2006b. Promoting declines in the prevalence of late-life disability: Comparisons of three potentially high-impact interventions. *Milbank Quarterly* 84 (3): 493–520.

Gallo, J. J., and B. D. Lebowitz. 1999. The epidemiology of common late-life mental disorders in the community: Themes for the new century. *Psychiatric Services* 50 (9): 1158–66.

Lakdawalla, D., D. P. Goldman, and B. Shang. 2005. The health and cost consequences of obesity among the future elderly. *Health Affairs* 24:R30–42.

Langa, K. M., M. Chernew, M. Kabeto, A. R. Herzog, M. B. Ofstedal, R. Willis, R. Wallace, L. Mucha, W. Straus, and A. M. Fendrick. 2001. National estimates of the quantity and cost of informal caregiving for the elderly with dementia. *Journal of Geriatric Internal Medicine* 16 (11): 770–78.

Langa, K. M., M. A. Valenstein, A. M. Fendrick, M. U. Kabeto, and S. Vijan. 2004. Extent and cost of informal caregiving for older Americans with symptoms of depression. *American Journal of Psychiatry* 161:857–63.

Lawlor, E. F. 2003. *Redesigning the Medicare contract: Politics, markets, and agency.* Chicago: University of Chicago Press.

Lubitz, J., L. Cai, E. Kramarow, and H. Lentzner. 2003. Health, life expectancy, and health care spending among the elderly. *New England Journal of Medicine,* 349 (11): 1048–55.

Neumann, P. J., A. B. Rosen, and M. C. Weinstein. 2005. Medicare and cost-effectiveness analysis. *New England Journal of Medicine* 353 (14): 1516–22.

Rowe, J. E. 1999. Geriatrics, prevention, and the remodeling of Medicare. *New England Journal of Medicine* 340 (9): 720–21.

Russell, L. B. 1998. Prevention and Medicare costs. *New England Journal of Medicine* 339 (16): 1158–60.

Sommers, L. S., K. I. Marton, J. C. Barbaccia, and J. Randolph. 2000. Physician, nurse, and social worker collaboration in primary care for chronically ill seniors. *Archives of Internal Medicine* 160:1825–33.

Wagner, E. H., B. T. Austin, C. Davis, M. Hindmarsh, J. Schaefer, and A. Bonomi. 2001. Improving chronic illness care: Translating evidence into action. *Health Affairs* 20 (6): 64–78.

13

Long-Term Care Policy as an Investment in Baby Boomers and Future Generations

MICHELLE PUTNAM

NATIONAL PLANS FOR MEETING BABY BOOMERS' CHRONIC CARE AND DISABILITY NEEDS

As a nation, we are rather behind and generally unprepared for baby boomer aging. We have no national long-term care policy and a relatively small trained professional long-term care workforce, and most boomers have only modest retirement savings—likely not enough to privately pay for their own long-term care needs. This is the unfortunate truth. As it stands, chronic care and disability in old age (as in younger years) are uninsured, private responsibilities. Medicare insures long-term care for only short periods of time (up to 90 days) and for medical requirements only (U.S. Department of Health and Senior Services 2007a). A relatively small proportion of individuals have private long-term care insurance (an estimated six million individuals as of 2002), but it is often expensive, hard to access, and limited in its coverage and payment (Coronel 2004).

Medicaid is the default national long-term care insurer for persons with chronic care and disability needs who have spent their private savings; who are still in need of treatment, equipment, services, and/or supports; and who medically and financially qualify in their state. For those without insurance, care and supports must be privately funded and/or informally provided by family members and friends. For those with insurance, private funds and informal supports are also important supplements, but they generally do not cover the total cost of care (Cohen 2003).

This poor state of "readiness" (to borrow a term from the Federal Emergency Management Agency) is provoking national concern by state governments worried that Medicaid long-term care costs are financially unsustainable as the older population grows (National Governors Association 2007). Medicaid consumed an average of 17 percent of state budgets in 2005, and costs are projected to rise through 2010 (Smith et al. 2005). There are few alternate policies to fill the void of a dedicated long-term care policy. The Older Americans Act (OAA) programs attempt to do so through case management, home and community-based care, transportation, nutrition, and caregiver support services for persons age 60 and older. But for the size and scope of its mission, appropriations under the OAA remain remarkably low. Using 2005 population estimates (the most recent), the 2008 appropriation represents an allotment of roughly 27 cents for each eligible person (Administration on Aging 2007). A second federal program, the Rehabilitation Act, offers some peer and personal assistance supports through Centers for Independent Living for people of all ages with disabilities. State and local vocational rehabilitation, disability, and aging programs (public and private) also offer a range of services, but they are usually quite modest and in short supply. Thus, as it stands, the United States is not in a strong position to meet the care and support needs of baby boomers as they enter old age.

Why are we so far behind in our planning in the long-term care arena? One explanation lies in the lack of political interest and will to create large-scale long-term care policy for older adults, a group seen as already having their fair share of entitlements. The passage (in 1988) and later repeal (1989) of the Medicare Catastrophic Care Act set back long-term care policy initiatives and sparked debates of intergenerational equity in the media that continue to present day. The more recent battle for Medicare prescription drug coverage spent most of the remaining political capital for old-age issues, and increasing estimates of program costs for this so-called Part D program regularly remind Americans of how expensive large-scale social welfare benefits directed at older people have become.

A second explanation may be that we may have been excessively optimistic about the levels of health and wealth the baby-boom cohort will enjoy. However, boomers self-report lower health status levels than did their parents at the same age (Soldo et al. 2006). And, while baby boomer net worth is higher than their parents' generation, significant disparities in wealth exist based on race, marital status, and level of education. These disparities, in turn, translate into high levels of inequality in retirement savings (Lusardi and Mitchell 2007).

A third reason may lie in our lack of prior exposure to and extensive experience with chronic care, disability supports, and long-term care needs. Baby boomers' parents are the first generation to live long enough to need extended care and supports en masse. Thus aging, disability, and health care infrastructure—in both the public and private sectors—is still maturing as the baby boomers approach old age.

Acknowledging these shortcomings and the potential factors behind them, the question at hand is, what do we do now? Taking an optimistic view, this lack of formal attention to long-term care becomes an opportunity to thoughtfully develop chronic care, disability, and long-term care policies that support not only the medical needs of baby boomers but their individual, social, and economic concerns as well. Of course, moving forward will require us to think more critically than we have in the past about the purpose of long-term care and more imaginatively about our assumptions regarding what older adults, and those experiencing disabilities in particular, can contribute to our society. We will need to measure policy outcomes in terms of not just what types and amounts of care and supports are provided but also what people are able to do and contribute to their families and communities once care and supports are provided. In sum, we need to break out of the existing mode of thinking and, instead, understand long-term care policy as an investment in older adults.

DEMOGRAPHIC AND SOCIAL TRENDS SUPPORTING AN INVESTMENT STRATEGY IN LONG-TERM CARE

For many, investing in older adults with chronic care and disability-support needs may seem to be an unusual idea. However, certain demographic and social trends suggest this approach may match well with the needs and interests of many current older adults and those of the baby boomers as they enter old age.

Greater Disability-Related Diversity within Middle-Aged and Older Generations

Since 1950, the early life-course period of the baby boom, life expectancy has continually increased. From 1950 to 2004, life expectancy for the total population from birth increased from 68.2 to 77.8 years and rose from 13.9 to 18.7 years at age 65 (Centers for Disease Control and Prevention 2007). In addition, functional impairment has declined among the general over-60 population, and disability has become more compressed into later ages (Cai and Lubitz 2007). Of particular note, life expectancy has increased for persons with chronic conditions and those experiencing physical, mental, and developmental disabilities. With improvements in medical treatment, technology, pharmaceuticals, and self-care procedures, the accidents, injuries, diseases, and acute conditions that previously shortened life have increasingly segued into chronic conditions (Kemp and Mosqueda 2007). Thus, for persons with such conditions as spinal cord injury, cancer, developmental disability, multiple sclerosis, HIV/AIDS, and cerebral palsy, among others, years of life beyond the age of onset have been extended. Each of these trends demonstrates success, but they also help account for the increasing levels of diversity of disability now being experienced by older adults. While some will not experience chronic illness or disability until the very end of their lives, others may experience it for much of their lives, and a few even for a majority of their lives.

As they age, baby boomers bring still more disability-relevant factors to the older population. Boomers have higher rates of chronic illnesses and conditions such as diabetes and obesity than prior generations (Soldo et al. 2006). Maturing to midlife in an era of rapidly advancing technology, baby boomers are benefiting from earlier detection and more effective treatment of conditions like cancer, Alzheimer's, and Parkinson's. Early detection increases the number of persons living "post-onset" of disease, and a growing proportion of such individuals are now among the baby boomers. Finally, the last decade has seen greater recognition of mental health and illness and increasing parity in treatment. As baby boomers grow older, this widens the range of conditions available to categorize their chronic care or disability-related needs.

Older Adults' Expectations of Participation and Engagement Are Changing

Traditionally, our conceptualizations of life stages have been linear (education, work, retirement) and paired by a dependency ratio status (noncontributor, contributor, noncontributor). Challenges to these models are being made by current older adults who are making new pathways in old age beyond traditional retirement by remaining in the formal workforce as employees or business owners, volunteering, seeking additional education, or taking on new family roles (Freedman 2006). Baby boomers show signs of following in the footsteps of their parents and older relatives by seeking to remain engaged and active participants in their families and communities (Wilson and Simson 2006). There is no reason to assume that their desire for community participation will decrease due to the presence of chronic conditions or disability. Certainly, there will always be a small minority of older adults who are ill, frail, and medically unable to engage in activities with family, friends, and the wider community. However, for most adults with disabilities, barriers to participation are not only the expense, or cost, of care but more perniciously the stereotypes that ghettoize such individuals as ill and frail and with little capacity to contribute. As older adults' expectations of what one does in old age change, their expectations for chronic care and disability supports that enhance community involvement rather than only assuring residency at home will increase as well.

Technology Is Adding New Ways to Meet Chronic Care and Disability-Related Needs

In previous generations, human interventions constituted the majority of informal and formal support provided to meet chronic care and disability needs. With the advancement of computers, information technology, and other sciences, the last two decades have seen technology begin to replace, complement, and even supersede human-provided assistance (Freedman et al. 2006). Low-technology devices like canes, bath chairs, and ramps remain important and in widespread use. Now, however, high technology such as Ibot chairs that permit users to climb stairs and roll on unpaved trails, voice and eye command computer devices, smart houses that interact with occupants, and automobiles adapted for user capabilities are increasingly available to consumers.

Baby boomers belong to the first high-tech generation, engaging in widespread computer and technology use in their daily lives. They continue to readily adopt new technologies such as in-ear cell phones, global positioning systems in automobiles, and programmable home appliances and electronics that respond to owner needs, preferences, and safety concerns. The capacity to produce technology that meets chronic care and disability-related needs is increasing and more readily brought to mass markets through the Internet. Baby boomers will likely find innovative ways for new and everyday technologies to meet their needs.

Baby Boomers Are Becoming Savvy Long-Term Care Consumers

In the baby-boomer generation, caregiving for older parents is seemingly ubiquitous. Boomers are the first generation of caregiver consumers—they have experience with aging and disability services, support programs, organizations, and policies that their parents, if they served as caregivers, did not have before they entered old age. As caregivers, boomers' work was estimated in value at $350 billion in 2006 (Gibson and Houser 2007) and ranged from direct assistance to case management to financial planning. As they interact with aging and disability systems, long-term care insurance providers, and practice professionals, baby boomers are gaining firsthand knowledge of what is and is not working within both acute and long-term care for persons experiencing chronic illness and disability. With long-term care a private concern, caregivers are becoming a powerful consumer group in the marketplace and a broad stakeholder constituency in long-term care policy.

As they enter old age, baby boomers will likely be more informed, savvy consumers, having previously been through the insurance systems, service networks, and resource centers. Thus they should, first, be able to ask more critical, probing questions about what options are available for meeting their chronic care and disability-support needs (which may be more accurately self-defined); second, have a better sense of what the best value for their money is; and third, be capable of seeking and finding alternatives if the options provided are unsatisfactory to them. Should they need help in procurement, it is probable that the next caregiver generation—boomer children (generations X and Y)—will be even more adept at deciphering real and virtual marketplace options as instant access to global information and communication are hallmarks of their aging cohorts.

REDEFINING MEASURES OF COST AND BENEFIT IN AN INVESTMENT EQUATION

The economic value of investing in chronic care and disability supports for older adults is an unsavory topic. Yet pretending it is not an underlying issue only stymies dialogue about measures of costs and benefits. The sheer size of the baby-boomer generation is predicted to double the absolute numbers of older adults with chronic care and disability needs (Johnson, Toohey, and Wiener 2007). Costs of long-term care are projected to quadruple between 2000 and 2040, with estimated costs as high as $379 billion—with one-third of that amount ($132 billion) paid for through public insurance (Allen 2005). Private costs include long-term care premiums and copayments, informal family provided care, and other costs such as in-kind and intrafamily resources transfers. Placed into an economic cost-benefit analysis, public and private financing of baby boomers' chronic care and disability-related needs are predicted to be hefty, particularly when defined broadly (i.e., to include transportation, nutrition, assistive technology, a personal attendant, home and community care, skilled nursing, and so on). Thus long-term care is seen as posing a serious strain on both public and private budgets.

If the return on long-term care spending is viewed exclusively in financial terms, most economists would suggest it is minimal at best. Thus public spending is targeted to those people who are "most vulnerable" or most "at risk," and private long-term care insurance benefits are capped. This public and private policy approach tends to give people the minimal amount of care and support they need to get by in basic life activities. Additionally, by default, those in need of publicly insured long-term care benefits through Medicaid are either in or induced to enter poverty by virtue of Medicaid's income and asset restrictions. The hard outcome measures of this residual policy approach are tied to immediate physical and, somewhat less often, mental health needs, with other measures that assess quality of life and life satisfaction having less salience. This approach represents a limited way to conceptualize long-term care outcomes, with the benefits it yields being limited to the restricted range of care interventions it encompasses.

A more inclusive nonresidual approach would examine return on the care investment not just economically but socially and psychologically as well. Chronic care and disability supports would be provided to ensure that older adults could engage and participate in the activities and roles they desired. As such, outcome measures may evaluate care and support utilization, but they would also measure participation and social inclusion. This investment approach ideologically borrows from theories of capability (Sen 1999;

Nussbaum 2006) and models of social return on investment (Glaeser, Laibson, and Sacerdote 2002).

The aging of the baby-boom generation brings this discussion center stage. As the population of older adults diversifies, has greater expectations for engagement, finds new ways to meet its needs through technology, and is more knowledgeable about long-term care policies, there is less reason to assume older adults with chronic care and disability-related needs are unable to make contributions to their families and communities. The sheer size of the baby-boom generation makes this point more visible as the number of older adults experiencing chronic conditions and disabilities grows. The way we measure community engagement and contribution and ultimately social inclusion must be well matched with how we evaluate economic costs so that return on investment is readily seen. Small steps are being made in this direction currently that will likely serve as the foundation for investment-oriented long-term care policy.

QUIET LONG-TERM CARE "INVESTMENT" REVOLUTIONS ALREADY UNDER WAY

Despite the fact that we as a nation are functioning on de facto long-term care policies heavily reliant on informal care and supports for persons with chronic care and disability-related needs, quiet revolutions are taking place in aging and disability policy. The demographic and social trends noted above offer support for these changes, but for now the marketplace alone has not yet had enough power to generate a sea change. A powerful push has come from federal government entities in response to external and internal pressures. This is leveraging legislative and administrative change, bringing with it a new focus that is beginning to shift the nature and purpose of long-term care policy.

Deinstitutionalization of Long-Term Care

Over the past two decades, the combined trends of increased outpatient treatment and more quantity and greater variety of home and community-based care have meant that more people with chronic conditions (of all ages) are living in our communities, including those with significant cognitive, physical, and emotional conditions. There are many factors that support these changes, including patterns of insurance reimbursement and consumer preferences. The industry shift toward deinstitutionalization of long-term care as public policy, however, is driven largely by civil rights rather than market interests.

Compliance with the Americans with Disabilities Act (ADA) and the Supreme Court's 1999 ruling in *Olmstead v. LC* has forced a radical change in course for provision of chronic care and disability supports. The Court ruling deemed mandatory institutional care to be discriminatory against persons with disabilities, requiring that community-based care choices must be made available to those who preferring it (Teitelbaum, Burke, and Rosenbaum 2003). This ruling paralleled years of disability rights advocacy work pushing for greater community integration and inclusion. President George W. Bush's 2001 executive order implementing the New Freedom Initiative mandated immediate, demonstrated compliance with the *Olmstead* ruling by all federally funded entities (U.S. Department of Health and Human Services 2003).

In less than a decade since the ruling and the order, a visible shift can be seen in federal, state, and local program directives and structures. Prime examples include "Systems Change," "Real Choices," "Money Follows the Person," and Aging and Disability Resource Centers grants provided through the Centers for Medicare and Medicaid Services (CMS) and the Administration on Aging. Many model programs and policy demonstrations have been completed, with others still currently ongoing, such as Cash and Counseling demonstration, which is jointly funded by CMS (Centers for Medicare and Medicaid Services), DALTP (Office of Disability, Aging, and Long-Term Care Policy), and the Robert Wood Johnson Foundation (see www.cashandcounseling.org).

Many of the innovations that have been produced were created through administrative regulations with minimal public or legislative discourse. For example, the 2005 Budget Reconciliation Act permits Medicaid to offer home and community-based services without a CMS waiver—prior law funded only institutionally provided long-term care (Tritz 2006). Some lawmakers are actively seeking to legislate long-term care policy changes that would codify into law program options supporting broader options for home and community-based services that keep older adults engaged in their communities. Senators Tom Harkin and Arlen Spector have taken the lead, introducing the Community Choice Act of 2007 (GovTrack 2008).

Addition of Social and Economic Outcomes

Deinstitutionalization efforts, whether explicitly stated or not, tend to have outcome measures that go beyond function and health and begin to examine engagement and inclusion. For many Medicaid beneficiaries with chronic conditions and/or those experiencing disability, provision of care and supports facilitate engagement in family, community, and work roles. In the past, this has been a more vocalized aim of younger persons with disabilities, but with the noted role expansion, it is increasingly an aim of older adults as well (Stevens-Ratchford and Diaz 2003). This can be seen in the redesign of Medicaid's insurance coverage for younger and older persons with disabilities through its waiver options and demonstration programs (e.g., Waivers 1115c and 1918b, Cash and Counseling). These programs have increased the level of choice and control beneficiaries have in selecting and using supports and services within home and community-based care.

For many beneficiaries, this has meant having more opportunity to ensure formal care and supports that complement existing informal and personal resources. When redundancy is decreased, resources are freed to facilitate larger social and economic goals. For example, in the Cash and Counseling program, a person unable to prepare meals may have them delivered by a relative instead of cooked by a chore worker paid for by Medicaid insurance. Funds saved may be applied to cover transportation costs to volunteer engagements instead.

A more explicit example of this hybrid purpose is the Social Security Administration's (SSA) Ticket to Work program, which permits continuation of Medicare health insurance for persons with disabilities returning to the formal workforce without employer provided health insurance (see http://www.ssa.gov/work/aboutticket.html). This program has had limited success, however, as states have reduced their Medicaid partner funding (which pays for long-term care) in the face of competing budget priorities, and persons with disabilities have had difficulty in sustaining employment due to medical reasons or nonreceptive working environments (Craig et al. 2007). Despite these challenges, the multipurpose or coordinated program aims are becoming more of a focus of CMS's and SSA's long-term disability policies (Social Security Advisory Board 2006).

Public Bolstering of Informal Care and Private Long-Term Care Insurance

Slowly we are seeing shifts in the valuation of informal care provided by family members to older adults with chronic care and disability-related needs. As caregiving costs have become better measured, offsets have gradually appeared in various forms, including state tax credits, caregiver wages, and in-kind caregiver supports (including the Administration on Aging's Family Caregiver Support Program and state and local programs). Information and assistance for caregivers and persons with chronic care, disability, and long-term care needs are also of elevated priority. Single-entry points into finding and using care and services meant to reduce consumer burden are appearing across the nation, for instance, in the form of Aging and Disability Resource Centers and the United Way's central call number 211. These centralized information centers are intended to support informal caregivers and help enable many states to better leverage private supports to reduce unnecessary Medicaid-funded nursing home admissions (see www.aoa.gov and www.211.org).

Perhaps unintentionally, yet in tandem, reforms in private long-term care insurance are being introduced. To this point, long-term care insurance has been largely unregulated and unstable, and coverage has often been hard to access (Kofman and Thompson 2004). One solution being proposed in several states is public-private partnerships that create "tiered" insurance schemes with private insurance as the primary insurer (until exhausted) followed by public insurance (Medicaid) as the second insurer. Under some proposals, private insurance premiums are 100 percent tax deductible, and asset caps for Medicaid eligibility are raised to match the amount of private insurance coverage purchased (http://www.rwjf.org/files/publications/other/ Longtermcare_052007.pdf). The bolstering of private resources creates a stronger market orientation of long-term care, which as noted earlier is creating strong consumer constituencies. To the extent that private resources offer greater flexibility and independence to older adults and support to families in meeting chronic care and disability needs, these are seemingly positive developments.

Institutionalizing Role Changes in Old Age

While changes in Medicaid, caregiver, and long-term care insurance policies have targeted audiences, the Older Americans Act has a universal mandate to facilitate health and well-being for all adults over age 60. Through its continued reauthorization and funding, the OAA has built a thin national infrastructure of supports to facilitate health and wellness, social engagement, and economic participation for over forty years. Resolutions coming from the 2005 White House Conference on Aging extend its programmatic reach farther than ever before by including as a priority issue the creation of meaningful volunteer and civic engagement experiences for older adults. The 2006 reauthorization of the OAA reflected this broadened agenda to foster inclusion and participation of older adults in our communities.

As noted in the introduction to this chapter, however, the budget allotted for OAA programs remains proportionally small in relation to the number of persons eligible for them. Thus, while ideologically significant, minimal funding is available to develop new or model programs. Related programs that would facilitate community participation and engagement for persons with chronic care and disability-related support needs such as transportation, home modifications, and the development of livable communities allowing persons to age in place are also short on funding. This, then, is perhaps the cusp of institutionalizing role changes in old age that emphasize social inclusion. While the Administration on Aging's Strategic Action Plan for 2007–2012 continues to stress meeting the more basic needs of older adults, the extended scope of the Older Americans Act suggests a wider focus for funding is possible in the future (U.S. Department of Health and Human Services 2007b).

PRECURSORS, EXPECTATIONS, AND INFLUENCES ON ADOPTION OF AN INVESTMENT APPROACH TO LONG-TERM CARE

A positive discussion of long-term care policy as an investment in baby boomers and future generations hinges on a reduction in the prevalence of

Decade	Selected health, chronic care, aging, and disability policy events
1930s	Social Security Act passed (1935)
	National Health Act of 1939 proposed
1940s	Wagner-Murray-Dingell bill proposed health care coverage for all (1943, reintroduced 1949)
	LaFollette-Barden Vocational Rehabilitation Act (1944)
	GI Bill of Rights (1944)
	Hill-Burton Act (Hospital Survey and Construction Act) (1946)
	Truman proposes national health insurance to Congress (1945 and 1949)
	Taft-Smith-Ball bill proposed grants to states for health care for poor (1946)
1950s	Medical Facilities Survey and Construction Act of 1954 aids construction of nursing homes, institutions for chronically ill, and rehabilitation facilities (1954)
	Social Security Disability Insurance enacted (1956)
1960s	Kerr-Mills Act grants aid to states for medical care of elderly poor (1960)
	First White House Conference on Aging (1961)
	Mental Retardation Facilities and Community Health Centers Construction Act (1963)
	Civil Rights Act (1964)
	Medicare, Medicaid, Older Americans Act (1965)
	Age Discrimination Act (1967)
	Architectural Barriers Act (1968)
	HEW's Task Force Report on Medicare Prescription Drug coverage (1969)
1970s	Supplemental Security Income established (1972)
	Rehabilitation Act of 1973 prohibits discrimination based on disability in federally funded programs and services (1973)
	Education for All Handicapped Children Act of 1975
	Developmentally Disabled Assistance and Bill of Rights Act (1975)
	Rehabilitation Act Amendments of 1978 establish Independent Living Centers
1980s	Omnibus Budget Reconciliation Acts 1980: Nursing Home Reform
	Omnibus Budget Reconciliation Act of 1981 establishes 1915(c) waivers permitting coverage of HCBC for persons at risk of institutionalization
	Medicare Channeling Demonstration (1984)
	Mental Illness Bill of Rights Act (1985)
	Air Carrier Access Act prohibited disability-based discrimination (1988)
	Fair Housing Act amendments prohibit disability-based discrimination (1988)
	Medicare Catastrophic Care Act of 1988 (repealed 1989)
1990s	Americans with Disabilities Act (1990)
	Clinton administration begins approving Medicaid 1115 waivers to states (1993)
	Family Medical Leave Act (1993)
	State Children's Health Insurance Program enacted (1997)
	Ticket to Work and Work Incentives Act (1999)
	Olmstead v. L.C., Supreme Court decision (1999)
2000s	Senior Citizens Freedom to Work Act (2000)
	Family Caregiver Support Program (2000)
	CMS Cash & Counseling Demonstration begins
	New Freedom Initiative (2001)
	Medicare Prescription Drug, Modernization Act (2003)
	First baby boomer OASI claim filed (October 15, 2007)

(Left margin vertical labels: Baby boomer parents; Baby boomers; Baby boomers' children)

FIGURE 13-1.   Policy Timeline Leading to Discussions of Long-Term Care
Sources: Disability Social History Project, Social Security Administration, Rehabilitation Research and Training Center on Independent Living Management, Temple University.

the belief that people experiencing chronic conditions and disability have less to offer or contribute to our communities than people not experiencing these conditions. Without this attitudinal change, selling chronic care and disability supports as continued investments in the human capital of older adults will continue to be an extremely difficult challenge. Additionally, prejudice and discrimination based on age must be reduced. If old age is thought to be synonymous with disability and/or stagnant development, arguments for investment in individuals across the life course are equally problematic. Extending the purpose of providing chronic care and disability supports beyond medical needs to also include social participation and engagement as primary goals addresses a growing concern about social inclusion. Arguably this is becoming a more defined interest of older adults, albeit stated in softer terms and restricted to specific activities, such as the emphasis on volunteering and civic engagement as noted above.

Figure 13-1 presents a selected list of health, aging, and disability policy events set against the lifetimes of three generations—the parents of baby boomers, baby boomers, and baby boomers' children. It shows both steady, incremental development of social welfare policies supporting older adults and persons with disabilities as well as some significant leaps forward in these policies over the lifetime of the baby boomers' parents. When viewing this trajectory, it appears we are slowly heading toward wider discussions of long-term care.

Whether or not the aging of the baby-boom generation will jump-start political and policy discourse is unclear. It seems unlikely that we will see the creation of any new entitlement program for older adults until concerns about the financial futures of Social Security and Medicare are addressed. However, given their legal directive, we should expect that the current "quiet revolutions" in long-term care will continue within Medicaid. Perhaps we will also see some extension of long-term care benefits within Medicare (see chapter 12 in this volume). Additionally, pressures may continue to build for the improvement of caregiver supports and reform of private long-term care insurance. In all of these efforts, we have the choice to revalue the benefit of long-term care as an investment in baby boomers and future populations of older adults. This seems a topic worthy of significant discussion.

REFERENCES

Administration on Aging. 2007. Legislation and budget. Available at http://www.hhs.gov/budget/07budget/aoa.html.

Allen, K. 2005. Long-term care financing: Growing demand and cost of services are straining federal and state budgets. Testimony presented on April 27, 2005, before the Subcommittee on Health, Committee on Energy and Commerce, House of Representatives. Available at http://www.gao.gov/new.items/d05564t.pdf.

Cai, L., and J. Lubitz. 2007. Was there compression of disability for older Americans from 1992 to 2003? Demography 44 (3): 479–95.

Centers for Disease Control and Prevention. 2007. Life expectancy at birth at 65 years of age, and at 75 years of age, by race and sex: United States, selected years 1900–2004 (Table 27). Available at http://www.cdc.gov/nchs/data/hus/hus07.pdf#fig18.

Cohen, M. 2003. Private long-term care insurance: A look ahead. *Journal of Aging and Health* 15 (1): 74–98.

Coronel, S. 2004. *Long-term care insurance in 2002*. Washington, DC: America's Health Insurance Plans.

Freedman, M. 2006. The social-purpose encore career: Baby boomers, civic engagement, and the next state of work. *Generations* 30 (4): 43–46.

Freedman, V. A., E. M. Agree, L. G. Martin, and J. C. Cornman. 2006. Trends in the use of assistive technology and personal care for late-life disability, 1992–2001. *Gerontologist* 46 (1): 124–27.

Gibson M. J., and A. N. Houser. 2007. Valuing the invaluable: A new look at the economic value of family caregiving. AARP Issue Brief 82. Available at http://www.assets.aarp.org/rgcenter/il/ib82_caregiving.pdf.

Glaeser, E., D. Laibson, and B. Sacerdote. 2002. An economic approach to social capital. *Economic Journal* 112 (483): F437–F458.

GovTrack. 2008. S. 799: Community Choice Act of 2007. Http://www.govtrack.us/congress/bill.xpd?bill=s110-799.

Johnson, R., D. Toohey, and J. Wiener. 2007. Meeting the long-term care needs of the baby boomers: How changing families will affect paid helpers and institutions. Retirement Project. Washington, DC: Urban Institute.

Kemp, B., and L. Mosqueda. 2007. Introduction to *Aging with disability: What the clinician needs to know*, ed. B. Kemp and L. Mosqueda, 1–8. Baltimore: Johns Hopkins University Press.

Kofman, M., and L. Thompson. 2004. Consumer protection and long-term care insurance: Predictability of premiums. Georgetown University Long-Term Care Financing Project. Available at http://www.ltc.georgetown.edu/pdfs/consumer.pdf.

Lusardi, A., and O. Mitchell. 2007. Baby boomer retirement security: The roles of planning, financial literacy, and housing wealth. *Journal of Monetary Economics* 54 (1): 205–44.

National Governors Association. 2007. The fiscal survey of states. Available at http://www.nasbo.org/Publications/PDFs/Fiscal%20Survey%20of%20the%20States%20June%202007.pdf.

Nussbaum, M. 2006. *Frontiers of justice: Disability, nationality, species membership*. Boston: Harvard University Press.

Sen, A. 1999. *Development as freedom*. Oxford: Oxford University Press.

Smith, V., K. Gifford, E. Ellis, A. Wiles, R. Rudowitz, and M. O'Malley. 2005. Medicaid budgets, spending and policy initiatives in state fiscal years 2005 and 2006: Results from a 50-state survey. Kaiser Commission on Medicaid and the Uninsured. Available at http://www.kff.org/medicaid/upload/Medicaid-Budgets-Spending-and-Policy-Initiatives-in-State-Fiscal-Years-2005-and-2006-report-executive-summary.pdf.

Social Security Advisory Board. 2006. A disability system for the 21st century. Washington, DC: Social Security Administration. Available at http://www.ilr.cornell.edu/edi/publications/PolicyForum/PolicyForum-Bios_2007-01-12.pdf.

Soldo, B., O. Mitchell, R. Tfaily, and J. McCabe. 2006. Differences in health on the verge of retirement. National Bureau of Economic Research (NBER) Working Paper No. 12,762. Cambridge, MA: NBER.

Stevens-Ratchford, R., and T. Diaz. 2003. Promoting successful aging through occupation: An examination of engagement in life; A look at aging in place, occupation and successful aging. *Activities, Adaptation & Aging* 27 (3/4): 19–37.

Teitelbaum, J., T. Burke, and S. Rosenbaum. 2003. *Olmstead v. L.C.* and the Americans with Disabilities Act: Implication for public health policy and practice. *Public Health Report* 119 (3): 371–74.

Thornton, C., G. Livermore, T. Fraker, D. Stapleton, B. O'Day, D. Wittenburg, R. Weathers, N. Goodman, T. Silva, E. Martin, J. Gregory, D. Wright, and A. Mamun. 2007. Evaluation of the Ticket to Work Program: Assessment of Post-Rollout Implementation and Early Impacts, Vol. 1. Princeton: NJ: Mathematica Policy Research, Inc.

Tritz, K. 2006. Medicaid's home and community-based services state plan option: Section 6068 of the Deficit Reduction Act of 2005. Washington, DC: Congressional Research Service. Available at http://www.nacdd.org/images2/pdfs/CRS%20report%20HCBS%20Option.pdf.

U.S. Department of Health and Human Services. 2003. The New Freedom Initiative. Http://www.hhs.gov/newfreedom/init.html.

———. 2007a. Medicare Coverage. Available at http://www.medicare.gov/Coverage/Home.asp.

———. 2007b. U.S. Administration on Aging strategic plan, 2007–2012. Available at http://www.scribd.com/doc/356862/AoA-Strategic-Action-Plan-20072012.

Wilson, L., and S. Simson, eds. 2006. *Civic engagement and the baby boom generation: Research, policy, and practice perspectives.* New York: Haworth Press.

14

Differential Treatment by Age: Age Discrimination or Age Affirmation?

JOHN MACNICOL

S ince its hesitant beginnings in the early years of the twentieth century, the discipline of gerontology has grown and flourished, influencing many areas of social and public policy (Achenbaum 1995; Katz 1996). It has concerned itself with improving the lot of older people, campaigning for better social security and pension provision for those who have retired from labor market activity or child care duties. It has sought special recognition and resource allocation for the particular health care needs of older people, via geriatric medicine. It has exposed the conditions under which many old people have to live when in institutional care. And it has countered the negative portrayal and treatment of older people in all areas of social life, including the discriminations they suffer merely on account of their age. At a grassroots level, many organizations of older people themselves—often collectively termed the "gray lobby"—have likewise pressured governments to recognize the particular needs of old age. Old people have never been passive victims: they have always campaigned for their rights (Pratt 1976; Blaikie 1990).

In doing so, campaigners have operated from a position that is often seen as inherently contradictory. On the one hand, many gerontologists wish to dispense with age as a categorization and work toward an "age-irrelevant," "age-neutral," or "ageless" society—one in which individuals will be judged by the content of their character, and not according to their chronological age. Examining old age as a discrete period is held to be misguided since no physical or cognitive significance can be attached to the age of 65, which emerged from the late nineteenth century onward as the age at which most state pensions were paid. Quite rightly, defining one particular age as the onset of "old age" is often criticized for being too much based upon biomedical or welfarist approaches. Interestingly, many gray lobby pressure groups have rejected such rigid demarcations, believing that the young, middle-aged, and old should work together for a common cause: the old are "our future selves." For example, campaigns by labor organizations or unmarried women in the United Kingdom in the 1920s and 1930s sought a reduction in the state pension age to 60 or even 55, as a recognition of the diminishing incomes suffered by many working-class people in late middle age. And in the United States, membership in AARP (formerly the American Association of Retired Persons) is open to all above the age of 50.

Yet while pleading the cause of "agelessness," gerontology demarcates old age as a protected territory, and argues for greater resource allocation to the end of the chronological life course via policies that "single out, stigmatize and isolate the aged from the rest of society" (Estes 1979, 2) in a way that can be seen as subtly ageist (Bytheway 1995, 97). The alternative suggested by newer life course perspectives is to dispense with the idea of the life cycle (since it is held to be inherently ageist to divide life into discrete stages) and to examine aging as a long and gradual *process* from birth to death, affected by such cross-cutting variables as class, gender, and ethnicity. However, this approach is scarcely more helpful, since controlling for all the variables involved would present a task so challenging as to be well-nigh impossible.

As the large baby-boom cohorts pass across the age-65 frontier in all advanced industrial societies, this central dilemma is moving beyond the pages of gerontology texts and becoming a major problem of social policy: Should we dispense with differential treatment by age, in the name of anti-ageism? Should we recognize that it is absurd to identify the age of 65 as the threshold of "old age"? Should state pension ages be raised, given that health status and working capacity must have improved? Should public policies become needs based rather than age based? Or should we acknowledge old age as a separate and potentially vulnerable stage of life that requires statutory protection via age-based policies (Neugarten 1982)?

In rejecting biological determinism, many gerontologists argue that it is necessary to distinguish between different kinds of "time" or "age." *Chronological age* (or "calendar time") refers quite simply to an individual's date of birth and involves an interaction between biographical time (an individual's life history) and historical time (the historical context within which an individual ages, affected by different cohort and generational experiences). *Social age* encapsulates socially ascribed identity or status differentiation by age, according to the age norms, age expectations, age-appropriate behaviors, and age divisions that prevail in any particular society at any given point in time, and are strongly internalized. *Physiological* or *biological age* denotes one's physical or cognitive status, as measured by tests of functional ability, mobility, strength and dexterity, bone density, organ reserve, intellectual performance, and so on. Finally, *psychological age* is an individual's self-assessment of his or her own age.

Chronological age per se is therefore meaningless: it is always mediated through prevailing social attitudes, ideologies, and structured inequalities and only attains significance in a particular cultural setting. In certain contexts, the biology of aging can be subject to a radical reevaluation. For example, in both the United Kingdom and the United States, the economic recession and high unemployment of the 1930s caused older workers to be judged industrially obsolescent, and the prevailing view was that they should be encouraged to leave the labor market in the name of economic efficiency. Yet once World War II had begun, labor shortages necessitated the retraining of older workers for key skilled positions in the wartime economy, and their importance was fully acknowledged. Indeed, in both countries the perceived value of older workers has changed over the past seventy years, with pendulum-like swings in the 1930s, 1970s, and 1980s. When technological innovation and economic restructuring necessitated workforce downsizing, the emphasis was on encouraging their early exit from the labor force; yet since the 1990s, the emphasis has been as it was in the 1950s and 1960s, on expansion of labor supply, with the economic contribution of older workers greatly valued via policies aimed at their labor force retention. Many other examples could be cited where historically contingent circumstances have profoundly affected the social construction of old age.

THE IMPORTANCE OF AGING AND OLD AGE

Studying old age is important for a variety of reasons. First, the aging process affects us all and is a source of constant fascination. It is deeply ingrained in our patterns of thought: we all live by "social clocks" that determine the "right" time to leave school, start work, marry, become a parent, retire, and so on (Neugarten 1996). So much of our popular culture is age based, and age is a vital element in the construction of individual identity. At both the macro level of society at large and the micro level of the extended family, we are enmeshed within complex hierarchies of age that profoundly affect our sense of self.

Second, old age and death present enormous spiritual and existential challenges (Cole 1992). Not surprisingly, mankind has always been intrigued by longevity, and even today medical breakthroughs that promise to extend life are newsworthy. The debate between biologists (who argue that, if only cell deterioration could be delayed, human beings could live for hundreds of years) and demographers (who argue that the maximum human life span is probably fixed at about 120 years) is at the core of aging studies.

Interestingly, old age is also a major reason for the existence of advanced welfare states, since the cost of social security and health care for older people is one of the largest items in welfare budgets. Western societies face the prospect of aging populations from the second decade of the twenty-first century, necessitating large increases in health and social care expenditure. For example, in the United Kingdom, a recent estimate is that cases of dementia may rise from 560,000 at present to 1,400,000 by 2051 (National Audit Office 2007). Much will depend on the uncertain balance of positive and negative forces determining health status in old age: positive factors (such as improvements in medical technology) may be offset by negative ones (such as a rising incidence of obesity).

Age is also a powerful social division, a determinant of many social phenomena, and the basis for social judgments (even if this is insufficiently acknowledged). The age structure of a population is one variable that affects its social characteristics: for example, youthful populations have a high propensity toward criminal behavior, unemployment, violent or traumatic deaths, out-of-wedlock births, and other social problems potentially more expensive than pension systems.

Finally, age is a source of discrimination. Indeed, many argue that ageism is as damaging and corrosive as racism or sexism, even if it may be qualitatively different, more complex and subtle—and therefore more problematic to demonstrate. The problem of age discrimination has also been addressed somewhat belatedly in Western societies. In order to understand why this is so, one needs to consider the meanings of discrimination in general and age discrimination in particular.

SOME PROBLEMS INHERENT IN DISCRIMINATION

All discrimination involves the application of assumed group characteristics to an individual, regardless of that individual's actual personal characteristics. A class of persons is identified, and all its members are assumed to have similarity. Such generalizations may have a rough accuracy, but they overlook the diversity and difference that exists within members of that class. Much depends upon the accuracy of the generalization.

The modern meaning of *discrimination* is intimately associated with the slow transition to liberal-democratic capitalist societies, with greater emphasis on individual rights. In the nineteenth century, both the United Kingdom and the United States possessed quasi-feudal social structures. There were very wide disparities of wealth and income, upward social mobility was restricted, only a few adult males possessed the right to vote, and inequality before the law (for example, with regard to women or ethnic minorities) was accepted. Discrimination was widespread and little commented on. The idea of individual rights was therefore undeveloped, and the term *discrimination* had a neutral meaning—to "differentiate."

However, the spread of democracy over the past hundred years has solidi-fied individual rights and transformed our conceptualization of discrimina-tion. It has taken on normative meanings, both positive and negative. Negative discrimination implies that harm is inflicted by one individual on another via a restriction of their rights; it can also be "a social pattern of ag-gregate behavior" inflicted by one group upon another (Banton 1994, 5).

Discrimination is viewed as an aberration in modern liberal-capitalist soci-eties, which pay lip service to the principle of equality of opportunity. However, legislative action against discrimination still tends to apply only to the public sphere—in areas such as employment, education, housing, or selection for public office. In our private worlds, we still enjoy considerable freedom to discriminate by making choices based upon our preferences or even prejudices—for example, in selecting friends or an area in which to live.

There are also two other elements in the modern meaning of discrimination—particularly employment discrimination—that raise thorny issues. First, it has long been a central principle of free market economics that discrimination is logically impossible in a truly capitalist economy. In conditions of perfect market competition, it is argued, an employer would always behave rationally, and it would be economically irrational to select an employee on productivity-irrelevant qualities such as gender, race, religion, or age: an employer's profits would suffer in consequence (Epstein 1992, 445, 452). Of course, in the real world, as opposed to the hypothetical abstraction of a pure market economy, an employer may indeed be willing to suffer some drop in profits in order to indulge his or her "taste for discrimination"—quite how much of a drop is the key question (Becker 1957, 6). Nevertheless, the argument emanating from free market economists is interesting and can instructively be adapted. While they would maintain that discrimination has naturally lessened as capitalism has evolved, it can just as convincingly be argued that state policies against employment discrimination are an essential part of the transition to a more competitive free market economy. It is interesting that in the United Kingdom and the United States, effective laws against employment discrimination are a post-1960s phenomenon, coinciding with the move away from a manufac-turing-based economy and toward a more service-oriented and white-collar employment base with more insecure, "flexible" jobs and a culture of com-petitive individualism that has characterized Western economies in the last forty years.

Second, most definitions of employment discrimination maintain that true discrimination occurs when a personnel decision is made on grounds other than productivity. If a personnel decision can be proven to be produc-tivity related, the likelihood of discrimination diminishes considerably (and, in the legal process, the onus of proof then falls on the plaintiff). A com-monly cited instance is the workplace policy of "no beards." If this were to exist for health and safety reasons, it would not be considered discrimina-tory; if, however, it merely reflected the prejudices of an employer against

Sikh men, it would be discriminatory. Employment discrimination laws do not prevent employers from firing employees who are unproductive. Indeed, such laws may be a way of streamlining workforces and improving productivity by ensuring that employment decisions are made on rational economic grounds. Only the most economically valuable workers are hired and retained. Outlawing "irrational" employment discrimination certainly solidifies individual rights, but it also maximizes economic efficiency.

Both of the above points need to be borne in mind when considering action against age discrimination. The late twentieth-century "discovery" of age discrimination and consequent legislative action may signal a new recognition of the rights of older people. On the other hand, it may—paradoxically—herald an era in which age protection is diminished, state pension ages will rise, and there will be workfarist policies designed to force older people into the kinds of new low-grade, poorly remunerated jobs that modern economies are generating. That is the dilemma.

AGEISM AND AGE DISCRIMINATION IN EMPLOYMENT

Ageism is generally taken to denote those attitudes, actions, and vocabularies that serve to accord people a diminished social status solely by reference to their age. To pass judgment on an individual, and thereby define his or her social worth, on the basis of a morally irrelevant characteristic such as age is held to be an affront to natural justice. As Erdman Palmore (1999, 7–8) has argued, "The democratic ideal is that each person should be judged on the basis of individual merit rather than on the basis of group characteristics such as race, sex and age." Although ageism can of course apply at any age, it is when it is directed at older people that it seems most objectionable. It is manifest in everyday linguistic expression, discourses, jokes, visual imagery, advertising, fashion, patterns of thinking, popular culture, and so on. Contemptuous epithets like "mutton dressed as lamb," "old codger," or "greedy geezer" are all too commonplace.

Ageism as a concept is of relatively recent origin (although prejudice against older people has long been researched), dating from Robert Butler's celebrated invention of the term in 1969 (Butler 1969). It therefore drew inspiration from the civil rights agitation of the 1960s and has infused the discipline of gerontology ever since. By contrast, age discrimination in employment has a very long history: there has been discussion since at least the 1930s of the question of whether the labor market disadvantages of older workers are caused primarily by discrimination per se or by other factors (notably economic restructuring and a contraction of those labor market sectors with high age profiles). Bodies such as the U.S. Department of Labor and the International Labour Organization researched the problems of older workers in the 1930s, including the discrimination they faced.

Age discrimination in employment involves the use of crude age proxies in personnel decisions relating to hiring, firing, promotion, demotion, retraining, (possibly) remuneration, and (most controversially) mandatory retirement. It is held to be inherently ageist to base individual personnel decisions upon age-based generalizations, since age is by itself not an accurate proxy for productivity. A truism in gerontology is that heterogeneity in health status and cognitive ability increases as cohorts age, rendering the use of age proxies morally dubious and economically dysfunctional.

Ageism is arguably more complex and nuanced than other forms of discrimination. Considerable debate has raged over its inherent dilemmas and contradictions (Nelson 2002; Macnicol 2006; Bytheway 2005). An immediate difficulty is whether ageism is like sexism or racism, and therefore whether it can be successfully combated by equal-opportunities legislation (Palmore and Manton 1973). Race and sex are often said to be immutable or unchanging characteristics, whereas age is a relative characteristic: it is arguably much more difficult to define victim and perpetrator in the case of the latter than the former. This is a particular problem if age discrimination laws apply at any age, since all citizens will be in the protected group. Indirect discrimination (discrimination that is not obvious, but that impacts adversely on a particular class of individuals) can be more difficult to demonstrate in the case of age: for example, the age profile of a firm will be determined by factors other than discrimination, and therefore statistical discrimination tests cannot be probative. Again, age discrimination in employment is often viewed as essentially irrational and prejudice-driven, perhaps stemming from employers' deep-seated fears of their own aging, decrepitude, and death. Employers may also suffer from "structural lag" in holding erroneous views about older workers' negative characteristics (absenteeism, slowness, skills deficiencies, unfamiliarity with new technology, and so on). However, many apparently ageist personnel policies may have a rational basis, such as the higher salary costs of an older employee or the fewer potential years of work that they can offer a firm (Levine 1988). The use of age proxies in personnel decisions may also be cheaper, more convenient, and less controversial than individual performance appraisal, just as mandatory retirement at age 65 treats every employee similarly, via a kind of rough justice (Palmore 1972).

A difficult problem is that there is a balance of positive and negative discriminations across the life course, and at any point in the life course. Much depends upon whether one takes a "synchronic," instantaneous perspective or a "diachronic," life span one (Daniels 1989). Health care allocation is an apposite example. There are many justified allegations that old people suffer negative discrimination in health care, as in a recent debate in the United Kingdom about the rationing of early-stage Alzheimer's drugs such as Aricept. However, it must also be recognized that, over the past fifty years, the proportion of health care expenditure allocated to old people has steadily risen in all Western societies. Illness management regimes (notably, through pharmaceuticals) have been so successful at lowering mortality and controlling morbidity in the young and middle-aged that all medicine is increasingly becoming geriatric medicine. It is possible to argue, therefore, that old people enjoy substantial *positive* discrimination in health and social care resource allocation. There is no doubt that certain age restrictions are widely supported and approved. These would include concessions to older people (such as free or subsidized public transport), laws that protect the young, age-based school curricula, mandatory retirement ages for civilian airline pilots, and so on.

A major conceptual difficulty in analyzing age discrimination is deciding exactly at what point our strongly internalized and widely accepted notions of "age-appropriate" behaviors become discriminatory. Is the choosing of friends or emotional partners of a similar age rational (based upon common interests or similar anticipated remaining life years), or is it discriminatory? Certain age divisions are considered reasonable and therefore widely accepted. In the rush to outlaw all ageism and age discrimination, should we dispense with age as a category? Or should we embrace age differences, just as we celebrate diversity and difference in other aspects of society?

Most of us enjoy living in a pluralistic, multicultural society (which offers us a much greater variety of music, restaurants, clothing styles, accents, and so on). To an extent, we also enjoy whimsically stereotypical images of ethnic diversity. Hopefully, we also appreciate living in an "age diverse" society, with age-based demarcation lines, and may thus occasionally enjoy slightly ageist stereotypes (most notably, the curmudgeonly characters in British television series like *One Foot in the Grave* or *The Last of the Summer Wine*). Age divisions and the complex working-out of intergenerational tensions also constitute a central theme of much popular culture and many television soap operas, such as *The Fresh Prince of Bel-Air*, *Frasier*, *Eastenders*, or *Neighbours* (hence, perhaps, their popularity with teenage children). There is, of course, a fine line between such good-humored, lighthearted stereotyping and overt racism, sexism, or ageism, and where that line should be drawn is the critical issue.

CURRENT POLICY IN THE UNITED KINGDOM

These dilemmas and difficulties are very evident in current policy in the U.K. and Britain, where two seemingly contradictory forces are at work. On the one hand, legislation outlawing age discrimination in employment (via the 2006 Age Regulations) has belatedly been introduced (some forty years after the United States' 1967 Age Discrimination in Employment Act) to provide improved employment protection and largely outlaw compulsory retirement before the age of 65 (unless "objectively justified"). The likelihood is that very soon retirement ages will be abolished for all but a few occupations. This has ostensibly been done as an enhancement of older people's "rights" and to remove the age-discriminatory barriers that allegedly worsen their employment opportunities. Interestingly, though, the first successful age discrimination case was brought by a woman discriminated against for being too *young* (Shaikh 2007).

Yet, on the other hand, more vigorous steps are being taken to push older economically inactive people into employment, as part of the "responsibilities" agenda. The British government has set a target of getting a million more people aged 50 and over back into work, as part of its aim of achieving an overall employment rate of 80 percent among people of working age. To this end, reforms of Incapacity Benefit (a major source of income for jobless older men, particularly in deindustrialized areas) are being implemented to make claiming it more difficult. Workfare will undoubtedly become more proactive in the future, with greater sanctions being applied to benefit claimants of all ages (Freud 2007). In addition, following the recommendations of the Pensions Commission (chaired by Lord Turner) the decision has been made to raise the state pension age incrementally to 68 by 2046. Interestingly, the Pensions Commission argued that improving life expectancy at age 65 justified raising the state pension age, thereby articulating for the first time an entirely new principle—that people shall only be allowed, on average, a fixed period of time in pension-funded retirement. This radical change has been little debated in the United Kingdom, but arguably it represents a significant erosion of the welfare rights of older people.

The ostensible reasons for this policy shift are several, and they relate to the economic challenge posed by the baby-boom generation moving into retirement. First, the United Kingdom faces the prospect of an aging population from the second decade of the twenty-first century, with the proportion of the 65-and-over population projected to rise from 16 percent at present to 23 percent by 2031. Projections suggest that by 2022 there will be three million more people of working age over the age of 50, and a million fewer under the age of 50, making it imperative that everything possible be done to improve the job prospects of older workers (Whiting 2005, 287).

As with all population forecasting, however, there is much uncertainty over future trends in birthrates, life expectancy at age 65, and immigration—so much so that, at the time of writing, projections for the size of the UK population are regularly being revised upward, owing to unexpectedly high levels of immigration. An increase in population size from sixty million now to more than seventy million by 2051 is being projected, and, since these extra numbers will mainly be in the younger age groups, the demographic problem posed by the baby boomers will be lessened: the tax base will expand and National Insurance revenues will increase.

Second, there was a fall in the employment rates of British men aged 50 and over from the early 1970s to the mid-1990s, and only a small rise in those of women. Although older people's employment rates have risen since 1994, as a consequence of an improving economy, it is still the case that one in three British people between 50 and state pension age is jobless. A future economic downturn could cause their employment rates to fall again.

A third reason for encouraging increased labor force activity of older people is the perceived need to improve the basic state pension, combined with (as already indicated) a raising of the state pension age. In addition, falling stock market values have caused many final-salary occupational pension schemes to close, and the incomes yielded by money-purchase schemes are generally inadequate. Unless older people are to languish on other welfare benefits until the age of 68, they will have to be retained longer in their existing jobs, and (perhaps rather unconvincingly) protection against age discrimination in employment is seen as one way of achieving this (Department for Work and Pensions 2006, 65–66). There is also some concern over loss of skills through early retirement.

A final impulse behind the push to extend working lives is the New Labour government's broader macroeconomic strategy of expanding labor supply and achieving noninflationary economic growth by lowering employers' wage costs. As a recent government report on combating age discrimination argues, "More people competing for jobs means that people are less keen to demand wage increases" (Cabinet Office 2000, 39).

What are prospects for getting the baby boomers to work later in life? The United States has had its Age Discrimination in Employment Act since 1967, and this Act has been subject to several important amendments (notably the uncapping of the mandatory retirement age for nearly all occupations) that have undoubtedly improved job protection for older workers. However, it may not have had much effect on older people's labor force participation rates, despite claims made for it (Adams 2004), since these have fallen since the 1970s and risen slightly since the mid-1990s in precisely the way they have in other industrialized countries (Macnicol 2007, 35–39). Compared with the European Union, the United States displays less inclination to apply labor market activation to older people: there, fertility rates are higher, population growth is faster, and Social Security appears relatively more solvent (Rix 2006, 10–11). Since the 1930s, the labor force participation rates of older American men have been markedly higher than those in the United Kingdom; for example, the rate for men aged 65 and over was 17.7 percent in the United States (in 2000) compared with only 7.5 percent in Britain (in 2001) (Macnicol 2007, 36).

The current policy prescriptions in the United Kingdom appear to be limited almost exclusively to supply-side solutions, yet the employment difficulties of older people have been caused more by lack of labor market demand. In other words, while there exists a minority of middle-class early retirees who have chosen to leave the labor force before the age of 65 because of relatively generous occupational pensions, the majority of early retirements are blue-collar and involuntary, caused by the disappearance of a job or by ill health (Whiting 2005, 287–88). An analysis of older workers' joblessness predicated on the assumption that age discrimination is the principal cause is one that is confined to the level of the individual firm, locating the problem as arising from the "prejudices" of employers: the rather limited solution is seen as effecting a "cultural change" by disabusing employers of their age-discriminatory attitudes.

However, the real cause is the complex supply-demand mismatches of age, gender, skill, region, and sector that have always characterized modern economies and have intensified since the 1970s. For example, there are pronounced regional variations in the employment rates of people aged between 50 and state pension age: the highest levels of older people's joblessness are in the economically depressed, deindustrialized areas such as Wales and the North East of England. Again, part-time working and self-employment become more pronounced with every year after the age of 50: two-thirds of men who still work after age 65 do so part-time, and four out of ten are self-employed. Part-time jobs have increased massively in the British economy since World War II—from 831,000 jobs in 1951 to 7,412,000 in 2006—and it seems likely that much future employment growth will be on this basis, and at the bottom end of the labor market. It is difficult to see how this can form a viable basis for later-life employment.

CONCLUSION

Differential treatment by age has hitherto protected older people via age-based social security and other entitlements—admittedly, sometimes at the cost of ghettoizing and marginalizing old age and encouraging the non-old to view our elders as a passive, unproductive fiscal burden. Yet the removal of such age-based protections in the name of "agelessness" and as part of a superficially appealing strategy of countering age discrimination carries equal dangers—that of returning to a nineteenth-century old-age experience, in which many poorer citizens will be compelled, through economic necessity and the withdrawal of pension support, to work later in life at low-paid, menial jobs. Such coercion would be a high price to pay for the achievement of an "ageless society."

REFERENCES

Achenbaum, W. 1995. *Crossing frontiers: Gerontology emerges as a science.* Cambridge: Cambridge University Press.

Adams, S. 2004. Age discrimination legislation and the employment of older workers. *Labor Economics* 11 (2): 219–41.

Banton, M. 1994. *Discrimination.* Buckingham, UK: Open University Press.

Becker, G. 1957. *The economics of discrimination.* Chicago: University of Chicago Press.

Blaikie, A. 1990. The emerging political power of the elderly in Britain, 1908–1948. *Ageing and Society* 10 (1): 17–39.

Butler, R. N. 1969. Age-Ism: Another form of bigotry. *Gerontologist* 9 (4): 243–46.

Bytheway, B. 1995. *Ageism.* Buckingham, UK: Open University Press.

———. 2005. Ageism. In *The Cambridge Handbook of Age and Ageing,* ed. M. L. Johnson, 338–45. Cambridge: Cambridge University Press.

Cabinet Office. Performance and Innovation Unit. 2000. *Winning the generation game: Improving opportunities for people aged 50–65 in work and community activity.* London: The Stationery Office.

Cole, T. R. 1992. *The journey of life: A cultural history of aging in America.* Cambridge: Cambridge University Press.

Daniels, N. 1989. Justice and transfers between generations. In *Workers versus pensioners: Intergenerational justice in an ageing world,* ed. P. Johnson, C. Conrad, and D. Thomson, 57–79. Manchester, UK: Manchester University Press.

Department for Work and Pensions. 2006. *A new deal for welfare,* Cm. 6730. London: The Stationery Office.

Epstein, R. A. 1992. *Forbidden grounds: The case against employment discrimination laws.* Cambridge, MA: Harvard University Press.

Estes, C. 1979. *The aging enterprise.* San Francisco: Jossey-Bass.

Freud, D. 2007. *Reducing dependency, increasing opportunity: Options for the future of welfare to work. An independent report to the Department for Work and Pensions.* London: Department for Work and Pensions.

Katz, S. 1996. *Disciplining old age: The formation of gerontological knowledge.* Charlottesville: University Press of Virginia.

Levine, M. L. 1988. *Age discrimination and the mandatory retirement controversy.* Baltimore: Johns Hopkins University Press.

Macnicol, J. 2006. *Age discrimination: An historical and contemporary analysis.* Cambridge: Cambridge University Press.

————. 2007. The American experience of age discrimination. In *The future of older workers: New perspectives,* ed. W. Loretto, S. Vickerstaff, and P. White, 27–41. Bristol, UK: Policy Press.

National Audit Office. 2007. *Improving services and support for people with dementia.* London: The Stationery Office.

Nelson, T. D., ed. 2002. *Ageism: Stereotyping and prejudice against older persons.* Cambridge, MA: MIT Press.

Neugarten, B. L., ed. 1982. *Age or need? Public policies for older people.* Beverly Hills, CA: Sage.

————. 1996. Age distinctions and their social functions. In *The meanings of age: Selected papers of Bernice L. Neugarten,* ed. D. A. Neugarten, 56–71. Chicago: University of Chicago Press.

Palmore, E. B. 1972. Compulsory versus flexible retirement: Issues and facts. *Gerontologist* 12 (4): 343–48.

————. 1999. *Ageism: Negative and positive.* New York: Springer.

Palmore, E. B., and K. Manton. 1973. Ageism compared to racism and sexism. *Journal of Gerontology* 28 (3): 363–69.

Pratt, H. J. 1976. *The gray lobby.* Chicago: University of Chicago Press.

Rix, S. E. 2006. Age discrimination in the United States. Paper presented to the International Federation of Ageing Conference, Copenhagen, May 30–June 2.

Shaikh, T. 2007. Woman, 20, sacked for being too young wins bias case. *Guardian.* November 13.

Whiting, E. 2005. The labour market participation of older people. *Labour Market Trends* 113 (7): 285–95.

15

Aging Policy as Family Policy: Expanding Family Leave and Improving Flexible Work Policies

STEVEN K. WISENSALE

O n October 17, 2007, in Manchester, New Hampshire, presidential candidate Hillary Rodham Clinton (D-NY) delivered a speech at a forum hosted by the local YWCA. The senator reiterated what had appeared in a news release issued by her office the previous day in which she proposed that the federal government provide $1 billion annually in grants to encourage states to develop paid family leave programs. "Too many Americans today feel trapped between being there for their kids and being there for their employer, and our government policies have just not kept up with the realities of American life," she said. "We can make life a little easier for everyone—for mothers and for fathers—to do the most important job in any society: raising and nurturing the next generation" (Office of Senator Hillary Rodham Clinton 2007, 1).

Although immediately heralded by many for putting work and family near the top of the political agenda, Clinton also generated some discomfort among experts in aging who see a much different picture of "the realities of American life." Loaded with references to "kids" and "mothers and fathers" and "nurturing the next generation," the senator's comments contained no references to an aging society that depends heavily on family caregivers. Will such an expansion of the Family and Medical Leave Act (FMLA), which originally included elder care, continue to include paid leave for caregivers of aging parents or will it be limited to child care? After all, in 1999 President Bill Clinton also proposed paid leave under the FMLA by permitting states to tap surplus funds in their Unemployment Insurance programs, but in doing so he emphasized child care, not elder care. Consequently, he more or less amputated the intergenerational "family care" component of the very act he had signed in 1993. And only a handful of states included elder care in their push for paid leave (Wisensale 2003). So, if even the liberal politicians in our society can address work and family issues without mentioning elder care, what does the future hold for aging policy in general and for family care of the old and frail in particular?

The purpose of this chapter is to answer a fourfold set of questions. First, to identify the extent to which caregivers of the elderly must balance work and family responsibilities: Who are they and how do their experiences affect their time, income, and career paths? Second, what are the strengths and weaknesses of the major public policies designed to assist family caregivers? Third, how has the private sector reacted to the challenge of work and family balance, and more specifically, how responsive have corporations been to the expressed needs of employees who care for elderly family members? And fourth, what strategies and recommendations should be put forth to improve family leave and flexible work policies? In light of a new administration assuming the White House in 2009, the timing could not be better for taking a new look at an old problem.

CAREGIVERS AT WORK

The research literature is saturated with endless references to employees being overworked and underappreciated, often subjected to insensitive managers and supervisors who are blind to their workers' responsibilities at home. We learn that in comparison to other industrialized societies, Americans now work more than 1,800 hours a year, surpassing Japan, which held the top spot for more than a decade. Yet, the United States has neither implemented nor seriously considered adopting policies that reduce work time (Heymann and Beem 2005). Rather than family-work advocates confronting this problem head-on and lobbying for a mandated workweek of less than forty hours, they have chosen instead to focus their attention on the need for child care, paid leave, and more flex time. What's more, while workers in the European Union are granted between twenty-five and thirty-three days of paid vacation per year (amounting to a total of five or six weeks off), the United States has no such laws on the books, nor is the issue even on the national agenda for discussion (Gornick, Heron, and Eisenbrey 2007).

We also learn that between 1979 and 2004 the employment rate of women, the primary caregivers in American society, increased from 47.5 percent to 56 percent and continues to rise (Gornick, Heron, and Eisenbrey 2007). Further, the U.S. Department of Labor reports that three-fourths of all mothers with children under age 18 are now in the labor force and 65 percent with children under 6 are working full-time (U.S. Bureau of Labor Statistics 2005). And, from the perspective of dual-earner families, we learn that 65 percent of families with children are headed by two employed parents, and one out of eight couples works as much as 100 hours per week—all amidst the growing phenomenon of two-parent households working full-time on two different shifts. This is in sharp contrast to the 1960s, when 70 percent of families with children had at least one parent at home full-time (Boots 2004).

If not completely overlooked in the research literature, caregivers of the elderly are frequently relegated to secondary status when discussions revolve around policy recommendations for addressing the issue of work and family balance. In turn, the mass media and politicians have followed suit, as illustrated by Senator Clinton's comments in the opening paragraph of this chapter. But at least two facts in particular cannot be ignored. One is that the population is aging and millions of baby boomers are on the verge of retirement. The other is that, with each passing day, there are more people in the labor force who have elderly relatives in need of assistance of some sort. Indeed, according to a study by the Conference Board, *Juggling the Demands of Dependent Care*, 37 percent of U.S. workers are more concerned about caring for an elderly relative than a child. Equally significant, beginning in 1999–2000, 60 percent of the labor force was composed of women over 40, the primary caregivers of the elderly, and nearly 40 percent of all American workers fell into the 40-to-54 age group, considered by many to be the prime age range for adult children assisting elderly parents (ProQuest Information and Learning Company 1999).

According to a study completed by the Sloan Work and Family Research Network (2002), 35 percent of wage and salaried workers said they had provided care for an elderly relative aged 65 or older in the past year. A more recent study concluded that at least six out of ten employed caregivers reported that they had made some work-related adjustments as a result of their caregiving responsibilities, and 52 percent of women and 34 percent of men indicated that they had experienced workday interruptions as a result of caregiving responsibilities for older relatives (MetLife Mature Market Institute and National Alliance for Caregiving 2007).

This much we know: In 2006, somewhere between 30 million and 38 million adult caregivers provided care to adults who had at least one limitation in an activity of daily living (ADL) or an instrumental activity of daily living (IADL) (AARP Public Policy Institute 2006). Although it is generally assumed that most caregivers are women (the average caregiver in America is a 46-year-old woman who works outside the home), a 2004 study found that nearly four in ten caregivers of the elderly are men who work full-time while assisting someone over 50 (National Alliance for Caregiving and AARP 2004). Another fact worth noting is that a quarter of the men and 28 percent of women employees reported they shared a residence with the elderly they were helping (National Alliance for Caregiving and the Center for Productive Aging at Towson University 2003).

It is further estimated that caregivers of the elderly provide an average of twenty-one hours of care per week, or 1,080 hours per year, and about half also contribute financially, spending between $200 and $324 a month out of pocket to cover groceries, medications, and other related items. All told, the commitment to caregiving alone converts to an economic value of approximately $350 billion annually, a figure that exceeds the total annual expenditures of Medicare ($342 billion in 2006) as well as the total sales of two of the world's largest corporations: Wal-Mart ($349 billion in 2006) and ExxonMobil ($335 billion) (AARP Public Policy Institute 2006). Viewed another way, it is projected that the annual cost of replacing informal caregiving with paid home care would range between $45 billion and $94 billion, with most of the expense being shouldered by American taxpayers (U.S. Department of Health and Human Services 2002).

But the cost of providing informal unpaid caregiving does not end with financial calculations alone. It can also be measured in terms of career disruption for workers and lost productivity for businesses. With respect to workers, due to caregiving obligations, 83 percent report arriving late or leaving early, 41 percent having to take a leave of absence, 37 percent going from full-time to part-time work, 14 percent turning down a promotion, and 12 percent taking early retirement (National Alliance for Caregiving and AARP 2004).

Businesses are also affected by caregiving in terms of lost productivity. With almost one-fifth of all workers (19 percent) serving as informal caregivers, productivity losses to U.S. businesses due to caregiving activities have been estimated to exceed $33.6 billion (AARP Public Policy Institute 2006). Viewed from a micro perspective, the cost to employers per full-time-employed caregiver currently ranges from $2,110 to $2,441 annually, depending on the level of commitment and intensity of the care (MetLife Mature Market Institute and National Alliance for Caregiving 2007).

Therefore, not only can employees benefit from expanded leave policies and more flexible work schedules, but so too can employers. Such an approach can quickly become a win-win situation, with employees saving taxpayers billions of dollars through informal caregiving, and employers cutting losses in productivity. Such a convergence, in turn, would contribute to the cultivation of a vibrant and healthy economy. Policies currently in place and the extent to which they should be revamped to enhance this convergence are the focus of the remainder of this chapter.

PUBLIC POLICIES GEARED TOWARD ASSISTING CAREGIVERS OF THE ELDERLY

Currently, there are several major policies in place at the federal level designed to assist caregivers of the elderly. They fall under four distinct categories:

1. The Older Americans Act and Title XX of the Social Security Act, which includes the Social Services Block Grant program

2. Tax policy, including the Dependent Care Tax Credit (DCTC) and the Dependent Care Assistance Program (DCAP)
3. The National Family Caregivers Support Program (NFCSP)
4. The Family and Medical Leave Act (FMLA)

A fifth but lesser known policy, the Alternative Work Schedules Act (AWSA), is supportive of family caregivers but is limited to federal employees only. In short, it offers workers flextime that usually consists of some combination of compressed workweeks, variable hours per day, and individually negotiated arrival and departure times at the workplace (Liechty and Anderson 2007). Equally obscure and also confined to federal employees is the Family Friendly Leave Act of 1994, which permits workers to use their sick leave to care for ill family members.

The Older Americans Act and Title XX

A variety of programs are funded through the Older Americans Act and Title XX of the Social Security Act that support caregivers through information and referral services, respite care programs, and caregiver training and support. Other programs, such as adult day health care, access to assistive devices, transportation, and home-delivered meals, either supplement services already being provided by unpaid family caregivers or substitute for them. Also included is funding for the National Eldercare Locator Service, which, among other things, helps long-distance caregivers access information about available services in other parts of the country, and Aging and Disability Resource Centers, which offer information to caregivers about community and institutionally based long-term care services. More than forty states also have received special funding through the Administration on Aging to design and implement innovative caregiver support programs, including respite care.

Tax Policy

Many caregivers of the elderly can qualify under two different tax programs. The DCTC offers caregivers a tax credit to offset the costs of providing services to a spouse or dependent who lives with the caregiver but is physically or mentally incapable of self-care. The program is limited to situations in which the one filing for the credit requires such a service in order to remain employed. Expenses for providing the care must total at least $3,000 per year. Dependent care can be provided by either a private individual (e.g., a personal care attendant or a home health aide) or a care center that meets specified regulations, such as an adult cay health center. On average, a household with an income of $50,000 and caregiving expenses that exceed $3,000 will be eligible for a credit of $600 (Scott 2005).

Under the DCAP, caregivers who work for employers that offer this benefit may exclude up to $5,000 of their earnings from taxes. A taxpayer in the

10 percent bracket would save $500 on average, while one in the 25 percent bracket would save about $1,250 (Lyke and Whittaker 2007). Taxpayers can use both the DCTC and the DCAP in the same year, but not for the same expenses. But regardless of the type of tax credit selected, compensation for the caregiver tends to be minimal.

The National Family Caregivers Support Program

The NFCSP was created in 2000 by the Administration on Aging and implemented in 2001. Funds totaling about $113 million were allocated to states through a congressionally mandated formula based on a proportionate share of a state's population aged 70 years or older. Under the program, all states are responsible for working closely with area agencies on aging as well as local community service providers to offer five basic services designed to support caregivers:

- information about available services in the community
- assistance to caregivers in gaining access to supportive services
- creation of individual counseling programs, formation of support groups, and offering of caregiving workshops
- respite care and other temporary relief for caregivers
- various other supplemental services on a limited basis

Under the NFCSP, three types of caregivers are eligible to receive assistance: family caregivers of older adults; grandparents caring for grandchildren; and other family members—such as aunts, uncles, and cousins. Intergenerational in structure, the program gives priority to those in greater social and economic need, such as poor minorities and older individuals who are providing care and support to those with developmental disabilities.

Despite its good intentions, a 2004 study completed by the Family Caregiver Alliance in cooperation with the National Conference of State Legislatures found four major weaknesses in the program: inadequate resources at the state level; insufficient funding by the federal government; little consensus among the fifty states on "best practices"; and insufficient emphasis on assessing caregivers' needs (Family Caregiver Alliance and the National Conference on State Legislatures 2004). Nonetheless, the NFCSP represented "the first federally-funded program implemented at the state level designed specifically to support the needs of family caregivers of older people," according to Feinberg and Newman (2004, 760).

The Family and Medical Leave Act

While the programs discussed above may benefit caregivers in a variety of ways through the delivery of social services, tax relief, and counseling and training, none of them intersect directly with the growing challenge of balancing work and family responsibilities. The FMLA, on the other hand, was designed for that very purpose. Passed and implemented in 1993, the FMLA was the very first bill signed by newly elected President Bill Clinton. Its adoption marked the end of eight years of congressional debate and two vetoes by Clinton's predecessor, George H. W. Bush.

The law allows a worker to take up to twelve weeks of unpaid leave in any twelve-month period for the adoption of a child; to care for a sick child, spouse, or *parent* (not in-laws) with a serious health condition; or for the worker's own health condition. The law further guarantees job security in that an employee is entitled to return to the same or comparable job and requires the employer to maintain health benefits as if the employee never took leave in the first place. The law applies only to companies with fifty or more employees and to workers who have been employed for at least one year or 1,250 hours. Consequently, the FMLA applies to only about 6 percent of the corporations and 60 percent of the labor force (Wisensale 2001).

With respect to structure, the FMLA has three major characteristics that place it in sharp contrast to typical models in other industrialized nations. First, the leave is unpaid. All industrialized countries except Australia and the United States provide some form of wage replacement for those taking leave. Second, the U.S. model has a family focus. That is, unlike its European counterparts, which are designed primarily for new parents, the U.S. law is intergenerational in structure, thus allowing time off from work for the birth or care of a child as well as care for an elderly parent. And third, unlike other industrialized countries, the United States links eligibility for leave to company size (fifty or more employees). It should be emphasized here that one of the major explanations for the FMLA's intergenerational component is the role played by AARP in lobbying on its behalf. In short, AARP agreed to throw its weight behind the bill once it was expanded from child to family care. However, in doing so, any dreams of including paid leave ended abruptly when a majority of legislators concluded that the cost of coverage for elder care would be excessive (Elving 1995; Wisensale 2001).

Unfortunately, because the FMLA is often discussed in terms of child care, little attention has been devoted to its potential for addressing major long-term care demands. However, as the boomer generation retires and becomes afflicted with multiple chronic illnesses fifteen to twenty years later, more families will be called upon to address the personal health care needs of their elderly relatives. Between 2000 and 2002, more than half of the states introduced legislation to provide paid leave to family caregivers through the use of state unemployment insurance (UI) trust funds. However, almost all of the state initiatives limited the coverage to "baby care." That is, in pushing for paid leave, only five of twenty-six states included care of an elderly parent in their proposals. The other states, none of which succeeded, opted to limit their initiatives to baby care (National Partnership for Women and Families 2004). In short, the original intergenerational structure of the FMLA was slowly being dismantled by well-intentioned state legislators who were seeking to provide paid leave. This development can be particularly problematic in light of future projections of the long-term care needs of an aging population (Wisensale 2003).

However, one success story for paid-leave advocates took place in 2002. California, by expanding its state disability insurance program from maternal to family care, became the first state to adopt a comprehensive paid family and medical leave insurance policy. Workers can receive a partial wage replacement (55–60 percent of wages) with a cap during six weeks of leave per year to care for a newborn or newly adopted or foster child, or to care for a seriously ill family member, including an *elderly parent* or a domestic partner. Funded solely by employee contributions, the average annual cost per worker is about $27 (Wisensale 2006). It should also be noted that in 2006 the state of Washington became the second state to adopt paid leave. However, when it goes into effect in 2009, it will *not* include elder care.

But families and the government should not be expected to shoulder the entire burden of family care of the elderly. The private sector must also recognize and fulfill its obligations in addressing this issue. After all, in this age of privatization when greater responsibility is being shifted from the public to the private sector and from the collective to the individual—what Hacker (2006) refers to as the "great risk shift"—corporations cannot be permitted to take a pass on this. They must be held at least partially accountable for the rising number of stressed-out, dysfunctional families that fuel the world's highest divorce rate. Therefore, through whatever means are necessary, the business sector needs to be brought into discussions of work and family balance more frequently and become more invested in finding a solution to this problem. Such an approach will not only address the needs of employees but also contribute to greater productivity and higher profits for the company.

THE ROLE OF THE PRIVATE SECTOR

In October 2007, *Working Mother* magazine published its twenty-second annual "100 Best Companies" edition, in which it lists, but does not rank, the 100 top family-friendly companies in the United States. Corporations are judged across a variety of categories, including health care coverage, on-site child care, domestic partner benefits, employee assistance programs, and paid *parental* (not family) leave, among others. There are several categories in particular that pertain directly to caregivers of the elderly and clearly distinguish the Top 100 companies from all the others. For example, all of the Top 100 offer flextime and telecommuting (part-time) to their employees, compared to just 58 and 33 percent, respectively, for those companies not included in the Top 100. Similarly, 97 percent of the Top 100 companies offer a compressed workweek and elder care resource and referral services, compared to only 38 and 22 percent, respectively, of other firms.

With respect to elder care, obviously it has migrated into the boardrooms of some, if not all, corporations. Aware of the fact that by 2020 one in three households will be responsible for caring for an elderly relative, compared to one in four today, companies are slowly beginning to recognize the needs of their employees (Medical News Today 2006). A 2005 study found that 29 percent of employers provide employees with information about elder care services (Galinsky et al. 2005). Perhaps even more important, the trend appears to be upward rather than downward. That is, in 2005 employers were more likely (34 percent) to report that they offered elder care resource and referral services than employers in 1998 (23 percent) (Galinsky et al. 2005). But whether or not the corporate sector is moving quickly enough to address the concerns of their employees is quite another matter. When prioritized, the most common needs expressed by working caregivers of the elderly are flexibility in work schedules, information and referral services, more support from coworkers and supervisors, and assistance in making decisions about care options (Wagner 2003).

Not only do unresolved elder care issues result in lost productivity, but there is also growing evidence that companies with more comprehensive family-friendly policies consistently outperform the Standard & Poor's 500 index and report a turnover rate that is half the national average (Healy 2005). Similarly, other studies have shown that companies with employee-friendly cultures and an assortment of job-flexibility policies have a 3.5 percent greater market value than companies that lack such policies (Reed and Clark 2004). In 2001, a survey conducted by Watson Wyatt (2007) concluded that the stock value of employee-friendly companies increased by 64 percent between 1996 and 2001, compared to 21 percent for the least employee-friendly ones.

In 1996, a feature article in *Business Week* entitled "Balancing Work and Family: Big Returns for Companies Willing to Give Family Strategies a Chance" introduced readers to First Tennessee National Bank, a frequent member of *Working Mother*'s Top 100. Efforts to balance work and family there resulted in an improved employee retention rate that converted to a $106 million profit gain over two years. Aetna Life and Casualty cut its resignations in half by extending its unpaid parental leave to six months, saving the company $1 million a year in hiring and training expenses. Other companies, including DuPont, Eddie Bauer, Marriott, and Motorola offer comparable family-friendly benefits that have produced similar results (Wisensale 2001). More recently, in a two-year study of 1,400 workers, 70 percent of managers and 87 percent of employees reported that workplace flexibility enhanced productivity (Levin-Epstein 2006) Equally significant, managers of six major U.S. firms (Amway, Bristol-Myers Squibb, Honeywell, Kraft, Lucent Technologies, and Motorola) reported that flexible work schedules enhanced retention rates (Burke and Collison 2004).

Clearly, some businesses "get it" when it comes to addressing work and family issues, and particularly with respect to employees providing care for elderly relatives. However, too few companies have followed suit, and too many are apparently content in maintaining the status quo. The extent to which government should intervene and mandate specific family-friendly policies is open for debate, of course, but in the current political climate, the success of such an approach is highly unlikely. What may be effective in the end is a combination of government jawboning and Top 100–type companies producing a steady drumbeat of effective "best practices" that produce greater worker retention, enhance productivity, and increase profits—all crucial components of a successful corporation in a highly competitive globalized economy.

The remainder of this chapter will be devoted to a review of possible strategies that can be employed to address the growing demands of America's caregivers in general and caregivers of the elderly in particular. Specific policy recommendations will also be discussed.

STRATEGIES AND RECOMMENDATIONS FOR EXPANDING LEAVE AND FLEXTIME POLICIES

In light of the facts and statistics presented so far, there are numerous options available to both the public and private sectors to expand existing leave and flextime policies. There is also plenty of room for innovation and the introduction of new ideas for meeting the growing demands of employed caregivers of the elderly. Therefore, echoing the work of Gornick and Meyers (2003), Heymann and Beem (2005), Levin-Epstein (2006), and Wisensale (2001, 2006), six specific recommendations for expanding leave and flextime policies in the workplace are put forth here for discussion and consideration:

1. Providing paid family and medical leave
2. Adopting paid sick leave
3. Mandating annual leave for vacations
4. Identifying and encouraging model workplace flexibility policies
5. Promoting "soft touch" workplace flexibility laws
6. Generating and supporting state initiatives geared to family caregivers of the elderly in particular

Each is discussed below.

Provide Paid Family and Medical Leave

With the Family and Medical Leave Act about to celebrate its fifteenth anniversary, the time is long past for adopting paid leave. As stated previously, the United States and Australia stand alone as the two remaining industrialized nations that have not adopted paid leave. Other than five states (California, Rhode Island, Hawaii, New Jersey, and New York) that cover paid maternity leave through state temporary disability insurance in which a pregnancy is viewed as a disability, and California, which expanded its disability insurance model to include family care, only Washington State has adopted paid leave (as of 2009) without employing a temporary disability insurance funding mechanism.

With respect to funding a wage replacement under the FMLA, Congress has several options. It can, for example, revisit the use of surplus UI trust funds, a policy that Canada has employed for more than a decade with few if any negative ramifications as a result. A second possibility would be to tax employees and employers directly to create a federal trust fund that can be tapped to cover caregiving responsibilities. In California, only employees pay such a tax, which averages around $30 a year. Or, Congress can consider Senator Clinton's proposal (originally introduced by Senator Chris Dodd [D-CT] as the Family and Medical Leave Expansion Act) that would jump-start state legislative activity by offering federal funds for a series of model demonstration projects, including paid leave. This may, of course, result in a patchwork of paid leave policies scattered across the country, but it may also serve as a laboratory for exploring the strengths and weaknesses of various players and funding mechanisms.

Since its inception, there have been only two major attempts to reform the FMLA. The first came in 1999 when President Clinton recommended through an executive order that states employ their UI trust funds to cover paid leave—a policy proposal that was never adopted by any state and was quickly rescinded when George W. Bush assumed the White House in 2001. The second major attempt occurred in 2006 when the Military Families Leave Act (MFLA) was passed by Congress but was lost in a presidential veto that killed the expansion of the State Children's Health Insurance Program (SCHIP). If adopted, the MFLA will provide military families up to six months of leave to care for their combat-injured loved ones. Note, however, that paid leave was not included in the original MFLA bill, and it will only apply to a relatively small and younger cohort.

But beyond providing a wage replacement, the FMLA can and should be expanded in at least five other ways. First, make it more accessible to workers so that those in firms with as few as twenty-five employees, or even fifteen, can take leave to care for a child, spouse, or elderly relative. Second, broaden the definition of a caregiver to include in-laws (such as daughters- and sons-in-law) and thus replace the current constricting policy definition of *parent*. Third, allow grandchildren to provide care to grandparents, which is not covered by the FMLA as it exists today. We should always foster more intergenerational relationships and responsibilities when given the opportunity. Fourth, expand the length of leave from twelve weeks to eighteen or twenty-four weeks and include a provision that recognizes the need for providing intermittent care coverage among caregivers of the elderly. And finally, expand the law further to cover same-sex partners who have the same caregiving responsibilities, including spousal and elder care, as traditional families.

Whatever options are selected and strategies employed, it is imperative that advocates for the aged remind themselves that elder care must be included in any reform efforts. If there are any agnostics or nonbelievers in the crowd, they should consult my earlier article "Two Steps Forward, One Step Back: Family Leave as Retrenchment Policy" (Wisensale 2003) for a reminder of how quickly elder care was jettisoned from the original FMLA when states pushed toward paid leave in 2000–2001. Simply put, coverage of elder care cannot be viewed as a sand castle that is left to the mercy of a rapidly shifting political surf.

Adopt Paid Sick Leave

The federal government should establish a national standard for paid sick days, a benefit that is quite common in other industrialized countries. However, currently there are no state or federal laws that require employers to provide paid sick days. Consequently, when illness strikes, 57 million Americans, or about 50 percent of the nation's labor force, do not have a single paid sick day available. Only one in three has paid sick days for doctors' appointments and the situation worsens as one looks at lower income brackets. Within the lowest quartile of wage earners, nearly 80 percent have no paid sick leave. This is despite the fact that an overwhelming majority of Americans believe employees deserve time off from work to address their own or their families' health care needs (National Partnership for Women and Families 2007). But only recently has Congress moved to address this issue.

In April 2005, Senator Ted Kennedy (D-MA) and Representative Rosa DeLauro (D-CT) introduced the Healthy Families Act (HFA), which would require employers with fifteen or more employees to provide seven paid sick days to care for their own and their families' medical needs. Passage of the Act, which has failed three times so far despite Democrats having taken control of Congress in 2006, would instantly benefit 66 million Americans, many of whom are caregivers of the elderly. By the federal government adopting such legislation, all states and businesses would automatically be forced to operate within the same set of rules. However, under no circumstances should the HFA become a substitute for an expanded FMLA or serve as an inoculation against future attempts to adopt paid family leave. Further, in passing the HFA, it is essential that paid sick leave include time off for the care of elderly relatives.

Mandate Annual Leave for Vacations

Unlike employees in most other industrialized countries, workers in the United States get very little paid vacation time. According to Heymann and

Beem (2005), at least ninety-six nations have adopted some degree of statutory annual leave, and eighteen mandate a minimum of at least twenty paid vacation days a year. Workers in Finland and France, for example, are guaranteed thirty paid vacation days by law; in Sweden, they get twenty-five days and in Germany twenty-four. All European countries must give their workers at least twenty paid vacation days plus national holidays (Allegretto 2005; Levin-Epstein 2006). Such policies are in sharp contrast to the United States, where most workers have to be employed for twenty-five years before they qualify for twenty paid vacation days. The United States does have ten national holidays, but they are not mandatory and more employees work on those days with each passing year.

In recommending the passage of a federal law that establishes a minimum standard for paid vacation leave, I urge advocates and policy makers to avoid the temptation to view paid family leave and vacation time as interchangeable benefits. If anything, paid vacation time for caregivers should be viewed as respite care, not an extension of the FMLA or HFA. Until all three of these initiatives are adopted individually and stand alone as separate options for family caregivers, they should not be combined to address caregiving demands. Otherwise, the three policies will blur into one, devoted advocates for each will disband, efforts to expand the programs will be hindered, and ultimately support for family caregivers will atrophy. Therefore, the mission is clear: view leave policy as a three-pronged strategy: family leave, sick leave, and mandated vacation time.

Identify and Encourage Model Workplace Flexibility Policies

Either the government or a very effective private nonprofit organization should recognize innovative flexibility policies in the workplace and serve as a clearinghouse where other corporations can explore various models of flex-work and exchange ideas. Flextime programs geared specifically to caregivers of the elderly should be highlighted and best practices identified. Examples of such flex-work policies include creative part-time work arrangements, job sharing, a compressed workweek, flexibility in starting and ending the workday, and greater use of telecommuting. But if companies are not already motivated by their employees' caregiving responsibilities, concerns over a world flu pandemic has forced some corporations to devise innovative work schedules and telecommuting strategies that can be employed to keep the business afloat. Corporate executives may not only be enlightened about the value of flex-work by such exercises but may also consider adopting such policies when public health concerns are *not* a top priority.

The government can play several roles in transforming the culture of the workplace, including offering tax incentives to corporations who establish themselves as family-friendly by adopting generous leave policies, providing resource and referral programs, and offering flexible work schedules so employees can address family needs. By assuming a government-as-shepherd role, the public sector can do much to influence the behavior of the private sector without alienating it. For example, in Japan the Ministry of Health, Labor, and Welfare launched a special website where employers can post examples of their success stories in helping their employees balance work and family obligations. Australia and New Zealand have established similar websites (Levin-Epstein 2006).

There are a few government websites in the United States geared to work and family issues, including the Department of Labor's Flex Options for Women Project, but more informative sites are needed. Meanwhile, the federal government can not only follow in Japan's footsteps and create a similar website but also remind corporations that it has been in the vanguard of the workplace flexibility movement by permitting each executive agency to establish its own approaches to flex-work (Levin-Epstein 2005). For example, all full-time workers in federal agencies are guaranteed thirteen paid sick days each year, and telecommuting is becoming more common for those employees who are not in direct contact with the public daily.

Promote "Soft Touch" Workplace Flexibility Laws

An emerging strategy that may prove effective in convincing corporations to create and maintain a flexible workplace is the adoption of soft-touch laws. Developed first in Great Britain, the soft-touch law promotes employee and employer dialogue by legally empowering employees with the right to request a flexible work schedule in order to address family caregiving needs. In submitting the formal document, the employee is required to respond to a list of questions that asks how can the employer accommodate the employee without harming the business. The employer is then required to discuss the matter with the employee and either approve or disapprove the request in writing (Levin-Epstein 2006). Currently, the British model applies only to parents of children under age 6 and disabled children under age 18. However, the United States could adopt a similar law and extend it to include caregivers of the elderly.

Generate and Support State Initiatives Geared to Family Caregivers

Although it is implied here that most of the proposed strategies should emerge from the federal government, this does not have to be the case. Through careful funding of very selective demonstration projects, the federal government can encourage states to adopt paid-leave laws, flex-work policies, soft-touch policies, and other family-friendly initiatives that cut across the life span. And clearly, the states have been very active with respect to work and family legislation.

Between January 2005 and May 2006, the Sloan Work and Family Research Network identified a total of 234 bills and 530 statutes related to work and family issues. Twenty-seven states introduced three or more work-family bills, nineteen states were classified as having a particularly high number of work-and/or family-related committees, and sixteen had both a high number of bills and a high number of such committees (Sloan Work and Family Research Network 2006). Legislatures in both New York and New Jersey have introduced paid family leave bills, for example, and almost twenty states have established respite care programs geared specifically to caregivers of the elderly. In Massachusetts, all employers must provide a minimum of seven paid sick days per year, which employees can use to care for an elderly relative. Rhode Island and Pennsylvania guarantee employees up to fourteen and twenty-four hours of unpaid leave, respectively, during any twelve-month period to care for an elderly relative. Compared to where we were twenty years ago, this represents significant progress (Wisensale and Allison 1988).

Either through a traditional carrot-and-stick approach initiated by the federal government or various other means, states should be encouraged to adopt more family-friendly legislation aimed at supporting caregivers of the elderly. Perhaps the time has come for applying an abbreviated version of a "family impact statement" to legislative proposals that concern work and family. That is, prior to passing any law on this issue in the future, state and federal lawmakers should be required to pause and respond to at least one very important question in particular: Will this legislation benefit caregivers of the elderly? This question is also appropriately attired for corporate boardrooms.

CONCLUSION

At this point, it is customary to summarize much of what has been written in the preceding pages and conclude the chapter with a series of recommendations. Yes, services under the Older Americans Act and Title XX should be broadened and their funding increased. Yes, tax credit programs should be expanded so more people can participate. Of course the Family and Medical Leave Act should include a respectable wage replacement and be made more accessible to more workers. And yes, the Healthy Families Act should be passed, the budget for the National Family Caregivers Support Program should be doubled, and more states and corporations should adopt a variety of family-friendly policies, including soft-touch laws. I wholeheartedly support all of these endeavors. Calculations can be made and costs for taking such action can be projected with a fairly high degree of accuracy. However, a very disturbing pair of questions lurk in the shadows: What is the cost of inaction, and who will pay the price?

REFERENCES

AARP Public Policy Institute. 2006. *Valuing the invaluable: A new look at the economic value of family caregiving.* Issue Brief No. 82. Washington, DC: AARP.

Allegretto, Sylvia. 2005. *U.S. workers enjoy far fewer vacation days than Europeans.* Washington, DC: Economic Policy Institute.

Boots, Shelly W. 2004. *The way we work: How children and their families fare in a 21st century workplace,* Washington, DC: New America Foundation. Available at http://www.newamerica.net/publications/policy/the_way_we_work.

Burke, Mary Elizabeth, and Jessica Collison. 2004. *U.S. job recovery and retention poll findings.* Arlington, VA: Society for Human Resources Management.

Business Week. 1996 (Sept. 16). Balancing work and family: Big returns for companies willing to give family strategies a chance. Available at http://www.businessweek.com/1996/38/b34931.htm.

Elving, Ron. 1995. *Conflict and compromise: How Congress makes the law.* New York: Simon & Schuster.

Family Caregiver Alliance and the National Conference of State Legislatures. 2004. *The state of the states in family caregiver support: A fifty-state study.* San Francisco: Family Caregiver Alliance.

Feinberg, Lynn, and Sandra Newman. 2004. A study of 10 states since passage of the national family caregiver support program: Policies, perceptions, and program development. *Gerontologist* 44 (3): 760–69.

Galinsky, Ellen, James Bond, Stacey Kim, and Erin Brownfield. 2005. *Overwork in America: When the way we work becomes too much.* New York: Families and Work Institute.

Gornick, Janet, Alexandra Heron, and Ross Eisenbrey. 2007. The work-family balance: An analysis of European, Japanese, and U.S. work-time policies. Washington, DC: Economic Policy Institute.

Gornick, Janet, and Marcia Meyers. 2003. *Families that work: Policies for reconciling parenthood and employment.* New York: Russell Sage Foundation.

Hacker, Jacob S. 2006. *The great risk shift: The assault on American jobs, families, health care, and retirement and how you can fight back.* Oxford: Oxford University Press.

Healy, Cathy. 2005. *A business perspective on workplace flexibility: When work works—an employer strategy for the 21st century.* New York: Families and Work Institute.

Heymann, Jody, and Christopher Beem, eds. 2005. *Unfinished work: Building equality and democracy in an era of working families.* New York: New Press.

Levin-Epstein, Jodie. 2005. How to exercise flexible work: Take steps with a soft touch law. Work-Life Balance Series Brief No. 3. Washington, DC: Center for Law and Social Policy. Available at http://www.clasp.org/publications/work_life_brf3.pdf.

———. 2006. *Getting punched: The job and family clock.* Washington, DC: Center for Law and Social Policy.

Liechty, Janet, and Elaine Anderson. 2007. Flexible workplace practices: Lessons from the federal Alternative Work Schedules Act. *Family Relations* 56 (3): 314–17.

Lyke, Robert, and Julie Whittaker. 2007. *Tax benefits for health insurance and expenses: Overview of current law and legislation, 2007.* CRS Report RL33505. Washington, DC: Congressional Research Service.

Medical News Today. 2006. Companies increasingly offering workplace benefits for employees who provide elder care. http://www.medicalnewstoday.com/articles/48255.php.

MetLife Mature Market Institute and National Alliance for Caregiving. 2007. *The MetLife Caregiving Cost Study: Productivity losses to U.S. business.* Westport, CT: MetLife Mature Market Institute.

National Alliance for Caregiving and the Center for Productive Aging at Towson University. 2003. *The MetLife study of sons at work: Balancing employment and eldercare.* Westport, CT: MetLife Mature Market Institute.

National Partnership for Women and Families. 2004. *Get well soon: Americans can't afford to get sick.* Washington, DC: National Partnership for Women and Families.

———. 2007. Everyone gets sick; not everyone has time to get better. http://www. nationalpartnership.org/site/PageServer?pagename=psd_index.

Office of Senator Hillary Rodham Clinton. 2007. Hillary Clinton's agenda for working families: Helping parents balance work and family. Press release, October 16. Available at http://www.hillaryclinton.com/news/release/view/?id=3743.

ProQuest Information and Learning Company. 1999. Elder-care: A growing workplace issue. *Growth Strategies,* November 15. Available at http://findarticles.com/ p/articles/mi_qa3908/is_199911/ai_n8861049.

Reed, Patricia, and Shirley Clark. 2004. *Win-win workplace practices: Improved organizational results and improved quality of life.* Washington, DC: Women's Bureau, U.S. Department of Labor.

Scott, Christine. 2005. *Dependent care: Current tax benefits and legislative issues.* CRS Report RS21466. Washington, DC: Congressional Research Service.

Sloan Work and Family Research Network. 2002. Questions and answers about elder care. http://wfnetwork.bc.edu/pdfs/elder_care_91707.pdf.

———. 2006. The 2005–2006 legislative summary sheet of elder care bills introduced into state legislatures. http://wfnetwork.bc.edu/pdfs/flexschedbills.pdf.

U.S. Bureau of Labor Statistics. 2005. Women in the labor force. http://www.bls.gov/ cps/wlf-databook2005.htm.

U.S. Department of Health and Human Services. 2002. Informal caregiving: Compassion in action. http://aspe.hhs.gov/search/daltcp/reports/Carebro2.pdf.

Wagner, Donna. 2003. *Workplace programs for family caregivers: Good business and good practice.* San Francisco: Family Caregiver Alliance.

Watson Wyatt. 2007. *The business case for superior people management.* http://www. watsonwyatt.com/strategyatwork/article.asp?articleid=9521.

Wisensale, Steven K. 2001. *Family leave policy: The political economy of work and family in America.* Armonk, NY: M. E. Sharpe.

———. 2003. Two steps forward, one step back: The family and medical leave act as retrenchment policy. *Review of Policy Research* 20 (2): 135–51.

———. 2006. California's paid leave law: A model for other states? *Marriage and Family Review* 39 (2): 177–95.

Wisensale, Steven K., and Michael Allison. 1988. An analysis of the 1987 state family leave legislation: Implications for caregivers of the elderly. *Gerontologist* 28 (3): 779–84.

About the Editor and Contributors

THE EDITOR

Robert B. Hudson, Ph.D., editor of this two-volume set, is professor and chair of the Department of Social Policy, Boston University School of Social Work. He has written widely on the policies and politics of aging, his work having appeared in *Social Service Review, Milbank Quarterly, International Social Security Review, Journal of Health Politics, Policy and Law*, and *Handbook of Aging and the Social Sciences*, among other publications. He currently serves as editor-in-chief of *Public Policy and Aging Report*, the quarterly publication of the National Academy on an Aging Society. Dr. Hudson is a fellow of the Gerontological Society of America (GSA) and an elected member of the National Academy of Social Insurance (NASI), where he chairs the John A. Heinz Dissertation Award Committee. He has received the Donald Kent Award from GSA and the Arthur S. Flemming Award from the National Association of State Units on Aging. His most recent book is *The New Politics of Old Age Policy* (Johns Hopkins University Press). He received his doctorate in political science from the University of North Carolina at Chapel Hill.

CONTRIBUTORS

W. Andrew Achenbaum, Ph.D., is professor of history and social work at the University of Houston's Graduate College of Social Work. Author of five books and coeditor of eleven others, he is currently working with H. R. Moody on a book tentatively entitled *Leaving a Legacy*, which will address baby boomers' responsibilities to pass on to rising cohorts a sounder social-insurance system and global environment.

Robert H. Binstock, Ph.D., is professor of aging, health, and society at Case Western Reserve University. A former president of the GSA, he has served as director of the White House Task Force on Older Americans and as chairman and member of a number of advisory panels to the federal, state, and local governments and foundations. He is also a former chair of the Gerontological Health Section of the American Public Health Association. He has frequently testified before the U.S. Congress. Professor Binstock has published some three hundred articles, book chapters, monographs, and books, most dealing with politics and policies affecting aging. The latest of his twenty-five books is *Aging Nation: The Economics and Politics of Growing Older in America* (2006), coauthored with James H. Schulz.

Christine Bishop, Ph.D., is Atran Professor Labor Economics at the Heller School of Social Policy and Management, Brandeis University, where she also directs the doctoral program. She is an economist whose research spans policy-related problems in health services supply, demand, and financing, focusing on services for older adults. Her current studies concern the reorganization of work in nursing homes to provide more person-centered care and the impact of Medicare's prescription drug benefit on elders eligible for both Medicare and Medicaid. She earned her doctorate in economics from Harvard University.

Jeffrey Burr, Ph.D., received his doctorate in sociology from the University of Texas at Austin. He is currently associate dean of the McCormack Graduate School of Policy Studies and professor of gerontology at the University of Massachusetts–Boston. He is a fellow in the UMass Boston Gerontology Institute, a fellow of the GSA (Behavioral and Social Sciences Section), and a member of Sigma Phi Omega (the national gerontological honor society). Dr. Burr's research interests include the social demography of aging, household composition and living arrangements, race and ethnicity in aging populations, labor force participation in later life, and productive activity in later life.

Craig Copeland, Ph.D., is a senior research associate with the Employee Benefit Research Institute (EBRI). He has been with EBRI since 1997, where he is the director of the EBRI's Social Security Reform Evaluation Research Program. In addition to Social Security, his research has focused on employment-based retirement plans and individual retirement accounts. Dr. Copeland has authored more than fifty EBRI Issue Briefs and *EBRI Notes* articles. In addition, he also has authored chapters in books and articles in journals, most recently, "Increasing Debt Risk of Those Age 55 or Older, 1992–2004" in *Public Policy and Aging Report*. He received a B.S. in economics from Purdue University and a Ph.D. in economics from the University of Illinois at Urbana–Champaign.

John Gist, Ph.D., is senior advisor for fiscal and economic affairs in AARP's Public Policy Institute (PPI). Prior to his tenure at AARP, he was a professor of political science and public affairs from 1973 until 1987 at the University of Illinois–Springfield, the University of Georgia, and Virginia Tech. He was a visiting scholar at the U.S. Department of Housing and Urban Development in 1977–1979 and 1985–1986. He holds a Ph.D. in political science from Washington University in St. Louis. Dr. Gist has published numerous articles on federal budget, entitlement spending, and tax policy issues in the *Milbank Quarterly, Gerontologist, Journal of Aging and Social Policy, Journal of Urban Economics, American Political Science Review, Midwest Journal of Political cal Science, Journal of Politics*, and *Policy Studies Journal*. His recent PPI studies include publications on boomers' inheritances and savings adequacy, personal debt among people aged 50 and older, the distributional effects of tax policies, entitlement spending and the economy, and income growth and inequality. His current work concerns baby boomers' housing wealth, refinancing, and consumption of housing equity.

Karen C. Holden, Ph.D., is professor of public affairs and consumer science at the University of Wisconsin–Madison. She is a fellow of the GSA, a member of NASI, and an associate of the Fellows Program of EBRI. Dr. Holden's broad area of research is the effect of social security and pension policy on economic status after retirement and widowhood. Her most recent research is on retirement savings adequacy and, using the Wisconsin Longitudinal Study, the relationship between economic and psychological well-being (or "happiness") among older women and men. She has also published in the area of disability, welfare reform, mandatory retirement policies, and risk of nursing home care. She received her B.A. from Barnard College and her doctorate in economics from the University of Pennsylvania.

Edward F. Lawlor, Ph.D., is the dean and William E. Gordon Professor at the George Warren Brown School of Social Work at Washington University in St. Louis. Dean Lawlor conducts research and writes on access to health care, health care reform, policy analysis, and aging. A national Medicare expert, he is the author of *Redesigning the Medicare Contract: Politics, Markets, and Agency*. He is founding editor of the *Public Policy and Aging Report*. Prior to joining the Brown School, he served as dean at the School of Social Service Administration at the University of Chicago from 1998 to 2004. From 1990 to 1998, he was the director of both the Center for Health Administration Studies and the Graduate Program in Health Administration and Policy at the University of Chicago. For ten years, Dr. Lawlor was a member and secretary of the Chicago Board of Health, and he has served on numerous policy and advisory bodies in the fields of health care and aging.

John Macnicol, M.A., Ph.D. (Edin.), is visiting professor in social policy at the London School of Economics. He has published extensively on current social policy and the history of social policy. His recent publications include *The Politics of Retirement in Britain, 1878–1948* (Cambridge University Press, 1998); *Paying for the Old: Old Age and Social Welfare Provision* (editor; Thoemmes Press, 7 vols., 2000); and *Age Discrimination, an Historical and Contemporary Analysis* (Cambridge University Press, 2006; winner of the UK Social Policy Association's award for Best New Publication, 2006–2007). He is currently working on the rise of the U.S. neoconservatives and their influence on social policy in the United Kingdom.

Jan E. Mutchler, Ph.D., received her doctorate in sociology from the University of Texas at Austin. She is currently professor of gerontology and associate director for social and demographic research at the Gerontology Institute, University of Massachusetts–Boston. She is a fellow of the GSA (Behavioral and Social Sciences Section). Dr. Mutchler's current research focuses on intergenerational family relationships, racial and ethnic diversity, household and family demography, and health disparities in later life.

Greg O'Neill, Ph.D., is director of the National Academy on an Aging Society, the public policy institute of the GSA. The academy conducts research on issues related to population aging and publishes the quarterly *Public Policy and Aging Report*. He directs GSA's Civic Engagement in an Older America project (www.civicengagement.org), an initiative funded by the Atlantic Philanthropies to promote the study of civic engagement by experts in the field of aging. Dr. O'Neill's publications include *The State of Aging and Health in America*, a national and state-by-state report card on healthy aging. He received his Ph.D. in sociology with a concentration in population studies from Duke University in 1998.

Michelle Putnam, Ph.D., is assistant professor at Simmons College School of Social Work in Boston. She is a nationally recognized expert in the area of aging and disability policy and the population of people aging with long-term disability. Dr. Putnam has published numerous articles and book chapters on the intersections of aging and disability, socioeconomic and policy issues related to independent living and long-term care, and collaboration and coalition-building across aging and disability organizations and service networks. She is a frequent reviewer for the National Institute of Disability and Rehabilitation Research. Dr. Putnam has led multiple research and knowledge translation studies funded by organizations such as AARP, the John A. Hartford Foundation, and the National Institute on Aging. She is a frequent keynote speaker on the topic of aging with disability around the United States and abroad.

Sara E. Rix, Ph.D., is a strategic policy advisor with the Economics Team of the AARP PPI, where she focuses on the economics of aging, labor force and demographic trends, employment and retirement policy, and older worker employment issues. She has written and spoken extensively on aging issues for more than thirty years. Dr. Rix has been involved in numerous national and international activities that focus on an aging world, including serving as a lecturer in the Economics and Financial Aspects of Aging training program of the UN's International Institute on Ageing in Malta. She is a fellow of NASI, the GSA, and the Royal Society for the Encouragement of Arts, Manufactures and Commerce (RSA). In her spare time, she volunteers as a primate interpreter at the National Zoo.

Jack L. VanDerhei, Ph.D., is a faculty member at Temple University's Fox School of Business and Management (Department of Risk, Insurance, and Healthcare Management). He has authored more than one hundred publications devoted to employee benefits and insurance; his major areas of research focus on the financial aspects of private defined benefit and defined contribution retirement plans. In his capacity as the research director of EBRI's Fellows Program, he is currently analyzing a database with annual observations since 1996 of over 20 million 401(k) participants from more than 50,000 plans. He has won the American Risk and Insurance Association award for the best feature article in the *Journal of Risk and Insurance* and the James S. Kemper Foundation Award for the best feature article in *Risk Management and Insurance Review*. VanDerhei serves as editor of *Benefits Quarterly*, is a member of NASI, and serves on the Advisory Board of the Pension Research Council at the Wharton School of the University of Pennsylvania.

Diane M. Watts-Roy received her M.A. degree in sociology from the College of William and Mary in Williamsburg, Virginia. Her previous work includes serving as the director of an Alzheimer's respite program. She is currently a doctoral student in the Department of Sociology at Boston College. Her dissertation research explores the consumer perspective on regimens associated with extending the life span and/or delaying aging.

John B. Williamson, Ph.D., received his B.S. degree from MIT and his doctorate in social psychology from Harvard University, and he is currently a professor of sociology at Boston College. He has published sixteen books and more than 120 journal articles and book chapters. Among his books are *The Generational Equity Debate*; *The Senior Rights Movement*; *Age, Class Politics and the Welfare State*; *Old Age Security in Comparative Perspective*; and *The Politics of Aging*. He is currently chair of the Social Research, Policy, and Practice section (and a vice president) of the GSA. He is affiliated with the Center for Retirement Research and with the Center for Work and Aging, both at Boston College. The focus of his current research is on the comparative international study of social security systems.

Steven K. Wisensale, Ph.D., is professor of public policy in the Department of Human Development and Family Studies at the University of Connecticut. His primary teaching responsibilities and research interests are in family policy and aging policy, and he is the recipient of the University of Connecticut's Excellence in Teaching Award. He is the author of more than seventy-five journal articles, book chapters, and policy briefs. Dr. Wisensale has published three books, including *Family Leave Policy: The Political Economy of Work and Family in America*. He has received two Fulbright Fellowships—one in Germany, the other in the Czech Republic—and is a former research fellow of the GSA. In 1999, he was a consultant to the United Nations on world population aging. Dr. Wisensale serves on the Board of Directors of the Council on Contemporary Families and is a member of the Public Policy Committee of the GSA.

Index